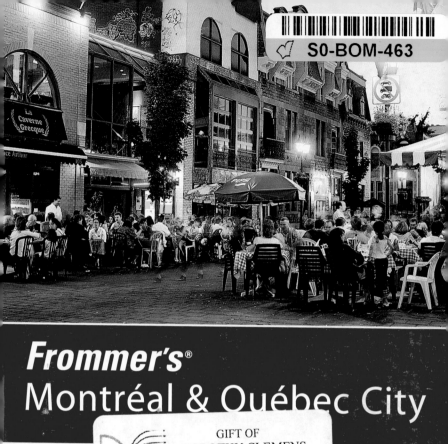

S0-BOM-463

Frommer's®
Montréal & Québec City

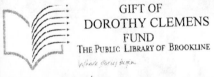

GIFT OF
DOROTHY CLEMENS
FUND
THE PUBLIC LIBRARY OF BROOKLINE

My Montréal & Québec City
by Leslie Brokaw

ON MY FIRST VISIT TO QUÉBEC, HALF A LIFETIME AGO, I TOOK FULL advantage of the local sidewalk cafes. Nowhere else can a visitor more readily absorb the distinctive customs and rhythms of another culture. It was in just such a cafe, in Québec City, looking out over the silvered expanse of the St. Lawrence River and up to the peaked copper roofs of the Château Frontenac, that I began to understand what this singular province was all about. The couple at the next table was in deep conversation. She spoke only French, he only English, and yet they understood each other perfectly.

That's the key to Québec's self-labeled "distinct society." French and British traditions exist side by side, peppered with an internationalism that reflects Canada's liberal immigration policies. Old Francophones still play petanque in the parks on warm days, and in winter their grandchildren bobsled down the run from the capital's fortress to its grand château, the Frontenac. Unilingual Anglophones take high tea in Montréal's grand hotels of the privileged, while their progeny speak Franglish in *boîtes de nuit,* where the singers sound like Piaf and Azvanor. The two cities compete in mounting shoulder-to-shoulder festivals that celebrate everything from jazz to winter to comedy to film.

The photographs on the following pages are just a taste of the many reasons to put Montréal and Québec City on your list of must-see destinations.

© Nicholas Reuss/Lonely Planet Images

MONTMORENCY FALLS (left) are higher than Niagara—as anyone is sure to be told, several times, upon visiting. Back in the 18th century, British and French forces lobbed cannonballs at each other from entrenchments on both banks. These days, fireworks, sometimes seen above the falls, are strictly for fun, and launched during annual festivals.

In this view from the east end of the **MONTREAL'S OLD PORT (above)**, the silver-domed 1847 Bonsecours building is in the foreground, with Colonial-era Vieux Montréal surrounding it, and modern-day office towers rising behind. In summer, the rehabilitated park in front hosts concerts, rollerbladers, cyclists, sunbathers, and others who enjoy *le pic-nic*.

The high altar of the **BASILIQUE NOTRE-DAME (left)**, easily the most beautifully embellished of Montréal's hundreds of churches, is richly carved linden wood, as is most of the interior. The bell in the tower weighs 12 tons, and the floor rumbles when it rings. Orchestras perform here, drawn by the magnificent acoustics. The church's Protestant Irish-American architect, James O'Donnell, was so stirred by what he had wrought that he converted to Catholicism.

Pedestrian-only **RUE DU TRESOR (above)** in Québec City is an obligatory stop on every stroll through the old Upper Town. Artists line both sides of the narrow lane, their watercolors, prints, and drawings on display. There's no pressure to buy. Subject matter is mostly various vistas and details of their city, but some artists set up easels beside nearby outdoor cafes and offer to do portraits.

The historic district of Québec City is the only walled city north of Mexico. It's divided into two parts: Basse-Ville, the older part down by the river where the first European settlers built and farmed, and Haute-Ville, atop the steep-sided cliff to which the French citizens withdrew for greater safety from invaders. This **FUNICULAIRE (left)** connects the two, affording spectacular views and escape from the Breakneck Stairs, the other pedestrian route down the hill.

SUGARING-OFF (below) season is February through March, when sap is drawn from the vast stands of sugar maples with which the province is blessed. At first, the sap was merely processed, transformed into syrup and candies, and sent off to eager buyers. Then some canny Québecer decided to offer meals in his *cabane à sucre*—sugar shack. That evolved into an industry, and some sugar shacks stay open all year, providing gargantuan farm meals, live folkloric entertainment, simple lodgings, and even sleigh rides.

Boosters call Montréal the "City of Festivals," and justifiably so. Apart from a few bereft weeks here and there in the coldest months, it takes specific intent and careful planning to avoid celebratory events of one kind or another. Festivals throughout the year highlight comedy, film, cuisine, theater, cycling, motor racing, and fireworks. The greatest explosion of energy and talent, however, is during the annual **JAZZ FESTIVAL (above)**, with hundreds of performances in scores of venues, many of them free.

Montréal's **HÔTEL DE VILLE (right)** stands at the top of the Place Jacques-Cartier, which was the open-air market square of 19th-century Montréal. The extravagantly detailed French Second Empire style of the building is seen to best effect at night, and a dozen other impressive structures are similarly illuminated, constituting a rewarding—and safe—after-dark walking tour.

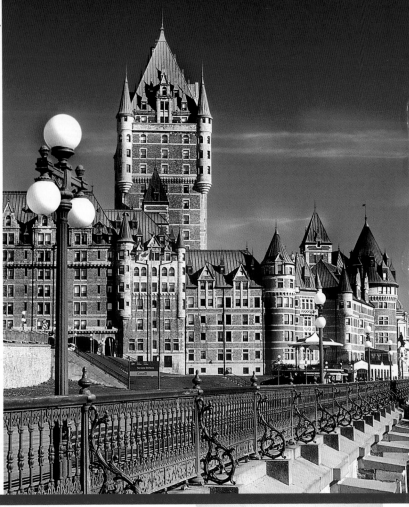

Few municipal symbols are as powerfully evocative as Québec's **CHATEAU FRONTENAC (above)**. In style, it is a Loire castle on steroids, one of a chain strung along the route of the Trans-Canada railway to encourage tourism at the start of the last century.

The long staircase leading down from the elevated La Citadelle to the promenade known as Terrace Dufferin is transformed into a **BOBSLED RUN (right)** during Québec City's annual winter carnival. No special skills or particular athleticism is required for the short but thrilling run, unless you count climbing up to the starting point.

Routinely designated the premier ski resort east of the Mississippi, **TREMBLANT** marches up the slopes of its namesake mountain. Active all year, Tremblant also offers water-sports on the town-mile lake at its base. Lodgings, dining, and nightlife range from economical to deluxe, and while kids are catered to, there are plenty of times and places for parents to get away for a few hours.

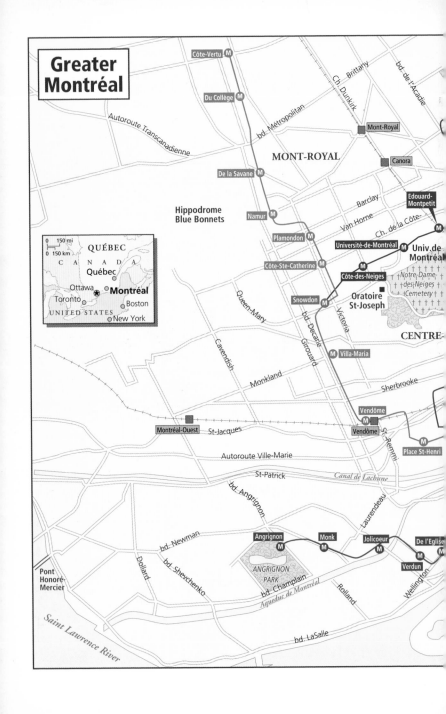

Greater Montréal

Côte-Vertu Ⓜ
Du Collège Ⓜ
Autoroute Transcanadienne
bd. Métropolitan
Ch. Dunkirk
Brittany
bd. de l'Acadie
Mont-Royal
MONT-ROYAL
Canora
De la Savane Ⓜ
Barclay
Edouard-Montpetit Ⓜ
Hippodrome
Blue Bonnets
Namur Ⓜ
Van Horne
Ch. de la Côte-
Plamondon Ⓜ
Université-de-Montréal Ⓜ
Univ.de Montréal
Côte-Ste-Catherine Ⓜ
Côte-des-Neiges Ⓜ
Notre-Dame-des-Neiges Cemetery
Snowdon Ⓜ
Oratoire St-Joseph
Queen-Mary
bd. Décarie
Victoria
CENTRE-
Ⓜ Villa-Maria
Girouard
Cavendish
Monkland
Sherbrooke
Vendôme Ⓜ
Montréal-Ouest
St-Jacques
Vendôme Ⓜ
St-Rémni
Ⓜ Place St-Henri
Autoroute Ville-Marie
St-Patrick
Canal de Lachine
bd. Angrignon
Laurendeau
Angrignon Ⓜ
Monk Ⓜ
Jolicoeur Ⓜ
De l'Église Ⓜ
bd. Newman
ANGRIGNON PARK
Verdun Ⓜ
Dollard
bd. Shevchenko
bd. Champlain
Aqueduc de Montréal
Rolland
Wellington
Pont Honoré-Mercier
Saint Lawrence River
bd. LaSalle

QUÉBEC
0 150 mi
0 150 km
CANADA
Québec
Ottawa
Montréal
Toronto
Boston
UNITED STATES
New York

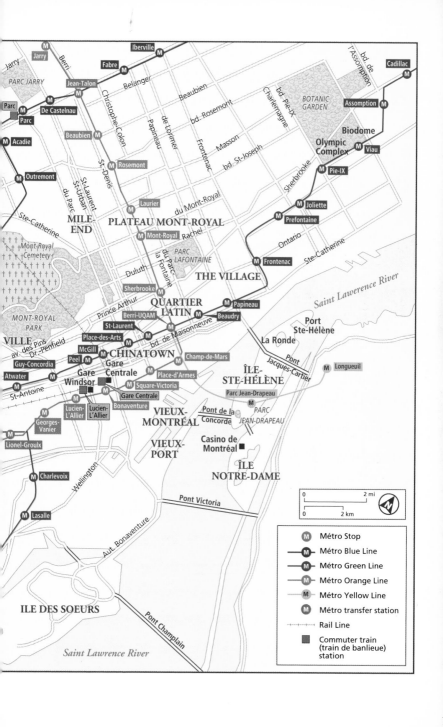

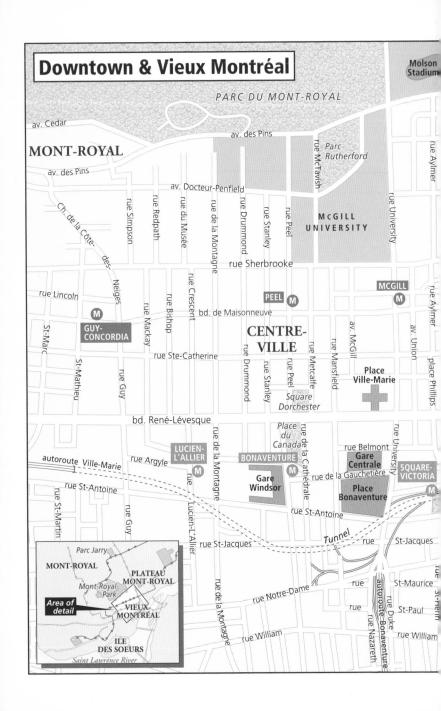

Downtown & Vieux Montréal

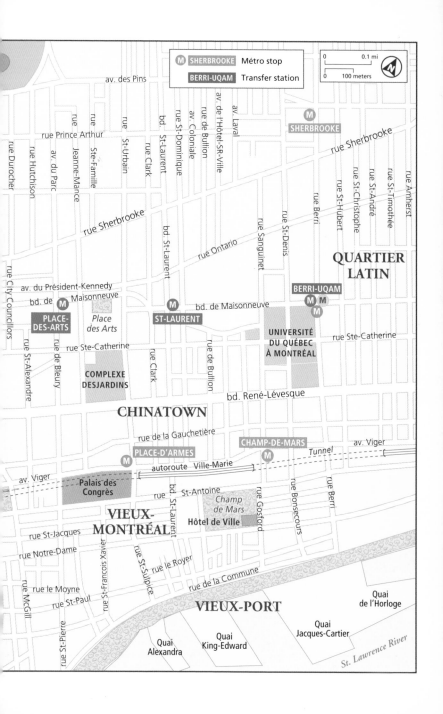

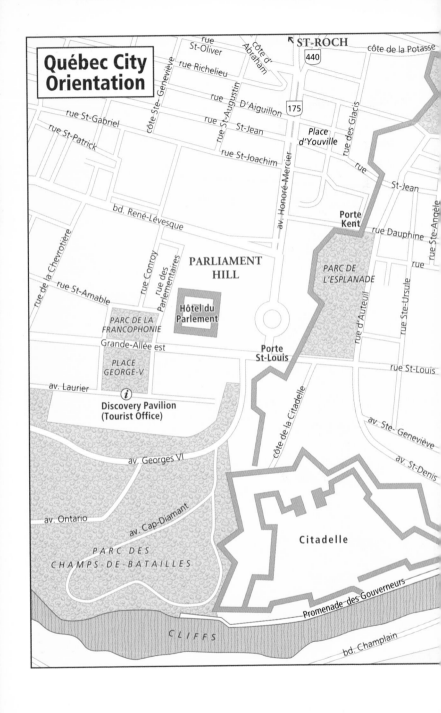

Québec City Orientation

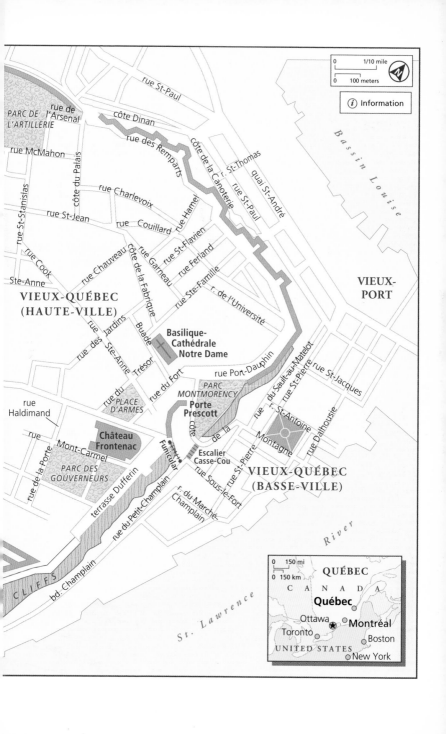

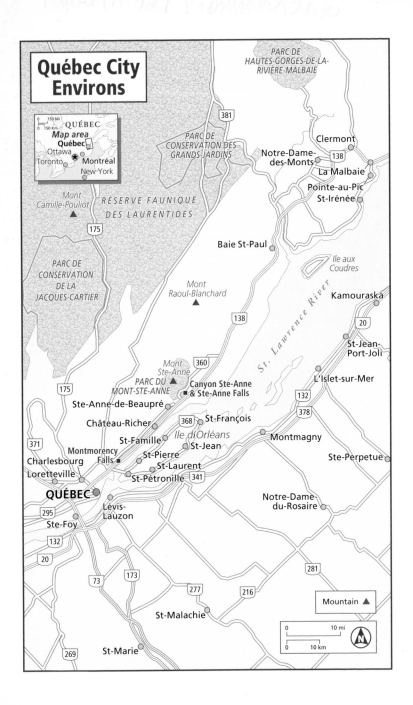

Québec City Environs

Frommer's®

Montréal & Québec City 2010

by Leslie Brokaw & Erin Trahan

WILEY

Wiley Publishing, Inc.

Travel 971.427 Frommer's 2010

ABOUT THE AUTHORS

Leslie Brokaw has been writing for *Frommer's* since 2006, authoring or contributing to recent editions of *Montréal Day by Day, Frommer's Canada,* and *Frommer's New England.* She is based in Boston and is a faculty member at Emerson College.

Erin Trahan is a writer and editor based in Boston.

Published by:

WILEY PUBLISHING, INC.

111 River St.
Hoboken, NJ 07030-5774

3 1712 01315 9754

ISBN 978-0-470-49731-9

Editor: Christine Ryan
Production Editor: Michael Brumitt
Cartographer: Andrew Murphy
Photo Editor: Richard Fox
Production by Wiley Indianapolis Composition Services

Front cover photo: Basilique Notre-Dame, Montréal ©Perry Mastrovito/Corbis
Back cover photo: Rue de la Barricade, Lower Town, Québec City ©Jeff Greenberg/ Alamy Images

For information on our other products and services or to obtain technical support, please contact our Customer Care Department within the U.S. at 877/762-2974, outside the U.S. at 317/572-3993 or fax 317/572-4002.

Wiley also publishes its books in a variety of electronic formats. Some content that appears in print may not be available in electronic formats.

Manufactured in the United States of America

5 4 3 2 1

CONTENTS

9 MONTRÉAL STROLLS 125

10 MONTRÉAL SHOPPING 146

11 MONTRÉAL AFTER DARK 158

12 SIDE TRIPS FROM MONTRÉAL 172

13 GETTING TO KNOW QUÉBEC CITY 204

14 WHERE TO STAY IN QUÉBEC CITY 212

21 FAST FACTS, TOLL-FREE NUMBERS & WEBSITES 289

INDEX 296

LIST OF MAPS

ACKNOWLEDGMENTS

This edition of the book continues to draw from more than 10 years of earlier versions written by Herbert Bailey Livesey, and still is influenced by his keen research and fine taste. Livesey continues to write about travel and food at www.akeyinthedoor.com. The authors also wish to acknowledge their husbands, Matthew Barber and Nate Van Houzen, who patiently lounged in hotel lobbies as the authors went on tours and who occasionally took notes at many of the meals and sights. Barber helped write the restaurant chapters of this book.

HOW TO CONTACT US

In researching this book, we discovered many wonderful places—hotels, restaurants, shops, and more. We're sure you'll find others. Please tell us about them, so we can share the information with your fellow travelers in upcoming editions. If you were disappointed with a recommendation, we'd love to know that, too. Please write to:

Frommer's Montréal & Québec City 2010
Wiley Publishing, Inc. • 111 River St. • Hoboken, NJ 07030-5774

AN ADDITIONAL NOTE

Please be advised that travel information is subject to change at any time—and this is especially true of prices. We therefore suggest that you write or call ahead for confirmation when making your travel plans. The authors, editors, and publisher cannot be held responsible for the experiences of readers while traveling. Your safety is important to us, however, so we encourage you to stay alert and be aware of your surroundings. Keep a close eye on cameras, purses, and wallets, all favorite targets of thieves and pickpockets.

FROMMER'S STAR RATINGS, ICONS & ABBREVIATIONS

Every hotel, restaurant, and attraction listing in this guide has been ranked for quality, value, service, amenities, and special features using a **star-rating system.** In country, state, and regional guides, we also rate towns and regions to help you narrow down your choices and budget your time accordingly. Hotels and restaurants are rated on a scale of zero (recommended) to three stars (exceptional). Attractions, shopping, nightlife, towns, and regions are rated according to the following scale: zero stars (recommended), one star (highly recommended), two stars (very highly recommended), and three stars (must-see).

In addition to the star-rating system, we also use **seven feature icons** that point you to the great deals, in-the-know advice, and unique experiences that separate travelers from tourists. Throughout the book, look for:

(Finds)	Special finds—those places only insiders know about
(Fun Facts)	Fun facts—details that make travelers more informed and their trips more fun
(Kids)	Best bets for kids, and advice for the whole family
(Moments)	Special moments—those experiences that memories are made of
(Overrated)	Places or experiences not worth your time or money
(Tips)	Insider tips—great ways to save time and money
(Value)	Great values—where to get the best deals

The following **abbreviations** are used for credit cards:

AE	American Express	DISC	Discover	V	Visa
DC	Diners Club	MC	MasterCard		

TRAVEL RESOURCES AT FROMMERS.COM

Frommer's travel resources don't end with this guide. Frommer's website, **www.frommers.com,** has travel information on more than 4,000 destinations. We update features regularly, giving you access to the most current trip-planning information and the best airfare, lodging, and car-rental bargains. You can also listen to podcasts, connect with other Frommers.com members through our active-reader forums, share your travel photos, read blogs from guidebook editors and fellow travelers, and much more.

The Best of Montréal & Québec City

If Montréal had a tagline, it could be "Any excuse for a party." An enormous joie de vivre pervades the way the city goes about its business. Its calendar is packed with festivals and events that bring out natives and guests from around the world year-round.

Since the 1967 World's Fair, known as Expo 67, put Montréal on the world stage, Montréal has become a modern city in every regard. Skyscrapers come in unexpected shapes and noncorporate colors. There's a beautifully preserved historic district. And the city's creative inhabitants have the ever-changing Plateau Mont-Royal and Mile End, large neighborhoods of artists' lofts, boutiques, cafes, and miles of restaurants.

American and European travelers will likely find Montréal an urban near-paradise. The subway system, called the Métro, is modern and swift. Streets are safe. And the best restaurants are unabashedly clever and stylish.

Québec City, more traditional and more French, is replacing its former conservatism with sophistication and playfulness. With an impressive location above the St. Lawrence River and carefully tended 18th- and 19th-century houses, this city is almost impossibly romantic—and unlike any other in North America.

1 UNFORGETTABLE TRAVEL EXPERIENCES

MONTREAL

- **Enjoy an Afternoon or Evening of Jazz:** In downtown, Old Town, and the Plateau, this is a favorite pastime of locals and visitors, especially in July during the renowned Festival International de Jazz. See "Music & Dance Clubs" in chapter 11.
- **Savor Gourmet Meals at Affordable Prices:** Experience all of French cuisine's interpretations—traditional, haute, bistro, Québécois—the way the locals do: by ordering the *table d'hôte* specials. You'll get to indulge in three or more courses for a fixed price that is only slightly more than the cost of a single main course. Most restaurants offer the option. See p. 76.

- **Explore Vieux-Montréal:** The city's oldest quarter has an overwhelmingly European flavor. Place Jacques-Cartier is the most popular outdoor square, and in any direction you'll find museums and churches worth savoring. A revitalized waterfront also inspires strolling or biking. A walking tour of the neighborhood is on p. 106.

QUEBEC CITY

- **Linger at an Outdoor Cafe:** Tables are set out at Place d'Armes in Upper Town, in the Quartier du Petit-Champlain in Lower Town, and along the Grande-Allée—a quality-of-life invention the French and their Québécois brethren have perfected. See chapter 15 for more information.

(Moments) **Romantic Québec City**

Every narrow street, leafy plaza, sidewalk cafe, horse-drawn calèche, pitched roof, and church spire breathes recollections of France's provincial towns. But to get the full Québec City treatment, amble those streets in the evening and find a bench on **Terrasse Dufferin,** the promenade alongside the Château Frontenac. The river below will be the color of liquid mercury in the moon's glow, and, on a clear night, you'll see a sky of stars. Faint music from the *boîtes* in Lower Town is a possibility. Romance is a certainty.

- **Soak Up Lower Town:** Once all but abandoned to the grubby edges of the shipping industry, the riverside neighborhood of Basse-Ville/Vieux-Port has been reborn. Antiques shops, bistros, and chic boutique hotels now fill rehabilitated 18th- and 19th-century buildings. See p. 255 for a walking tour.

- **Relax in Battlefields Park (Parc des Champs-de-Bataille):** This beautifully situated green space overlooks the St. Lawrence River and houses the Musée du Québec at its western end. It's particularly lively on weekends, when families and lovers come to picnic and play. See p. 239.

2 THE BEST SPLURGE HOTELS

MONTREAL

- **Hôtel Le St-James,** 355 rue St-Jacques ouest (℃ **866/841-3111** or 514/841-3111): This former 19th-century bank in Vieux-Montréal lets no detail escape its attention. From an opulent restaurant to marble-rich bathrooms to an immaculately trained staff, Hôtel Le St-James provides an experience that may well be the highlight of your visit. See p. 70.

- **W Montréal,** 901 rue Square-Victoria (℃ **877/946-8357** or 514/395-3100): Fancy yourself hip? Chic? On the fast track? If all that is you, then the W may be, too. It won't hurt if your platinum card is paid up and you don't need much sleep. There are three bars and lounges, a swank restaurant, and a clientele composed of knockouts of both genders. See p. 74.

QUEBEC CITY

- **Auberge Saint-Antoine,** 8 rue St-Antoine (℃ **888/692-2211** or 418/692-2211): Sure, there's the Château Frontenac, looming up above, the very symbol of the city. But for a more intimate visit, stay in Basse-Ville, or Lower Town. This hotel has grown into one of Québec's most desirable lodgings, with an arresting lounge and a top restaurant to boot. See p. 218.

- **Dominion 1912,** 126 rue St-Pierre (℃ **888/833-5253** or 418/692-2224): A key player in the redevelopment of the once dreary Vieux-Port, the Dominion has bedding so cozily enveloping that you may not want to go out. Do, though—for the fireplace, croissants, and café au lait in the lobby, if nothing else. See p. 219.

3 THE BEST MODERATELY PRICED HOTELS

MONTREAL

- **Auberge Bonaparte,** 447 rue St-François-Xavier (© **514/844-1448**): Even the smallest rooms in this fashionable urban inn are gracefully presented, and taking breakfast in the elegant **Bonaparte** restaurant (p. 86) is an especially civilized way to start the day. See p. 74.
- **Hôtel XIXe Siècle,** 262 rue St-Jacques ouest (© **877/553-0019** or 514/985-0019): Understated, tidy, and quiet, this Vieux-Montréal hotel offers spacious rooms and superior service. See p. 75.

QUEBEC CITY

- **Courtyard Marriott Québec,** 850 Place d'Youville (© **866/694-4004** or 418/694-4004): A hot property in recent years due to room renovations, friendly staff, and fair prices. Beds are piled with five pillows and sheet-cover duvets. See p. 220.
- **Hôtel Champlain,** 115 rue Ste-Anne (© **800/567-2106** or 418/694-0106): Even the smallest rooms boast silk curtains, king or queen beds, and 300-thread-count sheets. A self-serve espresso machine by the front desk ensures free cappuccinos at any time of day or night. See p. 217.

4 THE MOST UNFORGETTABLE DINING EXPERIENCES

MONTREAL

- **Europea,** 1227 rue de la Montagne (© **514/398-9229**): For the full treatment, order the ten-course *menu degustation.* You'll see why chef Jérôme Ferrer was named Chef of the Year by his colleagues and why Europea was named 2008 Restaurant of the Year by three local publications. See p. 80.
- **Toqué!,** 900 Place Jean-Paul-Riopelle (© **514/499-2084**): Superstar chef/owner Norman Laprise has been thrilling Montréal gourmands for years. In dishes of startling innovation, he brings together diverse ingredients that have rarely appeared before on restaurant plates. New menus come out frequently

enough to keep entrees from achieving signature status. See p. 85.

QUEBEC CITY

- **Laurie Raphaël,** 117 rue Dalhousie (© **418/692-4555**): Dazzling. Creative, Willy Wonka–style gourmet concoctions are artfully presented, with service that's friendly and correct and decor that's sophisticated with a touch of pizazz. See p. 230.
- **Panache,** 10 rue St-Antoine (© **418/692-1022**): Romance all the way, from the fireplace and velvet couches to the wrought-iron staircase leading to hideaway attic corners. French-Canadian cuisine with a kick. See p. 230.

5 THE BEST MUSEUMS

MONTREAL

- **Musée des Beaux-Arts,** 1339–1380 rue Sherbrooke ouest (© **514/285-2000**): Canada's first museum devoted

exclusively to the visual arts started out in 1912 in a neoclassical space on Sherbrooke's north side. It now has a newer pavilion on the opposite side and, new in 2011, the adjacent Erskine and American Church, which is being converted into a pavilion of Canadian art. Temporary exhibits have included a show about John Lennon and Yoko Ono, and another about fashion designer Yves Saint Laurent. See p. 102.

- **Pointe-à-Callière (Montréal Museum of Archaeology and History),** 350 Place Royale (© **514/872-9150**): A first visit to Montréal might best begin here. This strikingly modernistic structure at the edge of Vieux-Montréal marks the spot where the first European settlement put down roots in the city. It stands atop extensive excavations that unearthed not only remains of the French newcomers but also of the native bands that preceded them. On the self-guided tour, you wind your way through the subterranean complex. See p. 107.

QUEBEC CITY

- **Musée de la Civilisation,** 85 rue Dalhousie (© **418/643-2158**): Here is that rarity among museums: a collection of cleverly mounted temporary and permanent exhibitions that both children and adults find engrossing, without talking down or metaphysical maunderings. Make time for "People of Québec . . . Then and Now," a permanent exhibit that is a sprawling examination of Québec history. See p. 235.
- **Musée National des Beaux-Arts du Québec,** Parc des Champs-de-Bataille (© **866/220-2150** or 418/643-2150): Known simply as Musée du Québec, this museum highlights modern art (Jean-Paul Riopelle especially) and has a large, important collection of Inuit art, much produced in the 1980s and 1990s. See p. 239.

6 THE BEST OUTDOOR ACTIVITIES

MONTREAL

- **Traverse the Lachine Canal:** First constructed in the early 1800s to detour around the rapids of the same name, the canal was reopened for recreational use in 1997 after much renovation. It connects Vieux-Port with Atwater Market. You can explore the canal and its surroundings by guided boat tour, on foot, or on a rented bicycle. See chapter 8.
- **Bike the City:** Montréalers' enthusiasm for bicycling has provided the impetus for the ongoing development of bicycle paths that wind through downtown areas and out to the countryside—more than 560km (348 miles) at last count.

Rentals are available from shops and the new BIXI network, which has put thousands of bikes onto the streets for inexpensive borrowing. See p. 123.

QUEBEC CITY

- **Take a Walking Tour:** Combine immersion in Québec's rich history with a good stretch of the legs among the battlements and along the ancient city's cobblestoned streets. Use the walking tours in chapter 17 or go on a group tour. Information about meeting points, times, and routes is provided by the information center opposite Château Frontenac.

7 THE BEST ACTIVITIES FOR FAMILIES

MONTREAL

- **Visit the Biodôme de Montréal:** This is perhaps the most engaging attraction

in the city for children of any age. The Biodôme houses replications of four ecosystems: a Laurentian forest, the St.

Lawrence marine system, a polar environment, and, most appealingly, a tropical rainforest. See p. 109.

- **Spend a Day at the Centre des Sciences de Montréal:** Running the length of a central pier in Vieux-Port, this ambitious science center got a big overhaul in 2007. Attractions include interactive displays, multimedia challenges, and a popular IMAX theater. It's designed especially for ages 9 to 14. See p. 107.

QUEBEC CITY

- **Watch the Changing of the Guard:** La Citadelle is the fortress built by the British to repel an American invasion

that never came. It's still an active military post, and the ceremonial changing of the guard and beating the retreat are colorful and don't take too much time. See p. 238.

- **Thrill to a Waterfall:** A 15-minute car or bus ride north of the city is Montmorency Falls, a spectacular iron-tinged cascade. You can walk to the base or take a cable car to the top. A footbridge passes directly over the plunging water and is open to anyone brave-hearted enough to walk it. About a half-hour further north, Canyon Ste-Anne also has a thundering waterfall with footbridges that crisscross it and the canyon. See p. 276 and p. 279.

8 THE BEST OF MONTRÉAL & QUEBEC CITY ONLINE

- **Bonjour Québec** (www.bonjourquebec.com): The official site of Québec province is a comprehensive information bank. You'll find details about upcoming events and be able to search for hotels and reserve online.

- **Midnight Poutine** (www.midnightpoutine.ca): A terrific Montréal blog with more than a dozen contributors that provides "a personal ongoing

account of the city's happenings" and "a delicious high-fat source of rants, raves, and musings."

- *Hour* (www.hour.ca): A Montréal culture magazine available in print and online which includes entertainingly grumpy and often profane takes on current events. Restaurant and arts reviews are regularly updated.

2

Montréal & Québec City in Depth

Montréal and Québec City, the twin cities of the province of Québec, have a stronger European flavor than Canada's other municipalities. Most residents' first language is French, and a strong affiliation with France continues to be a central facet of the region's personality.

The defining dialectic of Canadian life is culture and language, and they're thorny issues that have long threatened to tear the country apart. Many Québécois have long believed that making Québec a separate, independent state is the only way to maintain their rich French culture in the face of the Anglophone (English-speaking) ocean that surrounds them. Québec's role within the Canadian federation has been the most debated and volatile topic of conversation in Canadian politics.

There are reasons for the festering intransigence, of course—about 250 years' worth. After France lost power in Québec to the British in the 18th century, a kind of linguistic exclusionism developed, with wealthy Scottish and English bankers and merchants denying French-Canadians access to upper levels of business and government. This bias continued well into the 20th century.

Many in Québec stayed committed to the French language and culture after British rule was imposed. Even with later waves of other immigrant populations pouring in over the cities, there was still a kind of bedrock loyalty held by many to the province's Gallic roots. France may have relinquished control of Québec to Great Britain in 1763, but France's influence, after its 150 years of rule, remained powerful—and still does. Many Québécois continue to look across the Atlantic for inspiration in fashion, food, and the arts. Culturally and linguistically, it is that tenacious French connection that gives the province its special character.

Two other important cultural phenomena have emerged over the past 10 years. The first is an institutional acceptance of homosexuality. By changing the definition of "spouse" in 39 laws and regulations in 1999, Québec's government eliminated all legal distinctions between same-sex and heterosexual couples and became Canada's first province to recognize the legal status of same-sex civil unions. Gay marriage became legal in all of Canada's provinces and territories in 2005. Montréal, in particular, has transformed into one of North America's most welcoming cities for gay people.

The second phenomenon is an influx of even more immigrants into the province's melting pot. "Québec is at a turning point," declared a 2008 report about the province's angst over the so-called reasonable accommodation of minority religious practices, particularly those of Muslims and Orthodox Jews. "The identity inherited from the French-Canadian past is perfectly legitimate and it must survive," the report continued, "but it can no longer occupy alone the Québec identity space." Together with 70,000 aboriginal people from 11 First Nation tribes who live in the province, immigrants help make the region as vibrant and alive as any on the continent.

The ancient walls that protected Québec City over the centuries are still in place today, and the town within their embrace has changed little, preserving for posterity the heart of New France.

Not so for Montréal. It was "wet" when the U.S. was "dry" due to Prohibition from 1920 to 1933. Bootleggers, hard drinkers, and prostitutes flocked to this large city situated so conveniently close to the American border, mixing with rowdy people from the port, much to the distress of Montréal's mostly upstanding citizenry. For 50 years, the city's image was decidedly racy, but in the 1950s, a cleanup began alongside a boom in high-rise construction and the restoration of much of the derelict Old Town. In 1967, Montréal welcomed international audiences to Expo 67, the World's Fair.

Today, much of what makes Montréal special is either very old or very new. The city's great gleaming skyscrapers and towering hotels, the superb Métro system, and the highly practical underground city date mostly from the 40 years since the Expo. The renaissance of much of the oldest part of the city, Vieux-Montréal, blossomed in the 1990s.

To understand the province's politics, you need to back up about 50 years. A phenomenon later labeled the Quiet Revolution began bubbling in the 1960s. The movement focused on transforming the largely rural, agricultural province into an urbanized, industrial entity with a pronounced secular outlook. French-Canadians, long denied access to the upper echelons of desirable corporate careers, started to insist on equal opportunity with the powerful Anglophone minority.

In 1968, Pierre Trudeau, a bilingual Québécois, became Canada's prime minister, a post he held for 18 years. More flamboyant, eccentric, and brilliant than any of his predecessors, he devoted much time to trying to placate voters on both sides of the French-English issue.

Also in 1968, the Parti Québécois was founded by René Lévesque, and the separatist movement began in earnest. Inevitably, there was a radical fringe, and it signaled its intentions by bombing Anglophone businesses. The FLQ (Front de Libération du Québec, or Québec Liberation Front), as it was known, was behind most of the terrorist attacks. Most Québécois separatists, of course, were not violent, but the bombings fueled passions and contributed to a sense that big changes were coming.

For decades, secession remained a dream for many Québécois. As recently as 1995, a referendum on sovereignty lost by a mere 1% of the vote.

During the 1990s, an unsettled mood prevailed in the province. Large businesses left town, anxious that if the province actually did secede, they would find themselves based outside of Canada proper. Economic opportunities were limited.

By 2000, though, things began to change. The Canadian dollar strengthened against the U.S. dollar. Unemployment, long in double digits, shrank to less than 6%, the lowest percentage in more than 20 years. Crime in Montréal, which was already one of the continent's safest cities, hit a 20-year low. The presence of skilled workers made Canada a favored destination for Hollywood film and TV production. The rash of FOR RENT and FOR SALE signs that disfigured Montréal in the 1990s was replaced by a welcome shortage of retail and office space.

In 2002, the 28 towns and cities on the island of Montréal merged into one megacity with a population of 1.8 million.

Today, the quest for separatism seems to be fading. Conversations with ordinary Québécois suggest they're weary of the argument. In March 2007, the Liberal

Party, headed by Jean Charest, won a minority government, with an out-of-nowhere second-place victory for the new Action Démocratique du Québec party and its young leader, Mario Dumont. The separatist Parti Québécois placed a distant third with just 28% of the vote. The moment marked, many think, the beginning of the end of the campaign for independence.

As significantly, the proportion of foreign-born Québec citizens continues to grow. After the arrival of 1.1 million immigrants to the country between 2001 and 2006, foreign-born nationals made up 20% of Canada's population, with Montréal, Toronto, Vancouver, and Calgary their prime destinations. In some areas of the country, Chinese dialects are outpacing French as the second most commonly spoken language; visitors to Montréal may notice large pockets of neighborhoods where the primary languages spoken are Mandarin and Cantonese.

2 LOOKING BACK AT MONTREAL & QUEBEC CITY

FIRST IMMIGRANTS

The first settlers of the region were the Iroquois, who spent time in what's now called Québec long before the Europeans arrived. The Vikings landed in Canada more than 1,000 years ago, probably followed by Irish and Basque fishermen. English explorer John Cabot stepped ashore briefly on the east coast in 1497, but it was the French who managed the first meaningful European toehold.

When Jacques Cartier sailed up the St. Lawrence in 1535, he recognized at once the tremendous strategic potential of Québec City's Cap Diamant (Cape Diamond), the high bluff overlooking the river. But he was exploring, not building an empire, and after stopping briefly on land, he continued on his trip.

Montréal, at the time, was home to a fortified Iroquois village called Hochelaga, composed of 50 longhouses. Cartier was on a sea route to China but was halted by the fierce rapids just west of what is now the Island of Montréal. (In a demonstration of mingled optimism and frustration, he dubbed the rapids "La Chine," assuming that China was just beyond them; even today, they're known as the Lachine.) He visited the Indian settlement in what's now Old Montréal before moving on.

Samuel de Champlain arrived 73 years later, in 1608, motivated by the burgeoning fur trade, obsessed with finding a route to China, and determined to settle Québec. He was perhaps emboldened after the Virginia Company founded its fledgling colony of Jamestown, hundreds of miles to the south, just a year before.

Called Kebec, Champlain's first settlement grew to become Québec City's Basse-Ville, or Lower Town, and then spread across the flat riverbank beneath the cliffs of Cap Diamant. In 2008, Québec City hosted major celebrations of the 400th anniversary of this founding.

Champlain would make frequent trips back to France to reassure anxious investors that the project, which he said would eventually "equal the states of greatest kings," was going apace. In truth, the first years were bleak. Food was scarce and scurvy ravaged many of the settlers. Demanding winters were far colder than in France. And almost from the beginning, there were hostilities, first between the French and the Iroquois, then between the French and the British (and, later, the Americans). At issue was control of the lucrative trade of the fur of beavers, raccoons, and bears, and the hides of deer, as the pelts were being shipped off to Paris fashion houses. The commercial battle lasted nearly a century.

To better defend themselves, the settlers in Québéc City constructed a fortress atop the cape and gradually the center of urban life moved to the top of the cliffs.

The French and British struggle for dominance in the new continent focused on their explorations, and in this regard, France outdid England. Their far-ranging fur trappers, navigators, soldiers, and missionaries opened up not only Canada but also most of what eventually became the United States, moving all the way south to the future New Orleans. At least 35 of the subsequent 50 U.S. states were mapped or settled by Frenchmen, who left behind thousands of city names to prove it, including Detroit, St. Louis, Duluth, and Des Moines.

Paul de Chomedey, Sieur de Maisonneuve, arrived in 1642 to establish a colony and to plant a crucifix atop the hill he called Mont Royal. He and his band of settlers came ashore and founded Ville-Marie, dedicated to the Virgin Mary, at the spot now marked by Place-Royale in the old part of the city. They built a fort, a chapel, stores, and houses. Pointe-à-Callière, the terrific Montréal Museum of Archaeology and History, is built on the site where the original colony was established.

Life was not easy. The Iroquois in Montréal had no intention of giving up land to the Europeans. Fierce battles raged for years. At Place d'Armes today, there's a statue of de Maisonneuve, marking the spot where the settlers defeated the Iroquois in bloody hand-to-hand fighting.

Still, the settlement prospered. Until the 1800s, Montréal was contained in the area known today as Vieux-Montréal. Its ancient walls no longer stand, but its long and colorful past is preserved in the streets, houses, and churches of the Old City.

ENGLAND CONQUERS NEW FRANCE

In the 1750s, the struggle between Britain and France had escalated. The latest episode was known as the French and Indian War (an extension of Europe's Seven Years' War), and strategic Québec became a valued prize. The French appointed Louis Joseph, marquis de Montcalm, to command their forces in the town. The British sent an expedition of 4,500 men in a fleet under the command of a 32-year-old general, James Wolfe. The British troops surprised the French by coming up and over the cliffs of Cap Diamant, and the ensuing skirmish for Québec, fought on September 13, 1759, became one of the most important battles in North American history: It resulted in a continent that would be under British influence for more than a century.

Fought on the Plains of Abraham, today a beautiful and much-used city park, the battle lasted just 18 to 25 minutes, depending on whose account you read. It resulted in 600 casualties, including both generals, who died as a result of wounds received. Wolfe lived just long enough to hear that the British had won. Montcalm died a few hours later. Today, a memorial to both men overlooks Terrasse Dufferin in Québec City and uniquely commemorates both victor and vanquished of the same battle. The inscription, in neither French nor English but Latin, is translated as, simply, "Courage was fatal to them."

The capture of Québec determined the war's course, and the Treaty of Paris in 1763 ceded all of French Canada to England. In a sense, this victory was a bane to Britain: If France had held Canada, the British government might have been more judicious in its treatment of the American colonists. As it was, the British decided to make the colonists pay the costs of the French and Indian War, on the principle that it was their home being defended. Britain slapped so many taxes on all imports that the infuriated U.S. colonists openly rebelled against the crown.

George Washington felt sure that French-Canadians would want to join the American revolt against the British crown, or at least be supportive. He was mistaken on both counts. The Québécois detested their British conquerors, but they were also devout Catholics and saw their contentious neighbors as godless republicans. Only a handful supported the Americans, and three of Washington's most competent commanders came to grief in attacks against Québec and were forced to retreat.

Thirty-eight years later, during the War of 1812, the U.S. army marched up the banks of the Richelieu River where it flows from Lake Champlain to the St. Lawrence. Once again, the French-Canadians stuck by the British and drove back the Americans. The war ended essentially in a draw, but it had at least one encouraging result: Britain and the young United States agreed to demilitarize the Great Lakes and to extend their mutual border along the 49th parallel to the Rockies.

THE RISE OF SEPARATISM IN QUEBEC

In 1867, the British North America Act created the federation of the provinces of Québec, Ontario, Nova Scotia, and New Brunswick. It was a kind of independence for the region from Britain, but was unsettling for many French-Canadians, who wanted full autonomy. In 1883, *"Je me souviens"*—an ominous "I remember"—became the province's official motto. From 1900 to 1910, 325,000 French-Canadians emigrated to the United States.

In 1968, the Parti Québécois was founded by René Lévesque, and the separatist movement began in earnest. One attempt to smooth ruffled Francophones (French speakers) was made in 1969, when federal legislation stipulated that all services across Canada were henceforth to be offered in both English and French, in effect declaring the nation bilingual.

That didn't assuage militant Québécois, however. They undertook to guarantee the primacy of French in their own province. To prevent dilution by newcomers, the children of immigrants were required to enroll in French-language schools, even if English or a third language was spoken in the home. This is still the case today.

"When I lived in Montréal in the '60s," wrote Ruth Reichl, editor of *Gourmet* magazine, in the March 2006 issue, "it was strangely segregated. The Anglophones I trailed through the staid streets were a proper lot, more English than the English, with their umbrellas and briefcases. They may not have been hurrying home to early tea, but I imagined they were. . . The Jewish community I found in another part of town was an entirely different experience. The people were boisterous, and their streets were rich with the scent of garlic, cloves, and allspice emanating from the mountains of pickles and deliciously rich smoked meat that I spied each time a restaurant door swung open. The French-Canadians had their own territory, too, and they stuck to themselves, speaking their own robust and expressive language. . . What struck me most, as a New Yorker accustomed to the hodgepodge piling up of one culture on another, was the barriers between them. They kept themselves strictly separate, each cleaving to their own language, rituals, and food."

In 1977, Bill 101 passed, all but banning the use of English on public signage. The bill funded the establishment of enforcement units, a virtual language police who let no nit go unpicked. The resulting backlash provoked the flight of an estimated 400,000 Anglophones to other parts of Canada.

In 1987, Canadian Prime Minister Brian Mulroney met with the 10 provincial premiers at a retreat at Québec's

March of the Language Police
(or La Police de Langue)

When the separatist Parti Québécois took power in the province in 1976, it wasted no time in attempting to make Québec unilingual. Bill 101 made French the provincial government's sole official language and sharply restricted the use of other languages in education and commerce. While the party's fortunes have fallen and risen and fallen, the primacy of Française has remained.

In the early days, agents of L'Office de la Langue Française fanned out across the territory, scouring the landscape for linguistic insults to the state and her people. MERRY CHRISTMAS signs were removed from storefronts, and department stores had to come up with a new name for Harris Tweed.

About 20% of the population spoke English as a primary language, and they instantly felt like second-class citizens. Francophones responded that it was about time *les Anglais* knew what second-class citizenship felt like.

Affected, too, was the food world. By fiat and threat of punishment, hamburgers became *hambourgeois* and hot dog was rechristened *chiens chaud*. And Schwartz's Montréal Hebrew Delicatessen (one of the city's fixtures since 1928)? It became Chez Schwartz Charcuterie Hébraïque de Montréal.

Meech Lake to cobble together a collection of constitutional reforms. The Meech Lake Accord, as it came to be known, addressed a variety of issues, but most important to the Québécois was that it recognized Québec as a "distinct society" within the federation. Manitoba and Newfoundland, however, failed to ratify the accord by the June 23, 1990, deadline.

As a result, support for the secessionist cause burgeoned in Québec. An election firmly placed the Parti Québécois in control of the provincial government again. A 1995 referendum on succession from the Canadian union was only narrowly defeated. The issue continued to divide families and dominate political discourse.

The year 2007 may have marked the beginning of the end the issue. In provincial elections, Parti Québécois placed third with just 28% of the vote. The election was perceived by many as the first step in closing the door on the campaign for independence.

As *Gourmet* editor Reichl wrote in that same March 2006 essay, "the city has completely transformed itself. Montréal is now the most bilingual city in the world, a place where every citizen seems equally at home in French and English. This change is about much more than mere language, however. Today, all the barriers seem to have melted away, allowing the inhabitants to come together and embrace one another's cultures."

Québécois, it must be said, are exceedingly gracious hosts. Montréal may be the largest French-speaking city outside Paris, but most Montréalers switch effortlessly from one language to the other as the situation dictates. Telephone operators go from French to English the instant they hear an English word, as do most store clerks, waiters, and hotel staff. This is less the case in country villages and in Québec City, but for visitors, there is virtually no problem that can't be solved with a few

The Separatist Movement in Brief

- In 1968, René Lévesque and fellow separatist movement members found the Parti Québécois (PQ) in an earnest attempt to make Québec independent from the rest of Canada.
- In 1976, the PQ come to power in Québec and retain leadership until 1985. The PQ regain power from the Liberals in 1994 and hold it more or less consistently through 2003.
- Forty years after its founding, the PQ suffers an anemic third-place showing in 2007 provincial elections. This is perceived by many as a crushing defeat for both the party and the separatist movement.

French words, some expressive gestures, and a little goodwill.

POLITICAL POWER FOR THE FIRST NATIONS

The French colonialists eventually came to realize that it was only through trade, alliances, and treaties—rather than force—that relations between them and native peoples could develop. From early on, formal alliances were part of the texture of the uneasy relationship between the two groups.

Describing and characterizing the long history of the treatment of native peoples is difficult. Assimilation of natives into European identity, for instance, was once perceived as a positive goal, but has been repudiated by natives, who are collectively known today as First Nations.

The 1876 Indian Act established federal Canadian authority over the rights and lands of "Indians" and set in place an assimilation process. Indians who wanted full rights as Canadians had to relinquish their legal Indian status and renounce their Indian identity. Participation in traditional dances, for instance, became punishable by imprisonment.

Those laws changed slowly. It was only in 1985, for instance, that an Indian woman who married a non-Indian would not automatically lose her Indian status. In 2007, the United Nations General Assembly adopted the Declaration on the Rights of Indigenous Peoples, recognizing the right of aboriginals to self-determination.

The interests of native peoples are today represented by the Assembly of the First Nations, which was established in 1985. Economic interests are represented in part by Société Touristique des Autochtones du Québec (STAQ), the aboriginal tourism corporation. STAQ puts out an official tourist guide annually, available at tourist offices. Other information is online at www.staq.net.

3 MONTREAL & QUEBEC CITY'S ART & ARCHITECTURE

Classic European art and architectural influences meet with an urbane, design-heavy aesthetic in Montréal and Québec City. Here are some art highlights:

FREDERICK LAW OLMSTED & PARC DU MONT-ROYAL

American landscape architect Frederick Law Olmsted created New York City's Central Park and also designed the park that surrounds the "mountain" in the center of Montréal. Parc du Mont-Royal opened in 1876. Olmsted's vision was to make the landscape seem more mountainous by using exaggerated vegetation—shade trees at the bottom of a path that climbs its side, for instance—to create the illusion of being in a valley at the lower elevations. Unfortunately, Montréal suffered a depression in the mid-1870s and many of the architect's plans were abandoned. The path was built but not according to the original plan, and vegetation ideas were abandoned. Still, Parc du Mont-Royal is an urban oasis and is used by many in all four seasons. For a walking tour of the park, see p. 140.

BRUCE PRICE & HIS CHATEAU FRONTENAC

It is an American architect, Bruce Price (1845–1903), who is responsible for the most iconic building of the entire Québec province: Château Frontenac, Québec City's visual center.

"The Château" opened as a hotel in 1893. With its castlelike architecture, soaring turrets, and romantic French-Renaissance mystery, it achieved the goal of becoming the most talked-about accommodation in North America. Today, it's a high-end hotel managed by the Fairmont chain.

The château was one of many similar-styled hotels commissioned by the bigwigs of the Canadian Pacific Railway in the late 19th century, when they were constructing Canada's first transcontinental railway. The company calculated that luxury accommodations would encourage travelers with money to travel by train.

Price also designed Montréal's Windsor Station as part of the same Canadian Pacific Railway project, as well as Dalhousie Station in Montréal, the facade of Royal Victoria College in Montréal, and the Gare du Palais train station in Québec City, whose turrets echo those of the Château Frontenac.

Architecture professor Claude Bergeron of Québec City's Univérsité Laval noted that as the leading practitioner of the Château style, Price "is sometimes credited with having made it a national Canadian style."

AVANT-GARDE VISION

In 1967, Montréal hosted the World's Fair, which it called Expo 67. The event was hugely successful—62 nations participated and over 50 million people visited. Overnight, Montréal was a star. With its avant-garde vision on display, it became a kind of prototype for a 20th-century city.

One of the most exhilarating buildings was Habitat 67, a 158-unit housing complex on the St. Lawrence river. Designed by Montréal architect Moshe Safdie, it looks like a collection of modular concrete blocks all piled together. The vision was to show what community housing could look like. It's not open to the public today, but it can be seen from the western end of Vieux-Port, and there are photos and information at Safdie's website, www.msafdie.com.

Palais des Congrès (Convention Center), at the northern edge of Vieux-Montréal,

---

Montréal Impressions

You cannot fancy you are in America; everything about it conveys the idea of a substantial, handsomely built European town, with modern improvements of half-English, half-French architecture.

—English Lt. Col. Burrows Willcocks Arthur Sleigh, writing about his time in Montréal in *Pine Forests and Hacmatack Clearings,* 1853

Geography 101: Telling Mountains from Molehills

Montréal is on an island that's part of the Hochelaga Archipelago. The island is situated in the St. Lawrence River near the confluence with the Ottawa River. At Montréal's center is a 232m (761-ft.) hill which natives like to think of as a mountain. It's called Mont Royal, and it's the geographic landmark from which the city takes its name.

Real mountains, though, rise nearby. The Laurentides, also called the Laurentians, comprise the world's oldest range and the playground of the Québécois. Their highest peak, Mont-Tremblant, is 968m (3,176 ft.). As well, the Appalachians' northern foothills separate Québec from the U.S., adding to the beauty of the Cantons-de-l'Est. This bucolic region on the opposite side of the St. Lawrence was once known as the Eastern Townships and is where many Montréalers have country homes.

is an unlikely design triumph, too. Built between 2000 and 2002 as part of a renovation and extension of the center, the building's transparent glass exterior walls are a crazy quilt of pink, yellow, blue, green, red, and purple rectangles. You get the full effect when you step into the inside hallway, when the sun streams in, it's like being inside a kaleidoscope. It's the vision of Montréal architect Mario Saia.

DESIGN MONTREAL

Montréal continues to be one of North America's most stylish cities. In 2006, UNESCO, the United Nations Educational, Scientific, and Cultural Organization, designated Montréal a "UNESCO City of Design" for "its ability to inspire synergy between public and private players." With the distinction, Montréal joined Buenos Aires and Berlin, other honorees, as a high-style city worth watching.

Design Montréal (www.designmontreal. com) is an organization devoted to celebrating and networking the city's arts and fashion communities. It holds design and architecture competitions, and its Design Montréal Open House, which debuted in 2007, is a 2-day event in May that opens the doors of the city's design-centric agencies and projects.

Much of what constitutes cutting-edge design is creative reuse of older buildings and materials. Among such venues is the industrial Darling Foundry, which houses in its raw, concrete space a contemporary art center and a small restaurant, the Cluny ArtBar (p. 90). Fashion also simmers, with an increasing number of innovative locals setting up shop. It all comes to a boil during early June's Montréal Fashion & Design Festival, which features fashion shows on outdoor stages in the heart of downtown, and during Montréal Fashion Week, in mid-October. Details are at www.sensationmode.com.

The city's aesthetic was well summed up by one fashionista in the *Montréal Gazette* a few years ago: "I'm all about the black, the white, and beige. Fall is about comfort—not that American style of sloppy comfort, but casual style."

INUIT ART

The region's most compelling artwork is indigenous. In Montréal, the Musée McCord has a First Nations room that displays objects from Canada's native population, including meticulous beadwork, baby carriers, and fishing implements. The city's annual First People's Festival, held in mid-June, highlights Amerindian and

Inuit cultures by way of film, video, visual arts, music, and dance. Visit www.native lynx.qc.ca or call ℂ 514/572-1799.

In Québec City, the Musée des Beaux-Arts du Québec is home to an important Inuit art collection assembled over many years by Raymond Brousseau. Also in Québec City, a permanent exhibition at the Musée de la Civilisation, "Nous, les Premières Nations" ("We, the First Nations"), provides a fascinating look at the history and culture of the Abenakis, Algonquins, Atikamekw, Crees, Hurons-Wendat, Inuit, Malecites, Micmacs, Innu, Mohawks, and Naskapis—the 11 First Nation tribes whose combined 70,000 members inhabit Québec today.

THOSE EXTERNAL STAIRCASES

Stroll through Montréal's Plateau Mont-Royal and Mile End neighborhoods and one of the first things you'll notice are the

outside staircases on the two- and three-story houses. Many are made of wrought iron, and most have shapely, sensual curves. One theory has it that they were first designed to accommodate immigrant families who wanted their own front doors even for second-floor apartments. Another has it that landlords put the stairs outside to cut down on common interior space that wouldn't count toward rental space.

The Catholic church, ever a force in the city, was originally all for the stairs because they allowed neighbors to keep an eye on each other. After the aesthetic tide turned, however, brick archways called loggia were built to hide the stairways. But the archway walls created ready-made nooks for teens to linger in, and the church helped push through legislation that banned new staircases entirely. That ban was lifted in the 1980s so that citywide efforts to maintain and renovate properties could keep the unique features intact.

4 MONTREAL & QUEBEC CITY IN POPULAR CULTURE

BOOKS & THEATER The late Jewish Anglophone Mordecai Richler inveighed against the excesses of Québec's separatists and language zealots in a barrage of books and critical essays in newspapers and magazines.

Richler wrote from the perspective of a minority within a minority and set most of his books in the working-class Jewish neighborhood of St. Urbain of the 1940s and 1950s, with protagonists who are poor, streetwise, and intolerant of the prejudices of other Jews, French-Canadians, and WASPs from the city's English-side Westmount neighborhood. His most famous book is *The Apprenticeship of Duddy Kravitz* (Pocket Books, 1959), which in 1974 was made into a movie of

the same name starring Richard Dreyfuss. In 2009 it was announced that Dustin Hoffman and Paul Giamatti would star in a film version of Richler's *Barney's Vision,* with filming in Montréal, the Laurentians, Rome, and New York City.

Legendary singer-songwriter Leonard Cohen wrote two novels set in Montréal: 1963's The Favorite Game (Vintage, 2003) and 1966's Beautiful Losers (Vintage, 1993).

Playwright Michel Tremblay, an important dramatist, grew up in Montréal's Plateau Mont-Royal neighborhood and uses that setting for much of his work. His *Les Belles-Sœurs (The Sisters-in-Law),* written in 1965, introduced the lives of working-class Francophone Québécois to the world. It was published in English by Talonbooks in 1992.

MUSIC   In 2008, the Putumayo World Music record label released a compilation CD called *Québéc Quebec* in honor of Québec City's 400th anniversary. It's a collection of 11 songs that reflect the province's rich musical diversity and provides a great introduction to Québécois music. Highlights include the upbeat, angelic-voiced Chloé Sainte-Marie ("Brûlots"); the pop band DobaCaracol ("Etrange"), which fuses a reggae groove with African rhythms and French-language pop; and the Celtic folk of La Bottine Souriante ("La Brunette Est Là"), the preeminent representatives of traditional Québécois music, which has its roots in French, English, Scottish, and Irish folk traditions. Samples of the songs can be heard at the Putumayo website (www.putumayo.com), where there's also a video of DobaCaracol.

Montréal has a strong showing of innovative musicians who hail from its clubs. Singer-songwriter Leonard Cohen is the best known. He grew up in the Westmount neighborhood and attended McGill University. He was inducted into the U.S. Rock and Roll Hall of Fame in 2008.

Rufus Wainwright, another singer-songwriter, grew up in Montréal and got his start at city clubs. Alternative rock bands from the city include Arcade Fire and Wolf Parade. (The band Of Montreal, however, is a U.S. band from Athens, Georgia.)

FILM & TELEVISION   Many U.S. films are made beyond the northern border for financial reasons, even when their American locales are important parts of the stories (*Brokeback Mountain,* for instance, was filmed in Alberta). Québécois films—made in the province, in French, for Québec audiences—can be difficult to track

down outside the region. Recent features worth seeking out include Jean-Marc Vallée's box-office hit *C.R.A.Z.Y.,* a gay coming-of-age story.

Alanis Obomsawin is an important documentarian. A member of the Abenaki Nation who was raised on the Odanak Reserve near Montréal, she began making movies for the National Film Board of Canada (www.nfb.ca) 40 years ago and has produced more than 30 documentaries about the hard edges of the lives of aboriginal people. In 2008, "the first lady of First Nations film"—as the commissioner of the National Film Board put it—received the Governor General's Performing Arts Award for Lifetime Artistic Achievement. A major retrospective of her work was shown at New York's Museum of Modern Art and Boston's Museum of Fine Art that same year.

Obomsawin has documented police raids of reservation lands, homelessness among natives living in cities, and a wrenching incident in 1990 that pitted native peoples against the government over lands that were slated to be turned into a golf course. That last event, detailed in the 1993 film Kanehsatake: 270 Years of Resistance, took place about an hour west of Montréal and included a months-long armed standoff between Mohawks and authorities.

"The land question and Mohawk sovereignty have been issues since the French and English first settled the area," Obomsawin has said. "A lot of promises were made and never kept. What the confrontation of 1990 showed is that this is a generation that is not going to put up with what happened in the past."

In 2007, the CBC television show *Little Mosque on the Prairie* began offering a peek into the religious and cultural issues faced by Canada's large immigrant population.

5 EATING & DRINKING IN MONTREAL & QUEBEC CITY

A generation ago, most Montréal and Québec City restaurants served only French food. A few *temples de cuisine* delivered haute standards of gastronomy, while numerous accomplished bistros served up humbler ingredients in less grand settings, and folksy places featured the hearty fare that long employed the ingredients available in New France—game such as caribou, maple syrup, and root vegetables. Everything else was considered "ethnic." Food crazes of the 1980s focusing on Cajun, Tex-Mex, and fusion didn't make much of a dent at the time: Québec province was French, and that was that.

Over the last 15 years, however, this attitude changed dramatically. The 1990s recession put many restaurateurs out of business and forced others to reexamine their operation. In Montréal, especially, immigrants brought the cooking styles of the world to the city.

Restaurants are colloquially called "restos," and they range from moderately priced bistros, cafes, and ethnic joints to swank luxury epicurean shrines.

MENU BASICS

One thing to always look for are *table d'hôte* meals. These are fixed-price menus, and with them, three- or four-course meals can be had for little more than the price of an a la carte main course. Even the best restaurants offer them, which means that you'll be able to sample some excellent venues without breaking the bank. *Table d'hôte* meals are often offered at lunch, when they are even less expensive; having your main meal midday instead of in the evening is the most economical way to sample many of the top establishments.

Remember that for the Québécois, *dîner* (dinner) is the noon meal, and *souper* (supper) is the evening meal. In this book, the word dinner is used in the common American sense—the evening meal. Note, too, that an *entrée* in Québec is an appetizer, while a *plat principal* is a main course. In fancier places, where a preappetizer nibble is proffered, it's called an *amuse bouche.*

Many higher-end establishments now offer tasting menus, with many smaller dishes over the course of a meal that offer a sampling of the chef's skills. Gaining popularity are surprise menus, also called "chef's whim," where you don't know what you're getting until it's there in front of you. It's becoming more common to find fine restaurants that offer wine pairings with meals as well, where the sommelier selects a glass for each course.

LOCAL FOOD HIGHLIGHTS

Be sure to try regional specialties. A Québécois favorite is *poutine:* french fries doused with gravy and cheese curds. It's ubiquitous in winter.

Game is popular, including venison, quail, goose, caribou, and wapiti (North American deer). Many menus feature emu and lamb raised north of Quebec City in Charlevoix. Mussels and salmon are also standard.

For sandwiches and snacks that only cost a few dollars, try any of the numerous places that go by the generic name *casse-croûte.* Menu items might include soup and *chiens chaud* (hot dogs).

Québec cheeses deserve attention, and many can only be sampled in Canada because they are often unpasteurized—made of *lait cru* (raw milk)—and therefore subject to strict export rules. Better restaurants will offer them as a final course. Of the more than 500 varieties available, you might look for Mimolette Jeune (firm, fragrant, orange), Valbert St-Isidor (similar to Swiss in texture), St-Basil de Port Neuf (buttery), Cru des Erables (soft, ripe), Oka (semisoft, made of cow's milk in a monastery), and Le Chèvre Noire (a sharp goat variety covered in black wax). Québec cheeses pick up armfuls of prizes each year in the American Cheese Society competition, North America's largest.

Cheeses with the *fromages de pays* label are made in Québec with whole milk and no modified milk ingredients. The label represents solidarity among artisanal producers and is supported by Solidarité Rurale du Québec, a group devoted to revitalizing rural communities. It's also supported by Slow Food Québec, which promotes sustainable agriculture and local production. Information is available at www.fromageduquebec.qc.ca.

BEER & WINE

Alcohol is heavily taxed, and imported varieties even more so than domestic versions, so if you're looking to save a little, buy Canadian. That's not difficult when it comes to beer, for there are many regional breweries, from Montréal powerhouse Molson to micro, that produce delicious products. Among the best local options are Belle Gueule and Boréal. The sign BIERES EN FUT means "beers on draft."

Wine is another matter. It is not produced in significant quantities in Canada due to a climate generally inhospitable to the essential grapes. But you might try bottles from the vineyards of the Cantons-de-l'Est region (just east of Montréal). Sample, too, the sweet "ice wines" and "ice ciders" made from fruit after the first frost. Many decent ones come from vineyards and orchards just an hour from Montréal.

One popular wine is L'Orpailleur, Seyval (www.orpailleur.ca). *L'orpailleur* refers to someone who mines for gold in streams—the idea being that trying to make good wine in Québec's cold climate is a similar leap of faith in an ability to defy the odds.

Planning Your Trip to Montréal & Québec City

The province of Québec is immense: It's the largest province in the second-largest country in the world (after Russia), covers an area more than three times the size of France, and stretches from the northern borders of New York, Vermont, and New Hampshire up almost to the Arctic Circle.

That said, most of the region's population lives in the stretch just immediately north of the U.S. border. Its major cities and towns, including Montréal and Québec City, are in this band of land, with the greater Montréal metropolitan area home to nearly half of the province's population. Québec City lies just 263km (163 miles) northeast of Montréal, commanding a stunning location on the rim of a promontory overlooking the St. Lawrence River, which is at its narrowest here. Most of the province's developed resort and scenic areas lie within a 3-hour drive of either city.

It can't be overstated how much the British and French struggle for dominance in the 1700s and 1800s for North America—the New World—continues to shape Québec's character today. A bit of history is in order (and you'll find yourself immersed in even more when you're touring the cities; it's inevitable). Samuel de Champlain arrived in Québec City in 1608, determined to settle the region as a French colony, a year after Britain's Virginia Company founded its fledgling colony of Jamestown, hundreds of miles to the south. French forces ruled the region until 1759, when British troops surprised the French by coming up and over the Cap Diamant cliffs in Québec City. The ensuing battle, fought on the city's Plains of Abraham on September 13, 1759, is one of the most important battles in North American history. Britain won, resulting in a continent that tilted away from France and was under British influence for more than a century. That influence carries on today, with Queen Elizabeth II's face still gracing all Canadian currency.

And yet, although most of Canada is English-speaking, 400 years of French tradition still hold strong in Québec. The first language of the vast majority of residents is French. There are areas of the province, outside of the cities, where the *only* spoken language is French. Much of the music and architecture feels French. And so Québec is a wholly unique blend of French and British inspiration. Much of the time the two halves blend. Sometimes they still do battle.

When you're planning a trip to Montréal and Québec City, imagine planning a trip to cosmopolitan European cities, where the old world rubs shoulders with new world. Accommodations range from modest inns to luxury hotels, and restaurants run the gamut from bistro-cozy to haute cuisine. Locals are lively and welcoming.

For additional help in planning your trip and more on-the-ground resources in Québec province, look through "Fast Facts" on p. 289.

High season in Québec province is June 24 (Jean-Baptiste Day) through early September (Labour Day). In Québec City, the period from Christmas to New Year's and February weekends during the big winter Carnaval are busy, too. Just north of Montréal, the Laurentian mountains do big ski business in the cold months. Hotels are most likely to be full and charge their highest rates in these periods.

Low season is during March and April, when few events are scheduled and winter sports start to be iffy. The late-fall months of October and November are also slow, due to their all-but-empty social calendars.

WEATHER

Temperatures are usually a few degrees lower in Québec City than in Montréal. Spring, short but sweet, arrives around the middle of May. Summer (mid-June through mid-Sept) tends to be humid in Montréal, Québec City, and other communities along the St. Lawrence River, and drier at the inland resorts of the Laurentides and the Cantons-de-l'Est. Intense, but usually brief, heat waves mark July and early August, but temperatures rarely remain oppressive in the evenings.

Autumn (Sept–Oct) is as short and changeable as spring, with warm days and cool or chilly nights. It's during this season that Canadian maples blaze with color for weeks.

Winter brings dependable snows for skiing in the Laurentides, Cantons-de-l'Est, and, north of Québec City, Charlevoix. Snow and slush are present from November to March. For many, Montréal's underground city is a climate-controlled blessing during this time.

For the current Montréal weather forecast, call ✆ **514/283-3010** or check www.weatheroffice.gc.ca.

Montréal's Average Monthly Temperatures (°F/°C)

	Jan	Feb	Mar	Apr	May	June	July	Aug	Sept	Oct	Nov	Dec
High (°F)	21	24	35	51	65	73	79	76	66	54	41	27
(°C)	–6	–4	2	11	18	23	26	24	19	12	5	–3
Low (°F)	7	10	21	35	47	56	61	59	50	39	29	13
(°C)	–14	–12	–6	2	8	13	16	15	10	4	–2	–11

Québec City's Average Monthly Temperatures (°F/°C)

	Jan	Feb	Mar	Apr	May	June	July	Aug	Sept	Oct	Nov	Dec
High (°F)	18	21	32	46	62	71	76	74	63	50	37	23
(°C)	–8	–6	0	8	17	22	24	23	17	10	3	–5
Low (°F)	2	5	16	31	43	53	58	56	46	36	25	9
(°C)	–17	–15	–9	–1	6	12	14	13	8	2	–4	–13

Note: To convert Celsius to Fahrenheit, multiply the Celsius reading by 1.8 and then add 32. For example, 17°C × 1.8 is 30.6 + 32 is 62.6°F.

MONTREAL & QUEBEC CITY CALENDAR OF EVENTS

Year-round, it's nearly impossible to miss a celebration of some sort in Montréal and Québec City. For an exhaustive list of events beyond those listed here, check http://events.frommers.com. You'll find a searchable, up-to-the-minute roster of what's happening in cities all over the world.

JANUARY

La Fête des Neiges (the Snow Festival), Montréal. Montréal's answer to Québec City's February winter Carnaval (see below) features dog-sled runs, a mock survival camp, street hockey, and tobogganing. The festival was canceled in 2008 for the first time in its 25-year history because of a labor dispute, but was back in 2009, over the last 2 weekends in January. Visit **www.fetedes neiges.com** or call © **514/872-6120** for 2010 details.

FEBRUARY

Carnaval de Québec, Québec City. Never mind that temperatures in Québec regularly plummet in winter to well below freezing. Canadians are extraordinarily good-natured about the cold and happily pack the family up to come out and play. A snowman called Bonhomme (Good Fellow) shuffles into town to preside over the merriment, and revelers descend upon the city to eddy around a monumental ice palace erected in front of the Parliament Building, to watch a dog-sledding race on Old Town's narrow streets, to play foosball on a human-size scale, to fly over crowds on a zipline, to ride down snowy hills in rubber tubes, and, not least of all, to dance at outdoor concerts.

The party is family-friendly, even considering the wide availability of plastic trumpets and canes filled with a concoction called caribou, the principal ingredients of which are cheap liquor and sweet red wine. Try not to miss the canoe race that has teams rowing, dragging, and stumbling with canoes across the St. Lawrence's treacherous ice floes. It's homage to how the city used to break up the ice to keep a path open to Lévis, the town across the river.

A C$10 pass provides access to most activities over the 17 days. Hotel reservations must be made well in advance.

Visit **www.carnaval.qc.ca** or call © 866/422-7628 or 418/621-5555 for details. January 29 to February 14, 2010.

Festival Montréal en Lumière (Montréal High Lights Festival). At the heart of this winter celebration are the culinary competitions and wine tastings. There are also multimedia light shows, classical and pop concerts, and a Montréal All-Nighter that ends with a free breakfast at dawn. Visit **www.montrealhighlights.com** or call © 888/477-9955 or 514/288-9955 for details. February 18 to 28, 2010.

APRIL

Bal en Blanc Party Week, Montréal. In 2009, an estimated 15,000 people came to the city for the 5-day rave/dance party—one of the biggest such events in the world. Last year's "White Party Week" was the 15th annual affair and featured house and trance D.J. events at Palais des Congrès and clubs such as Parking. Visit **www.balenblac.com**. Mid-April over Easter weekend.

MAY

Montréal Museums Day. Open house for most of the city's museums, with free admission and free shuttle buses. Visit **www.museesmontreal.org** or call the tourism office (© 877/266-5687 or 514/873-2015) for details. Last Sunday in May.

Montréal Bike Fest. For 8 days, tens of thousands of enthusiasts converge on Montréal to participate in cycling competitions that include a nocturnal bike ride (Tour la Nuit) and the grueling Tour de l'Île, a 52km (32-mile) race around the island's rim; it draws 30,000 cyclists, shuts down roads, and attracts more than 100,000 spectators. The nonprofit biking organization Vélo Québec (© 800/567-8356 or 514/521-8356) lists details at **www.velo.qc.ca**. Late May into early June.

Festival Transamériques, Montréal. Formerly the Festival de Théâtre des Amériques, this program was renamed and refocused in 2007, and now presents contemporary theater and dance works by companies from Canada and around the world. Visit **www.fta.qc.ca** or call ☏ **866/984-3822** or 514/842-0704. Late May into early June.

JUNE

Mondial de la Bière, Montréal. Yes, beer fans, this is a 5-day festival devoted to your favorite beverage. Admission is free and tasting coupons are C$1 each, with most tastings costing one to five coupons for 3 ounce samples. Showcased are world brands and boutique microbreweries, and "courses" lead to a "Diploma in Beer Tasting." Details at **www.festivalmondialbiere.qc.ca** and ☏ **514/722-9640.** Early June.

Saint-Ambroise Montréal Fringe Festival. For a long time, the main graphic at this event's website was a hand raising its middle finger. That gives you an idea of the attitude behind the Plateau Mont-Royal fest. It's 10 days of out-there theater with acts such as a one-man *Star Wars* stand-up, clowns gone bad, and drunken drag queens. The festival proclaims that there's "No Artistic Direction. Artists are selected by lottery… No Censorship. Artists have complete freedom to present ANYTHING." *Vive le fringe!* Check **www.montrealfringe.ca** or call ☏ **514/849-3378.** Mid-June.

Jean-Baptiste Day. Honoring St. John the Baptist, the patron saint of French-Canadians, this day is marked by far more festivities and enthusiasm throughout Québec than is Canada Day on July 1 (listed below). It's Québec's own *fête nationale* with fireworks, bonfires, music in parks, and parades. Visit **www.fetenationaleduquebec. com** for details. June 24.

L'International des Feux Loto-Québec (International Fireworks Competition), Montréal. Pitting the shows of different countries against each other, this annual fireworks competition is a spectacular event. Buy tickets to watch from the open-air theater in La Ronde amusement park on Île Ste-Hélène, or enjoy the pyrotechnics for free from almost anywhere overlooking the river (tickets have the added benefit of including admission to the amusement park). Kids, needless to say, love the whole explosive business. Go to **www. internationaldesfeuxloto-quebec.com** or call ☏ **514/397-2000** for details. In 2009, the festival celebrated its 25th anniversary over 11 Saturdays from June to August. Check for 2010 dates.

JULY

Canada Day. On July 1, 1867, three British colonies joined together to form the federation of Canada, with further independence from Britain coming in stages in the 1880s. Celebrations of Canada's birthday are biggest in Ottawa, though there are concerts, flag raisings, and family festivities in Montréal and Québec City. Get more information at **www.celafete.ca**. July 1.

Festival International de Jazz de Montréal. Since Montréal has a long tradition in jazz, this is one of the monster events on the city's calendar, celebrating America's art form since 1979. The 2009 edition featured performances by Tony Bennett, Ben Harper, Madeleine Peyroux, and Dave Brubeck. It costs serious money to hear stars of such magnitude, and tickets often sell out months in advance. Fortunately, 450 free outdoor performances also take place during the late-June/early July party, many right on downtown's streets and plazas. Visit **www.montreal jazzfest.com** or call ☏ **888/515-0515** or 514/871-1881. July 1 to 11, 2010.

Festival Juste pour Rire (Just for Laughs Festival), Montréal. Well-known comics including Bill Cosby, Whoopi Goldberg, and John Cleese have been featured, while smaller-name Francophone and Anglophone groups and stand-ups from around the world come to perform. It's held mostly along rue St-Denis and elsewhere in the Latin Quarter, both indoors and on the street. Check **www.hahaha.com** or call ☎ **888/244-3155** or 514/845-2322 for details. Held July 16 to 26, 2009; check for 2010 dates.

Festival d'Eté (Summer Festival), Québec City. The world's largest Francophone music festival happens in the heart of Vieux-Québec and, since 2007, in the St-Roch neighborhood. More than 400 performances of rock, jazz, reggae, and classical take place at both indoor and outdoor venues. Check **www.infofestival.com** or call ☎ **888/ 992-5200** or 418/523-4540. July 8 to 18, 2010.

Festival International Nuits d'Afrique, Montréal. A lively 13-day world-beat music showcase featuring musicians from the Caribbean, Africa, and the Americas. The festival also presents concerts year-round. Visit **www.festival nuitsdafrique.com** or call ☎ **514/499-9239.** Mid-July.

Les Grands Feux Loto-Québec, Québec City. Overlapping with Montréal's fireworks competition (see above), Québec's event uses the highly scenic Montmorency Falls 15 minutes north of the city center as its setting. Pyrotechnical teams are invited from countries around the world. Tickets get you admission to the base of the falls: there are 6,000 reserved bleacher seats and 22,500 general-admission tickets. Go to **www.quebecfireworks.com** or call ☎ **888/523-3389** or 418/523-3389 for details. Wednesdays and Saturdays. July 24 to August 11, 2010.

Divers/Cité Festival, Montréal. In partnership with government agencies and sponsored by major corporations, Divers/Cité is one of North America's largest parties for gay, lesbian, bisexual, and transgendered people. It's 8 days of dance, drag, art, and music concerts, and nearly everything is outdoors and free. Details at **www.diverscite.org** or ☎ **514/285-4011.** July 24 to August 1, 2010.

Les FrancoFolies de Montréal. Since 1988, this music fest has featured French-language pop, hip-hop, electronic, world beat, and *chanson.* There are 70 indoor shows and twice as many that are outdoors and free. Check **www. francofolies.com**. Late July into early August.

Festival International de Courses de Bateaux-Dragons de Montréal. The annual dragon boat festival welcomes some 200 teams that pour into the Olympic Basin on Île Notre-Dame. In addition to races, there are drawing contests for children and opportunities to try paddling on the ancient Chinese crafts. Details are at **www.montreal dragonboat.com**. Two days in late July.

AUGUST

Festival des Films du Monde (World Film Festival), Montréal. This festival has been an international film event since 1977. A strong panel of actors, directors, and writers from around the world make up the jury each year, giving the event a weight that many festivals lack. Various movie theaters play host. Check **www.ffm-montreal.org** or call ☎ **514/848-3883** for details. Late August to early September.

SEPTEMBER

Fall Foliage. Starting midmonth, the maple trees blaze with color and a walk in the parks of Montréal and Québec City is a refreshing tonic. It's also a perfect time to drive to the Laurentians or Cantons-de-L'Est (both near Montréal) or Île d'Orléans or Charlevoix (both easy drives from Québec City).

OCTOBER

Black & Blue Festival, Montréal. One of the biggest gay events on the planet, this party was, a few years ago, named the best international fest by France's Pink TV Awards, beating out even Carnival in Rio. And when we say big, we mean *big:* The main event is an all-night party at Olympic Stadium. There's also a Jock Ball, a Leather Ball, and a Military Ball. Visit **www.bbcm.org** or call © **514/875-7026.** Seven days in mid-October.

Festival du Nouveau Cinéma, Montréal. Screenings of new and experimental films ignite controversy, and forums discuss the latest trends in cinema and video. Events take place at halls and cinemas throughout the city. Check **www.nouveaucinema.ca** or call © **514/844-2172.** Twelve days in mid-October.

DECEMBER

Christmas through New Year's, Québec City. Celebrating the holidays *a la française* is a particular treat here, where the streets are almost certainly banked with snow and nearly every ancient building sports wreaths, decorated fir trees, and glittery white lights.

2 ENTRY REQUIREMENTS

PASSPORTS

Passport rules for travelers from the U.S. to Canada are now similar to rules for all other international travelers to the country: A passport, passport card, or Western Hemisphere Travel Initiative document is required for entry. For U.S. citizens, the passport requirement has been an evolving change over the past few years implemented as part of the U.S. Intelligence Reform and Terrorism Prevention Act of 2004. Since January 2007, all air travelers have been required to present a valid passport, and as of June 1, 2009, the same requirements apply to everyone 16 years old and up traveling by land or sea, including trips by car, bus, or cruise ship. U.S. citizens under 16 will be able to continue using a U.S. birth certificate or naturalization certificate (original only, not a photocopy) at land and sea borders. Details are online at the U.S. Department of State website, **www.travel.state.gov**.

Lawful permanent residents of the U.S. must have their permanent resident cards (green cards) with them to enter Canada and reenter the U.S. More details are available from U.S. Customs and Border Protection (**www.cbp.gov**).

If you are driving into Canada, be sure to have your car's registration with you. U.S. citizens do not need an international driver's license—a state-issued license is fine.

Frequent travelers from the U.S. may want to consider a **NEXUS membership,** which gets you preapproved by U.S. Customs and Border Protection and can speed the trip across the border (when driving, for instance, there is a special lane for NEXUS members). Details are at www.cbp.gov or © **866-NEXUS26** (639-8726).

Note on DWIs: If you have ever been convicted for driving while intoxicated, you may be denied entrance. An approval of rehabilitation may be obtained for a fee from a Canadian consulate in the U.S.

Note for young travelers: Anyone 18 and younger and traveling without a parent must have proof of citizenship and a letter from both parents (or guardians) detailing the length of stay, providing the parents' telephone number, and authorizing the person waiting for them to take care of them while they are in Canada. Note that while the U.S. defines a minor as 16 years or younger, Canada defines a minor as 18 years or younger.

Note for parents traveling with children: Because of international concerns about child abduction, if you are divorced, separated, or traveling without your spouse and are bringing your children to Canada, you will need proof of custody or a notarized letter from the other parent giving permission for foreign travel. The letter should include addresses and phone numbers where the parents or guardians can be reached and identify a person who can confirm that the children are not being abducted or taken against their will. Passport requirements apply to children of all ages.

For information on how to obtain a passport, read "Passports" in the "Fast Facts" section of chapter 21.

VISAS

Citizens of the U.S., U.K., Australia, Ireland, and New Zealand do not need visas to enter Canada. Citizens of many other countries must have visas, which they'll need to apply for well in advance at their nearest Canadian embassy or consulate. Information is available at the **Citizenship and Immigration Canada** website, www. cic.gc.ca.

CUSTOMS
What You Can Bring into Canada

Visitors can expect at least a probing question or two at the border or airport. Normal baggage and personal possessions should be no problem, but plants, animals, and other products may be prohibited or require additional documents before they're allowed in.

For specific information about Canadian rules, check with the **Canada Border**

Services Agency (© **506/636-5064** from outside the country or 800/461-9999 within Canada; www.cbsa-asfc.gc.ca). Search for "bsf5082" to get a full list of visitor information.

Tobacco and alcoholic beverages face strict import restrictions: Individuals 18 years or older are allowed to bring in 200 cigarettes, 50 cigars, or 200 grams of tobacco; and 1.14 liters of liquor, 1.5 liters of wine, or 24 cans or bottles of beer. Additional amounts face hefty taxes.

Possession of a car radar detector is prohibited, whether or not it is connected. Police officers can confiscate it and fine the owner C$500 to C$1,000.

A car driven into Canada can stay for the duration allowed the visitor, which is up to 6 months unless the visitor has arranged permission for a longer stay.

Visitors can temporarily bring recreational vehicles, such as snowmobiles, boats, and trailers, as well as outboard motors, for personal use.

If you do not declare goods or falsely declare them, they can be seized *along with the vehicle in which you brought them.*

What You Can Take Home from Canada

For information on what you're allowed to bring home, contact the following agencies:

U.S. Citizens: U.S. Customs and Border Protection (CBP), 1300 Pennsylvania Ave., NW, Washington, DC 20229 (© **877/287-8667;** www.cbp.gov).

U.K. Citizens: HM Customs & Excise at © **0845/010-9000** (from outside the U.K., 020/8929-0152); www.hmce.gov.uk.

Australian Citizens: Australian Customs Service at © **1300/363-263;** www. customs.gov.au.

New Zealand Citizens: New Zealand Customs, The Customhouse, 17–21 Whitmore St., Box 2218, Wellington (© **04/473-6099** or 0800/428-786; www. customs.govt.nz).

If you're traveling with expensive items such as laptops or musical equipment, consider registering them before you leave your country to avoid challenges at the border on your return.

MEDICAL REQUIREMENTS

Inoculations or vaccinations are not required for entry into Canada.

3 GETTING TO MONTREAL & QUEBEC CITY

Served by highways, transcontinental trains and buses, and several airports, Montréal and Québec City are easily accessible from the U.S. and overseas.

For more information on navigating each city once you've arrived, see the "Getting Around" sections in chapters 5 and 13.

ARRIVING BY PLANE

Most of the world's major airlines fly into the **Aéroport International Pierre-Elliott-Trudeau de Montréal** (airport code YUL; © **800/465-1213** or 514/394-7377; www.admtl.com), more commonly known as Montréal-Trudeau Airport. It used to be called Montréal-Dorval, which you'll find on older maps.

In Québec City, the teeny **Jean Lesage International Airport** (airport code YQB; © **418/640-2600;** www.aeroportdequebec. com) is served by a number of major airlines. Most air traffic comes by way of Montréal, although there are some direct flights from U.S. cities, including Chicago (on United Airlines), Newark and Cleveland (on Continental Airlines), and Detroit (on Delta Airlines). *Tip:* Save time by arranging your flights so that your custom entry will take place at your final Canadian destination, when possible. For instance, if you are flying from the U.S. and have to make one or more stops en route to Canada, make the transfer in the U.S. Otherwise, when you land in Canada you'll have to collect your bags, pass through customs, and then check your bags again before continuing on to your final destination, which may lengthen your overall transit.

To find out which airlines travel to the region, please see "Airline, Hotel & Car-Rental Websites," p. 294.

Getting from the Airports to the Cities

Montréal-Trudeau is served by the shuttle bus **L'Aérobus** (© 514/631-1856), which travels between the airport and downtown, stopping at Berri Terminal, the city's main bus terminal, also known as the Station Centrale d'Autobus. Buses run daily every 30 minutes from 9am to 8:30pm and every hour from 9pm to 9am. One-way fares are C$15 for adults, C$14 for seniors, and C$12 for children. The ride takes about 30 minutes.

A taxi trip to downtown Montréal costs a flat fare of C$38 plus tip. Call © **514/394-7377** for more information.

From Québec City's airport, a taxi to downtown is a fixed-rate C$33. Bus service is no longer available between the airport and Québec City.

Renting a Car on Arrival

Terms, cars, and prices for car rentals are similar to those in U.S. and Europe, and all the larger American companies operate in Canada. Basic rates are about the same from company to company, although a little comparison shopping can unearth modest savings. A charge is usually levied when you return a car in a location other than the one in which it was rented.

Québec is the first Canadian province to mandate that residents have radial snow tires on their cars in winter. The law, which debuted in late 2008, runs from mid-December until March 15. Rental car agencies are required to provide snow tires on car rentals during that period, and many charge an extra, non-negotiable fee.

The minimum age to rent a vehicle in Canada ranges from 21 to 25 years old. Many companies require renters be at least 25 years of age, or they may charge additional fees for those under 25. Persons under 25 may be asked for a major credit card in the same name as their driver's license.

For listings of major **car-rental agencies** in Québec, please see "Airline, Hotel & Car-Rental Websites," p. 294.

ARRIVING BY CAR

All international drivers must carry a valid driver's license from their country of residence. A U.S. license is sufficient as long as you are a visitor and actually are a U.S. resident. A U.K. license is sufficient as well. If the driver's license is in a language other than French or English, an additional International Driver's Permit is required.

Driving north to Montréal from the U.S., the entire journey is on expressways. From New York City, all but the last 40 or so miles of the 603km (375-mile) trip are within New York state on Interstate 87. I-87 links up with Canada's Autoroute 15 at the border, which goes straight to Montréal.

If you come over Pont Champlain, the main bridge into Montréal, you'll likely be greeted by one of its charming LED messages, such as "Someone loves you, drive with care" or "Carpooling is an interesting energy saver."

From Boston, I-93 goes up through New Hampshire's White Mountains and merges into I-91 to cross the tip of Vermont. At the border, I-91 becomes Autoroute 55. Signs lead to Autoroute 10 west, which goes into Montréal. Boston to Montréal is 518km (322 miles).

Québec City is 867km (520 miles) from New York City and 644km (400 miles) from Boston. From New York,

follow the directions to Montréal and then pick up Autoroute 20 to Québec City. From Boston, follow the directions to Montréal, but at Autoroute 10, go east instead of west to stay on Autoroute 55. Get on Autoroute 20 to Québec City and follow signs for the Pont Pierre-Laporte, the major bridge into the city. Turn right onto Boulevard Wilfrid-Laurier (Rte. 175) shortly after crossing the bridge. It changes names first to Boulevard Laurier and then to Grande-Allée, a main boulevard that leads directly into the central Parliament Hill area and the Old City. Once the street passes through the ancient walls that ring the Old City, it becomes rue St-Louis, which leads straight to the famed Château Frontenac on the cliff above the St. Lawrence River.

Another appealing option when you're approaching Québec City from the south is to follow Route 132 along the river's southern side to the town of Lévis. A car ferry there, **Traverse Québec-Lévis** (② 877/787-7483 or 418/643-2019; www.traversiers.gouv.qc.ca), provides a 10-minute ride across the river and a dramatic way to see the city, especially for the first time. Though the schedule varies substantially through the year, the ferry leaves at least every hour from 6am to 2am. One-way costs C$6.25 for the car and driver, C$2.75 for each additional adult, and C$11 for a car with up to six passengers.

When driving between Québec City from Montréal, there are two options: Autoroute 40, which runs along the St. Lawrence's north shore, and Autoroute 20, on the south side (although not hugging the water at all). The trip takes about 3 hours.

In Canada, highway distances and speed limits are given in kilometers (km). The speed limit on the autoroutes is 100kmph (62 mph). There's a stiff penalty for neglecting to wear your seatbelt, and all passengers must be buckled up.

> **Tips Fill Up Before Crossing Over**
>
> Gasoline in Canada is expensive by American standards, even considering the rising prices in the U.S. Gas is sold by the liter, and 3.78 liters equals 1 gallon. Recent prices of C93¢ per liter are equivalent to about C$3.52 per gallon, or US$2.85. If you're driving from the U.S., fill up before you come over the border.

Note on radar detectors: Radar detectors are prohibited in Québec province. They can be confiscated, even if they're not being used.

It is illegal to turn right on a red light on the island of Montréal. It is permitted in the rest of Québec and Canada.

In 2008, Québec became the first province to mandate that residents have radial snow tires on their cars in winter. Visitors and their cars are exempt, but the law does give an indication of how seriously rough the winter driving can be. Consider using snow tires when traveling in the region from December through March.

Members of the American Automobile Association (AAA) are covered by the Canadian Automobile Association (CAA) while driving in Canada. See p. 289 in chapter 21.

ARRIVING BY TRAIN

Montréal is a major terminus on Canada's **VIA Rail** network (© **888/842-7245** or 514/989-2626; www.viarail.ca). Its station, **Gare Centrale,** at 895 rue de la Gauchetière ouest (© **514/989-2626**), is centrally located downtown. The station is connected to the Métro subway system at **Bonaventure Station.** (Gare Windsor, which you might see on some maps, is the city's former train station. It's a beautiful castlelike building now used for offices.) Québec City's train station, **Gare du Palais,** is in Lower Town at 450 rue de la Gare-du-Palais. Many of the hotels listed in this book are up an incline from the station, so a short cab ride might be necessary.

VIA Rail trains are comfortable—all major routes have Wi-Fi, and some trains are equipped with dining cars and sleeping cars.

Amtrak (© **800/872-7245;** www.amtrak.com) has one train per day into Montréal from New York that makes intermediate stops. Called the *Adirondack,* it's very slow, but its scenic route passes along the Hudson River's eastern shore and west of Lake Champlain. It takes 11 hours from New York if all goes well, but delays aren't unusual.

The train ride between Montréal and Québec City takes about 3 hours.

ARRIVING BY BUS

Montréal's central bus station, called **Station Centrale d'Autobus** (© **514/842-2281**), is at 505 bd. de Maisonneuve est. It has a restaurant and an information booth. Beneath the terminal is **Berri-UQAM Station,** the junction of several Métro lines. (UQAM—pronounced "*Oo-kahm*"—stands for Université de Québec à Montréal.) Alternatively, **taxis** usually line up outside the terminal building.

Québec City's bus terminal, at 320 rue Abraham-Martin (© **418/525-3000**), is just beside the train station. As from the train station, it's an uphill climb or short cab ride to Upper Town or other parts of Lower Town.

ARRIVING BY BOAT

Both Montréal and Québec City are stops for cruise ships that travel along the St. Lawrence River (in French, Fleuve Saint-Laurent). The Port of Montréal, where ships dock, is part of the lively Vieux-Port neighborhood and walking distance from restaurants and shops.

Similarly, in Québec City, ships also dock in the Vieux-Port neighborhood,

where, again, there is an abundance of restaurants and shops in walking distance.

4 MONEY & COSTS

Frommer's lists exact prices in the local currency. The currency conversions quoted above were correct at press time. However, rates fluctuate, so before departing consult a currency exchange website such as **www. oanda.com/convert/classic** to check up-to-the-minute rates.

It's always advisable to travel with money in a variety of forms: cash, credit or debit cards, and ATM cards.

If you're flying in and don't have Canadian dollars, you can withdraw money upon arrival at an airport ATM to cover transportation to your hotel, tipping, and other airport incidentals.

Avoid exchanging money at commercial exchange bureaus and hotels, which often have the highest transaction fees.

CURRENCY

Canadian money comes in graduated denominations of dollars and cents. Aside from the $2 coin, Canadian coins are similar to their U.S. counterparts: 1¢, 5¢, 10¢, 25¢. Bills—$5, $10, $20, $50, $100—are all the same size but different colors, depending on the denomination. The gold-colored $1 coin (called a "loonie" by Canadians because of the depiction of a loon on one side) has replaced the $1 bill. A $2 coin, with a bronze center surrounded by a nickel disk, has replaced the $2 bill. The $2 coin is sometimes called a "twonie," a reference to the next-smaller coin.

ATMS

The easiest way to get cash is from an ATM (automated teller machine). As ubiquitous in Québec and the rest of Canada as they are elsewhere, ATMs in French are called GABs, or *guichet automatique bancaire*. They're sometimes referred to as cash machines or cashpoints. ATMs are found outside or inside bank branches, in malls, at train stations, and in small shops, and are as common in small villages as they are in the cities.

Note about PINs: PINs (personal identification numbers) can only be four digits at Canadian ATMs. If your PIN has more numbers, change it before departing, otherwise it will not work.

Note about bank fees: Many banks impose a fee each time you use a card at another bank's ATM, and that fee can be higher for international transactions. U.S. banks sometimes charge US$5 or more for Canadian withdrawals. Check with your bank about its international withdrawal fees before your trip. In addition, the machine from which you get cash is likely to charge its own fee.

Be sure you know your daily withdrawal limit before traveling.

CREDIT & DEBIT CARDS

Credit and debit cards are another safe and easy way to travel. They are accepted at nearly all hotels, restaurants, shops, and attractions. They provide a convenient

The Value of the Canadian Dollar vs. Other Popular Currencies

C$	US$	UK£	Euro€	A$	NZ$
1	0.81	.56	0.62	1.19	1.48

What Things Cost in Québec Province

City hotel room, moderate rate, summer	C$180
Montréal Métro ticket	C$2.75
Table d'hôte 3-course dinner (without alcohol)	C$25
Double espresso	C$3.50
Museum pass for 3 days	C$45
Gasoline: per liter	C93¢
per gallon equivalent	C$3.52

record of all your expenses and generally offer decent exchange rates. Note that many credit card companies assess a "transaction fee" of 1% to 3% on *all* charges incurred abroad.

You can withdraw cash advances from credit cards at banks or ATMs, though high fees make credit card cash advances a pricey way to get cash. Keep in mind that you'll pay interest from the moment of your withdrawal, even if you pay your monthly bill on time.

MasterCard and Visa are most commonly accepted at hotels, restaurants, and shops in the province. American Express, Diners Club, and Discover are taken less often.

CURRENCY EXCHANGE

Main branch banks and *caisses populaires* (credit unions) will exchange most foreign currencies. Tourism offices can often exchange money or point you to a place that will.

5 HEALTH

GENERAL AVAILABILITY OF HEALTHCARE

Canada has a state-run health system, and Québec hospitals are modern and decently equipped, with well-trained staffs.

You are unlikely to get sick from Canada's food or water. The U.S. **Centers for Disease Control and Prevention** (✆ **800/232-4636;** www.cdc.gov/travel) provides up-to-date information on health hazards by region or country and offers food-safety tips.

WHAT TO DO IF YOU GET SICK AWAY FROM HOME

Hospitals are listed on p. 290. Reliable medical clinics around the world are listed at the **International Society of Travel Medicine** (www.istm.org).

Medical treatment in Canada isn't free for foreigners, and doctors and hospitals will make you pay at the time of service. See p. 290 in chapter 21 for suggestions about medical insurance.

Familiar over-the-counter medicines are widely available in Canada. **Drugstores & Pharmacies** are listed on p. 290. If there is a possibility that you will run out of prescribed medicines during your visit, take along a prescription from your doctor. Carry the generic name of prescription medicines in case a local pharmacist is unfamiliar with the brand name.

Remember to pack your medications in your carry-on luggage and have them in their original containers with pharmacy labels—otherwise, they may not make it through airport security. If you're entering Canada with syringes used for medical reasons, bring a medical certificate that shows they are for medical use and be sure to declare them to Canadian Customs officials.

If you suffer from a chronic illness, consult your doctor before departure.

Additional **emergency numbers** are listed in the "Fast Facts" section of chapter 21.

6 SAFETY

STAYING SAFE

Montréal and Québec City are extremely safe cities, and far safer than their U.S. or European counterparts of similar size. Montréal in 2008, for instance, had 29 homicides for the entire year, the lowest number since police began collecting statistics. Street gang wars, which plague many cities, are nonexistent here.

Still, common sense insists that visitors stay alert and observe the usual urban precautions. It's best to stay out of parks at night and to take a taxi when returning from a late dinner or nightclub.

There have been reports of escalating road-rage incidents, so think twice before expressing impatience or anger with the actions of other drivers.

Québec is one of Canada's more liberal provinces. Mass demonstrations are rare and political violence is unusual.

Tolerance of others is a Canadian characteristic, and it's highly unlikely that visitors of ethnic, religious, or racial minorities will encounter even mild forms of discrimination. That applies to sexual orientation as well, especially in Montréal, which has one of the largest and most visible gay communities in North America.

7 SPECIALIZED TRAVEL RESOURCES

In addition to the destination-specific resources listed below, please visit Frommers. com for additional specialized travel resources.

GAY & LESBIAN TRAVELERS

Québec province is a destination for international gay travelers. Gay life here is generally open and accepted (gay marriage is legal in Québec), and gay travelers are heavily marketed to. The **Tourisme Montréal** website, www.tourisme-montreal. org, has a "Gay and Lesbian" minisite which lists gay-friendly accommodations, events, websites for queer meet-ups, and more. Travelers will find the rainbow flag prominently displayed on the doors and websites of many hotel and restaurants in all the city's neighborhoods.

In Montréal, many gay and lesbian travelers head straight to **the Village** (also known as "the Gay Village"), a neighborhood located primarily along rue Ste-Catherine est between rue St-Hubert and rue Papineau. Here there are antiques shops, bars, B&Bs, and clubs, clubs, clubs. The Beaudry Métro station is at the heart of the neighborhood and is marked by the rainbow flag. (As the Tourisme Montréal website says, "Rainbow columns on a subway station entrance? I've got a feeling we're not in Kansas anymore!")

The Village is action central on any night, but it especially picks up during the weeklong celebration of sexual diversity known as **Divers/Cité** (www.diverscite. org) in late July and early August and the **Black & Blue Festival** (www.bbcm.org), probably the world's largest circuit party with a week of entertainment and club dancing; it's held in October. They're both listed in the calendar earlier in this chapter. In 2006, Montréal added a pink feather to its cap by hosting the first World Outgames, attracting more than 16,000 athletes.

The Village Tourism Information Centre at 249 rue St-Jacques, Ste. 302 (© 888/595-8110 or 514/522-1885), is open Tuesday through Thursday in the summer and weekdays the rest of the year. It provides information about everything from wine bars to yoga classes. It's operated by the Québec Gay Chamber of Commerce (www.ccgq.ca). Gay Line (© 888/505-1010 or 514/866-5090; www.gayline.qc.ca) is a help line offering advice on over 550 accommodations, events, and services.

Of several local queer publications, the most thorough is *Fugues* (www.fugues.com), which describes current and future events and lists gay-friendly lodgings, clubs, saunas, and other resources. Free copies are available at tourist offices and in racks around the city.

Gay.com has a special section about Montréal at www.gay.com/travel.

In Québec City, the community is much smaller. Geographically, it's centered in Upper Town just outside the city walls, on rue St-Jean and the parallel rue d'Aiguillon, starting from where they cross rue St-Augustin and heading west. Le Drague Cabaret Club at 815 rue St-Augustin (© 418/649-7212; www.ledrague.com), or "the Drag," is a central gathering place with a cabaret and two dance rooms.

In early September, Québec City hosts a 3-day gay-pride fest, Fête Arc-en-Ciel (www.glbtquebec.org), which attracts thousands of people to Place d'Youville.

For more gay and lesbian travel resources, visit www.frommers.com/planning.

TRAVELERS WITH DISABILITIES

Québec regulations regarding wheelchair accessibility are similar to those in the U.S., including requirements for curb cuts, entrance ramps, designated parking spaces, and specially equipped bathrooms. However, access to the restaurants and inns housed in 18th- and 19th-century buildings, especially in Québec City, is often difficult or impossible.

Advice for travelers with physical limitations is provided in the French-language guide *Le Québec Accessible* (2005), which lists more than 1,000 hotels, restaurants, theaters, and museums. It costs C$20 and is available from Kéroul (© 514/252-3104; www.keroul.qc.ca). Kéroul also publishes an English-language brochure called *The Accessible Road* which has information about everything from how to get a handicapped parking sticker to which top attractions are most accessible. It's available as a free download at www.keroul.qc.ca.

When you're out and about, look for the Tourist and Leisure Companion Sticker (T.L.C.S.) at tourist sites. It designates that companions of travelers with disabilities can enter for free. A list of participating enterprises is online at www.vatl-tlcs.org.

For more on organizations that offer resources to travelers with disabilities, go to www.frommers.com/planning.

FAMILY TRAVEL

Montréal and Québec City offer an abundance of family-oriented activities. Many of them are outdoors, even in winter. Watersports, river cruises, fort climbing, and fireworks displays are among summer's many attractions, with dog sledding and skiing the top choices in snowy months. Québec City's walls and fortifications are fodder for imagining the days of knights and princesses. In both cities, many museums make special efforts to address children's interests and enthusiasms.

For accommodations, restaurants, and attractions that are particularly kid-friendly, look for the "Kids" icon throughout this guide. Also see chapter 8's "Especially for Kids" on p. 115 and chapter 16's "Especially for Kids" on p. 243.

Children who speak French or are learning French might like a guidebook of their own. The fun *Mon Premier Guide de Voyage au Québec* (Ulysse, 2009) has 96 pages of photos, mini-essays, and activities for kids age 6 to 12. You can find it in provincial bookshops.

For a list of more family-friendly travel resources, visit www.frommers.com/planning.

SENIOR TRAVEL

Mention the fact that you're a senior citizen when you make your travel reservations. Many Québec hotels still offer discounts for older travelers.

Throughout the province, theaters, museums, and other attractions offer reduced admission to people as young as 60.

Show your **AAA** card if you have one: Members of the American Automobile Association get the same discounts as members of the CAA. That means reduced rates at many museums, hotels, and restaurants.

Many reliable agencies and organizations target the 50-plus market. **Elderhostel** (© **800/454-5768;** www.elderhostel. org) arranges worldwide study programs for those aged 55 and older and offers a variety of trips to Québec City and Montréal.

The 2009–2010 edition of the bestselling paperback *Unbelievably Good Deals and Great Adventures That You Absolutely Can't Get Unless You're Over 50* (McGraw-Hill) by Joann Rattner Heilman includes information about Canadian travel.

For even more information and resources about travel for seniors, check www.frommers.com/planning.

VEGETARIAN TRAVEL

Le Commensal is a popular vegetarian restaurant in both Montréal and Québec City (p. 84 for Montréal information; p. 233 for Québec City). **Aux Vivres** (p. 98) is a popular vegan spot in Montréal's Plateau neighborhood.

Two websites list other vegetarian options in Montréal and Québec City: **HappyCow's Vegetarian Guide** (www. happycow.net) and **VegDining.com**.

For more vegetarian-friendly travel resources, go to www.frommers.com/planning.

TRAVELERS WITH PETS

Pets with proper rabies vaccination records may be admitted to Canada, but review the necessary procedures with the **Canada Border Services Agency** (© 506/636-5064; www.cbsa-asfc.gc.ca). Certified assistance dogs are exempt from import restrictions when the person assigned the dog accompanies it to Canada.

Americans who want to ensure a smooth border crossing back into the U.S. need to check with **U.S. Customs and Border Protection** before departing. The useful brochure "Pets and Wildlife: Licensing and Health Requirements" is available as a PDF from the Customs website at www.customs.gov.

From the famed Château Frontenac and the high-end boutique hotels of the Groupe Germain to chains such as Loews, many hotels now accept pets. Some even offer walking services and little beds for dogs. There are often restrictions regarding the size of animals, and most must not be left alone in the hotel room. Most hotels charge an extra fee of C$25 or more per day *or* per stay.

For more resources about traveling with pets, go to www.frommers.com/planning.

8 SUSTAINABLE TOURISM

Montréal walks the walk when it comes to green living—or, more accurately, it bikes the bike. Its new BIXI system, a self-service bicycle rental program that debuted in the spring of 2009, began (somewhat absurdly) picking up awards even before a single bike hit the roads: the prestigious Edison Best New Products Awards gave it a Gold award for best product of 2009 in the Energy & Sustainability category, and *Time* magazine named it one of the Best Inventions of 2008.

High praise for a service that had yet to satisfy even one customer. But the vision is big: BIXI, an abbreviation of the words Bicyclette and Taxi, is similar to popular programs in Berlin, Paris, and Barcelona, where users pay a small fee to pick up bikes from designated bike stands and drop them off at any other. (Helmets are not included.) Modular bike-rack stations are Web-enabled and solar-powered, and the bicycles are, as *Time* magazine put it, "designed with tons of sealed components to resist the savage beatings they will undoubtedly receive, and they're equipped with RFID tags so they're easily trackable." Projections called for 3,000 BIXI bikes on the road in 2009 and 300 stations in Montréal's central boroughs. BIXI touts that it will be the most environmentally friendly means of transportation in the city. It's most economical for short trips (that's what it's designed for); visitors who want a

General Resources for Green Travel

In addition to the resources for Québec listed above, the following websites provide valuable wide-ranging information on sustainable travel. For a list of even more sustainable resources, as well as tips and explanations on how to travel greener, visit www.frommers.com/planning.

- In Canada, **www.greenlivingonline.com** offers extensive content on how to travel sustainably, including a travel and transport section and profiles of the best green shops and services in Toronto, Vancouver, and Calgary.
- **Responsible Travel** (www.responsibletravel.com) is a great source of sustainable travel ideas; the site is run by a spokesperson for ethical tourism in the travel industry. **Sustainable Travel International** (www.sustainable travelinternational.org) promotes ethical tourism practices, and manages an extensive directory of sustainable properties and tour operators around the world.
- In the U.K., **Tourism Concern** (www.tourismconcern.org.uk) works to reduce social and environmental problems connected to tourism. The **Association of Independent Tour Operators** (**AITO;** www.aito.co.uk) is a group of specialist operators leading the field in making holidays sustainable.
- In Australia, the national body which sets guidelines and standards for ecotourism is **Ecotourism Australia** (www.ecotourism.org.au). **The Green Directory** (www.thegreendirectory.com.au), **Green Pages** (www.thegreen pages.com.au), and **Eco Directory** (www.ecodirectory.com.au) offer sustainable travel tips and directories of green businesses.

bike for a full day or weekend will probably find it cheaper to rent from a shop. BIXI fees and details are listed at **www.bixi.com/home**.

In the warm months, Montréal closes off large sections of main streets for pedestrian-only traffic, including, in Vieux-Montréal, rue St-Paul, and, in the Village, rue Ste-Catherine. In 2009, the Plateau neighborhood unveiled a 15-year plan to create more pedestrian-only streets, wider sidewalks, and a tramway line on av. du Parc, which runs north-south through the eastern side of Parc du Mont-Royal. It's all part of grander effort to reduce traffic, encourage public transport, and make life easier for walkers.

The Hotel Association of Canada (HAC) oversees the **Green Key Eco-Rating Program,** which awards a rating of one to five green keys to hotels that minimize waste and reduce their ecological footprint. The voluntary, self-administered audit assesses five areas within hotel management, including housekeeping and food services. Recipients often display a Green Key plaque in a prominent location alongside other commendations. While HAC does not currently verify the audits on a national scale, the **Corporation de l'industrie touristique du Québec** (www.citq.info) does so within Québec province. To read a description of each award tier and to locate Green Key hotels, visit www.hacgreenhotels.com.

Restaurants throughout the region tout locally-sourced food on their menus, with much of the region's food grown, raised, or caught within 100 miles. At the high-end **Aix Cuisine du Terroir** (p. 86) in

- **Carbonfund** (www.carbonfund.org), **TerraPass** (www.terrapass.org), and **Carbon Neutral** (www.carbonneutral.org) provide info on "carbon offsetting," or offsetting the greenhouse gas emitted during flights.

- **Greenhotels** (www.greenhotels.com) recommends green-rated member hotels around the world that fulfill the company's stringent environmental requirements. **Environmentally Friendly Hotels** (www.environmentallyfriendlyhotels.com) offers more green accommodation ratings. The **Hotel Association of Canada** (www.hacgreenhotels.com) has a Green Key Eco-Rating Program, which audits the environmental performance of Canadian hotels, motels, and resorts.

- **Sustain Lane** (www.sustainlane.com) lists sustainable eating and drinking choices around the U.S.; also visit **www.eatwellguide.org** for tips on eating sustainably in the U.S. and Canada.

- For information on animal-friendly issues throughout the world, visit **Tread Lightly** (www.treadlightly.org). For information about the ethics of swimming with dolphins, visit the **Whale and Dolphin Conservation Society** (www.wdcs.org).

- **Volunteer International** (www.volunteerinternational.org) has a list of questions to help you determine the intentions and the nature of a volunteer program. For general info on volunteer travel, visit **www.volunteerabroad.org** and **www.idealist.org**.

Montréal, for instance, *terroir* refers to soil and the restaurant's allegiance to products grown in the immediate region. You can also find "biodynamic," or organic, wines at many restaurants.

You'll want to bring carry bags when you go shopping: BYOB took on a new meaning—Bring Your Own Bag—in early 2009, when the province's *Société des alcools du Québec* (SAQ) liquor stores stopped using single-use plastic and paper bags. "It's a green action," said a spokesperson. "It's really a big statement for sustainable development." The initiative was easy to push through at the wine and hard liquor stores because the province has a monopoly on them. The hope is that, by setting the bar high in SAQ stores, other retailers will follow suit. Shoppers who don't have bags will be able to buy reusable ones for C75¢ to C$4, depending on the size.

9 SPECIAL INTEREST TRIPS & ESCORTED GENERAL INTEREST TOURS

ADVENTURE TRIPS

Bike touring is wildly popular and well accommodated in Québec. The province inaugurated the **Route Verte (Green Route),** a 4,000km (2,485-mile) bike network, in the summer of 2007. Many inns and restaurants along the route actively work to accommodate the nutritional, safety, and equipment needs of cyclists. See "Biker's Paradise: The 4,000km Route Verte" on p. 179 for details and contact information.

Vélo Québec (© 800/567-8356 or 514/521-8356; www.velo.qc.ca) was behind the development of the Route Verte and offers excellent biking information. It also offers guided bike tours throughout the province, coordinating meals, accommodations, and baggage transport.

The gorgeously rural Charlevoix region, an hour north of Québec City, is the perfect place in which to take an ecotour. Charlevoix was designated a protected UNESCO World Biosphere Reserve in 1988 and is subject to balanced development and cross-disciplinary research into conservation. For tour suggestions, check with **Aventure Ecotourisme Québec** (www.aventure-ecotourisme.qc.ca), an association of tour operators that provides outdoor adventure programs with a focus on environmental care and preservation. It has stringent operational standards and is partner to Leave No Trace Center for Outdoor Ethics (www.lnt.org), which educates operators and tourists about how to minimize the environmental impact of recreation. Aventure Ecotourisme also offers vacation planning.

One association member is **Mer et Monde Ecotours** (© 866/637-6663 or 418/232-6779; www.mer-et-monde.qc. ca), which puts on kayak trips in Charlevoix that take clients close to the whales who converge in the region each summer. For more information, see p. 287.

FOOD & WINE CLASSES

In Montréal, **Europea** restaurant (p. 80; © 514/398-9229; www.europea.ca) offers 1-hour cooking lessons for C$45 per person (click on "L'Atelier" at the website). Europea knows of which it teaches: The title of Chef of the Year was bestowed on chef Jérôme Ferrer by the Société des Chefs, Cuisiniers et Pâtissiers du Québec in 2007.

Also in Montréal, the Italian cooking classes of Elena Faita-Venditelli, who runs the packed-to-the-rafters cookware shop **Quincaillerie Dante** (© 514/271-2057), are often booked months in advance. In 2008 Faita-Venditelli was named "l'Ordre national," the most prestigious honorary distinction in the province.

In the Laurentians, about an hour north of Montréal on the way to Mont-Tremblant, guests of **L'Eau à la Bouche** (p. 178) can opt for a weekend package that includes hands-on kitchen training with chef/owner Anne Desjardins. Call © **888/828-2991** or 450/229-2991 or visit www.leaualabouche.com.

In Québec City, the famed restaurant **Laurie Raphaël** (p. 230; © **418/692-4555;** www.laurieraphael.com) underwent major renovation a few years ago that not only spiffed up its space but added a fancy public kitchen. From September to May, chef/owner Daniel Vézina gives 3- to 4-hour cooking classes in that kitchen on Saturday afternoons for C$185 per person (cost includes a meal plus wine).Also in Québec City, **Les Artistes de la Table** (© **418/694-1056;** www.lesartistesdela table.com) offers 4-hour custom cooking classes in the first floor of a gorgeous neo-classical building from 1850. Serious cooks will want to walk by just to peek at the kitchen through the vast windows. Cost is about C$120 per person.

If you have a car, the **Route des Vins (Wine Route),** 103km (64 miles) southeast of Montréal, is a pleasant vineyard tour that goes past **Vignoble de l'Orpailleur** (© **450/295-2763;** www.orpailleur.ca),

Domaine Pinnacle (© 450/298-1226; www.icecider.com), and **Le Cep d'Argent** (© **877/864-4441** or 819/864-4441; www.cepdargent.com), all within the region that specializes in cider and ice wine. See the box "Cantons-de-l'Est: Wine (& *Cidre de Glace*) Country" on p. 196.

ACADEMIC TRIPS & LANGUAGE CLASSES

If you're itching to dust off your notebooks from high school French class, the **Université du Québec à Montréal (UQAM;** © 514/987-3000 ext. 5621; www.langues.immersion.uqam.ca) offers French immersion courses for 3 weeks in either July or August. Students can opt for on-campus housing or stay with a host family. One session integrates French instruction with jazz events during the renowned Festival International de Jazz de Montréal. Programs are geared for persons 18 and up, beginners through intermediate.

Adults and teens alike can combine an array of activities with French language immersion in Québec City through **Edu-Inter** (© **418/575-4137;** www.learning frenchinquebec.com). Year-round sessions can quench an *amour pour le français* by combining language programs with skiing, cooking, horseback riding, or sight-seeing.

10 STAYING CONNECTED

TELEPHONES

The Canadian telephone system, operated by Bell Canada, closely resembles the U.S. model. All operators speak English and French and respond in the appropriate language as soon as callers speak to them. In Canada, dial © **00** to reach an **operator.**

A local call at a pay phone in Québec province costs C50¢. **Directory information** calls (dial © **411**) are free of charge.

When making a local call within Québec province, you must dial the area code before the seven-digit number.

Toll-free numbers: Phone numbers that begin with 800, 888, 877, and 866 are toll-free. That means they're free to call within Canada and from the U.S. You need to dial 1 first.

Remember that both local as well as long-distance calls usually cost more from hotels—sometimes a lot more, so check

Tips **What's in a Name? Understanding Affiliations**

Many tourist businesses in the province are members of groups that offer seals of approval. Here's a quick primer of what some memberships signify:

- **Aventure Ecotourisme Québec** is an association of tour operators who provide outdoor-adventure programs with a focus on environmental care and preservation. It requires stringent operational standards and is a partner of the Leave No Trace Center for Outdoor Ethics (www.lnt.org), which educates operators and tourists about how to minimize the environmental impact of recreation. It also offers vacation planning. Sample member: The kayaking company Mer et Monde Ecotours (p. 287). **www.aventure-ecotourisme.qc.ca**.
- **Hôtellerie Champêtre** is a membership group of 26 Québec inns and resorts that are big on personality and often (but not always) midrange in price. They have to have at least three (out of five possible) stars from the Québec tourist authorities. Many are housed in historic buildings or have access to a dramatic outdoors spot. Sample member: Auberge La Camarine (p. 278), whose structure dates from 1750. **www.hotelleriechampetre.com**.
- **Relais and Châteaux** is a collection of high-end gourmet restaurants and luxury hotels around the world. The group is exclusive, with fewer than 500 properties in 56 countries. Members receive secret visits by reviewers and can be expelled if standards aren't met. Sample member: La Pinsonnière (p. 285), one of Canada's first hostelries to be invited into the prestigious organization. **www.relaischateaux.com**.

before dialing. Some hotels charge for all phone calls you make, including toll-free ones.

To call Québec province from the U.S.: Calls between Canada and the U.S. do not require the use of country codes. Simply dial the 3-digit area code, then the seven-digit number. *Example:* To call the Infotouriste Centre in Montréal, dial 514/873-2015. **To call Québec from the U.K./Ireland/Australia/New Zealand:** Dial the international access code 00 (from Australia, 0011), then the Canadian country code 1, then the area code, and then the seven-digit number. *Example:* To call the Infotouriste Centre in Montréal, dial 00-1-514/873-2015. **To call the U.S. from Québec:** Simply dial the three-digit

area code and seven-digit number. *Example:* To call the U.S. Passport Agency from Québec province, dial 202/647-0518. **To call the U.K./Ireland/Australia/New Zealand from Québec:** Dial 011, then the country code (U.K. 44, Ireland 353, Australia 61, New Zealand 64), then the number.

CELLPHONES & PREPAID SERVICES

Visitors from the U.S. should be able to get roaming service that allows them to use their cellphones in Canada.

Some wireless companies let you adjust your plan to get cheaper rates while traveling. Sprint, for instance, has a "Canadian roaming" option for US$3 per month that reduces the per-minute rate. Ask your provider for options.

Europeans and most Australians are on the **GSM** (Global System for Mobile Communications) network with removable plastic SIM cards in their phones. Call your wireless provider for information about traveling. You may be able to purchase pay-as-you-go SIM cards in Canada with local providers.

Cellphone rentals are not common in Canada, so if you end up traveling without a phone, **pre-paid phone services** are your best option. With **OneSuite.com** (© 866/417-8483; www.onesuite.com), for instance, you prepay an online account for as little as US$10. You then dial a toll-free or local access number when traveling, enter your PIN, and then dial the number you're calling. Calls from Canada to mainland U.S. cost just US2.5¢ to US3.5¢ per minute. Calls to the U.K. cost 2p per minute to a landline and 17.5p per minute to a mobile.

INTERNET CALLS

Cheaper still are phone calls conducted over the Web. If you're traveling with a computer, consider signing up for a broadband-based telephone service (in technical terms, Voice-over Internet Protocol, or VoIP). Companies such as **Skype** (www. skype.com) allow you to make international calls from your laptop. Calls to people who also have the program on their computers are free. You can call people who don't have the service, although fees apply.

INTERNET & E-MAIL
With Your Own Computer
Many hotels, *auberges,* and cafes now offer **Wi-Fi** (wireless fidelity). Some also still offer high-speed Internet access through cable connections.

Without a Computer
Most hotels maintain business centers with computers for use by guests or outsiders, or at least have one computer available for guest use.

Cybercafes are fading from the Canadian scene with the rise of Wi-Fi, but there are still a few around. In Vieux-Montréal, **Café-Bistro Van Houtte** (© 514/288-9387), 165 rue St-Paul ouest, has a bank of computers and pre-paid Internet access cards for C$5.65 per hour. In Québec City, **Centre Internet,** 52 Côte du Palais (© 418/692-3359), does good business in Old Québec's Upper Town, just a block off of the main rue St-Jean. You can purchase access in increments of 20 minutes (C$2.50 for 20, C$4.50 for 40, C$6.50 for 60).

11 TIPS ON ACCOMMODATIONS

Both Montréal and Québec City have familiar international hotel chains as well as small B&Bs hosted by locals. In between are the boutique hotels, which combine high-end service with plush room accommodations and decor that ranges from Asian minimalist to country luxury. A good room in one of these smaller hotels could provide the best memories of your trip.

Most Québec hotels offer online specials and package deals that bundle rooms with meals or sightseeing activities. In many cases, this can result in rates significantly below what's quoted in this book.

Tip: Always check hotel websites before calling to make a reservation.

Some properties in the Laurentians and Charlevoix offer meal plans. The European Plan (EP) is for the room alone, with no meals. The Continental Plan (CP) includes breakfast. The Modified American Plan (MAP) includes breakfast and one dinner. The American Plan (AP) is a room plus all three meals each day.

Because the region is so intensely cold so many months of the year, tourism here is cyclical. That means that prices drop—often steeply—for much of the September-through-May period. While rooms are less expensive these times of year, some of the essential vibrancy and *joie de vivre* of the region goes into hibernation as well.

See the introductions of "Where to Stay in Montréal" on p. 62 and "Where to Stay in Québec City" on p. 212 for further details.

Suggested Montréal & Québec City Itineraries

Public transportation in Montréal and Québec City is excellent, so you won't need a car for the tours listed below. The suggested itineraries focus on each city individually.

1 THE BEST OF MONTREAL IN 1 DAY

This exploration of cosmopolitan Montréal allows ample time for random exploring, shopping, or lingering in sidewalk cafes. While many suggestions are for warm weather, there are periodic suggestions for inside stops during the winter months. If you're staying only 1 night, book a room in one of Vieux-Montréal's boutique hotels. Visitors find themselves drawn to the plazas and narrow cobblestone streets of this 18th- and 19th-century neighborhood, so you might as well be based there. *Start: Vieux-Montréal.*

❶ Place d'Armes ★★★
Begin your day in the heart of **Vieux-Montréal ★★★**, at the site of the city's oldest building, the **Vieux Séminaire de St-Sulpice** (p. 126), erected by Sulpician priests who arrived in 1657. Next to it is the **Basilique Cathedral Notre-Dame de Québec ★★★** (p. 106), an 1824 church with a stunning interior of intricately gilded rare woods. Its acoustics are so perfect that the late, famed opera star Luciano Pavarotti performed here several times. From here, consider taking the walking tour on p. 125, which takes you past every historic structure in Vieux-Montréal.

❷ Pointe-à-Callière ★★★
Otherwise, head down the slope from the basilica to the district's riverside edge and **Pointe-à-Callière (Museum of Archaeology and History).** After viewing the multimedia show above the ruins, descend below the streets to discover remnants of Amerindian camps and early French settlements. See p. 107.

❸ OLIVE ET GOURMANDO
A couple of cobblestone blocks away is Olive et Gourmando, which started as a bakery and evolved into a full-service, French-feeling cafe. Eat in or put together a picnic lunch to carry to the nearby park. 351 rue St-Paul ouest (☏ **514/350-1083**). See p. 92.

❹ Musée McCord ★
Take a cab or the Métro to Peel Station and walk to the **Musée McCord,** which sits across the street from McGill University. The permanent exhibition "Simply Montréal: Glimpses of a Unique History" justifies a trip all on its own. See p. 103.

❺ Musée des Beaux-Arts ★★★
West on rue Sherbrooke from Musée McCord is the city's most important fine-arts museum. Permanent exhibits are free, and temporary shows have included a full-career retrospective of Yves Saint Laurent and an exploration of Cuban art history. See p. 102.

4

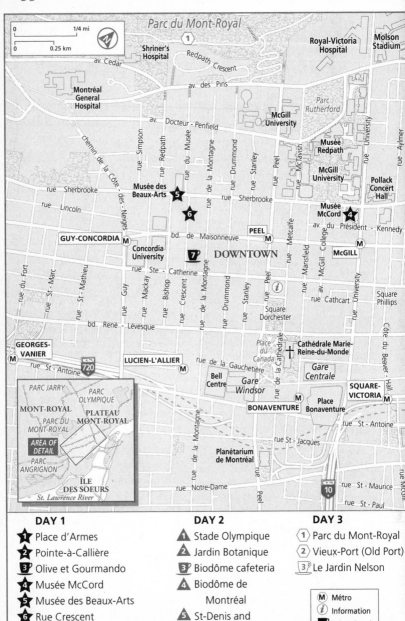

DAY 1
1. Place d'Armes
2. Pointe-à-Callière
3. Olive et Gourmando
4. Musée McCord
5. Musée des Beaux-Arts
6. Rue Crescent
7. Sir Winston Churchill Pub

DAY 2
1. Stade Olympique
2. Jardin Botanique
3. Biodôme cafeteria
4. Biodôme de Montréal
5. St-Denis and St-Laurent

DAY 3
1. Parc du Mont-Royal
2. Vieux-Port (Old Port)
3. Le Jardin Nelson

Ⓜ Métro
ⓘ Information
☕ Take a break

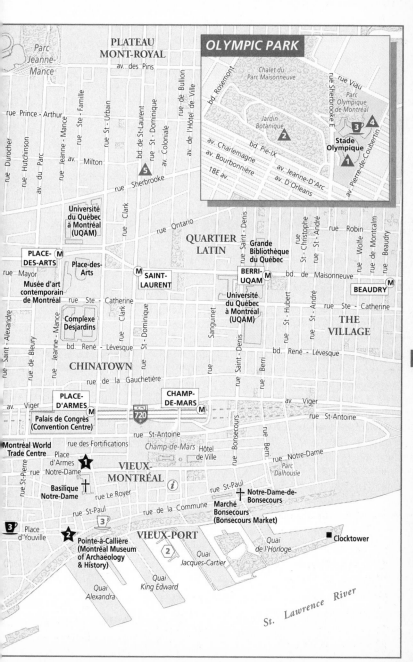

6 Rue Crescent ★★

By this point, you're likely craving a sit-down. Walk south on rue Crescent to get to downtown's primary nightlife district. If it's warm, take a seat on a terrace.

To decide where to go for dinner, peruse the listings in chapter 7 of the worthy restaurants downtown.

> **7 SIR WINSTON CHURCHILL PUB**
> Epicenter of the rue Crescent scene for ages, this pub is filled with chatty 20- to 40-somethings. It's a good spot to nurse a pint or two of cold beer while taking in the passing parade. 1459 rue Crescent near rue Ste-Catherine (**℃ 514/288-3814**). See p. 167.

2 THE BEST OF MONTREAL IN 2 DAYS

With the absolute essentials of historic Old Montréal and downtown Anglophone cultural institutions under your belt, prepare to take a journey into French Montréal. Just before Montréal hosted the 1976 Olympics, municipal authorities erected some principal venues in the city's eastern, overwhelmingly Francophone precincts, which is where we start. *Start: Viau Métro station.*

1 Stade Olympique

The controversial Olympic Stadium was scorned as the "Big Owe" and then "Big Woe" due to cost overruns that provoked elevated taxes. It now houses five public pools and sports an inclined tower that's more than 175m (574 ft.) high. There's also a funicular that scoots to the observation level at the top in seconds. See p. 110.

In the summer, a shuttle van is available to transport you to the Jardin Botanique.

2 Jardin Botanique ★★★

Lush and romantic year-round, this botanical garden encompasses 75 hectares (185 acres) of plants and flowers and 10 large greenhouses. Japanese and Chinese gardens feature hideaway pavilions and courtyards. See p. 109. Inside the garden is also the **Insectarium,** which has live exhibits of scorpions, tarantulas, honey bees, hissing cockroaches, and the like. It's closed for renovations until early February, 2010. See p. 115.

If it's available, take the shuttle back to the Stade Olympique and walk to the adjacent Biodôme.

> **3 LA BRISE**
> You might want to eat before you take on the Biodôme (see below), which can easily occupy another hour, especially if you have youngsters in tow. This in-house, self-serve cafeteria at the Biodôme offers sandwiches and the like.

4 Biodôme de Montréal ★★

Originally a velodrome (cycling track) built for the 1976 Olympics, this unique facility replicates four ecosystems, complete with tropical trees and golden lion tamarin monkeys that swing on branches overhead. See p. 109.

Take the Métro to Square Victoria or Place d'Armes.

5 St-Denis & St-Laurent ★★

After all this, it might well be time to get back to your hotel for a recuperative rest.

But if you're ready to continue on, take the Métro to Sherbrooke and walk one block west to rue St-Denis. Head north into the lower precincts of Plateau Mont-Royal. There are no must-see sights along this route, just cafes and shops, so surrender to the heart of French Montréal's color and vitality.

The walking tour on p. 136 provides guidance to some options along the way.

The Main, as boulevard St-Laurent is locally known, is 8 short blocks to the west. It also is lined with amiable places at which to bend an elbow and listen to music. The best stretch is from rue Sherbrooke on the south to avenue du Mont-Royal on the north.

3 THE BEST OF MONTREAL IN 3 DAYS

If you've followed the above itineraries, you've already visited Montéal's primary must-see sights. On this third day, slack off a bit, with idylls in the park and a ride on the St. Lawrence—tranquil or thrilling, your choice. *Start: Take the Métro to Peel Station (if you're in reasonably good shape) or a taxi to Lac des Castors (Beaver Lake) in Parc du Mont-Royal.*

❶ Parc du Mont-Royal ★

The hill that rises behind downtown is the small "mountain," Mont Royal, that gave the city its name.

Its rounded crest became a public park somewhat according to plans by architect **Frederick Law Olmsted.** Throngs of people come for its woods, paths, and meadows in all four seasons. You can join them with a stroll up from Peel station (see p. 140 for a walking tour), or a taxi ride to Lac des Castors (Beaver Lake). See p 106.

Make your way by Métro or taxi back to the southern end of the city, the Vieux-Port.

❷ Vieux-Port ★★

Though it was a gray, ragged industrial harbor less than 20 years ago, the Old Port at the edge of Vieux-Montréal has been transformed into a broad, vibrant park. Principal among the attractions is the **Centre des Sciences de Montréal** (p. 107), on quai (pier) King Edward. It contains a popular IMAX theater in addition to interactive computer-driven displays sure to enthrall your inner geek.

At the park's east end, near the old clock tower, is the departure point for **Les**

Sautes-Moutons (✆ **514/284-9607**). The company entices adventurous spirits with special flat-bottomed boats that travel upriver in wet and wild challenges on the roiling Lachine Rapids. Other companies provide more sedate river cruises. See p. 120 for options.

You can also rent **bicycles and in-line skates** by the hour or day from here, and head out to the peaceful **Lachine Canal,** a nearly flat 11km (6.8-mile) bicycle path that's open year-round. See p. 123.

> **3** LE JARDIN NELSON
> Vieux-Montréal is home to a considerable number of restaurants catering to most tastes and wallets. One of the most popular is **Le Jardin Nelson** on the main square, Place Jacques-Cartier. It's open in the warm months and has a lovely garden where jazz musicians perform throughout the day and evening. The menu offers soups, sandwiches, pizzas, and a delectable roster of main-course and dessert crepes. 407 Place Jacques-Cartier (✆ **514/ 861-5731**).

4 THE BEST OF QUEBEC CITY IN 1 DAY

The capital of this singular province bears scant resemblance to Montréal. The oldest walled city north of Mexico's Campeche sustains the look of a provincial European village that keeps watch over the powerful St. Lawrence River. Entrancing in all seasons, it lays out a yearlong banquet of festivals and celebrations. To take greatest advantage of all the city has to offer, book a hotel or B&B within the walls of the Haute-Ville (Upper Town) or in the revitalized Basse-Ville (Lower Town). *Start: Château Frontenac.*

❶ **Terrasse Dufferin** ★★★

First thing after unpacking, get to **Château Frontenac** ★★★ (p. 213)—its peaked copper roofs are visible from everywhere in the city. Tours of this hotel are available (p. 241), and it has a posh bar and pretty cafe to take in the views, but if the weather's nice just go to the long riverside promenade, the Terrasse Dufferin. It affords panoramic views of the Old City's **Basse-Ville (Lower Town)** ★★★. In good weather, street performers often entertain passersby; in winter, an old-fashioned toboggan run is set up on the steep staircase at the south end.

❷ **Funicular** ★

Take the cliffside elevator down from the Terrasse Dufferin's north end. Traveling at a steep angle, it's enclosed in glass to take advantage of the views. (See p. 209.)

An alternative descent is via **L'Escalier du Casse-Cou,** which translates as "Breakneck Stairs." Either route gets you to the top of rue du Petit-Champlain, a pedestrian street of shops and cafes populated largely by tourists.

Walk down rue Sous-le-Fort and make the first left turn.

❸ **Place-Royale** ★★★

This small but picturesque square was the site of the first European colony in Canada and is surrounded by restored 17th- and 18th-century houses. The church on one side is **Eglise Notre-Dame-des-Victoires,** built in 1688. The Centre d'Interprétation de Place-Royale is here, too. At the end of

the block, turn around to view a *trompe l'oeil* mural depicting citizens of the early city. See p. 238.

Continue past the mural and turn right on rue de la Barricade toward the river. Turn left on rue Dalhousie and walk a couple of blocks to:

❹ **Musée de la Civilisation** ★★★

A city highlight. This ambitious museum, filled with fascinating exhibits, can easily fill 2 or 3 hours. Take in the permanent exhibit, "People of Québec . . . Then and Now," which explores the province's roots as a fur-trading colony and gives visitors a rich sense of Québec's daily life over the generations. See p. 235.

Leaving the museum, turn left on rue Dalhousie, left on rue St-Paul, and then left on rue du Sainte-au-Matelot.

❺ **A BOUNTY OF BISTROS**
Within a block of the corner of rues St-Paul and du Sault-au-Matelot are some of the city's best bistros and casual eating places. Almost any of them will do for a snack or a meal, but our top choice is **L'Echaudé** ★★, 73 rue du Sault-au-Matelot (ⓒ **418/692-1299**). It offers excellent value for classic French dishes and puts out sidewalk tables in summer. See p. 231.

After eating, continue west along rue St-Paul.

❻ **Rue St-Paul** ★

This is a great street to browse for antiques and collectibles. See p. 259 in the walking tour for some highlights.

Turn right at rue St-Thomas and cross quai St-André.

❼ Marché du Vieux-Port

This large market is open year-round. Produce and other agricultural products

of the farming island of Île d'Orléans (p. 270) are sold here. See p. 265.

5 THE BEST OF QUEBEC CITY IN 2 DAYS

During the repeated conflicts with the British in the 18th century, the residents of New France moved to the top of the cliffs of Cap Diamant that rise behind the river-level Basse-Ville. Over the years, they threw up fortifications with battlements and artillery emplacements that eventually encircled the city as it existed at that time. Most of these fortifications remain, albeit restored repeatedly. Along with the narrow streets, leafy plazas, and leaning houses that compose the Old Town, these historic defenses are the reason to spend the day within the walls. ***Start:*** *Terrasse Dufferin.*

❶ La Citadelle ★★

Today, walk south to the end of Terrasse Dufferin. At the end, go up the staircase to the **Promenade des Gouverneurs.** To the right and at the top is La Citadelle, a partially star-shaped fortress built in anticipation of an American invasion that never happened. When you reach the top, walk around the rim. The fortress has a low profile, dug into the land rather than rising above it, and is still occupied by troops. Look for the courtyard where a ceremonial changing of the guard occurs at 10am every day in summer. It can be viewed from here, saving the admission fee. See p. 238.

Walk down the hill to av. St-Denis, and take it to the left to where it meets the corner of rue St-Louis, the main road into the Old Town.

❷ Porte St-Louis and the Walls

Rue St-Louis passes through the main gate in the city walls, which is called the Porte St-Louis. The long greenway on the inside of the walls is known as **Parc l'Esplanade.** Stroll along it and down a steep hill to the other main gate in the wall, **Porte St-Jean** (it is, sad to say, a 20th-century re-creation). Next to it is the entrance to **Parc de**

l'Artillerie, where you can view an officer's mess and quarters and an old iron foundry.

Walk west on rue St-Jean through the gate and outside. This is **Place d'Youville,** a plaza with hotels, a concert hall, vending stalls, and an open-air venue for the concerts of the city's many festivals.

Bear right around the plaza.

> **❸ RISTORANTE IL TEATRO**
> A good bet for lunch or dinner, especially if you can snare a table under the umbrellas on the sidewalk. Pasta and risotto are specialties. The restaurant is part of Le Capitole, a hotel-theater complex. 972 rue St-Jean (☏ **418/694-9996**).

After lunch, walk back to the gate and along bustling rue St-Jean.

❹ Rue St-Jean

One of the liveliest of Vieux-Québec's Haute-Ville streets, rue St-Jean is lined with an ever-updated variety of shops, cafes, pubs, and restaurants. Some of the shopping possibilities here are listed in chapter 18.

SUGGESTED MONTRÉAL & QUÉBEC CITY ITINERARIES

THE BEST OF QUÉBEC CITY IN 2 DAYS

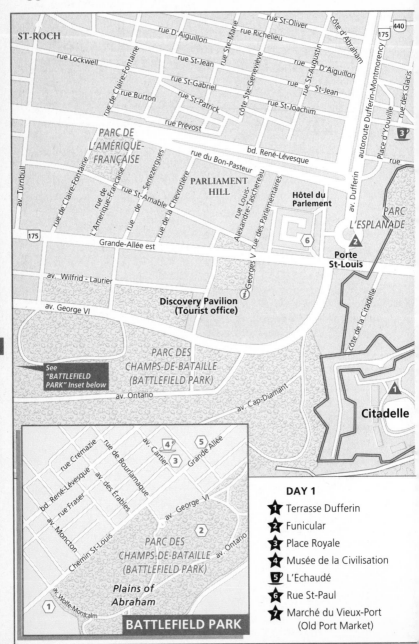

DAY 1

1. Terrasse Dufferin
2. Funicular
3. Place Royale
4. Musée de la Civilisation
5. L'Echaudé
6. Rue St-Paul
7. Marché du Vieux-Port (Old Port Market)

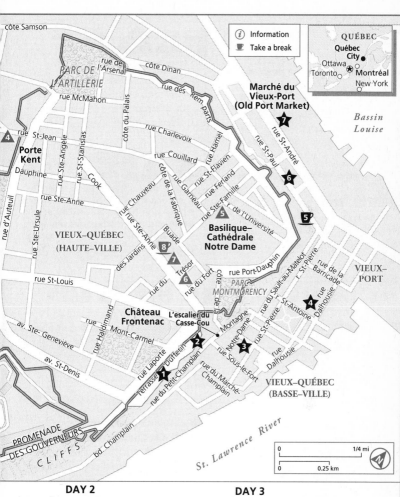

DAY 2

1. Citadelle
2. Porte St-Louis and the Walls
3. Restaurante Il Teatro
4. Rue St-Jean
5. Basilique Notre-Dame
6. Rue du Trésor
7. Québec Expérience
8. Le Pain Béni

DAY 3

1. Musée des Beaux-Arts du Québec
2. Parc des Champs-de-Bataille
3. Avenue Cartier
4. Café Krieghoff
5. Grande-Allée
6. Hôtel du Parlement

At the end of rue St-Jean, bear right up Côte de la Fabrique. At the end is the:

❺ Basilique Cathedral Notre-Dame de Québec ★

What with bombardments, fires, and repeated rebuilding, this representative of the oldest Christian parish north of Mexico is nothing if not perseverant. Parts of it, including the bell tower, survive from the original 1647 building, but most of what remains is from a 1771 reconstruction. Step inside to see the blindingly bright gold leaf. See p. 240.

Leaving the church, walk left along rue Baude and turn right on:

❻ Rue du Trésor

A narrow pedestrian alley that cuts up to the Place d'Armes, Trésor is lined with the etchings, drawings, and watercolors of artists

seeking tourist dollars. Nearly all the renderings are of Québec City scenes, and they make worthwhile souvenirs. See p. 262.

Directly on the street at no. 8, go inside for the:

❼ Québec Expérience

This 3D show re-creates in vivid detail some of the grim realities of being a settler. Guns and cannons explode at audiences, a simulated bridge crashes down, walls of water simulate storms at sea. Kids love it. See p. 242.

> **⑧ LE PAIN BÉNI**
> Snag an outdoor table at this restaurant in the Auberge Place d'Armes (p. 216). You can try Québécois classics with modern twists, such as wild boar over creamy risotto, or more simple pizzas and pastas. 24 rue Ste-Anne (☎ **418/694-9485**).

6 THE BEST OF QUEBEC CITY IN 3 DAYS

While the romance of the capital is largely contained within Vieux-Québec's Lower and Upper Towns, there's much to experience outside the Old City. And though the suggested itineraries for the first 2 days can easily be extended over 3 days, especially if children and those with limited mobility are involved, try to make time for at least one or two of the following attractions. ***Start:*** *Musée des Beaux-Arts.*

❶ Musée des Beaux-Arts du Québec ★★★

At the southwestern end of the Parc des Champs-de-Bataille (Battlefields Park, which contains the Plains of Abraham), the capital's most important art museum focuses on Inuit art and the works of Québec-born painters and sculptors. Galleries also feature works of provincial artists from the earliest days of the colony to the present. The original 1933 museum is connected to a newer structure by a glass-roofed pavilion that houses the reception area, museum shop, and cafe. For children, there's a craft-projects room. See p. 239.

Walk outside and around back to:

❷ Parc des Champs-de-Bataille ★★

Get some fresh air with a stroll through the 108 hectares (267 acres) that comprise Canada's first national urban park and the city's playground. Within its rolling hills are two Martello towers, cylindrical stone defensive structures built between 1808 and 1812, as well as cycling and roller-blading paths and picnic grounds. See p. 239.

Head to the main street, Grand-Allée, and cross over to the perpendicular street:

❸ Avenue Cartier

Nearly opposite the museum, avenue Cartier is a street of intriguing shops and restaurants. Foodies will want to check out **Halles du Petit-Cartier,** 1191 av. Cartier, 1 block off Grand-Allée. The indoor mall has about a dozen merchants who sell cheeses, pâtés, terrines, pastries, and fancy picnic items. There's also a small grocery store in back. See p. 261.

4 CAFÉ KRIEGHOFF
This cheerful cafe has an outdoor terrace a few steps up from the sidewalk. On weekend mornings it's packed with artsy locals of all ages, whose tables get piled high with bowls of café au lait and huge plates of egg dishes, sweet pastries, or classics like *steak frites.* 1091 av. Cartier (✆ **418/522-3711**). See p. 233.

5 Grande-Allée
Walk back to Grande-Allée and turn left to get back to the Old City. There's a gentle slope that goes downhill. After about 3 blocks, the shoulder-to-shoulder

rows of cafes and clubs begin. One of the largest clubs is on the right, **Maurice** (p. 268). Keep it in mind for the evening; it's a one-stop dining and entertainment emporium with terrace bars, a good restaurant, **VooDoo Grill** ★ (p. 232), and a disco.

Continue on Grand-Allée to the commanding Second Empire château on your left:
6 Hôtel du Parlement
This august structure houses the provincial legislative body that Québécois proudly proclaim their National Assembly. Guided tours are available weekdays year-round from 9am to 4:30pm and weekends in summer from 10am to 4:30pm. Among the best sights are the Assembly Chamber and the Room of the Old Legislative Council. See p. 243.

As you exit the Parlement building, the walls of the Old City will be directly in front of you.

Getting to Know Montréal

Getting oriented in Montréal is remarkably easy. The airport is only 23km (14 miles) from downtown, and the Métro (subway) is fast and efficient. Walking, of course, is the best way to enjoy and appreciate this vigorous, multidimensional city. Take it in, neighborhood by neighborhood.

1 ORIENTATION

ARRIVING

For information about arriving in Montréal by plane, train, car, or bus, see "Getting to Montréal & Québec City," p. 26 in chapter 3.

VISITOR INFORMATION

The main tourist center for visitors in downtown Montréal is the large **Infotouriste Centre,** at 1255 rue Peel ((C) **877/266-5687** or 514/873-2015; Métro: Peel). It's open daily and the bilingual staff can provide suggestions for accommodations, dining, car rentals, and attractions.

In Vieux-Montréal, there's a small **Tourist Information Office** at 174 rue Notre-Dame est, at the corner of Place Jacques-Cartier (Métro: Champ-de-Mars). It's open daily in warmer months, Wednesday through Sunday in winter, and proffers brochures, maps, and a helpful staff.

The city of Montréal maintains a terrific website at **www.tourisme-montreal.org**.

CITY LAYOUT

MAIN ARTERIES & STREETS In downtown Montréal, the principal east-west streets include boulevard René-Lévesque, rue Ste-Catherine (*rue* is the French word for "street"), boulevard de Maisonneuve, and rue Sherbrooke. The north-south arteries include rue Crescent, rue McGill, rue St-Denis, and boulevard St-Laurent, which serves as the line of demarcation between east and west Montréal. Most of the downtown areas featured in this book lie west of boulevard St-Laurent.

In Plateau Mont-Royal, northeast of the downtown area, major streets are avenue du Mont-Royal and avenue Laurier.

> **Map Tip**
>
> For a map of greater Montréal, see the color insert at the front of this guide.

In Vieux-Montréal, the main thoroughfares are rue St-Jacques, rue Notre-Dame, and rue St-Paul, along with rue de la Commune, the waterfront road that hugs the promenade bordering the St. Lawrence River.

Tips **Montréal: Where the Sun Rises in the South**

For the duration of your visit to Montréal, you'll need to accept local directional conventions, strange as they may seem. The city borders the St. Lawrence River, and as far as locals are concerned, that's south, with the U.S. on the other side. Never mind that the river, in fact, runs almost north and south at this point. For this reason, it has been observed that Montréal is the only city in the world where the sun rises in the south. Don't fight it: Face the river. That's south. Turn around. That's north. All is clear?

To ease the confusion, the directions given throughout the Montréal chapters conform to this local directional tradition. However, the maps in this book also have the true compass on them.

When examining a map of the city, note that prominent thoroughfares such as rue Ste-Catherine and boulevard René-Lévesque are said to run either "east" or "west," with the dividing line being boulevard St-Laurent, which runs "north" and "south." For streets that run east and west, the numbers start at St-Laurent and then *go in both directions*. They're labeled either *est*, for east, or *ouest*, for west. That means, for instance, that the restaurant Chez l'Epicier, at 311 rue St-Paul *est*, is actually 1km (about a half mile, or 13 short blocks) from the restaurant Marché de la Villete, at 324 rue St-Paul *ouest*—and not directly across the street.

In addition to the maps in this book, neighborhood street plans are available online at www.tourisme-montreal.org and from the information centers listed above.

FINDING AN ADDRESS As explained in "Montréal: Where the Sun Rises in the South," above, boulevard St-Laurent is the dividing point between east and west (*est* and *ouest*) in Montréal. There's no equivalent division for north and south (*nord* and *sud*)—the numbers start at the river and climb from there, just as the topography does. Make sure you know your east from your west, and confirm the cross street for all addresses.

In earlier days, Montréal was split geographically along cultural lines. Those who spoke English lived predominantly west of boulevard St-Laurent, while French speakers were concentrated to the east. Things still do sound more French as you walk east: Street names and Métro station names change from Peel and Atwater to Papineau and Beaudry.

THE NEIGHBORHOODS IN BRIEF

Centre Ville/Downtown This area contains the Montréal skyline's most dramatic elements and includes most of the city's large luxury and first-class hotels, principal museums, corporate headquarters, main transportation hubs, and department stores.

The district is loosely bounded by rue Sherbrooke to the north, boulevard René-Lévesque to the south, boulevard St-Laurent to the east, and rue Drummond to the west.

Within this neighborhood is the area often called "the Golden Square Mile," an Anglophone district once characterized by dozens of mansions erected by the wealthy Scottish and English merchants and industrialists who dominated the city's political and social life well into the 20th century. Many of those stately homes were torn down when skyscrapers began to rise here after World War II, but some remain.

At downtown's northern edge is the urban campus of prestigious McGill University, which retains its Anglophone identity.

Vieux-Montréal The city was born here in 1642, down by the river at Pointe-à-Callière. Today, especially in summer, most people converge around Place Jacques-Cartier, where cafe tables line narrow terraces. This is where street performers, strolling locals, and tourists congregate.

The area is larger than it might seem at first. It's bounded on the north by rue St-Antoine, once the "Wall Street" of Montréal and still home to some banks. Its southern boundary is the Vieux-Port (Old Port), a waterfront promenade bordering rue de la Commune that provides welcome breathing room for cyclists, in-line skaters, and picnickers. To the east, Vieux-Montréal is bordered by rue Berri and to the west, by rue McGill.

Several small but intriguing museums are housed in historic buildings, and the district's architectural heritage has been substantially preserved. Restored 18th- and 19th-century structures have been adapted for use as shops, boutique hotels, studios, galleries, cafes, bars, offices, and apartments. In the evening, many of the finer buildings are beautifully illuminated. In the summer, sections of rue St-Paul and rue Notre-Dame turn into pedestrian-only lanes. The neighborhood's official website is **www.vieux.montreal.qc.ca**. It sometimes has a live webcam of Place Jacques-Cartier.

Plateau Mont-Royal This is where Montréalers feel most at home—away

from downtown's chattering pace and the more touristed Vieux-Montréal. It's where they come to shop, dine, and play.

Bounded roughly by rue Sherbrooke to the south, boulevard St-Joseph to the north, rue St-Urbain to the west, and avenue Papineau to the east, the Plateau has a vibrant ethnic atmosphere that fluctuates with each new immigration surge.

Rue St-Denis runs the length of the district and is to Montréal what boulevard St-Germain is to Paris, while boulevard St-Laurent, running parallel, has a more polyglot flavor.

Known as "the Main," St-Laurent was the boulevard first encountered by foreigners tumbling off ships at the waterfront. They simply shouldered their belongings and walked north, peeling off into adjoining streets when they heard familiar tongues or smelled the drifting aromas of food reminiscent of the old country. New arrivals still come here to start their lives in Canada.

Without its gumbo of languages and cultures, St-Laurent would be an urban eyesore. But its ground-floor windows are filled with glistening golden chickens, collages of shoes and pastries and aluminum cookware, curtains of sausages, and the daringly far-fetched garments of designers on the forward edge of Montréal's active fashion industry.

Many warehouses and former tenements have been converted to house this panoply of shops, bars, and high- and low-cost eateries, their often-garish signs drawing eyes away from the still-dilapidated upper stories. See p. 136 for a walking tour of this fascinating neighborhood.

Parc du Mont-Royal Not many cities have a mountain at their core. Reality insists that Montréal doesn't either, as what it calls a "mountain" would be seen as a very large hill by many other people. Still, Montréal is named for this outcrop—the "Royal Mountain."

The park here is a soothing urban pleasure to drive or walk in. You can take a horse-drawn calèche to the top for a view of the city and its river.

On its northern slope are two cemeteries, one that used to be Anglophone and Protestant, the other Francophone and Catholic—reminders of the linguistic and religious division that persists in the city.

With its trails for strolling, hiking, and cross-country skiing, the park is well used by Montréalers, who refer to it simply and affectionately as "the Mountain."

Rue Crescent One of Montréal's major dining and nightlife districts lies in the western shadow of the massed phalanxes of downtown skyscrapers. While the first street on its northern end houses luxury boutiques in Victorian brownstones, its southern end holds dozens of restaurants, bars, and clubs of all styles, spilling over onto neighboring streets.

The quarter's Anglophone origins are evident in the street names here: Stanley, Drummond, Crescent, Bishop, and MacKay.

The party atmosphere that pervades after dark never quite fades, and it builds to crescendos as weekends approach, especially in warm weather. That's when the area's 20- and 30-something denizens spill out into sidewalk cafes and onto balcony terraces.

The Village Also known as the Gay Village, the city's gay and lesbian enclave is one of North America's largest. This compact but vibrant district is filled with clothing stores, antiques shops, dance clubs, and cafes.

It runs along rue Ste-Catherine from rue St-Hubert to rue Papineau and onto side streets.

For the last few years, the city has made the length of rue Ste-Catherine in the Village pedestrian-only for the entire

summer. Bars and restaurants build ad-hoc terraces into the street, and a summer-resort atmosphere pervades.

A rainbow, the symbol of the gay community, marks the Beaudry Station, which is on rue Ste-Catherine in the heart of the neighborhood.

St-Denis Rue St-Denis, which runs from the Latin Quarter downtown near rue Ste-Catherine est and continues north into the Plateau Mont-Royal district, is the thumping central artery of Francophone Montréal, thick with cafes, bistros, offbeat shops, and lively nightspots.

At its southern end, near the concrete campus of the Université du Québec à Montréal (UQAM), the avenue is decidedly student oriented, with indie rock cranked up in the inexpensive bars, and young adults in jeans and leather swapping philosophical insights and telephone numbers. It is rife with the visual messiness that characterizes student and bohemian quarters.

Farther north, above rue Sherbrooke, a raffish quality persists along the rows of three- and four-story Victorian houses, but the average age of residents and visitors nudges past 30. Prices are higher, and some of the city's better restaurants are here.

This is the district in which to take in the pulse of Francophone life. There are no museums or important galleries on St-Denis, nor is the architecture notable, which relieves visitors of the chore of obligatory sightseeing. Take in the passing scene—just as the locals do—over bowls of café au lait at any of the numerous terraces that line the avenue.

Mile End Adjoining Plateau Mont-Royal at its upper west corner, this blossoming neighborhood is contained by rue St-Laurent on the east, avenue Du Parc on the west, boulevard St-Joseph on the south, and rue Bernard in the north. Though it's outside of the usual tourist orbit, it has a growing number of retail attractions, including designer clothing stores, places at which to buy household goods, and many worthwhile restaurants.

Mile End has pockets of many ethnic minineighborhoods, including Italian, Portuguese, Armenian, Hassidic, and Greek. There's an area some still call Greektown along avenue du Parc, largely in the form of restaurants and taverns.

Île Ste-Hélène & Île Notre-Dame St. Helen's Island in the St. Lawrence River was altered extensively to become the site of Expo 67, Montréal's very successful World's Fair in 1967. In the 4 years before the Expo, construction crews doubled its surface area with landfill and then went on to create an island beside it that hadn't existed before: Île Notre-Dame. Much of the earth for this was dredged from the bottom of the St. Lawrence, and 15 million tons of rock from the excavations for the Métro and the Décarie Expressway were carried in by truck.

When the World's Fair was over, the city preserved the site and a few of its exhibition buildings. Parts were used for the 1976 Olympics, and today, Île Ste-Hélène is home to an amusement park, La Ronde (p. 116), as well as the popular Casino de Montréal (p. 169).

Connected by two bridges, the islands now comprise the recently designated **Parc Jean-Drapeau,** which is almost entirely car-free and accessible by Métro.

Quartier International When Route 720 was constructed some years ago, it left behind a desolate swath of derelict buildings, parking lots, and empty spaces smack-dab between downtown and Vieux-Montréal.

Bounded, more or less, by rue St-Jacques on the south, avenue Viger on the north, rue St-Urbain on the east, and rue University on the west, this no-man's land is slowly being spruced up with new parks, office buildings—notably agencies or businesses with an international focus—and a recently expanded **Palais des Congrès (Convention Center).**

The convention center, in fact, is a design triumph, as unlikely as that seems. Transparent glass exterior walls are a crazy quilt of pink, yellow, blue, green, red, and purple rectangles. You can step into the inside hallway for the full effect when the sun streams in, it's like being inside a huge children's kaleidoscope. The walls are the vision of Montréal architect Mario Saia.

A small plaza opposite the convention center's west end is named for Jean-Paul-Piopelle, a prominent Québec artist. One of his sculptures stands here.

The Quartier incorporates the World Trade Center Montréal, a complex of brokerage houses, law firms, and import-export companies.

Chinatown Tucked just north of Vieux-Montréal, centered on the intersection of rue Clark and the pedestrianized section of rue de la Gauchetière, Chinatown is mostly comprised of restaurants and a tiny park. The fancy gates to the area on boulevard St-Laurent are guarded by white stone lions. Community spirit is strong and inhabitants remain faithful to their traditions despite the encroaching modernism all around them.

The Underground City During Montréal's long winters, life slows on the streets of downtown as people escape into *la ville souterraine,* a parallel subterranean universe. Down there, in a controlled climate that recalls an eternal spring, it's possible to arrive at the railroad station, check into a hotel, shop for days, and go out for dinner—all without donning an overcoat or putting on snow boots.

This underground city evolved when major downtown developments—such as Place Ville-Marie (the city's first skyscraper), Place Bonaventure, Complexe Desjardins, Palais des Congrès, and Place des Arts—put their below-street-level areas to profitable use, leasing space for shops and other enterprises. Over time, in fits and starts and with no master plan, these spaces became connected with Métro stations and then with each other. It became possible to ride long distances and walk the shorter ones through mazes of corridors, tunnels, and plazas. Today, there are over 1,000 retailers and eateries in or connected to the network.

Admittedly, the term "underground city" is not entirely accurate because of how some complexes funnel people through their own spaces. In Place Bonaventure, for instance, passengers may leave the Métro and wander on the same level only to find themselves peering out a window several floors above the street.

The city beneath the city has obvious advantages, including no traffic accidents and avoidance of winter slush. Natural light is let in wherever possible, which drastically reduces the feeling of claustrophobia that some malls evoke. However, the underground city covers a vast area, without the convenience of a logical street grid, and can be confusing. There are plenty of signs, but it's wise to make careful note of landmarks at key corners along your route. Expect to get lost anyway—but, being that you're in a maze, consider it part of the fun.

2 GETTING AROUND

Montréal is a terrific walking city. One thing to keep in mind when strolling is to cross only at street corners and only when you have a green light or a walk sign. City police began cracking down on jaywalkers in 2007 in an attempt to cut down on the number of accidents involving pedestrians, and newspapers continue to carry stories of fines being issued.

MONTREAL BY METRO

For speed and economy, nothing beats Montréal's **Métro system.** The stations are marked on the street by blue-and-white signs that show a circle enclosing a down-pointing arrow. Although showing its age (the system has run at a financial deficit in recent years), the Métro is relatively clean, and quiet trains whisk passengers through a decent network of underground tunnels. Information is online at **www.stm.info** or by phone at ℂ **514/786-4636.**

Fares are by the ride, not by distance. Single rides cost C$2.75. A card with six rides costs C$12.75, and a weekly pass, good for unlimited rides, is C$20. Reduced fares are available to children and, with special Métro OPUS cards, seniors and students. Sales are cash only. You can buy tickets from the booth attendant in any station or from a convenience store.

Tourist Cards can be a good deal if you plan to use the Métro more than three times in 1 day. You get unlimited access to the bus and Métro network for 1 day for C$9 or 3 consecutive days for C$17. The front of the card has scratch-off sections like a lottery card— you scratch out the month and day (or 3 consecutive days) on which you're using the card.

To enter the system, slip your ticket into the slot in the turnstile, show your pass to the booth attendant, or hand a ticket to the attendant. If you plan to transfer to a bus, take a transfer ticket *(correspondence)* from the machine just inside the turnstile. Every Métro station has one, and it allows you a free transfer to a bus wherever you exit the subway. Remember to take the transfer ticket at the station where you *first* enter the system. If you start a trip by bus and intend to continue on the Métro, ask the driver for a transfer.

The Métro runs from about 5:30am to 1am. If you plan to be out late, check the website at www.stm.info or call ℭ **514/786-4636** for the exact times of each line's last train.

The system is not immune to transit strikes, and convenient as it is, there can be substantial distances between stations. Accessibility is sometimes difficult for people with mobility restrictions or parents with strollers.

MONTREAL BY BUS

Bus fares are the same as fares for Métro trains, and Métro tickets are good on buses, too. Exact change is required if you want to pay in cash. Although they run throughout the city and give tourists the advantage of traveling aboveground, buses don't run as frequently or as swiftly as the Métro. If you start a trip on the bus and want to transfer to the Métro, ask the bus driver at the start of the ride for a transfer ticket.

Montreal by TaxThere are plenty of taxis run by many different companies. Cabs come in a variety of colors and styles, so their principal distinguishing feature is the plastic sign on the roof. At night, the sign is illuminated when the cab is available. The initial charge is C$3.30. Each additional kilometer (⅔ mile) adds C$1.60, and each minute of waiting adds C60¢. A short ride from one point to another downtown usually costs about C$7. Tip about 10% to 15%. Members of hotel and restaurant staffs can call cabs, many of which are dispatched by radio. They line up outside most large hotels or can be hailed on the street.

Montréal taxi drivers range in temperament from unstoppably loquacious to sullen and cranky. Some know their city well, others have sketchy knowledge and poor language skills, so it's a good idea to have your destination written down—with the cross street—to show your driver.

MONTREAL BY CAR

Montréal is an easy city to navigate by car, although traffic during morning and late afternoon rush hour can be horrendous. If you'll be doing much driving, you may want to pick up the pocket-size atlas published by JDM Géo and MapArt (www.mapart.com), sold at gas stations throughout Canada. The map offers more detail than most, especially in the areas outside the primary tourist orbit. The company also sells good maps for the Laurentians and Cantons-de-l'Est regions discussed in chapter 12.

It can be difficult to park for free on downtown Montréal's heavily trafficked streets, but there are plenty of metered spaces. Look around before walking off without paying. Traditional meters are set well back from the curb so they won't be buried by plowed snow in winter. Metered parking costs C$3 per hour, and meters are in effect weekdays until 9pm and weekends until 6pm.

If there are no parking meters in sight, you're not off the hook. Computerized Pay 'N Go stations are quickly replacing meters. Look for the black metal kiosks: They're columns about 6 feet tall with a white "P" in a blue circle. Press the "English" button, enter

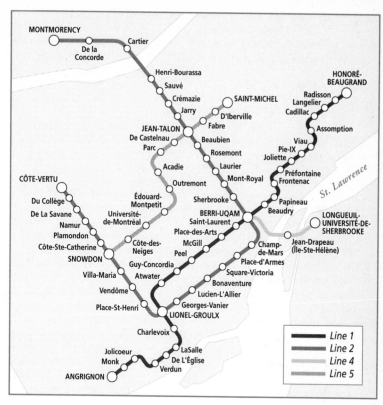

the letter from the space where you are parked, and then pay with cash or a credit card, following the onscreen instructions.

Check for signs noting parking restrictions, usually showing a red circle with a diagonal slash. The words LIVRAISON SEULEMENT mean "delivery only." Most downtown shopping complexes have underground parking lots, as do the big downtown hotels. Some hotels offer in and out privileges, letting you take your car in and out of the garage without a fee—useful if you plan to do some sightseeing by car.

The limited-access expressways in Québec are called *autoroutes,* with distances given in kilometers (km) and speed limits given in kilometers per hour (kmph). Because French is the province's official language, some highway signs are only in French, though Montréal's autoroutes and bridges often bear dual-language signs.

One traffic signal function often confuses newcomers: Should you wish to make a turn and you know that the street runs in the correct direction, you may be surprised to initially see just a green arrow pointing straight ahead instead of a green light permitting the turn. The arrow gives pedestrians time to cross the intersection. After a few moments, the light will turn from an arrow to a regular green light and you can proceed with your turn.

Fun Facts **July 1: Citywide Moving Day**

Montréal is an island of renters, and close to 100,000 people move from old apartments to new ones every July 1—on that date, and only that date. It coincides with Canada's National Day, ensuring that separatist-minded Francophone Québécois won't have time to celebrate a holiday they have no intention of observing anyway.

All but certain to be miserably hot and humid, July 1 is a trial that can, nevertheless, be hilarious to observe. See families struggle to get bedroom sets and large appliances down narrow outdoor staircases! Watch sidewalks become obstacle courses of baby cribs, bicycles, and overflowing cardboard boxes! Listen to the cacophony of horns as streets become clogged with every serviceable van, truck, and SUV!

Later in the day, hundreds of people arrive at their new digs and discover gifts of junk no longer desired by their predecessors—busted furniture, pantries of old food, pitiful plants.

No one can explain why reason didn't prevail long ago in the form of a mandated staggered schedule. Unless you're interested in observing the mayhem or taking advantage of the best trash-picking of the year, you'll want to be someplace else on that day.

A blinking green light means that oncoming traffic still has a red light, making it safe to make a left turn.

Turning right on a red light is prohibited on the island of Montréal, except where specifically allowed by an additional green arrow. Off the island, it is legal to turn right after stopping at red lights, except where there's a sign specifically prohibiting that move.

While most visitors arriving by plane or train will want to rely on public transportation and cabs, a **rental car** can come in handy for trips outside of town or if you plan to drive to Québec City.

In Québec, the highway speed limit is 100 kmph (62 mph) and toll roads are rare. For listings of major **car-rental agencies** in Québec, please see "Airline, Hotel & Car-Rental Websites," p. 294.

MONTREAL BY BIKE

Montréal has an exceptionally great system of bike paths, and bicycling is common not just for recreation but for transportation as well.

Most Métro stations have large bike racks. In some neighborhoods, sections of the street where cars would normally park are fenced off for bike racks.

Passengers can take bicycles on the Métro from 10am to 3pm and after 7pm on weekdays and all day on Saturday, Sunday, and holidays. This rule is suspended, however, on special-event days when the trains are too crowded. Bikers should board the first car of the train, which can hold a maximum of four bikes (if there are already that many bikes on that car, you have to wait for the next train). Details are online at **www.stm.info/ English/metro/a-velo-met.htm**.

The nonprofit biking organization **Vélo Québec** (© **800/567-8356** or 514/521-8356; www.velo.qc.ca) has the most up-to-date information on the state of bike paths and offers guided tours throughout the province (*vélo* means "bicycle" in French).

Several taxi companies participate in the **Taxi+Vélo** program. You call, specify that you have a bike to transport, and a cab with a specially designed rack arrives. Up to three bikes can be carried for an extra fee of C$3 each. The companies are listed on a PDF at www.velo.qc.ca (search the French-language pages for *"taxi"* or *"transport en commun"*). They include **Taxi Diamond** in Montréal (© 514/271-6331) and Taxi Union Longueuil in Rive-Sud (© 450/679-6262).

Bicycle rentals are available from shops around the city. One of the most centrally located for visitors is **ÇaRoule/Montréal on Wheels** (© **877/866-0633** or 514/866-0633; www.caroulemontreal.com) at 27 rue de la Commune est, the waterfront road bordering Vieux-Port.

In May 2009, the city initiated a long-awaited self-service bicycle rental program called BIXI, an abbreviation of the words *bicyclette* and *taxi*. It's similar to programs in Paris, Barcelona, and Berlin, where users pick up BIXI bikes from designated stands throughout the city and drop them off at any other stand, for a small fee. Some 3,000 bikes were to be in operation by the end of 2009 with some 300 stations in Montréal's central boroughs. For short trips (under 2 hr.), it's economical, but if you want a bike for a half-day or longer, it's may be cheaper to rent from a shop. BIXI fees and details are listed at **www.bixi.com**.

GETTING TO KNOW MONTRÉAL

5

GETTING AROUND

6

Where to Stay in Montréal

Accommodations in Montréal range from skyscrapers on grand boulevards to converted row houses to stylish inns and boutique luxury hotels—the latter of which are found in ever-increasing numbers in Vieux-Montréal. See "Tips on Accommodations" in chapter 3 for suggestions on securing the right venue and best deal for you.

STAR SYSTEM The tourist authorities in Québec province apply a six-level rating system (zero to five stars) to seven categories of establishments that host travelers. An ocher-and-brown shield bearing the assigned rating is posted near the entrance to most hotels and inns. The Québec system is based on quantitative measures such as the range of services and amenities. No star is assigned to properties that meet only the basic minimum standards, while five stars are reserved for establishments deemed exceptional. Most of the recommendations below have gotten at least three stars from the state system. Details are at www.citq.info.

The stars you see in the reviews in this book are based on Frommer's own rating system, which assigns between zero and three stars. The Frommer's ratings are more subjective than the state's, taking into account such considerations as price-to-value ratios, quality of service, ambience, location, helpfulness of staff, and the presence of such facilities as spas and exercise rooms.

RATES The rates quoted in the listings in this chapter are "rack rates"—the standard rates charged for double-occupancy rooms. These rates are used to divide the hotels into four price categories, ranging from "Very Expensive" to "Inexpensive," for easy reference. Remember that rack rates are only guidelines and that you can often find better deals.

Hotel rates are highest during the region's busiest times, from May to October, reaching a peak in July and August. Rates also inflate during the frequent summer festivals, annual holidays (Canadian *and* American), and winter carnivals in January and February. (Festivals and dates are listed on p. 20 in chapter 3.) For those periods, reserve well in advance, especially if you're looking for special prices or packages.

Except in B&Bs, visitors can almost always find discounts and package deals. That's especially the case on weekends, when business clients leave town.

CATEGORIES The hotels listed below are near most attractions in downtown and Vieux-Montréal. The listings are categorized first by neighborhood, then by price.

All rooms have private bathrooms unless otherwise noted. Many of the more luxurious hotels have stopped providing in-room coffeemakers, so ask in advance if this feature is important to you. Most hotels provide Wi-Fi in either part of or all of their facilities, although this continues to be a work in progress for some properties. Ask about the most current Internet options when reserving a room.

Most Montréal hotels are entirely nonsmoking. Those that aren't have a limited number of smoking rooms available.

TAXES Most goods and services in Canada are taxed 5% by the federal government (the GST, or Goods and Services Tax). On top of that, the province of Québec adds an additional 7.5% tax (the TVQ). A 3% accommodations tax (which goes toward promoting tourism) is in effect in Montréal. Prices listed in this book do not include taxes.

B&BS Bed-and-breakfasts boast cozier settings than many hotels and are often (but not always) lower priced than comparable hotels. They also give visitors the opportunity to get to know a Montréaler or two, since their owners are among the most outgoing and knowledgeable guides one might want. The Association des Gites Touristiques de Montréal (the Bed & Breakfast Association of Montréal) at 1933 rue Panet ($\mathcal{C}$ 514/510-7976; www.agtm.ca) lists B&Bs and guest houses that are approved by the province's tourist board. You can also find B&Bs at www.tourisme-montreal.org.

Accommodations and rules at B&Bs can vary significantly, so ask upfront whether children are welcome or if bathrooms are shared.

1 BEST HOTEL BETS

- **Best Boutique Hotels (Downtown): Hôtel Le Germain,** 2050 rue Mansfield ($\mathcal{C}$ 877/333-2050 or 514/849-2050), is luxurious and contemporary, and since 2007 has been home to restaurant **Laurie Raphaël Montréal.** The **Loews Hôtel Vogue,** 1425 rue de la Montagne ($\mathcal{C}$ 888/465-6654 or 514/285-5555), also hosts guests with warmth and style. See p. 64 and p. 65.
- **Best Boutique Hotel (Vieux-Montréal):** The **Hôtel Le St-James,** 355 rue St-Jacques ouest, Vieux-Montréal ($\mathcal{C}$ 866/841-3111 or 514/841-3111), raises the bar to an almost impossibly high level and has a superbly Sybaritic spa and gorgeous grand hall for dining. See p. 70.
- **Best Historic Hotel:** While devoid of external artifice (it looks pretty darn plain from the outside), **Fairmont The Queen Elizabeth,** 900 bd. René-Lévesque ouest ($\mathcal{C}$ 866/540-4483 or 514/861-3511), marked its 50th anniversary in 2008, reminding the world that it was one of North America's first hotels with escalators, central air-conditioning, and direct-dial phones in each room. Its reception lobby still impresses. (The venerable **Ritz-Carlton Montréal,** at 1228 rue Sherbrooke ouest, is under renovation and expected to reopen sometime in 2010.) See p. 64 and p. 68.
- **Best Hotel for Business Travelers (Expensive): Sofitel Montréal Golden Mile,** 1155 rue Sherbrooke ouest ($\mathcal{C}$ 514/285-9000), the first Canadian branch of the pervasive French luxury hotel chain, has floor-to-ceiling windows, convenient desks, a well-appointed exercise room, and a good restaurant with a pretty bar and terrace. See p. 68.
- **Best Hotel for Business Travelers (Discount): Hôtel Le Dauphin Montréal-Downtown,** 1025 rue de Bleury ($\mathcal{C}$ 888/784-3888 or 514/788-3888), adjacent to the convention center and a few blocks from Vieux-Montréal's northern end, offers big-hotel touches at small-budget prices. See p. 70.
- **Best Hotels for a Romantic Getaway:** So many options. **Hostellerie Pierre du Calvet,** 405 rue Bonsecours ($\mathcal{C}$ 866/544-1725 or 514/282-1725), has ancient cut-stone walls, swags of velvet and brocade, and tilting floors that Benjamin Franklin once trod upon. Meanwhile, **Auberge du Vieux-Port,** 97 rue de la Commune est ($\mathcal{C}$ 888/660-7678 or 514/876-0081), offers a more contemporary retreat, with many bedrooms offering unobstructed views of the waterfront. See p. 72 and 71.

- **Best Design Hotels: Hôtel St. Paul,** 355 rue McGill (✆ **866/380-2202** or 514/380-2222), softens its austere lines with pale-cream walls, while the **Hotel Gault,** at 449 rue Ste-Hélène (✆ **866/904-1616** or 514/904-1616), leaves its raw concrete uncovered and incorporates candy-colored furniture. See p. 73 and 72.

- **Best Bet for a Long Stay:** Rooms in the converted warehouse, **Le Square Phillips Hôtel & Suites,** 1193 Square Phillips (✆ **866/393-1193** or 514/393-1193), provide ample space and everything you need to be home away from home. A pool and rooftop terrace are nice bonuses. See p. 70.

- **Best B&B:** In a 1723 structure in Vieux-Montréal, **Auberge Les Passants du Sans Soucy,** 171 rue St-Paul ouest (✆ **514/842-2634**), is more upscale and stylish than most of its peers, and it's near the Old City's top restaurants and clubs. See p. 75.

- **Best Hotel Breakfast:** At **Auberge Bonaparte,** 447 rue St-François-Xavier (✆ **514/844-1448**), morning meals are large and served in the elegant Bonaparte restaurant. See p. 74.

- **Best Service at a Hotel:** It's tough to choose between the troops at the wildly luxurious **Hôtel Le St-James,** 355 rue St-Jacques ouest, Vieux-Montréal (✆ **866/841-3111** or 514/841-3111), and the team at the understated **Hôtel XIXe Siècle,** 262 rue St-Jacques ouest (✆ **877/553-0019** or 514/985-0019). Both display grace and care when it comes to tending to their guests. See p. 70 and 75.

2 CENTRE VILLE/DOWNTOWN

EXPENSIVE

Fairmont The Queen Elizabeth (Le Reine Elizabeth) ★★ (Kids) Montréal's largest hotel—it has more than 1,000 rooms—stacks its 21 floors atop VIA Rail's Gare Centrale, the main train station, with the Métro and popular shopping areas such as Place Ville-Marie and Place Bonaventure accessible through underground arcades. This desirable location makes "the Queen E" a frequent choice for heads of state and touring celebrities, even though other hotels in town offer more luxurious pampering. The Fairmont Gold 18th and 19th floors are the best choice, offering a private concierge lounge with complimentary breakfasts and cocktail-hour canapés. Less exalted rooms on floors 4 through 17 are satisfactory, furnished traditionally, and feature easy chairs, ottomans, and bright reading lamps. May 2009 marked the 40th anniversary of John Lennon and Yoko Ono's weeklong "Bed-in for Peace" in suite no. 1742.

900 bd. René-Lévesque ouest (at rue Mansfield), Montréal, PQ H3B 4A5. ✆ **866/540-4483** or 514/861-3511. Fax 514/954-2296. www.fairmont.com/queenelizabeth. 1,039 units. C$189–C$359 double; C$289 and up suite. Children 18 and under stay free in parent's room. Packages available. AE, DC, MC, V. Valet parking C$26. Métro: Bonaventure. Pets accepted for fee. **Amenities:** 3 restaurants; 2 bars; babysitting; concierge; executive-level rooms; exceptional health club & spa w/Jacuzzi and instructors; pool (indoor); room service; Wi-Fi (in lobby, C$14 per day). *In room:* A/C, TV, hair dryer, Internet (C$14 per day).

Hôtel Le Germain ★★★ This undertaking by the owner of Québec City's equally desirable boutique hotel, **Dominion 1912** (p. 219), is a big shot of panache in the downtown lodging scene. It jazzed things up even more with the 2007 opening of the in-house **Laurie Raphaël Montréal,** an offshoot of the much-esteemed restaurant of the same name in Québec City. The hotel vibe is stylish loft, mixing Asian minimalism with Western comforts. Bedrooms have super-comfy bedding, marshmallowy-plush reading chairs, ergonomic work areas with eye-level plugs and ports, windows that open, and a variety of lighting options. A glass partition between the bed and the shower is standard. Self-serve breakfasts include perfect croissants and café au lait, and there's a free espresso machine in the lobby. Near constant renovations and sprucing of paint, bedding, and amenities keeps this boutique hotel at the top of its game.

2050 rue Mansfield (at av. du President-Kennedy), Montréal, PQ H3A 1Y9. (✆) **877/333-2050** or 514/849-2050. Fax 514/849-1437. www.hotelgermain.com. 101 units. C$210–C$475 double. Rates include breakfast. Packages available. AE, DC, MC, V. Valet parking C$25. Métro: Peel. Pets accepted, C$30 a night. **Amenities:** Restaurant; bar; babysitting; concierge; exercise room; room service. *In room:* A/C, TV, movie library, hair dryer, minibar, MP3 docking station, Wi-Fi (free).

Le Centre Sheraton Montréal Hotel ★ Ever bustling, this branch of the familiar brand goes about its business with efficiency and surety of purpose. That figures, since earnest people in suits make up most of the clientele. They gravitate toward the Club Rooms, which include a free breakfast and a private lounge with expansive views and evening hors d'oeuvres. Regular guest rooms are decorated in modest corporate style but are clean and have good beds. The health club includes an indoor pool, sauna, whirlpool, a fully equipped fitness center with skylights, a massage studio, and summer terrace. True to its name, this hotel has a central downtown location that's near Dorchester Square, Gare Centrale (the main train station), and the high-stepping rue Crescent dining and nightlife district.

1201 bd. René-Lévesque ouest (btw. rue Drummond and rue Stanley), Montréal, PQ H3B 2L7. (✆) **800/325-3535** or 514/878-2000. Fax 514/878-3958. www.sheraton.com/lecentre. 825 units. C$189–C$599 double; C$539 and up suite. Children 18 and under stay free in parent's room. Packages available. AE, DC, DISC, MC, V. Valet parking C$26, self-parking C$20. Métro: Bonaventure. If you're driving, note that the entrance is on rue Drummond. Pets accepted. **Amenities:** Restaurant; bar; babysitting; concierge; executive-level; health club w/spa and sauna; pool (indoor w/whirlpool); room service; Wi-Fi (in lobby, free). *In room:* A/C, TV, hair dryer, Wi-Fi (C$15 per day).

Loews Hôtel Vogue ★★ (Kids) When the Vogue opened in 1990, it instantly joined the Ritz-Carlton at the top tier of the local luxury-hotel pantheon. Twenty years on, confidence and capability continue to resonate from every member of its staff, and luxury permeates the hotel from the lobby to the well-appointed guest rooms. Feather pillows and duvets dress oversize beds, and huge marble bathrooms are fitted with Jacuzzis—double-size in suites—and separate shower stalls. Rooms all have consistent decor, so what you see on the website is what you'll get when you arrive. The hotel's **L'Opéra Bar** is a two-story room with floor-to-ceiling windows and is open until 2am. Packages that include room service breakfast are worth the splurge.

1425 rue de la Montagne (near rue Ste-Catherine), Montréal, PQ H3G 1Z3. (✆) **888/465-6654** or 514/285-5555. Fax 514/849-8903. www.loewshotels.com. 142 units. C$229–C$329 double, C$429 suite; from C$189 low season. Children 17 and under stay free in parent's room. Packages available. AE, DC, DISC, MC, V. Valet parking C$32. Métro: Peel. Pets accepted for fee. **Amenities:** Restaurant; 2 bars; babysitting; children's programs; concierge; exercise room (24-hr.) and discounted access to Club Sportif MAA gym and pool; room service, Wi-Fi (in lobby, free). *In room:* A/C, TV/DVD, CD player, hair dryer, minibar, MP3 docking station, Wi-Fi (C$15 per day).

Opus Montréal Hotel ★ One of Montréal's nightlife epicenters is the Opus's restaurant and bar, **Koko** (p. 169), which boasts the city's most expansive terrace. Hotel guests can cut its notoriously long lines and sip neon drinks among the clubbing elite, where heel height regularly exceeds 5 inches. Bedrooms are designed for this crowd: the concrete ceilings and sugarplum walls look better in evening light, showers are lit from

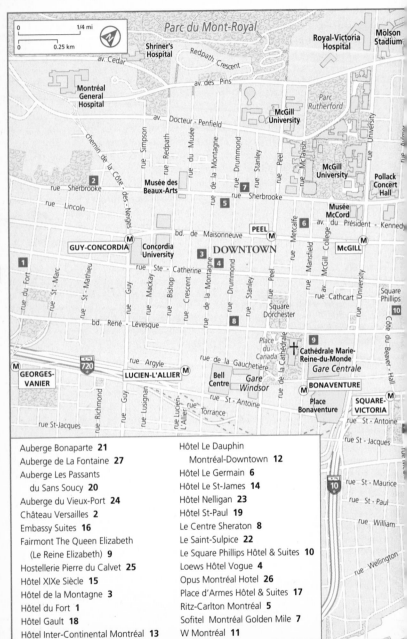

Auberge Bonaparte **21**
Auberge de La Fontaine **27**
Auberge Les Passants
  du Sans Soucy **20**
Auberge du Vieux-Port **24**
Château Versailles **2**
Embassy Suites **16**
Fairmont The Queen Elizabeth
  (Le Reine Elizabeth) **9**
Hostellerie Pierre du Calvet **25**
Hôtel XIXe Siècle **15**
Hôtel de la Montagne **3**
Hôtel du Fort **1**
Hôtel Gault **18**
Hôtel Inter-Continental Montréal **13**

Hôtel Le Dauphin
  Montréal-Downtown **12**
Hôtel Le Germain **6**
Hôtel Le St-James **14**
Hôtel Nelligan **23**
Hôtel St-Paul **19**
Le Centre Sheraton **8**
Le Saint-Sulpice **22**
Le Square Phillips Hôtel & Suites **10**
Loews Hôtel Vogue **4**
Opus Montréal Hotel **26**
Place d'Armes Hôtel & Suites **17**
Ritz-Carlton Montréal **5**
Sofitel Montréal Golden Mile **7**
W Montréal **11**

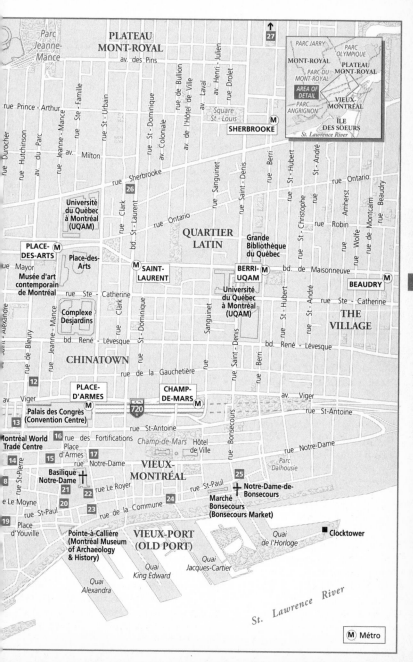

Tips   Keep Up Your Workout Schedule

If you're staying at a hotel that doesn't have a fitness center or whose exercise room is modest, keep **Club Sportiff MAA** in mind (📞 **514/845-2233;** www.clubsportifmaa.com). Located centrally downtown at rue Peel between rue Sherbrooke and boulevard de Maisonneuve, the luxury facility has a 743-sq.-m (8,000-sq.-ft), state-of-the-art gym with cardio and strength training equipment, a lap pool, and a full schedule of classes—everything from spinning to Pilates to Ashtanga yoga. A few hotels, like Loews Hôtel Vogue, provide discounted passes to their overnight guests. For everyone else, day passes are available for C$20 for adults and C$10 for children 17 and under.

below, and linens are silky soft. Guests often need the earplugs found on every nightstand. The structure began life in 1914 as the first poured concrete building in North America and was a boutique hotel named for its architect, Joseph-Arthur Godin, until the Opus group purchased it in 2007. Though technically downtown, the hotel borders Plateau Mont-Royal, where city dwellers both live and party. A free drop-off service can whisk you downtown or to Vieux-Montréal for a stroll along the harbor.

10 Sherbrooke ouest, (near rue St-Laurent), Montréal, PQ H2X 4C9. 📞 **866/744-6346** or 514/843-6000. Fax 514/843-6810. www.opushotel.com. 136 units. C$229–C$249 double; C$369–C$669 suite. Children 18 and under stay free in parent's room. Packages available. AE, DC, DISC, MC, V. Valet parking C$26. Pets accepted for fee. Métro: St-Laurent. **Amenities:** Restaurant; bar; babysitting; concierge; health club; room service; Wi-Fi (in lobby, free). *In room:* A/C, TV, CD player, hair dryer, Internet (C$15 per day), minibar.

Ritz-Carlton Montréal ★★   The Ritz and its restaurants were closed for all of 2009 and are expected to reopen in November, 2010. Since its launch in 1912, the luxe hotel has been a favorite for both accommodations and dining, with **Café de Paris** favored for high tea and **Le Jardin du Ritz** for its duck pond and ducklings. The C$100-million renovation project started in June 2008. Check the hotel's website for updates and pricing details.

1228 rue Sherbrooke ouest (at rue Drummond), Montréal, PQ H3G 1H6. 📞 **800/363-0366** or 514/842-4212. www.ritzmontreal.com.

Sofitel Montréal Golden Mile ★★   The French luxury hotel chain transformed a bland 1970s downtown office tower into a coveted destination for visiting celebrities and the power elite. It wows from the moment of arrival, from the light-filled stone-and-wood lobby to the universally warm welcome visitors get from the staff. The 100 standard rooms (called Superior) have floor-to-ceiling windows, furnishings made from Québec-grown cherrywood, down duvets, and a soothing oatmeal-cream decor featuring black-and-white photos of Montréal by local photographers. Though chairs with right-angled backs are a bit too overdesigned for comfort, the desks, which attach to the wall, are easy to use from either side. Bathrooms have rain showers but not bathtubs. The ambitious **Renoir** restaurant (p. 81) features an upscale bar and outdoor terrace. Catering to the international and business guests whose bodies are still operating on different time zones, the exercise room is open 24 hours per day.

1155 rue Sherbrooke ouest (at rue Peel), Montréal, PQ H3A 2N3. ☏ **514/285-9000.** Fax 514/289-1155. www.sofitel.com. 258 units. C$215–C$290 double; from C$295 suite. Packages available. AE, DC, MC, V. Valet parking C$30. Métro: Peel. Pets accepted. **Amenities:** Restaurant; bar; babysitting; concierge; executive-level rooms; exercise room (24-hr, w/sauna); room service; Wi-Fi (common areas, C$15 per day). *In room:* TV, DVD player by request, CD player, hair dryer, Internet (C$15 per day), minibar, MP3 docking station.

MODERATE

Château Versailles ★ Official lodging of the **Musée des Beaux-Arts** (p. 102) and McGill University, the Versailles is near the museum but outside most of the tourist orbit. It began as a European-style pension in 1958 and expanded into adjacent pre-WWI town houses. The most spacious rooms have decorator treatment, with modern furnishings and Deco and Second Empire touches. Some have fireplaces. Loyal guests return for just this reason—every room is different. A buffet breakfast is served in the main living room, where you can sit at a small table or in an easy chair in front of a fireplace. One obstacle: the lack of an elevator by which to deal with the three floors. As well, at the time of our last visit, some bedding needed an upgrade. Across the street is sister property Le Meridien Versailles, 1808 rue Sherbrooke ouest (☏ **888/933-8111** or 514/933 8111; www.lemeridienversailleshotel.com), home to the well-regarded restaurant **Brontë.**

1659 rue Sherbrooke ouest (at rue St-Mathieu), Montréal, PQ H3H 1E3. ☏ **888/933-8111** or 514/933-8111. Fax 514/933-6967. www.versailleshotels.com. 65 units. C$169–C$220 double; from C$325 suite. Rates include breakfast. Packages available. AE, DC, DISC, MC, V. Valet parking C$24. Métro: Guy-Concordia. Pets accepted for fee. **Amenities:** Babysitting; concierge; exercise room (24-hr. w/sauna); room service. *In room:* A/C, TV, hair dryer, minibar, Wi-Fi (C$16 per day).

Hôtel de la Montagne Eras collide at this hotel, where an Art Deco lobby with giant tusked elephants and a fountain topped by a nude figure with stained-glass butterfly wings opens onto a jazz piano cabaret lounge. Just a few steps further and you're in the giant singles watering hole **Thursday's** (p. 167), which has a terrace opening onto lively rue Crescent. In warmer months, patrons from all over the city stand in line for the rooftop pool and bar (both open till 3am). Factor in the trio of slot machines and discothèque, and you could be in Vegas, baby! After that, the relatively serene bedrooms, all with balconies, seem downright bland, but they're clean and include good-size bathrooms and high-end bedding. Some rooms have benefited from a sleek update in the last 2 years (they cost more). All in all, the hotel offers a competent staff and bit of old-fashioned pizazz.

1430 rue de la Montagne (north of rue Ste-Catherine), Montréal, PQ H3G 1Z5. ☏ **800/361-6262** or 514/288-5656. Fax 514/288-9658. www.hoteldelamontagne.com. 142 units. C$175–C$249 double. Children 12 and under stay free in parent's room. Packages available. AE, DC, DISC, MC, V. Valet parking C$16, for SUV C$32. Métro: Peel. Pets accepted for fee. **Amenities:** 2 restaurants; 3 bars; babysitting; concierge; pool (heated, outdoor); room service. *In room:* A/C, TV, hair dryer, minibar, Wi-Fi (free).

Hôtel du Fort (Kids) While hardly grand, this reliable hotel takes as its primary duty providing lodging to longer-term business travelers. That includes providing a fitness room (newly renovated) sufficient enough for a thorough workout, basic kitchenettes with fridges and microwave ovens in every room (the concierge can have groceries delivered), and a wheelchair-accessible underground parking garage. Because all rooms are a good size and many have sofas with hide-a-beds, they're good for small families or persons who use wheelchairs. A buffet breakfast is served in the lounge. In a nod toward sustainability, kitchenettes feature energy-efficient appliances with Energy Star designation.

1390 rue du Fort (at rue Ste-Catherine), Montréal, PQ H3H 2R7. ✆ **800/565-6333** or 514/938-8333. www. hoteldufort.com. 124 units. C$179–C$225 double; C$219–C$305 suite. Children 11 and under stay free in parent's room. Packages available. AE, DC, MC, V. Self-parking C$18. Métro: Guy-Concordia. **Amenities:** Babysitting; concierge; exercise room; room service. *In room:* A/C, TV, hair dryer, kitchenette, Wi-Fi (C$11 per day).

Le Square Phillips Hôtel & Suites ★ ⟨**Value**⟩   The three advantages here are space, livability, and locale. Originally designed as a warehouse by the noted Québec architect Ernest Cormier, the building was converted to its present function in 2003. The vaguely cathedral-like spaces were largely retained, making for capacious studio bedrooms and suites fully equipped for long stays. Full kitchens in every unit come with all essential appliances—toasters, fridges, stoves, dishwashers, crockery, and pots and pans. There's a rooftop pool with a lovely view and an exercise room; a laundry room is also available for guest use. The location, at the edge of the downtown shopping district, is ideal and an easy walk to Vieux-Montréal and the rue Crescent nightlife district.

1193 Square Phillips (south of rue Ste-Catherine), Montréal, PQ H3B 3C9. ✆ **866/393-1193** or 514/393-1193. Fax 514/393-1192. www.squarephillips.com. 160 units. C$179–C$199 double; C$199–C$355 suite. Discounts for stays of 7 or more days. Rates include breakfast. AE, DC, DISC, MC, V. Valet parking C$20. Métro: McGill. Pets accepted. **Amenities:** Babysitting, concierge, exercise room, pool (heated, indoor, rooftop). *In room:* A/C, TV, hair dryer, kitchen, Wi-Fi (free).

INEXPENSIVE

Hôtel Le Dauphin Montréal-Downtown ⟨**Value**⟩   This member of the small Dauphin hotel chain opened in 2007 and presents a terrific option for travelers on a budget. Room furnishings are simple and clean if somewhat dorm-room functional. On the other hand, bathrooms are sleek (black counters, slate floors, and glass-walled shower stalls), beds are comfy, and—get this—all units are equipped with a computer terminal and free Internet access. Rooms also have bigger-hotel touches: flatscreen TVs, in-room safes large enough to hold a laptop, large refrigerators (unstocked), and morning newspaper delivery. A key is required to access the elevator, for an added bit of safety. There are four extra-large rooms. The location, next to the convention center on the northern end of Vieux-Montréal, is central, though the immediate surroundings are nondescript.

1025 rue de Bleury (near av. Viger), Montréal, PQ H2Z 1M7. ✆ **888/784-3888** or 514/788-3888. Fax 514/788-3889. www.hoteldauphin.ca. 72 units. C$129–C$159 double. Rates include breakfast. AE, MC, V. Métro: Place d'Armes. Self-parking C$15. **Amenities:** Exercise room. *In room:* A/C, TV/DVD, fridge, hair dryer, Wi-Fi (free) & in-room computer w/free Internet.

3 VIEUX-MONTREAL (OLD MONTREAL)

VERY EXPENSIVE

Hôtel Le St-James ★★★   In a word, gorgeous. Montréal's surge of designer hotels spans the spectrum from minimalist to ornate, and Le St-James sits squarely at the elegantly ornate end of the range. It began life as a merchant's bank in 1870 and the opulence of that station has been retained. The grand hall, replete with Corinthian columns and balconies with gilded metal balustrades, now houses the hotel's high-end **XO Le Restaurant,** and all three meals plus afternoon tea (2:30 to 5pm) are served here on the finest of china. Sumptuous rooms are furnished with entrancing antiques and impeccable reproductions, and bathrooms offer a sea of white marble. The stone-walled, candlelit **Le**

Spa specializes in full-body water therapy. A member of the Leading Small Hotels of the World, Le St-James represents a triumph of design and preservation for visiting royalty— or those who want to be treated like it.

355 rue St-Jacques ouest (near rue St-Pierre), Montréal, PQ H2Y 1N9. © **866/841-3111** or 514/841-3111. Fax 514/841-1232. www.hotellestjames.com. 61 units. C$425–C$475 double; C$525 and way up for suites. Packages available. AE, DC, DISC, MC, V. Valet parking C$30. Métro: Square Victoria. Pets accepted. **Amenities:** Restaurant; babysitting; concierge; exercise room; room service. *In room:* A/C, TV, hair dryer, minibar, MP3 docking station, Wi-Fi (free).

Le Saint-Sulpice Hôtel ★★ (**Kids**) Open since 2002 and part of the wave of high-style boutique hotels that has washed across Vieux-Montréal, Le Saint-Sulpice impresses with an all-suites configuration, an ambitious eatery called **S Le Restaurant,** and courtly service. Though independently owned and operated, the hotel is a member of Hotels & Preference, and easily meets that brand's demanding, sophisticated standards. Three levels of suites come with myriad conveniences and gadgets, including minikitchens with microwave ovens, stoves, and fridges. Some have fireplaces. The largest suites, at the executive level, sleep six and are often taken by film crews in town for movie productions. There's an outdoor terrace where lunch, dinner, and drinks are served facing the gardens of the Sulpician Seminary. Children's services include gaming consoles in every room, board games, kid-friendly TV programming, a children's menu, and day care.

414 rue St-Sulpice (next to the Basilique Notre-Dame), Montréal, PQ H2Y 2V5. © **877/785-7423** or 514/288-1000. Fax 514/288-0077. www.lesaintsulpice.com. 108 units. Summer C$429–C$474 for superior and deluxe suites; winter C$329 and up. Rates include full breakfast. Children 11 and under stay free in parent's room. Packages available. AE, DC, DISC, MC, V. Valet parking C$25 or C$32 for SUV. Métro: Place d'Armes. Pets accepted for fee. **Amenities:** Restaurant; bar; babysitting; children's services, concierge; health club & spa w/ sauna; room service. *In room:* A/C, TV, kitchenette, minibar, Wi-Fi (free).

EXPENSIVE

Auberge du Vieux-Port ★★ Terrifically romantic, this tidy luxury inn is housed in an 1882 building facing the waterfront, and many of the rooms as well as a rooftop terrace offer unobstructed views of Vieux-Port—a particular treat on summer nights when there are fireworks on the river or in winter when it's snowing. Exposed brick and stone walls, massive beams, polished hardwood floors, and windows that open define the hideaway bedrooms; number 403, for instance, allows expansive views, space to stretch out, and a king bed. In the late afternoon, guests get a complimentary glass of wine with cheese in **Narcisse,** the small, sophisticated wine bar off the lobby, with live jazz adding to the mood Thursday through Saturday starting at 6:30pm. The *auberge* also runs the **Lofts du Vieux-Port** (www.loftsduvieuxport.com), renovated in 2009, with suites that have kitchenettes and other amenities for longer stays.

97 rue de la Commune est (near rue St-Gabriel), Montréal, PQ H2Y 1J1. © **888/660-7678** or 514/876-0081. Fax 514/876-8923. www.aubergeduvieuxport.com. 27 units. C$179–C$285 double. Rates include full breakfast and afternoon wine and cheese. Children 11 and under stay free in parent's room. AE, DC, DISC, MC, V. Valet parking C$24. Métro: Champs-de-Mars. **Amenities:** Bar; babysitting; concierge; exercise room at sister hotel; room service. *In room:* A/C, TV, CD player, CD library, hair dryer, minibar, Wi-Fi (free).

Embassy Suites ★ Along with the **W Montréal** (p. 74), the **InterContinental Montréal** (see below), and the new **Le Westin Montréal,** this recent entry from the Hilton empire helps constitute an expanding hotel row opposite the Palais des Congrès (Convention Center). While it is the most moderately priced and least flashy of the four—don't expect 600-count Egyptian cotton sheets or complimentary limo service—it is as welcoming a place for families as it is for executive road warriors. As befits an establishment in the area on the northern edge of Vieux Montréal that tourism authorities call the "Quartier Internationale," guests range widely over diverse nationalities and ethnicities. Cooked-to-order breakfasts are free, as are evening cocktails, which can add up to a significant savings. All but 20 of the units are bona fide suites, with pull-out sofas, big-screen TVs, and kitchens with microwave ovens, fridges, and, in pricier suites, ranges.

208 rue St-Antoine ouest (at rue St-François-Xavier), Montréal, PQ H2Y 0A6. ⓒ **514/288-8886.** Fax 514/288-8899. www.embassysuitesmontreal.com. 210 units. C$204–C$280 double; Nov–Apr C$180–C$230 double. Rates include full breakfast. Children 17 and under stay free in parent's room. Packages available. AE, DC, DISC, MC, V. Self-parking C$19. Pets up to 25 pounds accepted for one-time fee of C$35. Métro: Place-d'Armes. **Amenities:** Restaurant; bar; babysitting; concierge; temporary fitness room (while large health club with pool is under construction); Wi-Fi (in lobby, free). *In room:* A/C, TV, fridge, hair dryer, kitchen (in some suites), Wi-Fi (C$10 per day).

Hostellerie Pierre du Calvet ★ Step from cobblestone streets into an opulent 18th-century home boasting velvet curtains, gold-leafed writing desks, and four-poster beds of teak mahogany. The wildly atmospheric public spaces are furnished with original antiques—not reproductions. Likewise, the voluptuous dining room, **Les Filles du Roy,** suggests a 19th-century hunting lodge. (If you've ever watched *Masterpiece Theatre* and thought, "What I wouldn't give to live in *that* country home," this hotel is for you.) Some of the nine bedrooms sport fireplaces, and room no. 6 even has a shower with stone walls. Door locks are awfully rickety so it's best to try to imagine them as romantic period pieces. In warm months, a walled-in outdoor courtyard with a small fountain is a hideaway dining terrace. Gaëten Trottier, whose family began the establishment in 1962, has converted a room into the **Musée du Bronze de Montréal;** it contains his sculpture and is well worth a look.

405 rue Bonsecours (at rue St-Paul), Montréal, PQ H2Y 3C3. ⓒ **866/544-1725** or 514/282-1725. Fax 514/282-0456. www.pierreducalvet.ca. 9 units. C$265–C$295. Rates include breakfast. Packages available. AE, MC, V. Métro: Champ-de-Mars. **Amenities:** Restaurant. *In room:* A/C, TV, hair dryer, Wi-Fi (free).

Hotel Gault ★★ This hotel explores the far reaches of minimalism, and design aficionados will likely love it. With raw, monumental concrete walls and brushed-steel work surfaces, Gault's structural austerity is stark but tempered by lollipop-colored reproductions of mod furniture from the 1950s and blonde woods, which keep things more playful than chilly. The large bedrooms on its five floors are all loft-style and large (the smallest are 29 sq. m/310 sq. ft.), and employ curtains instead of walls to define spaces. Bedding comes from the high-end Italian company FLOU, and hypoallergenic pillows are available. The first floor's Existential rooms feature the highest ceilings. Tubs aren't available in all rooms, but plush robes are. The sleek lobby, with its massive arched windows, also functions as a bar/cafe/breakfast area, and **Gault Restaurant** invites nonguests in for lunch, dinner, or 5 to 7pm happy hour.

449 rue Ste-Hélène (near rue Notre-Dame), Montréal, PQ H2Y 2K9. ⓒ **866/904-1616** or 514/904-1616. Fax 866/904-1717. www.hotelgault.com. 30 units. C$220–C$389 double; from C$489 suite. Rates include full breakfast. Children 12 and under stay free in parent's room. Packages available. AE, MC, V. Valet parking C$18–C$24. Métro: Square Victoria. Pets accepted for fee. **Amenities:** Restaurant; bar; babysitting; concierge; exercise room (24-hr.); room service; Wi-Fi (lobby, free). *In room:* A/C, TV/DVD, CD player, Internet (free).

Hôtel Nelligan ★ Occupying adjoining 1850 buildings, the Nelligan opened in 2002 and expanded in 2007 from 63 to 105 units, and more than half of the accommodations are now suites. Many of the bedrooms are dark-wooded, masculine retreats, with puffy duvets, heaps of pillows, and quality mattresses. The staff performs its duties admirably, and the building maintains beautiful public spaces, including **Verses** Restaurant (p. 86) on the ground floor, and Verses Sky Terrace, where drinks and light meals are served until 11pm. One distraction is that the hotel's indoor atrium can sometimes pull noise from the downstairs bar up to rooms. Still, claiming an enveloping lobby chair facing the open front to the street, with a book and a cold drink at hand, is one definition of utter contentment. The hotel is named for the 19th-century Québécois poet Emile Nelligan, whose lines are excerpted on the bedroom walls.

106 rue St-Paul ouest (at rue St-Sulpice), Montréal, PQ H2Y 1Z3. ⓒ **877/788-2040** or 514/788-2040. Fax 514/788-2041. www.hotelnelligan.com. 105 units. C$235–C$260 double; from C$365 suite. Rates include breakfast and afternoon wine and cheese. Packages available. AE, DC, DISC, MC, V. Valet parking C$24. Métro: Place d'Armes. **Amenities:** 2 restaurants; bar; babysitting; concierge; exercise room; room service, Wi-Fi (free). *In room:* A/C, TV/DVD, CD player, hair dryer.

Hôtel St. Paul ★★   The St. Paul has been a star to design and architecture aficionados since its 2001 opening and ranks among the most worthwhile of old buildings converted to hotels. Minimalism pervades, with simple lines and muted colors. Hallways are hushed and dark (truth be told, they border on pitch black) and open into bright rooms with furnishings in grounded tones. This being Canada, pops of texture come from pelt rugs. In the bathroom, marble sinks are square, and clear plastic cubes cover the toiletries. Special touches include locally-made chocolates delivered with turndown service and enormous soaking tubs. Many rooms face Vieux-Montréal's less touristed far western edge, with its mixture of stone and brick buildings (although the rumble of rue McGill's morning buses and commuters may keep you from sleeping in). A splashy restaurant, **Vauvert,** offers locally inspired French cuisine with a Mediterranean flair.

355 rue McGill (at rue St-Paul), Montréal, PQ H2Y 2E8. ⓒ **866/380-2202** or 514/380-2222. Fax 514/380-2200. www.hotelstpaul.com. 120 units. C$223–C$279 double; from C$439 suite. Rates include breakfast. Children 11 and under stay free in parent's room. Packages available. AE, MC, V. Valet parking C$20. Métro: Square Victoria. Pets accepted. **Amenities:** Restaurant; bar; babysitting; concierge; exercise room (24-hr.); room service; Wi-Fi (lobby and breakfast room, free). *In room:* A/C, TV, CD player, hair dryer, Internet (free), minibar.

InterContinental Montréal ★   Across the street from the convention center and a few minutes' walk from the **Basilique Notre-Dame** and Vieux-Montréal's restaurants and nightspots, this hotel opened in 1991 and in 2008 started a floor-to-ceiling renovation of its rooms, lobby, bar, restaurant, and reception area, all to better compete with a new **Le Westin Montréal,** which opened directly across the street in 2009. Client services struggled during construction, but one can presume that all will be in order in 2010. New guest rooms appeared spacious, quiet, spotless, well lit, and, in many cases, romantic. Guests of the club rooms get access to an exclusive lounge serving complimentary continental breakfast and afternoon hors d'oeuvres, beer, and wine. The hotel is adjacent to the restored 1888 Nordheimer building and has direct access to the underground city.

360 rue St-Antoine ouest (near rue de Bleury), Montréal, PQ H2Y 3X4. ⓒ **800/361-3600** or 514/987-9900. Fax 514/847-8730. www.montreal.intercontinental.com. 357 units. C$212–C$259 double; C$449–C$649 suite. Children 17 and under stay free in parent's room. Packages available. AE, DC, DISC, MC, V. Valet parking C$26, self-parking C$19. Métro: Square Victoria. Pets accepted for fee. **Amenities:** Restaurant; bar; babysitting; concierge; executive-level rooms; health club w/sauna and steam rooms, pool (lap, w/whirlpool); room service. *In room:* A/C, TV, DVD player on request, hair dryer, minibar, Wi-Fi (C$15 per day).

Place d'Armes Hôtel & Suites ★★ Elaborate architectural details of the late 19th and early 20th centuries are in abundant evidence inside the three cunningly converted adjoining buildings that make up this romantic hotel. Many bedrooms have high ceilings, richly carved capitals and moldings, or original brick walls, and all are decorated in contemporary fashion: deluxe bedding, slate floors in the bathrooms, spotlight lighting. Many bathrooms have disc-shaped rain-shower nozzles in the showers. The hushed **Rainspa** incorporates a *hammam*—a traditional Middle-Eastern steam bath—in addition to offering massages and facials. There are two terrific in-house dining options: the high-end **Aix Cuisine du Terroir** (p. 86), where meals are created around Québec ingredients, and the visually arresting **Suite 701** bar (p. 168), where guests are treated to complimentary wine and cheese each evening, when the *cinq-à-sept* (5 to 7) after-work crowd gathers.

55 rue St-Jacques ouest, Montréal, PQ H2Y 3X2. ✆ **888/450-1887** or 514/842-1887. Fax 514/842-6469. www.hotelplacedarmes.com. 135 units. C$225–C$285 double; from C$265 suite. Rates include breakfast and afternoon wine and cheese. Packages available. AE, DC, DISC, MC, V. Valet parking C$24. Métro: Place d'Armes. **Amenities:** Restaurant; bar; babysitting; concierge; exercise room (24-hr.); spa; room service. *In room:* A/C, TV, CD player, hair dryer, minibar, Wi-Fi (free).

W Montréal ★★★ Combining contemporary decor with in-house nightlife and attentive service, the W brand is unique on the hotel landscape, and the Montréal property follows suit. A dance club tone greets guests upon entry: neon lights around the doorway, a red glow in the front lobby. The hotel's newly renovated restaurant, **Otto,** attracts a sleek crowd of models, people who date models, and people who wish they were one or the other. So too does the intimate **W Café/Bartini,** which concocts specialty martinis and is often open until 3am, and the **Wunderbar,** which picks up the pace with beat-spinning DJs, also until 3am. Bedrooms follow through, with pillow-top mattresses, goose-down comforters, and 350-count Egyptian cotton sheets. That flatscreen TVs and DVD players are standard in even the basic (called Cozy) rooms is only to be expected. Open just since 2004, the W located where Vieux-Montréal meets downtown, both literally and figuratively.

901 Square-Victoria (at rue St-Antoine), Montréal, PQ H2Z 1R1. ✆ **877-W-HOTELS** (946-8357) or 514/395-3100. Fax 514/395-3150. www.whotels.com/montreal. 152 units. From C$299 double. Packages available. AE, DC, DISC, MC, V. Valet parking C$37. Métro: Square Victoria. Pets accepted (C$25 per day plus C$100 cleaning fee). **Amenities:** Restaurant; 3 bars; concierge; exercise room; room service; spa; Wi-Fi (lobby, free). *In room:* A/C, TV/DVD, hair dryer, Wi-Fi (C$20 per day).

MODERATE

Auberge Bonaparte ★ Even the smallest rooms in this fashionable urban inn are gracefully presented—they're sizeable, with comfortable, firm beds and bright decor. About half feature whirlpool tubs with separate showers. Guests can spend time on the rooftop terrace, which overlooks the Basilique Notre-Dame; one suite, on the top floor, offers superb views of the basilica's cloistered gardens. **Bonaparte** restaurant (p. 86) on the ground floor—romantic in a Left Bank sort of way—has long been one of our Vieux-Montréal favorites. Generous breakfasts are included in the cost of the room and served here, and sitting at one of the elegant window tables with a newspaper, a croissant, coffee, and an omelet feels like an especially civilized way to start the day.

447 rue St-François-Xavier (just north of rue St-Paul), Montréal, PQ H2Y 2T1. ✆ **514/844-1448.** Fax 514/844-0272. www.bonaparte.com. 31 units. C$170–C$215 double; C$355 suite. Rates include full breakfast. AE, DC, MC, V. Parking C$16 per calendar day. Métro: Place d'Armes. **Amenities:** Restaurant; babysitting; concierge; access to nearby health club; laptop w/Wi-Fi for borrowing (free); room service. *In room:* A/C, TV, hair dryer, Wi-Fi (free).

Auberge Les Passants du Sans Soucy ★ ⟨**Value**⟩ This cheery B&B in the heart
of Vieux-Montréal is a former 1723 fur warehouse gracefully converted into a tip-top
inn. Romantic rooms feature mortared stone walls, beamed ceilings, wrought-iron or
brass beds, buffed wood floors, jet tubs, flatscreen TVs, and electric fireplaces. Renovations in 2008 knocked out some walls and brought in sleeker furnishings to make four
smaller rooms larger. Breakfast is a special selling point: A sky-lit dining nook features
communal tables on either side of a fireplace imported from Bordeaux. The substantial
morning meals include chocolate croissants and made-to-order omelets. The marble-
floored front entry—unusual for a B&B—immediately sets a relaxed, urbane tone.

171 rue St-Paul ouest (at rue St-François-Xavier), Montréal, PQ H2Y 1Z5. ⓒ **514/842-2634.** Fax 514/842-
2912. www.lesanssoucy.com. 9 units. C$160–C$190 double, C$225 suite; early Jan–Apr from C$120. Rates
include full breakfast. AE, MC, V. Parking C$16 per calendar day. Métro: Place d'Armes. *In room:* A/C, TV,
hair dryer, Wi-Fi (free).

Hôtel XIXe Siècle ★★ In English, the name translates to "Hotel 19th Century"—
the building began life in 1870 as a bank in Second Empire style. Its interior reflects these
stately origins, starting with a lobby that looks like a Victorian library. Perhaps because
English-speakers don't know how to pronounce "XIXe Siècle," the hotel has dabbled with
renaming itself Hôtel 262. Whatever you call it, this tidy little hotel is worth seeking out
for its central location and superior service. Rooms are spacious, with 4.5m (15-ft.) ceilings, large windows, and functional work desks. Rooms facing the nondescript inner
courtyard may not be scenic, but they're nearly silent—perfect for light sleepers. Twenty
rooms on the first and second floors were renovated in 2008. Despite its faintly aristocratic air, the hotel gives nods to green living, with energy-saving light bulbs and recycling bins in each room.

262 rue St-Jacques ouest (at rue St-Jean), Montréal, PQ H2Y 1N1. ⓒ **877/553-0019** or 514/985-0019. Fax
514/985-0059. www.hotelxixsiecle.com. 59 units. C$185–C$220 double; C$195–C$250 suite. Children 12
and under stay free in parent's room. AE, DC, MC, V. Valet parking C$22. Pets accepted for fee. Métro: Place
d'Armes. **Amenities:** Bar; concierge; room service. *In room:* A/C, TV, DVD player on request, hair dryer,
Wi-Fi (free).

4 PLATEAU MONT-ROYAL

MODERATE

Auberge de La Fontaine ★ ⟨**Value**⟩ Colorful, quirky, and eminently competent, La
Fontaine has the feel of a cheerful hostel. It's located directly on the lovely Parc de La
Fontaine and one of the city's central bike paths. Bedrooms are done up in bright, funky
colors, and beds are comfortable. The downstairs kitchen, in addition to being stocked
with free tea, juices, cookies, and cheese, also has a microwave and a refrigerator for guest
use. The front desk sells beer and wine. A third floor terrace faces the park and is open
during the day, and one suite has a private park-side patio. For visitors who plan to spend
time at the restaurants and bars of Plateau Mont-Royal and who are looking for a casual
option, Auberge de La Fontaine can't be beat.

1301 rue Rachel est (at rue Chambord), Montréal, PQ H2J 2K1. ⓒ **514/597-0166.** Fax 514/597-0496.
www.aubergedelafontaine.com. 21 units. C$153–C$193 double, C$219–C$279 suite; Nov–Apr from
C$119. Rates include breakfast. Packages available. AE, DC, MC, V. Three parking spots plus free street
parking. Métro: Mont-Royal. **Amenities:** Bikes can be delivered; computer w/Internet. *In room:* A/C, TV,
hair dryer, Wi-Fi (free).

WHERE TO STAY IN MONTRÉAL

6

PLATEAU MONT-ROYAL

7

Where to Dine in Montréal

There was a time not so long ago when eating out in Québec meant eating French food, and that was that.

Over the last 15 years, however, this has changed dramatically. Partly, this is because of immigration: As the population diversified, an intermingling of styles, ingredients, and techniques was inevitable. Montréal is now as cosmopolitan in its offerings as any city on the continent. Indeed, in some eyes, it has taken Canada's lead role in gastronomy. Montréalers now routinely indulge in Portuguese, Indian, Moroccan, Thai, Turkish, Mexican, and Japanese cuisines, and a meal here can equal the best offered anywhere.

THE DINING SCENE Deciding where to dine among the many tempting choices can be bewildering. Keeping that in mind, we've highlighted the restaurants that are most honored, most special, or a great value.

Restaurants—colloquially called "restos"—are often clustered together in certain neighborhoods. Many moderately priced bistros offer outstanding food, congenial surroundings, and amiable service at reasonable prices. Nearly all have menus posted outside, making it easy to do a little comparison shopping.

It's wise to make a reservation if you wish to dine at one of the city's top restaurants, especially on a weekend evening. Unlike in larger American and European cities, however, a day or two in advance is sufficient for most places on most days. A hotel concierge can make the reservation, though nearly all restaurant hosts will switch immediately into English when they sense that a caller doesn't speak French.

Except in a handful of luxury restaurants, dress codes are all but nonexistent. But Montréalers are a fashionable lot and manage to look smart even in casual clothes. Save the T-shirts and sneakers for another city.

Always look for *table d'hôte* meals. These fixed-price menus with three or four courses usually cost just a little more than the price of a single à la carte main course. Restaurants at all price ranges offer them, and they represent the best value around. If you want to try many of the top restaurants, schedule some for noon-time meals if they offer *table d'hôte* menus at lunch. You'll get your best deal that way.

Remember that for the Québécois, the midday meal is called *dîner* (dinner) and the evening meal is *souper* (supper). An *entrée* is an appetizer, and a *plat principal* is a main course.

Insider websites featuring reviews and observations about the Montréal dining scene include **www.midnightpoutine.ca/food** and **www.endlessbanquet.blogspot.com**. *Montréal Gazette* restaurant critic Lesley Chesterman's has a terrific blog at **www.lesleychesterman.com** about the food scene.

For other tips about Québec food, see "Eating & Drinking in Montréal and Québec City," on p. 17 in chapter 2.

PRICES The restaurants recommended here are categorized by neighborhood and then by the cost of the main courses. Prices listed are for dinner unless otherwise indicated (lunch prices are usually lower) and do not include the cost of wine, tip, or the 5% federal tax and 7.5% provincial tax that are tacked on the restaurant bill. In all, count on taxes and tip to add another 30% to the bill.

PARKING Because parking space is at a premium in most restaurant districts, it's easiest to take the Métro or a taxi. If you're driving, find out whether valet parking is available.

SMOKING Québec has long had a smoking culture, but smoking in bars and restaurants has been banned since 2006.

TIPPING Montréalers consider 15% of the check (before taxes) to be a fair tip, increased only for exceptional food and service.

1 BEST DINING BETS

- **Best Classic French Bistro:** Plateau Mont-Royal's most Parisian spot, **L'Express,** 3927 rue St-Denis (at rue Roy; © **514/845-5333**), is where you come to see what the Francophone part of this city is all about. From the black-and-white-checkered floor to the grand, high ceilings to the classic cuisine, this is where Old France meets New France. See p. 95.
- **Best Exotic Downtown Restaurant:** In a city where French food and its derivations rule, the lush orange and blue Mediterranean decor at Portuguese **Ferreira Café,** 1446 rue Peel (© **514/848-0988**), not to mention its big, fleshy mounds of grilled squid and black cod, is downright sexy. See p. 81.
- **Best Restaurant to Eat So Much You Can't Move:** As the name—"The Pig's Foot"— suggests, **Au Pied de Cochon,** 536 rue Duluth est (© **514/281-1114**), is mostly about slabs of meat, especially pork. The PDC's Cut, weighing in at more than a pound, is emblematic. See p. 93.
- **Best Vegan:** A standard-bearer since 1997, Plateau Mont-Royal's **Aux Vivres** at 4631 bd. St-Laurent, near avenue du Mont-Royal (© **514/842-3479**) packs in vegans, vegetarians, and the meat eaters who love them. See p. 98.
- **Best Guilty Treat:** *Poutine* is a plate of french fries *(frites)* drenched with gravy afloat with cheese curds, and it's a bedrock Québec comfort food. **La Banquise,** 994 rue Rachel est (© **514/525-2415**), near Parc La Fontaine's northwest corner, offers upwards of 25 variations and is open 24 hours a day, 7 days a week. See p. 96.
- **Best for a Celebration: Nuances,** 1 av. du Casino (© **514/392-2708**), got a dazzling face-lift in 2007 and now looks as contemporary as the food on its plates. It's a gracious, multistarred *temple de cuisine* atop the Montréal casino on Île Ste-Hélène. See p. 99. Downtown, chef Jérôme Ferrer and his **Europea,** 1227 rue de la Montagne (© **514/398-9229**) provide sophisticated food in a sophisticated setting. See p. 80.
- **Best Breakfast:** The city has nine outposts of **Eggspectation,** and they all do brisk business serving funky, creative breakfasts with loads of egg options. The menu is extensive, prices are fair, and portions are huge. See p. 90.
- **Best Smoked Meat:** There are other contenders, but **Chez Schwartz Charcuterie Hébraïque de Montréal,** known simply as Schwartz's, at 3895 bd. St-Laurent, north of rue Roy in Plateau Mont-Royal (© **514/842-4813**), serves up the definitive version of regional brisket. See p. 95.
- **Best Burgers:** If you're looking for burgers on the inexpensive side, local wisdom holds that the best are assembled at the Latin Quarter's **La Paryse,** 302 rue Ontario est (© **514/842-2040**). See p. 99. If you want a higher end experience, **m brgr,** at 2025 rue Drummond (© **514/906-2747**) in downtown, is the new king. It was launched by steakhouse stalwart Moishes in 2008. See p. 93.

- **Best Bagel:** Even native New Yorkers give it up for Montréal's bagels, which are sweeter and chewier than those produced south of the border. Both **St-Viateur Bagel & Café,** at 1127 av. Mont-Royal est in Plateau Mont-Royal (© **514/528-6361**), and **Fairmont Bagel,** at 74 av. Fairmont ouest in Mile End (© **514/272-0667**), are the places to assess the comparison. See p. 96 and 98.
- **Best Restaurant at Which to Share Food:** The tapas phenomenon gave rise to **Pintxo,** in Plateau Mont-Royal at 256 rue Roy est (© **514/844-0222**), which does its own variations on the Spanish-Basque originals. See p. 95.
- **Best Touristy Joint:** The ratio of tourists to locals is high and the food isn't likely to be a highlight of your trip, but the three-leveled outdoor patio of **Le Jardin Nelson,** in Vieux-Montréal at 407 Place Jacques-Cartier (© **514/861-5731**) is pretty, the staff is uniformly friendly, and live jazz is featured both during the day and night. Huge upside-down umbrellas stand ready to funnel any rain away from diners. See p. 167.
- **Best Restaurant, Period:** Chef Normand Laprise and partner Christine Lamarche keep Vieux-Montréal's **Toqué!,** 900 Place Jean-Paul Riopelle, near rue St-Antoine (© **514/499-2084**), in a league of its own. This dazzlingly postmodern venue is now a deserving member of the gold-standard organization Relais & Châteaux. See p. 85.

2 RESTAURANTS BY CUISINE

The prices within each review refer to the cost in Canadian dollars of individual main courses, using the following categories: Very Expensive ($$$$), main courses at dinner average more than C$35; Expensive ($$$), C$25 to C$35; Moderate ($$), C$15 to C$25; and Inexpensive ($), C$15 and less. Restaurants are listed alphabetically at the end of the index in the back of this book.

Bakery
Nocochi (Downtown, $, p. 84)

Bistro
Boris Bistro ★ (Vieux-Montréal, $$, p. 89)
La Montée ★★ (Downtown, $$$, p. 81)
Leméac ★ (Mile End, $$$, p. 97)
L'Express ★ (Plateau Mont-Royal, $$, p. 95)
Marché de la Villete ★ (Vieux-Montréal, $, p. 91)

Breakfast
Café Cherrier (Plateau Mont-Royal, $, p. 95)
Eggspectation (Vieux-Montréal, $, p. 90)
Fairmont Bagel (Mile End, $, p. 98)

Contemporary French
Café Méliès (Plateau Mont-Royal, $$, p. 94)
Decca 77 ★★ (Downtown, $$$, p. 80)
Europea ★★★ (Downtown, $$$$, p. 80)
Le Local ★★ (Vieux-Montréal, $$$, p. 88)
Nuances ★★★ (Outer Districts, $$$$, p. 99)
Restaurant de l'Institut ★ (Plateau Mont-Royal, $$$, p. 94)
Toqué! ★★★ (Vieux-Montréal, $$$$, p. 85)
Verses Restaurant ★ (Vieux-Montréal, $$$$, p. 86)

Key to Abbreviations: $$$$ = Very Expensive $$$ = Expensive $$ = Moderate $ = Inexpensive

Contemporary Québécois

Aix Cuisine du Terroir ★★ (Vieux-Montréal, $$$, p. 86)

DNA ★★ (Vieux-Montréal, $$$, p. 88)

Le Club Chasse et Pêche ★ (Vieux-Montréal, $$$, p. 88)

Renoir (Downtown, $$$, p. 81)

Deli

Chez Schwartz Charcuterie Hébraïque de Montréal ★ (Plateau Mont-Royal, $, p. 95)

Fusion

Chez l'Epicier ★ (Vieux-Montréal, $$$, p. 86)

La Chronique ★★ (Mile End, $$$$, p. 96)

Ice Cream

Bilboquet (Mile End, $, p. 98)

Indian

Gandhi ★ (Vieux-Montréal, $$, p. 90)

Le Taj (Downtown, $$, p. 84)

Italian

BU (Mile End, $$, p. 97)

Buonanotte ★ (Plateau Mont-Royal, $$$, p. 93)

Cavalli (Downtown, $$$$, p. 80)

Globe ★ (Plateau Mont-Royal, $$$, p. 93)

Japanese

Jun-I ★ (Mile End, $$$, p. 97)

Lebanese

Boustan (Downtown, $, p. 84)

Light Fare

Café Cherrier (Plateau Mont-Royal, $, p. 95)

Claude Postel (Vieux-Montréal, $, p. 90)

Cluny ArtBar (Vieux-Montréal, $, p. 90)

Eggspectation (Vieux-Montréal, $, p. 90)

Fairmont Bagel (Mile End, $, p. 98)

La Banquise (Plateau Mont-Royal, $, p. 96)

MeatMarket Restaurant Café (Mile End, $$, p. 98)

McKiernan (Outer Districts, $, p. 101)

Nocochi (Downtown, $, p. 84)

Olive et Gourmando ★ (Vieux-Montréal, $, p. 92)

Patati Patata (Plateau Mont-Royal, $, p. 96)

St-Viateur Bagel & Café ★ (Plateau Mont-Royal, $, p. 96)

Titanic (Vieux-Montréal, $, p. 92)

Wilensky Light Lunch (Mile End, $, p. 99)

Mediterranean

Modavie ★ (Vieux-Montréal, $$$, p. 89)

Version Laurent Godbout ★★ (Vieux-Montréal, $$$, p. 89)

Pizza

Pizzédélic (Vieux-Montréal, $, p. 92)

Polish

Stash Café (Vieux-Montréal, $, p. 92)

Portuguese

Ferreira Café ★★★ (Downtown, $$$, p. 81)

Québécois

Au Pied de Cochon ★★ (Plateau Mont-Royal, $$$, p. 93)

Sandwiches

La Paryse (Latin Quarter, $, p. 99)

Olive et Gourmando ★ (Vieux-Montréal, $, p. 92)

Seafood

Ferreira Café ★★★ (Downtown, $$$, p. 81)

Joe Beef ★ (Outer Districts, $$$, p. 101)

Le Garde Manger (Vieux-Montréal, $$$, p. 88)

Maestro S.V.P. (Plateau Mont-Royal, $$$, p. 94)

Spanish
Pintxo ★★ (Plateau Mont-Royal, $$, p. 95)

Steakhouse
Joe Beef ★ (Outer Districts, $$$, p. 101)
Moishes ★ (Plateau Mont-Royal, $$$$, p. 93)

Thai
Chao Phraya (Mile End, $$, p. 98)

Traditional French
Bonaparte ★ (Vieux-Montréal, $$$, p. 86)
Julien (Downtown, $$, p. 84)
Le Bourlingueur (Vieux-Montréal, S$, p. 90)

Vegetarian/Vegan
Aux Vivres ★ (Mile End, $, p. 98)
Le Commensal (Downtown, $, p. 84)

3 CENTRE VILLE/DOWNTOWN

VERY EXPENSIVE

Cavalli ITALIAN   Employing a formula more common in the restaurants over on boulevard St-Laurent than here in the middle of the business district, the owners filled a glamorous space with striking young women in snug black dresses and hunky young men with requisite 4-day-old beards. It's like joining the after-party of a Hollywood premiere with 300 of the beautiful people. Being seen is top priority, but the food is noteworthy, too. Tempting as it is to simply make a meal of any of the dozen antipasti, that would mean ignoring such eminently worthwhile main events as the pine nut–crusted filet mignon or rack of lamb with oregano crust and olive *jus*. Prices are high, assuring a more prosperous crowd than usually found at similar emporia. The glowing pink bar turns into a heavy scene later in the evening.

2040 rue Peel (at bd. de Maisonneuve). ☎ **514/843-5100.** www.ristorantecavalli.com. Reservations recommended. Main courses C$34–C$46; *table d'hôte* lunch C$29–C$32. AE, MC, V. Mon–Fri noon–3pm and 6–10:30pm; Sat 6–10:30pm (bar open later). Métro: Peel.

Europea ★★★ CONTEMPORARY FRENCH   From outside, Europea looks like any of the city's multitude of low-brow brownstone eateries. But whether you ascend the spiral staircase or sit at a cozy table tucked in the cellar, you'll see why chef Jérôme Ferrer was named "Chef of the Year" by the Société des Chefs, Cuisiniers et Pâtissiers du Québec, in 2007, and why three local publications named Europea the 2008 restaurant of the year. The *amuse* arrives in a three-segment dish with foamy nibbles. Next comes a "teaser" demitasse of lobster cream cappuccino with truffle shavings. Gaps in the procession are short, leading to the main event—perhaps the roasted U10 scallops in beurre blanc emulsion. Leave room for dessert, which comes in small, delectable servings. For the full treatment, order the ten-course *menu dégustation*. For a bargain, come at lunch, when the *table d'hôte* starts at C$21.

1227 rue de la Montagne (near rue Ste-Catherine). ☎ **514/398-9229.** www.europea.ca. Reservations strongly recommended. Main courses C$30–C$44; *table d'hôte* lunch C$21–C$28, dinner C$57; 10-course *menu dégustation* C$87. AE, MC, V. Tues–Fri noon–2pm; daily 6–10pm. Métro: Peel.

EXPENSIVE

Decca 77 ★★ CONTEMPORARY FRENCH   The food is stunning, presented with both flair and perfection, yet it's difficult to see past this restaurant's drab setting in the lower corner of an office tower, even with the swaths of raspberry- and cappuccino-colored fabrics and high-design intent. Being steps from the Centre Bell presents a similar conundrum: handy location (and free valet parking after 5:30pm) but not atmospherically rewarding. But darn if the *pâté en croute* with marinated beets and asparagus milk emulsion wasn't divine. The same can be said of the bone marrow soup, the smoked trout with sweet corn, and the olive cake for dessert. *Magnifique.* Prix-fixe options for both lunch and dinner are good value.

1077 rue Drummond (at Réné-Lévesque). ☎ **514/934-1077.** www.decca77.com. Reservations recommended. Main courses C$24–C$40; *table d'hôte* lunch C$25, dinner C$35. AE, DC, MC, V. Mon–Fri 11:30am–2:30pm; Mon–Sat 5:30–10:30pm. Métro: Bonaventure or Lucien L'Aller.

Ferreira Café ★★★ SEAFOOD/PORTUGUESE   You'll feel transported to Portugal at this extremely popular downtown spot, where walls are embedded with a mosaic of broken white and cobalt ceramic plates. At lunchtime, customers are mostly middle-aged and dressed in business suits; at night, more festive diners come out to play. One highlight: *Cataplana,* which is the name of both a venerated Portuguese recipe and the hinged copper clamshell-style pot in which it is cooked. Ingredients vary depending on the chef, but here the dish is a fragrant stew of mussels, clams, potatoes, shrimp, *chouriço* sausage, and chunks of cod and salmon. A smaller late-night menu for C$24 is available every day from 10pm. As *Montréal Gazette* food critic Lesley Chesterman recently wrote, "Downtown Montréal may not be the coolest dining destination anymore, but at Ferreira on a sunny Friday night, I can think of few restaurants more impressive."

1446 rue Peel (near bd. de Maisonneuve). ☎ **514/848-0988.** www.ferreiracafe.com. Reservations recommended. Main courses C$26–C$40. AE, MC, V. Mon–Fri 11:45am–3pm; Mon–Wed 5:30–11pm; Thurs–Sat 5:30–midnight. Métro: Peel.

La Montée ★★ **Finds** BISTRO   La Montée began life as a compact bistro on the northern edge of Plateau Mont-Royal and moved to its current, swanker digs in 2008. It's no longer the elbow-to-elbow, casual/chic secret that it once was, now gussied up with curved white leather banquettes, wavy glass walls, and a 1960s style purple ceiling that adds pop to the beige and brown decor. It's become a venue for business dining and meals that are romantic if less casual. Pricing is simple: C$55 for four courses, C$65 for seven courses, or C$15 for each single item. The options at our visit were original: bison cannelloni with foie gras cream, blood pudding and mushroom risotto, beef short rib and *tartare* with "parsnip different ways." The menu changes regularly, so go in with open expectations.

1424 rue Bishop (near bd. de Maisonneuve). ☎ **514/289-9921.** www.lamontee.ca. Reservations recommended. C$55 for 4 courses; C$65 for 7 courses; C$15 for each single item. AE, MC, V. Mon–Fri 11:30am–2:30pm and 5–10pm; Sat 5–10pm. Métro: Guy-Concordia.

Renoir CONTEMPORARY QUEBECOIS   Lodged in the popular **Sofitel** hotel (p. 68), this ambitious restaurant calls its food "inspired." Make that "cautiously creative"—not ostentatious enough to halt conversation in midsentence, but worth an approving comment *en passant.* Plates are beautifully presented, with main events including filet mignon of deer and Chilean sea bass. Lunch is the busiest time, while dinner is quieter and populated mostly by well-dressed hotel guests. A large terrace thrusts out toward busy Sherbrooke. **Le Bar,** positioned prominently along the street-side windows in the same room as the restaurant, is a good spot for a sophisticated cocktail.

1155 rue Sherbrooke ouest (in the Sofitel hotel, at rue Stanley). ☎ **514/285-9000.** www.restaurant-renoir.com. Reservations recommended. Main courses C$34; *table d'hôte* lunch C$28–C$32, dinner C$54. AE, DISC, DC, MC, V. Mon–Fri 6am–11am and noon–3pm, 5–10:30pm; Sat–Sun 6am–4pm and 5–10pm. Métro: Peel.

Where to Dine in Downtown Montréal, Plateau Mont-Royal & Mile End

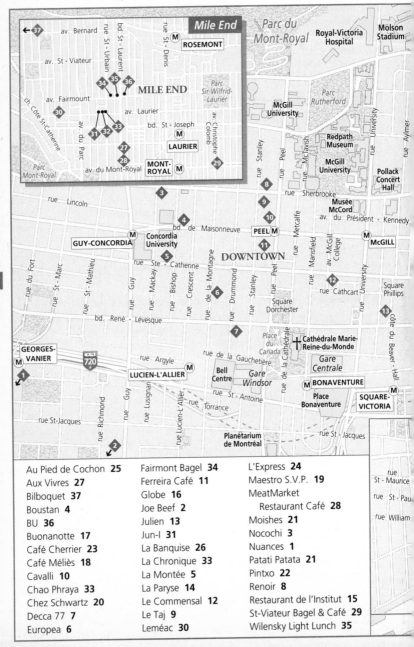

Au Pied de Cochon **25**	Fairmont Bagel **34**	L'Express **24**
Aux Vivres **27**	Ferreira Café **11**	Maestro S.V.P. **19**
Bilboquet **37**	Globe **16**	MeatMarket
Boustan **4**	Joe Beef **2**	Restaurant Café **28**
BU **36**	Julien **13**	Moishes **21**
Buonanotte **17**	Jun-I **31**	Nocochi **3**
Café Cherrier **23**	La Banquise **26**	Nuances **1**
Café Méliès **18**	La Chronique **33**	Patati Patata **21**
Cavalli **10**	La Montée **5**	Pintxo **22**
Chao Phraya **33**	La Paryse **14**	Renoir **8**
Chez Schwartz **20**	Le Commensal **12**	Restaurant de l'Institut **15**
Decca 77 **7**	Le Taj **9**	St-Viateur Bagel & Café **29**
Europea **6**	Leméac **30**	Wilensky Light Lunch **35**

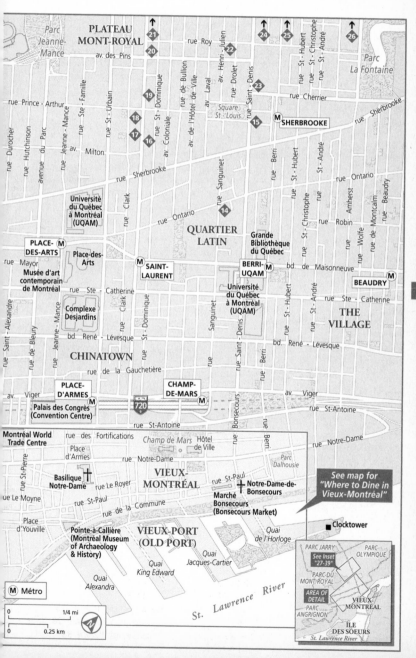

MODERATE

Julien TRADITIONAL FRENCH   A quiet downtown block in the financial district has been home to this relaxed Parisian-style bistro for years, hosting businesspeople at lunch and after-work cocktails and mostly tourists from nearby hotels in the evening. Much of the year, diners have the option of sitting at tables on the heated terrace. The menu, which offers generous-sized portions without the pyrotechnics, features classics such as steak or mussels with fries or the more imaginative linguini with shredded duck confit. There's always a vegetarian pasta option, too. Service is friendly and attentive.

1191 av. Union (at bd. René-Lévesque). ℂ 514/871-1581. www.restaurantjulien.com. Reservations recommended. Main courses C$17–C$31. AE, MC, V. Mon–Fri 11:30am–3pm; Mon–Sat 5:30–10pm. Métro: McGill.

Le Taj (Value) INDIAN   Still one of downtown's tastiest bargains. The price of the lunch buffet (C$13) has barely changed since the restaurant opened in 1985, and it's a real treat. The kitchen specializes in the Mughlai cuisine of the Indian subcontinent and seasonings tend more toward the tangy than the incendiary. Dishes are perfumed with turmeric, saffron, ginger, cumin, mango powder, and *garam masala* (a spice combination that usually includes cloves, cardamom, and cinnamon). Vegetarians have ample choices from the eight-page menu, with the chickpea-based *channa masala* among the most complex. Main courses arrive with the expected array of sauces and condiments in bowls, saucers, cups, and dishes. Evenings are quiet, and lunchtimes are busy but not hectic. On one large wall, a bas-relief mud wall depicts a village scene; that wall was part of the Indian Pavilion at Expo 67.

2077 rue Stanley (near rue Sherbrooke). ℂ 514/845-9015. www.restaurantletaj.com. Main courses C$20–C$30; lunch buffet C$13; *table d'hôte* dinner C$36. AE, DC, MC, V. Sun–Fri 11:30am–2:30pm and 5–10:30pm; Sat 5–11pm. Métro: Peel.

INEXPENSIVE

Boustan (Finds) LEBANESE   In the middle of the hubbub among the bars and clubs on rue Crescent, this Lebanese pizza parlor–style eatery, completely nondescript and consistently popular, has a line out the door at 2pm (office workers) and again at 2am (late-night partiers), all jonesing for its famed falafel, *shish taouk*, or *shawarma* sandwiches. Yes, that's former Prime Minister Pierre Trudeau in the photo at the cash register; he was a regular.

2020A rue Crescent (at bd. de Maisonneuve). ℂ 514/843-3576. Most items cost less than C$10. MC, V. Mon–Sat 11am–4am; Sun 6p–4am. Métro: Peel.

Le Commensal (Value) VEGETARIAN   Vegetarian fare is presented buffet-style here, with patrons helping themselves from dozens of options before paying the cashier by weight—about C$10 for an ample portion. Dishes include quinoa, garbanzo curry, several types of salads, a large variety of hot dishes, tofu with ginger sauce, and so on. Even avowed meat eaters are likely to not feel deprived. Beer and wine are available, too. With white tablecloths and a second-floor location tucked off rue Ste-Catherine, this is a satisfying spot to keep in mind when you're downtown. There's another branch at 1720 rue St-Denis (ℂ 514/845-2627).

1204 av. McGill College (at rue Ste-Catherine). ℂ 514/871-1480. www.commensal.com. Most meals cost less than C$10. A, MC, V. Daily 11:30am–10pm. Métro: McGill.

Nocochi BAKERY/LIGHT FARE   At a posh location on the corner of rue Sherbrooke a block west of the Musée des Beaux-Arts, this cute little cafe and patisserie is just the

> **(Fun Facts)** **Poutine, Smoked Meat & the World's Best Bagels**
>
> While you're in Montréal, indulge in at least a couple of Québec staples. Though you'll find them dolled up on some menus, these are generally thought of as the region's basic comfort foods:
>
> - **Poutine:** French fries doused with gravy and cheese curds.
> - **Smoked meat:** A maddeningly tasty sandwich component particular to Montréal whose taste hovers in the neighborhood of pastrami and corned beef.
> - **Cretons:** A pâté of minced pork, allspice, and parsley.
> - **Tourtière:** A meat pie of spiced ground pork often served with tomato chutney.
> - **Queues de Castor:** A deep-fried pastry the size of a man's footprint served with melted chocolate or cinnamon. The name means "beaver tails."
> - **Tarte au sucre:** Maple-sugar pie.
> - **Bagel:** A doughnut-shaped bread roll that in Montréal is smaller, chewier, and—it must be said—tastier than its New York brethren.

place for salads, sandwiches, or the house specialty pistachio muffin with afternoon tea. After museum-browsing or power-shopping, the all-white room, decorated with large close-up photos of decadent pastries, is a relief.

2156 rue Mackay (at rue Sherbrooke). © **514/989-7514.** Most meals cost less than C$8. MC, V. Daily 8am–7pm. Métro: Guy-Concordia.

4 VIEUX-MONTRÉAL (OLD MONTRÉAL)

VERY EXPENSIVE

Toqué! ★★★ CONTEMPORARY FRENCH   Toqué! is the gem that single-handedly raised the entire city's gastronomic expectations. A meal here is obligatory for anyone who admires superb, dazzlingly presented food. "Post-nouvelle" might be an apt description for chef Normand Laprise's creations. A short menu and top-of-the-bin ingredients, some of them rarely seen together—for example, cauliflower soup with foie gras shavings and milk foam, or smoked suckling pig cheek with maple-water sponge toffee, or olive oil sorbet with blood orange—ensure a unique tasting experience. If you choose one of the two seven-course tasting menus, you can opt for a wine pairing. The decor is 1960s loungey, with bulbous lamps hanging from the ceiling and low-back chairs. Most diners are prosperous-looking, so while the stated dress code is casual, you'll want to look sharp. Service, headed by co-owner Christine Lamarche, is efficient, helpful, and not a bit self-important.

900 Place Jean-Paul-Riopelle (at rue St-Antoine). © **514/499-2084.** www.restaurant-toque.com. Reservations required. Main courses C$41–C$47; tasting menus C$92 or C$104. AE, DC, MC, V. Tues–Sat 5:30–10:30pm. Métro: Square-Victoria.

Verses Restaurant ★ CONTEMPORARY FRENCH   The flowering of boutique hotels has given multiple jolts of glamour to Old Montréal, joining daring design with the preservation of historic buildings. Among them is the snazzy **Hôtel Nelligan** (p. 72), and the restaurant here, with ancient stone-and-brick walls, high ceilings, and a horseshoe bar, is welcoming and clubby. The ambience contributes to an active social scene after 5pm toward week's end, especially when the weather is warm enough to open the front doors or ascend to the rooftop **Verses Sky Terrace** (open daily until 11pm). Service is adroit and the pace of a meal is sedate. Dinner choices might include lamb *osso buco,* duck breast with juniper berry demi-glace, or a strip loin steak (though not everything works—a duo of mackerel and sturgeon in white-bean *velouté* was bland). The dessert menu features such playful options as a gooey pineapple upside-down cake.

100 rue St-Paul ouest (at St-Sulpice). ☎ **514/788-4000.** www.versesrestaurant.com. Reservations recommended. Main courses C$32–C$47; *table d'hôte* lunch C$25, dinner C$44–C$65. AE, DC, MC, V. Daily 6:30am–2:30pm and 5:30–10:30pm (until 11pm Fri–Sat). Métro: Place d'Armes.

EXPENSIVE

Aix Cuisine du Terroir ★★ CONTEMPORARY QUEBECOIS   Lodged in the high-end **Place d'Armes Hôtel** (p. 74), this resto (just call it "X") is a highlight of Vieux-Montréal dining. *Terroir* refers to soil, and a gastronomical allegiance to products grown in the immediate region dominates, evidenced in dishes like the roasted Québec duck breast and the veal chop from Charlevoix. An *amuse* of caviar with eggplant and aioli might set the course, and portions are generous enough that you could graze on a few appetizers alone (lobster bisque with shrimp quenelle and Abitibi caviar, for example, is quite filling). Restful tones, tan banquettes, and flickering gas lamps set an earthy mood. If you just need a snack or a more social atmosphere, head to the snazzy **Suite 701** bar, also in the hotel, where young professionals convene after work and into the evening. Food here—like the Kobe burger and fish and chips—comes from the same chef.

711 côte de la Place d'Armes (near rue St-Antoine). ☎ **514/904-1201.** www.aixcuisine.com. Main courses C$26–C$45; *table d'hôte* dinner C$48. AE, DC, DISC, MC, V. Mon–Fri 11:30am–2:30pm, Sat–Sun 11am–3pm, daily 5:30–11pm. Métro: Place d'Armes.

Bonaparte ★ TRADITIONAL FRENCH   In a city brimming with accomplished French restaurants, this is a personal favorite. The dining rooms run through the ground floors of two old row houses, with rich decorative details suggestive of the namesake's era. Adroit service is provided by schooled pros who manage to be knowledgeable without being stuffy. Highlights have included snails and oyster mushrooms in phyllo dough, Dover sole filet with fresh herbs, and mushroom ravioli seasoned with fresh sage. Lunches cater to an upscale business crowd, and the restaurant offers an early evening menu for theatergoers. The clean and bright 30-room **Auberge Bonaparte** (p. 74) is upstairs.

447 rue St-François-Xavier (north of rue St-Paul). ☎ **514/844-4368.** www.bonaparte.com. Main courses C$20–C$35; *table d'hôte* lunch C$16–C$23, dinner C$28–C$42; 7-course tasting menu C$62. AE, DC, MC, V. Mon–Fri noon–2:30pm; daily 5:30–10:30pm. Métro: Place d'Armes.

Chez l'Epicier ★ FUSION   This crisp little eatery opposite the Marché Bonsecours does double duty: It's simultaneously a high-end restaurant and a gourmet delicatessen with an abundance of tempting prepared foods and gourmet imports, so remember it when you're planning a picnic down the hill in Vieux-Port. The kitchen here is wont to fashionable, extravagant preparations, with creative flourishes equaled by only a few other local establishments. Global ingredients and techniques are part of the mix, as are witty surprises. For dessert? How about a chocolate club sandwich with pineapple fries?

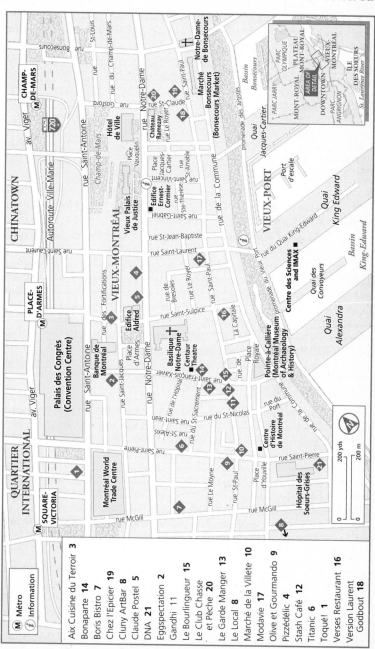

Legend

Ⓜ Métro
ⓘ Information

Aix Cuisine du Terroir **3**
Bonaparte **14**
Boris Bistro **7**
Chez l'Épicier **19**
Cluny ArtBar **8**
Claude Postel **5**
DNA **21**
Eggspectation **2**
Gandhi **11**
Le Bourlingueur **15**
Le Club Chasse et Pêche **20**
Le Garde Manger **13**
Le Local **8**
Marché de la Villette **10**
Modavie **17**
Olive et Gourmando **9**
Pizzédélic **4**
Stash Café **12**
Titanic **6**
Toqué! **1**
Verses Restaurant **16**
Version Laurent Godbout **18**

Success has nurtured ambition, and the chef-proprietor also runs **Version Laurent God-bout** (see below) a few doors away.

311 rue St-Paul est (at rue St-Claude). $\mathcal{C}$ **514/878-2232.** www.chezlepicier.com. Main courses C$27–C$40; 7-course tasting menu C$85. AE, MC, V. Mon–Fri 11:30am–2pm; daily 5:30–10pm. Métro: Champ-de-Mars.

DNA ★★ CONTEMPORARY QUEBECOIS   Blazing onto the Montréal restaurant scene in 2008, DNA suffuses concept dining with affable, expert service. Glass slabs divide the restaurant into nooks that allow the excitement of a packed house to bubble over without sacrificing intimacy or views of the building's architectural elements. Wondering about the origin of the fiddleheads or nettles? Servers will carry a basket of fresh and locally-grown ingredients to your table. This gesture adds charm to an evening out and can prompt gastronomic dialogue—so don't hesitate to ask questions. Since the chef buys whole animals, veal heart tartar mixed with foie gras is always on the menu, as are inventive recipes with ingredients like pork brain. The wine list overflows with Canadian options.

355 rue Marguerite D'Youville (at rue St-Pierre). $\mathcal{C}$ **514/287-3362.** www.dnarestaurant.com. Main courses C$24–C$36; 5-course tasting menu C$85; *table d'hôte* lunch C$20. AE, MC, V. Tues–Fri 11:30am–2:30pm and 6–10:30pm; Sat 6–10:30pm. Métro: Square Victoria.

Le Club Chasse et Pêche ★ CONTEMPORARY QUEBECOIS   The name "Hunting and Fishing Club" doesn't suggest fine dining, but here *chasse et pêche* more accurately means "new-school surf and turf." The contrast is apparent the moment you open the upholstered leather door—slate blue stucco walls and stuffed seating feel both retro and mod, cozy and sleek. The food follows suit: chilled sweet pea soup is garnished with fried oysters; a boar chop is drizzled with corn purée. This restaurant has continued to gain praise since its 2005 opening and works hard to keep attracting the crowds. The restaurant's website includes a quirky blog of reviews, YouTube films, and other stuff the staff likes, and hints at the establishment's loyal, hip following.

423 rue St-Claude (btw. rue St-Paul and Notre-Dame). $\mathcal{C}$ **514/861-1112.** www.leclubchasseetpeche.com. Reservations recommended. Main courses C$29–C$31. AE, MC, V. Tues–Fri 11:30am–2pm; Tues–Sat 6–10:30pm. Métro: Champ-de-Mars.

Le Garde Manger SEAFOOD   From the dark roadhouse decor to the moderately attentive baseball-capped servers to the rowdy slip of a bar, this giddy resto is a smackdown to its gentrified Vieux-Montréal neighbors. On the plus side, the food is pretty good and generously portioned. The menu changes nightly, but options might include spicy jerk snow crab, lobster *poutine,* or beef short ribs over arugula. The *assiette de fruits de mer* comes small or large, served in either three tasty tiers or in a wooden barrel perched sideways. You'll need a lead stomach to survive a whole portion of the signature dessert, a fried Mars bar, unless deafening rock music helps you digest. There's no sign outside, just a blank, white cube that glows pink when there's action inside.

408 rue St-François-Xavier (north of rue St-Paul). $\mathcal{C}$ **514/678-5044.** Reservations recommended. Main courses C$25–C$35. AE, MC, V. Tues–Sun 6–11pm; bar open until 3am. Métro: Place d'Armes.

Le Local ★★ CONTEMPORARY FRENCH   Whereas many of its counterparts have exquisite food but predictably styled atmosphere, or vice versa, Le Local musters originality in both arenas. The kitchen breathes new life into standards like surf and turf (theirs has BBQ ribs) and the concrete, wood, and glass interior feels remarkably current. Chef Charles-Emmanuel Pariseau trained locally before opening these doors in 2008 and sommelier Elyse Lambert has received regional and national recognition for her skills.

The *chiogga* beet salad with bacon, tomatoes, and truffle oil stood out as a starter; so, too, did the main course of a puff pastry tart with roasted scallops, chorizo, and blood pudding with pan-seared foie gras. But truly, one could roam the menu with great satisfaction. For a more casual night out or to sample highlights without the steep check, check out the bar and its lower-priced offerings.

740 rue William (at rue Prince). $\textcircled{C}$ **514/397-7737.** www.resto-lelocal.com. Reservations recommended. Main courses C$19–C$31; bar menu C$5–C$14. MC, V. Mon–Fri 11:30am–midnight; Sat 5:30pm–midnight; Sun 5:30–11:30pm. Métro: Square Victoria.

Modavie ★ MEDITERRANEAN   A highly visible location directly on the main pedestrian street no doubt helps keep this restaurant and wine bar full, but the management leaves little to chance. Live jazz is presented nightly from 7 until about 10pm, making this a comfortable place for singles as well as couples and groups. On summer nights, candles flicker in river breezes that flow in through the tall front and side windows. A handsome horseshoe-shaped bar with a dozen stools faces walls stacked with bottles of wine and single-malt scotches; ceiling fans twirl gently overhead. Food is put together well and generously portioned. Lamb is the house specialty and comes in six iterations, including a rack of lamb with Dijon mustard, rosemary, and thyme. Other options include bison medallion, tiger shrimp in Grand Marnier sauce, and ravioli stuffed with goat cheese.

1 rue St-Paul ouest (corner of rue St-Laurent). $\textcircled{C}$ **514/287-9582.** www.modavie.com. Reservations recommended. Main courses C$17–C$49; *table d'hôte* dinner C$27–C$32. AE, MC, V. Mon–Thurs 11am–10:30pm; Fri 11am–11pm; Sat 11:30am–11pm; Sun 11:30am–10:30pm. Métro: Place d'Armes.

Version Laurent Godbout ★★ MEDITERRANEAN   Chef-proprietor Laurent Godbout took on this space on the ground floor of the 19th-century Hotel Rasco following the success of his **Chez L'Epicier** (p. 86) just down the block. There's nothing 19th-century about the venue, though; it's furnished with thoroughly modern tables and sensibilities. Menu options could include veal filet served with goat cheese and eggplant, beef with fried clams, or pan-fried halibut with sundried tomatoes. There are only about 30 seats inside and a terrace out back, so it's an intimate restaurant. If you love the aesthetic, an on-site boutique sells the glassware, plates, and wooden wine buckets so you can re-create the look at home.

295 rue St-Paul est (at rue St-Claude). $\textcircled{C}$ **514/871-9135.** www.version-restaurant.com. Reservations recommended. Main courses C$26–C$36. AE, DC, MC, V. Tues–Fri 11:30am–2pm; Tues–Sat 5:30–10pm. Métro: Place d'Armes or Champ-de-Mars.

MODERATE

Boris Bistro ★ BISTRO   The outdoor space here stands out as especially pretty. In warm months, the restaurant opens its side doors to what feels like an adjacent vacant lot (the facade of a building that once stood here remains at one end), but there are leafy trees, large umbrellas, and, at night, subtle lighting and candles. It's filled with business folk and journalists by day—the *Montréal Mirror* newsweekly is in the same building—and all sorts at night: couples, families, and young adults. Cod is buttery and melty here, served over a basil-citrus risotto. French fries cooked in duck fat are a signature dish, and there's a choice of about a half-dozen *fromages du terroir,* local cheeses, along with sweet treats, to close a meal. The restaurant does big volume, but service is fast and efficient.

465 rue McGill (1 block south of rue Notre-Dame). $\textcircled{C}$ **514/848-9575.** www.borisbistro.com. Main courses C$14–C$20. AE, MC, V. In summer Mon–Fri 11:30am–11pm, Sat–Sun noon–11pm; in winter Mon–Fri 11:30am–2pm, Tues–Fri 5–9pm, Sat 6–9pm. Métro: Square-Victoria.

Gandhi ★ (Value) INDIAN   Classy but inexpensive enough to accommodate student and retiree budgets, Gandhi got so busy that the owners expanded into the adjacent building in 2007, doubling their seating space. The contiguous dining rooms are bright, and service is polite but brisk. Cooking is mostly to order and arrives fresh from the pot, pan, or oven. Biriyani and curry specialties are delicate and subtle, but ask that they be ramped up to spicier levels and the kitchen will oblige. (Request "madras hot" for medium heat.) Tandoori duck and lamb and chicken *tikka* are popular, and vegetarian dishes fill a large section of the card.

230 rue St-Paul ouest (near rue St-Nicolas). © **514/845-5866.** www.restaurantgandhi.com. Main courses C$10–C$20; *table d'hôte* lunch C$16–C$20. AE, MC, V. Mon–Fri noon–2pm; daily 5:30–10:30pm. Métro: Place d'Armes.

Le Bourlingueur (Value) TRADITIONAL FRENCH   Although it doesn't look especially promising at first, Le Bourlingueur is a keeper. The restaurant charges unbelievably low prices for several four-course meals daily. The blackboard menu changes depending on what's available at the market that day, making it possible to dine here twice a day for a week without repeating anything, except the uninteresting salad. Roast pork with applesauce, glazed duck leg, and *choucroute garnie* (sauerkraut with meat) are likely to show up, but the house specialty is seafood—look for the shrimp in Pernod sauce. The interior doesn't make the most of its stone walls and old beams, but the decor hardly matters at these prices.

363 rue St-François-Xavier (at rue St-Paul). © **514/845-3646.** www.lebourlingueur.ca. Reservations recommended on weekends. Main courses and *table d'hôte* lunch and dinner C$12–C$22. MC, V. Daily 11:30am–10pm. Métro: Place d'Armes.

INEXPENSIVE

Claude Postel LIGHT FARE   This sandwich shop started out as a patisserie and chocolatier, and then added some tables and a short menu of daily hot specials. Most customers seem to go for panini, pâtés, and pastries. Sandwiches are made to order, and breads are chewy and crusty in proper proportion. It's a logical place for a snack or a treat in the midst of a stroll through Vieux-Montréal.

75 rue Notre-Dame ouest (near rue St-Sulpice). © **514/844-8750.** www.claudepostel.com. Most items cost less than C$7. AE, MC, V. Mon–Fri 7am–7pm; Sat–Sun 9am–5pm. Métro: Place d'Armes.

Cluny ArtBar (Finds) LIGHT FARE   Artists and high-tech businesses are moving into the loft-and-factory district west of avenue McGill, at the edge of Vieux-Montréal, though the streets are still very quiet here. Among the pioneers is the Darling Foundry, an avant-garde exhibition space in a vast, raw, former foundry. Room is provided for Cluny, which serves coffee, croissants, and lunch, with such fare as vegetarian antipasto, cream of parsnip soup, and smoked salmon panini. Though it's called a bar, its main hours are during the daylight, when the sun streams in through mammoth industrial windows; it's open past 5pm only on Thursday. Tables are topped with recycled bowling alley floors, just so you know. Free Wi-Fi is available.

257 rue Prince (near rue William). © **514/866-1213.** www.fonderiedarling.org/louer_e/cluny.html. Main courses C$4–C$19. MC, V. Mon–Fri 8:30am–5pm (Thurs until 10pm). Métro: Square Victoria.

Eggspectation BREAKFAST/LIGHT FARE   Let the punny-funny name deter you and you'll miss a meal that may constitute one of your fondest food memories of Montréal,

(Moments) **Finding a Warm Corner After a Snowstorm**

Lots of people save their vacation time for summer to visit Montréal when it's flush with outdoor music festivals, sidewalk cafes, sunny-day street fairs, and easy biking and strolling.

But winter offers its own pleasures, especially if you're ensconced in the city after a big snowfall hits. In the early morning after such weather, Vieux-Montréal transforms into a wonderland blanketed in pure, white snow, still and quiet. Against the blank palette, the grey and black architecture of the 18th-century buildings stands out in high relief.

Compared to when the city is offering up all sorts of sensory experiences, it becomes easier with sound and color stripped away to try to imagine what life might have been like in the settlement's earliest days.

Cluny ArtBar (p. 90), on the far western end of Vieux-Montréal, is an excellent destination for a day like this. Classical music soars through the raw foundry space, and hot, frothy cappuccinos comfort you under a massive 1.2m (4-ft.) candelabra festooned with teeny Hindu gods and tea candles. Everything becomes new and old at the same time, cocooned by the awesome powers of Mother Nature.

especially if you're of the breakfast-is-best school of gastronomy. The atmosphere and food here are funky and creative, and prices are fair for the large portions. What's more, the kitchen knows how to deal with volume and turns out good meals in nearly lightning speed, even on packed weekend mornings. There are eight variations of eggs Benedict alone, as well as sandwiches, burgers, and pasta options. Dishes are tagged with names like "Eggiliration" and "Oy Vegg." This is a chain ("constantly eggspanding," as they put it), with nine locations in Greater Montréal.

201 rue St-Jacques ouest (at rue St-François-Xavier). © **514/282-0119.** www.eggspectation.ca. Most items cost less than C$12. AE, MC, V. Mon–Fri 6am–3pm; Sat–Sun 7am–4pm. Métro: Place d'Armes.

Marché de la Villete ★ (Value) BISTRO If you close your eyes and pretend the dangling plastic ham hocks and artificial ivy clinging to exposed pipes are real, you might convince yourself that there's a quiet French village outside of this simple shop-turned-restaurant. It started life as an atmospheric *boucherie* and charcuterie and the couple of tables in front multiplied quickly due to demand. Serving breakfast, snacks, and meals throughout the day, Marché de la Villete packs in tourists and office workers, especially between noon and 2pm. The staff is flirty and welcoming (even to guests who speak very little French). The several available platters of *merguez* and Toulouse sausages, various cheeses, and smoked meats are beguiling. Quiches, pâtés, and sandwiches are other possibilities. The *cassoulet de maison* is a must-try: It's full of duck confit, pork belly, homemade sausage, and silky smooth cassoulet beans, all topped with crunchy, seasoned bread crumbs.

324 rue St-Paul ouest (at rue St-Pierre). © **514/807-8084.** Reservations not accepted. Most items cost less than C$15. MC, V. Mon–Fri 9am–6pm; Sat–Sun 9am–5pm. Métro: Square Victoria.

Olive et Gourmando ★ SANDWICHES/LIGHT FARE   A local favorite. It started out as an earthy bakery painted in reds, pinks, and gold curlicues. Then it added table service and transformed itself into a full-fledged cafe. Regrettably, you can no longer take home a loaf of their near-perfect breads; instead sample (or just gaze at) the croissants, scones, biscuits, and brioche, all of which are better with good, strong coffee. As for lunch, choose from the menu's interesting sandwich compositions— maybe smoked trout with capers, sun-dried tomatoes, spinach, and herbed cream cheese on grilled bread, or caramelized onions, goat cheese and homemade ketchup on panini. Chocolates from local purveyor **Les Chocolats de Chloé** (p. 154) are also on the menu. The only pity is that this eminently appealing spot is not open Sunday, Monday, or evenings.

351 rue St-Paul ouest (at rue St-Pierre). ℂ **514/350-1083.** www.oliveetgourmando.com. Most items cost less than C$10. No credit cards. Tues–Sat 8am–6pm. Métro: Square-Victoria.

Pizzédélic (Kids) PIZZA   Pizza here runs the gamut from the traditional to the wildly imaginative, with toppings such as your basic tomato sauce and mozzarella to more startling concoctions involving black tiger shrimp and pickled ginger, or sea-food in cream sauce. The base crusts are thin and not quite crispy, and the selling point over ordinary pizzerias is the use of fresh, not canned, ingredients. Pastas and burgers are also available, and a breakfast menu is presented until 3pm daily. There's also a location at 3467 bd. St-Laurent (ℂ **514/845-0404**), about a block north of rue Sherbrooke.

39 rue Notre-Dame ouest (near bd. St-Laurent). ℂ **514/286-1200.** www.pizzedelic-montreal.com. Pizzas and pastas C$8.50–C$17. MC, V. Mon–Tues 11am–10pm; Wed–Sun 11am–11pm. Métro: Place d'Armes.

Stash Café (Value) POLISH   At this site for almost 30 years, this *restauracja polska* continues to draw throngs of enthusiastic returnees for its abundant offerings and low prices. The interior is composed of brick-and-stone walls, red-satin dome hanging lamps, wood refractory tables, and pews salvaged from an old convent. Roast wild boar has long been featured, along with *bigos* (a cabbage-and-meat stew) and *pierogis* (dumplings stuffed with meat, cheese, or cabbage)—as to be expected in a Polish restaurant. Filling options and sides include potato pancakes and borscht with sour cream. A jolly tone prevails, with animated patrons and such menu admonitions as "anything tastes better with wodka, even wodka."

200 rue St-Paul ouest (at rue St-François-Xavier). ℂ **514/845-6611.** www.stashcafe.com. Main courses C$11–C$17; *table d'hôte* dinner C$29–C$39. AE, DISC, DC, MC, V. Mon–Fri 11:30am–10pm; Sat–Sun noon–10pm. Métro: Place d'Armes.

Titanic (Finds) LIGHT FARE   Really good sandwiches are getting easier to find in Vieux-Montréal (see Olive et Gourmando, above), but they come to luscious life in Titanic's ramshackle rooms with overhead pipes. Freshly baked baguettes are split and filled with such savory combos as coarse country pâté with green peppercorns, or smoked ham and brie, or roast pork with chutney. There's a short cafeteria line of cold dishes and hot daily specials, or just stop in for a breakfast omelet and use the free Wi-Fi. Note that the restaurant closes at 4:30pm. The owners of Titanic also run the **Cluny ArtBar** (p. 90).

445 rue St-Pierre (1 block south of rue Notre-Dame). ℂ **514/849-0894.** www.titanicmontreal.com. Most items cost less than C$10. Cash only. Mon–Fri 8am–4:30pm. Métro: Place d'Armes.

VERY EXPENSIVE

Moishes ★ STEAKHOUSE   Those who care to spend serious money for a slab of beef should bring their platinum cards here. The oldest steak-and-seafood house in town is also arguably the finest. Positioned as a home for delicious classics, the menu features T-bones, chopped liver, and herring in cream sauce. Patrons include the trim new breed of up-and-coming executives (who are likely to go for the chicken teriyaki or arctic char) as well as those members of the older generation who didn't know about triglycerides until it was too late. The wine list is substantial, and the restaurant offers tasting evenings.

In 2008, Moishes opened a hip burger joint called **m brgr** in the heart of downtown, at 2025 rue Drummond (✆ **514/906-2747**; www.mbrgr.com). It has options for what it candidly terms "crazy expensive toppings" such as black truffle carpaccio. The "lunch box" deal is C$13 for a burger, fries, and soda.

3961 bd. St-Laurent (north of rue Prince Arthur). ✆ **514/845-3509**. www.moishes.ca. Reservations recommended. Main courses C$28–C$54. AE, DC, MC, V. Mon–Fri 5:30–11pm; Sat–Sun 5–11pm. Métro: Sherbrooke.

EXPENSIVE

Au Pied de Cochon ★★ QUEBECOIS   Packed to the walls 6 nights per week, this Plateau restaurant is a cult favorite, and we've drunk the Kool-Aid, too. As the name—which means "the pig's foot"—suggests, the menu here is mostly about slabs of meat, especially pork. The PDC's Cut, weighing in at more than a pound, is emblematic. Meats are roasted to the point of falling off the bone in a brick oven, and there's a grand selection of seafood, from oysters to lobster to softshell crab. Chef Martin Picard gets particularly clever with one pervasive product: foie gras. It comes in 10 combinations, including as a tart, with *poutine,* and in a goofy creation called Duck in a Can which does, indeed, come to the table with a can opener. When you feel like another bite will send you into a cholesterol-induced coma, sugar pie is the only fitting finish.

536 rue Duluth est (near rue St-Hubert). ✆ **514/281-1114**. www.restaurantaupieddecochon.ca. Reservations strongly recommended. Main courses C$19–C$45. AE, MC, V. Tues–Sun 5pm–midnight. Métro: Sherbrooke.

Buonanotte ★ ITALIAN   The high-ceilinged Buonanotte resembles something out of New York's SoHo: There's bass-heavy dance music, waitresses who look ready to depart to their next fashion shoot, patrons clad head to toe in black—it's all fabulous and dizzying. Though the food takes second place to the preening, the contemporary Italian dishes are good. The noise level cranks up after 7pm and the venue's real personality kicks in as a bar and nightclub with pretty people sipping drinks and DJs adjusting music to the crowd's mood.

3518 bd. St-Laurent (near rue Sherbrooke). ✆ **514/848-0644**. www.buonanotte.com. Reservations recommended. Main courses C$16–C$50. AE, DC, MC, V. Mon–Fri 11:30am–4pm and 5pm–3am; Sat–Sun 5pm–3am. Métro: St-Laurent.

Globe ★ ITALIAN   Like the nearby **Buonanotte** (see above), Globe is an erotically charged, high-end undertaking that starts with a hostess at the podium who looks like she's stopped by between runway gigs, continues with waitresses who bring food that's better than it has to be, and ends with dancing at midnight and lots of hooking up. There's a bar, where the activity intensifies after 9pm, and DJs who spin Thursday through Saturday. If you're here for the food, starters include charcuterie or calamari stuffed with goat cheese. After that, options include lobster Rockefeller mac n' cheese, braised Québec lamb shank, and soft shell crab BLT. A fun splurge is a *fruits de mer* platter, which starts at C$62 for two. A late-night menu is offered from midnight to 2am Thursday through Saturday.

3455 bd. St-Laurent (north of rue Sherbrooke). ℂ **514/284-3823.** www.restaurantglobe.com. Reservations recommended. Main courses C$24–C$49. AE, DC, MC, V. Sun–Wed 6–11pm; Thurs–Sat 6–midnight with a smaller menu available until 2am. Métro: St-Laurent.

Maestro S.V.P. SEAFOOD   Smaller and more relaxed than other restaurants in the 2 blocks of the Main north of Sherbrooke, the highlight of this storefront bistro is its oysters. The staff is happy to help you pick a few to taste; the PEI Raspberry Point, for instance, is particularly salty when contrasted with the smooth and creamy BC Kusshi (who knew?). Main-course options include grilled shrimp in a foie gras velouté with a fennel-and-spinach purée, and the Maestro Platter, an extravagant medley of clams, mussels, calamari, a half-lobster, *and* king crab. A 40-item tapas menu tantalizes Tuesday through Friday from 11am until 5pm, as well as all night on Tuesday and Wednesday, with most plates under C$10. An all-you-can-eat mussel special is available on Sunday and Monday nights for C$13 per person.

3615 bd. St-Laurent (at rue Prince Arthur). ℂ **514/842-6447.** www.maestrosvp.com. Reservations recommended. Main courses C$16–C$75; most under C$35. AE, DC, MC, V. Mon 5–11pm; Tues–Wed 11am–11pm; Thurs–Fri 11am–midnight; Sat 4pm–midnight; Sun 4–11pm. Métro: Sherbrooke.

Restaurant de l'Institut ★ CONTEMPORARY FRENCH   The Institut de Tourisme et d'Hôtellerie du Québec is a premiere training ground for city tour guides, hotel managers, front-of-the-room staff—and chefs. It runs two operations of particular interest to visitors: a **42-room training hotel** at this prime Plateau location, where rooms can be let for C$119 to C$185 per night, and a training restaurant where students practice innovative twists on classic dishes under the close eye of their teachers. The express menu at lunch is popular, and recently included gazpacho garnished with quinoa and *crème de bocconcini,* maple-and-chipotle-glazed pork chop with sautéed yams, and a delightful blueberry foam "cake." The dining room is elegant and proper, and service, not surprisingly, is attentive and friendly.

3535 rue St-Denis (1 block north of rue Sherbrooke). ℂ **514/282-5161.** www.ithq.qc.ca. Main courses lunch C$21–C$26, dinner C$33–C$42; *table d'hôte* lunch C$21. MC, V. Mon–Fri 7–9:30am, noon–1:30pm, and 6–8:30pm (closed Mon night); Sat 7:30–10:30am and 6–10:30pm; Sun 7:30–10:30am. Métro: Sherbrooke.

MODERATE

Café Méliès CONTEMPORARY FRENCH   In a section of the Main that bristles with hipness, this lower-key cafe-lounge sports electric-red decor that can best be described as "space-age submarine" (there are portholes throughout). A neighborhood favorite, it can be good for a quick dinner, but people also drop in for light or bountiful breakfasts on the weekends; a midday meal such as arugula lobster salad with asparagus, artichokes, and lemon vinaigrette; or simply espresso or a glass of wine. Steel, chrome, and glass define the generous space, updating the traditional bistro concept, and it's open nearly round-the-clock on the weekends.

3540 bd. St-Laurent (near av. des Pins). © **514/847-9218.** www.cafemelies.com. Main courses C$20–C$30; *table d'hôte* lunch C$22. AE, MC, V. Mon–Wed 11am–1am; Thurs–Fri 11am–3am; Sat–Sun 8:30am–3am. Métro: Sherbrooke.

L'Express ★ BISTRO No obvious sign announces L'Express, with its name only spelled out discreetly in white tiles in the sidewalk. There's no need to call attention to itself, since *tout* Montréal knows exactly where this most classic of Parisian-style bistros is. Eternally busy and open until 3am, the bistro's atmosphere hits all the right notes, from checkered floor to high ceiling to mirrored walls. Popular dishes include the ravioli *maison* (round pasta pockets filled with a flavorful mixture of beef, pork, and veal), the *soupe de poisson,* and the croque-monsieur, and kids will love the crepes. Though reservations are often necessary for tables, single diners and walk-ins can often find a seat at the zinc-topped bar, where full meals also are served. Service is usually good, although be prepared for very long waits during brunch hours.

3927 rue St-Denis (just north of rue Roy). © **514/845-5333.** Reservations recommended. Main courses C$9.75–C$23. AE, DC, MC, V. Mon–Fri 8am–3am; Sat–Sun 10am–3am. Métro: Sherbrooke.

Pintxo ★★ Ⓥalue SPANISH Pronounced "Peent-choo," the Basque word for tapas, this tucked-away resto draws from the Spanish Basque tradition, going in for exquisitely composed dishes at fair prices in pleasant surroundings. Cooking happens in an open kitchen in the middle of a two-part room with antique wood floors and brick walls. Each *pintxo* is true tapa size, only three or four bites, so order recklessly. Some of our favorites include the braised beef cheek, the seared foie gras on a bed of lentils, and the white asparagus with Serrano ham and fried onion cut so fine it looks like tinsel. Dinners aren't confined to meals composed solely of tapas presented on 4-inch tiles or slates, although that isn't a bad way to go. For C$30, the *menu dégustation* provides four chef's-choice *pintxos* and a main dish of your choice, in considerably larger proportion.

256 rue Roy est (2 blocks west of St-Denis). © **514/844-0222.** www.pintxo.ca. Main courses C$14–C$21; tapas C$6 or less; *menu dégustation* C$30. MC, V. Wed–Fri noon–2pm; Mon–Sat 6–11pm; Sun 6–10pm. Métro: Sherbrooke.

INEXPENSIVE

Café Cherrier BREAKFAST/LIGHT FARE The tables on the terrace that wraps around this corner building are filled whenever there's even a slim possibility that a heavy sweater and a bowl of café au lait will fend off frostbite. In summer, loyalists stay out until way past midnight, after the kitchen has closed. Brunch is popular even if the food is unexceptional, but do consider this place any time a snack is in order: Croques-monsieur, quiche, black pudding, and Toulouse sausage are all staples. Portions are ample and inexpensive, and an easygoing atmosphere prevails. It's popular with musicians, actors, and artists, so contrive to look mysterious or celebrated.

3635 rue St-Denis (2 blocks north of Sherbrooke). © **514/843-4308.** Main courses C$10–C$21; *table d'hôte* dinner C$19. MC, V. Mon–Fri 7:30am–10pm; Sat–Sun 8:30am–10pm. Métro: Sherbrooke.

Chez Schwartz Charcuterie Hébraïque de Montréal ★ DELI French–first language laws turned the name of this old-time delicatessen into a linguistic mouthful, but it's still known simply as Schwartz's to its ardent fans. Many are convinced it's the only place to indulge in the guilty treat of *viande fumée*—a kind of brisket that's called, simply, smoked meat. Housed in a long, narrow storefront, with a lunch counter and simple tables and chairs crammed impossibly close to each other, this is as nondescript a culinary landmark as you'll find. Any empty seat is up for grabs. Sandwich plates come heaped with smoked meat and piles of rye bread. Most people also order sides of fries and mammoth garlicky pickles. There are a handful of alternative edibles, but leafy green vegetables aren't among them. Schwartz's has no liquor license, but it's open late. It now has a take-out window, opened in 2008 in honor of its 80th birthday.

3895 bd. St-Laurent (just north of rue Roy). © **514/842-4813.** www.schwartzsdeli.com. Sandwiches and meat plates C$5.20–C$17. No credit cards. Sun–Thurs 8am–12:30am; Fri 8am–1:30am; Sat 8am–2:30am. Métro: Sherbrooke.

La Banquise LIGHT FARE   Open 24 hours a day in the heart of the Plateau on Parc La Fontaine's north end, this friendly, funky, hippy-meets-hipster diner is a city landmark for its *poutine:* La Banquise offers some two dozen variations on the standard french fries with gravy and cheese curds, with add-ons ranging from smoked sausage to hot peppers to smoked meat to bacon. "Regular" size is huge and enough for two. Also on the menu are steamed hot dogs ("steamies") served with hot cabbage coleslaw, burgers, omelets, and club sandwiches. Everything is best washed down with a local brew like Belle Gueule or Boréale. In warm weather there's an outside terrace.

994 rue Rachel est (near rue Boyer). © **514/525-2415.** www.restolabanquise.com. *Poutine* plates C$6.30–C$9.50; most other items cost less than C$11. No credit cards. Daily 24-hr. Métro: Mont-Royal.

Patati Patata LIGHT FARE   Tiny burgers, tiny prices, tiny space. Saying a harsh word against this beloved diner is nothing short of treason, because the staff is *that* friendly. Squeeze yourself onto a stool and watch the chefs sizzle concoctions for carnivores and vegetarians alike—there's even vegetarian *poutine* on this diverse and fairly priced menu. (Another plus is the cold draft beer.) Locals often avoid lines by ordering food to go, but visitors will want to wait in the notorious line-up to dine shoulder to shoulder with Montréalers who embrace value over personal space.

4177 St-Laurent (at rue Rachel). © **514/844-0216.** Most items cost less than C$7. No credit cards. Mon–Fri 8am–11p; Sat–Sun 11am–11pm. Métro: Mont-Royal.

St-Viateur Bagel & Café ★ LIGHT FARE   The bagel wars flare as hotly as Montréal's eternal smoked-meat battles, but this, an offshoot of the original bakery still at 263 rue St-Viateur ouest in the Mile End neighborhood, is among the top contenders. (We're also partial to **Fairmont Bagel,** p. 98.) Here, you can get bagels to go or to eat in, with sandwiches, soup, or salad. The company notes on its website that it uses the same old-fashioned baking techniques that founder Myer Lewkowicz brought with him from eastern Europe, including hand-rolling the bagels and baking them in a wood-burning oven. Although many varieties are available in the shops, the company's wholesale business keeps with tradition and only sells sesame and poppy seed, the two varieties that existed 40 years ago. Expect a short wait on weekends.

1127 Mont-Royal est (at av. Christophe-Colomb). © **514/528-6361.** www.stviateurbagel.com. Most items cost less than C$12. No credit cards. Daily 6am–11pm. Métro: Mont-Royal.

6 MILE END/AVENUE LAURIER

VERY EXPENSIVE

La Chronique ★★ FUSION   Montréal's top chefs have been recommending this modest-looking restaurant near Outremont for several years. It was feared that the resulting buzz might spoil the place, but the restaurant has only improved (while prices have gone way up). You'll discover how remarkable traditional recipes can be in the hands of a master. Presentations are so impeccable that you hate to disturb them, and flavors are so eye-rolling that you want to scrape up every last smear of food. Even diners leery of organ meats will find the veal sweetbreads a silky revelation. The menu features Mediterranean and Southwestern touches, as well as expensive ingredients like foie gras and caviar. A small but judicious selection of cheeses can precede or replace the tantalizing desserts, which look as if they might take flight.

99 av. Laurier ouest (at rue St-Urbain). ✆ **514/271-3095.** www.lachronique.qc.ca. Reservations recommended. Main courses C$36–C$45; 7-course tasting menu C$100. AE, DC, MC, V. Tues–Fri 11:30am–2pm; daily 6–10pm. Métro: Laurier.

EXPENSIVE

Jun-I ★ JAPANESE   Many give this the nod for best sushi in town. At first glance, it looks like a standard sushi bar—effusive greetings from the chefs behind the counter, traditional-looking *maki,* and other bits of fish and rice. But the eponymous chef, Junichi Ikematsu, has ideas that go far beyond what you probably consider typical. You won't soon forget the *unagi* dynamite roll—thick rounds of sticky rice encasing grilled eel, avocado, and rice crispies (a signature ingredient that reappears in other rolls). Stick with the sushi and you won't go wrong, although there are options of more conventional, but precisely grilled, meats and fish. The sake martini, with julienned cucumber and a side of ginger, is a refreshing winner.

156 av. Laurier ouest (near rue St-Urbain). ✆ **514/276-5864.** www.juni.ca. Reservations recommended on weekends. Main courses C$31–C$36; sushi C$5–C$12. AE, MC, V. Tues–Fri 11:30am–2pm; Mon–Thurs 6–10pm; Fri–Sat 6–11pm. Métro: Laurier.

Leméac ★ BISTRO   This sprightly restaurant on the far western end of the avenue Laurier scene has a long, tin-topped bar along one side, well-spaced tables, and a crew of cheerful waitstaff. While the bistro dishes sound conventional on the page, they are put together in freshly conceived ways. Two examples: An orange tomato gazpacho is topped with vegetable ratatouille, and the salmon *pot-au-feu* is a perfectly cooked filet laid over a healthful selection of small potatoes, carrots, tender Brussels sprouts, and their collective broth. The food is different but not startlingly so and is served in an atmosphere that invites lingering. Weekend brunch is popular, as is the C$22 appetizer-plus–main menu that kicks in at 10pm. The name comes from the publishing firm that used to occupy the building.

1045 av. Laurier ouest (corner of av. Durocher). ✆ **514/270-0999.** www.restaurantlemeac.com. Reservations recommended. Main courses C$19–C$38; late-night menu C$22; weekend brunch C$7.50–C$16. AE, DC, MC, V. Mon–Fri noon–midnight; Sat–Sun 10am–midnight. Métro: Laurier.

MODERATE

BU ITALIAN   Not only has BU won awards for its sleek decor, but it strikes just the right balance between wine and food. A handful of hot dishes are offered nightly, but the purpose of all the food is to complement, not do battle with, the wines. The long card of 500 selections eschews the same old bottlings, and even those who regard themselves as connoisseurs make delightful discoveries, guided by the knowledgeable staff. There are about 20 wines by the glass. Some come to this northern St-Laurent locale just for its silky rendition of *vitello tonnato*—veal and cream of tuna. The crowd gets younger as the night rolls on, and because the bar stays open late, off-duty chefs are often in the mix.

5245 bd. St-Laurent (at av. Fairmount). ✆ **514/276-0249.** www.bu-mtl.com. Reservations recommended. Antipasti and main courses C$4–C$25. AE, MC, V. Daily 5pm–1am. Métro: Laurier.

Chao Phraya (Finds) THAI   Open since 1988 and still a contender for the title of best Thai in town, Chao Phraya has a panache that sets it a few notches above most of its rivals. Named for a river in Thailand, Chao Phraya brightens its corner of the fashionable Laurier Avenue with white table linens and sprays of orchids. The most popular items include dumplings in peanut sauce as an appetizer and a mixed seafood dish composed of squid, scallops, shrimp, crab claws, mussels. One to three hot-pepper symbols grade hotness (two peppers are about right). A cooling cucumber salad helps, and you'll want a side of sticky rice, too. There is a good selection of vegetarian options. Everything comes in attractive bowls and platters, and the atmosphere is warm and cozy. All 12 pages of the menu are posted online.

50 av. Laurier ouest (1 block west of bd. St-Laurent). © **514/272-5339.** www.chao-phraya.com. Reservations recommended. Main courses C$10–C$20. AE, DC, MC, V. Thurs–Sat 5–11pm; Sun and Tues–Wed 5–10pm. Métro: Laurier.

MeatMarket Restaurant Café (Finds) LIGHT FARE   Neither a butcher shop nor a pickup joint, MeatMarket is actually a stylish sandwich-and-burger cafe. It's on a nondescript block of boulevard St-Laurent well north of the trendier restaurant action. There are vegetarian and salad options, but meats are the main attraction, including burgers and the Cuba Libre sandwich with grilled pork, plantain, Cuban marinade, and mint-and-mango ketchup. Led Zeppelin on the stereo adds exactly the right kick.

4415 bd. St-Laurent (just south of av. du Mont-Royal). © **514/223-2292.** www.meatmarketfood.com. Main courses C$6.50–C$29; most items cost less than C$14. AE, MC, V. Mon 11am–3pm; Tues–Sat 11am–11pm. Métro: Mont-Royal.

INEXPENSIVE

Aux Vivres ★ VEGAN   In business since 1997, this bright restaurant with white Formica tables, raw blonde walls, and pink Chinese lanterns has been humming and busy since moving into its current location in 2006. A large menu includes bowls of chili with guacamole, and bok choy with grilled tofu and peanut sauce. Other options include salads, sandwiches, desserts, and a daily chef's special. All foods are vegan, all vegetables are organic, and all tofu and tempeh are local and organic. In addition to inside tables, there is a juice bar off to one side and a back terrace.

4631 bd. St-Laurent (at av. du Mont-Royal). © **514/842-3479.** Most items cost less than C$12. No credit cards. Tues–Sun 11am–11pm. Métro: Mont-Royal.

Bilboquet (Kids) ICE CREAM   You can get a good croque-monsieur here, but the reasons to seek out this humble spot in Mile End's ritzy Outremont section are the splendid ice creams and sorbets. This *artisan glacier* makes its own sweet stuff, rich with caramel, nuts, fruit . . . whatever is fresh and available and strikes the chef's fancy. Flavors include maple taffy, passion fruit, chocolate-orange, and vanilla-raspberry. In warm weather, there's always a line. With just a few tables inside and benches outside, prepare to stroll with your cone. If you don't want to make the trek all the way north, you can also find Bilboquet ice cream at a push cart in the heart of Vieux-Port in warm months and in some cafes as well.

1311 rue Bernard ouest (at av. Outremont). © **514/276-0414.** Ice cream dishes less than C$8. No credit cards. Daily 11am–midnight. Closed Jan–Mar. Métro: Outremont.

Fairmont Bagel BREAKFAST/LIGHT FARE   Bagels in these parts of North America are thinner, smaller, and crustier than the cottony monsters posing as the real thing south of the border. They're hand-rolled, twist-flipped into circles, and baked in big wood-fired ovens right on the premises. Fairmont was founded in 1919 and now offers 20 types, including trendy options like muesli and (shudder) blueberry, but why opt for oddball tastes when you can get a perfect sesame version? A teeny shop, Fairmont sells its bagels and accouterments such as lox and cream cheese to go only. It's open 24 hours a day, 7 days a week—even on Jewish holidays.

74 av. Fairmont ouest (near rue St-Urbain). ✆ **514/272-0667.** www.fairmountbagel.com. Most bagels less than C$1. No credit cards. Daily 24-hr. Métro: Laurier.

Wilensky Light Lunch LIGHT FARE Wilensky's has been a Montréal tradition since 1932 and has its share of regular pilgrims nostalgic for its grilled-meat sandwiches, low prices, curt service, and utter lack of decor. This is Duddy Kravitz/Mordecai Richler territory, and the ambience can best be described as Early Jewish Immigrant. There are nine counter stools, no tables. The house special is grilled salami and bologna, with mustard, thrown on a bun and squashed on a grill, and never, for whatever reason, cut in two. You can wash it down with an egg cream or Cherry Coke jerked from the rank of syrups—this place has drinks typical of the old-time soda fountain that it still is. Enter Wilensky's to take a step back in time; we're talking tradition here, not cuisine.

34 rue Fairmount ouest (1 block west of bd. St-Laurent). ✆ **514/271-0247.** Most items cost C$4 or less. No credit cards. Mon–Fri 9am–4pm. Métro: Laurier.

7 QUARTIER LATIN

INEXPENSIVE

La Paryse ⟨**Value**⟩ SANDWICHES Only slightly larger than your basic hole in the wall, this Latin Quarter standby packs in students, profs, young execs, and middleagers. They come for the burgers, the consensus choice for "best in town." Unless you possess a really large appetite and a capacious mouth, you certainly won't need the double burger or the *frites grosse* (big fries). Wines are available by the glass. If you can, get a seat in the teeny venue, a sunny, funky place with handmade mosaic walls and yummy cakes displayed under glass domes. For vegetarians, there are tofu burgers and nut burgers that can be topped with blue cheese, apple slices, lettuce, and grilled mushrooms. The inevitable line moves quickly.

302 rue Ontario est (at rue Sanguinet). ✆ **514/842-2040.** All items cost less than C$10. MC, V. Tues–Fri 11am–11pm; Sat noon–10:30pm; Sun noon–10pm. Métro: Berri-UQAM.

8 OUTER DISTRICTS

VERY EXPENSIVE

Nuances ★★★ CONTEMPORARY FRENCH Nuances serves haute cuisine in a casino, as unlikely as that seems. Ensconced atop four floors of blinking lights and the crash of cascading jackpots, this dazzling entry into Montréal's gastronomic landscape got a face-lift in 2007 that made the decor as contemporary and elegant as the food. Gone is the dark presidential decor and in are creamy walls, white linen, and pale leather banquettes. Recent menu innovations have included Québec lamb wrapped in a savory crust with olives and creamy polenta and pan-fried black cod served with *koshi hikari* rice

Tips   **Late-Night Bites**

Most Montréal restaurants serve until 10 or 11pm, but sometimes you need something else—a meal or just a snack—a little later. Here are some places to keep in mind:

- **Boustan** (p. 84): In the middle of the late-night hubbub on downtown's rue Crescent, Boustan has lines out the door at 2am of night birds jonesing for a falafel or shawarma sandwich. Open until 4am daily.
- **Café Cherrier** (p. 95): This Plateau restaurant's kitchen typically closes at 10pm, but on warm summer nights, the terrace stays open to midnight or 1am.
- **Chez Schwartz** (p. 95): Also on the Plateau, Schwartz's meets all your smoked-meat needs until 12:30am every night, until 1:30am on Friday, and until 2:30am on Saturday.
- **Globe** (p. 93): Like its sister restaurant **Buonanotte** across the street (they share owners), this erotically charged restaurant at boulevard St-Laurent near rue Sherbrooke changes personality after about 10pm to something more akin to a nightclub. Thursday through Saturday, the regular menu is available until midnight, and a smaller menu kicks in from midnight until 2am.
- **La Banquise** (p. 96): Not only is Banquise known citywide for its *poutine*, but it's open 24 hours a day, 7 days a week—that is, whenever the urge strikes to indulge in any of 25 variations of french fries with gravy and cheese curds.
- **Leméac** (p. 97): This Mile End spot offers a special C$22 appetizer-plus–main menu from 10pm to midnight daily.
- **L'Express** (p. 95): Classic Paris-style food, available until 3am nightly.
- **m brgr** (p. 93): A chic little downtown burger joint whose name looks like a typo. You can get salads and sandwiches, but the noise is about the hamburgers. Open Friday and Saturday to midnight, Monday to Thursday until 11pm.
- **Rosalie** (1232 rue de la Montagne, ✆ 514/392-1970, www.rosalierestaurant. com): Out front is an active terrace and inside patrons lounge in leather sling chairs or perch along the long marble bar. Food is of the updated bistro style, and from 10pm to midnight the kitchen offers a three-course menu for C$27. By then, expect lights to dim and decibel levels to shoot up.

and kumquat chutney. For dessert there's lemongrass crème brûlée served with home-made churros, or warm chocolate cake. Dress code is businesslike, but women will feel equally comfortable in a little red dress. This is a room with real star power. Note that those younger than 18 are not admitted.

1 av. du Casino (in the Casino de Montréal, Île Ste-Hélène). ✆ **514/392-2708.** www.casinosduquebec. com. Reservations recommended. Main courses C$40–C$45; discovery menus C$95 and C$115. AE, DC, MC, V. Patrons must be 18 or older. Wed–Sun 5:30–11pm. Métro: Parc Jean-Drapeau.

EXPENSIVE

Joe Beef ★ SEAFOOD/STEAKHOUSE   This 28-seat beef-and-fish house opened in 2005 far from the brightest lights of downtown by folks who used to run those glamorous resto-clubs. In 2007 and 2008 the proprietors added two adjacent restaurants: **Liverpool House** (at no. 2501), an Italian gastropub, and **McKiernan** (no. 2485), a luncheonette and wine bar (see below). Chef David McMillan floats between the three venues; he's the big guy in the shorts and arm-sleeve tattoos. Atmosphere is moneyed roadhouse, with diners elbow to elbow and the restaurant's menu and wine list written on a big blackboard occupying one wall. Customary starters are oysters, and the menu might include *salade Joe Beef*, a tangy tangle of green beans, boiled potatoes, pickled beets, jicama, duck breast, and a poached egg. Mains often include suckling pig, cabbage stuffed with veal cheeks, and steak au poivre. With the Atwater Market just steps away, food is fresh and seasonal.

2491 rue Notre-Dame ouest (near rue Vinet). ✆ **514/935-6504.** www.joebeef.com. Reservations required. Main courses C$21–C$50. MC, V. Tues–Sat with seatings at 7 and 9:30pm. Métro: Lionel-Groulx.

INEXPENSIVE

McKiernan LIGHT FARE   Even the tragically hip must eat, and when they do, they head to the McKiernan luncheonette and wine bar, where chainsaws and Spam tins form the decor, and the wine chills in a stainless steel tub on the counter as you enter. This cramped outcropping by the proprietors of **Joe Beef** (see above) may feel inhospitable to persons not dressed like rock stars (and the waitstaff don't do much to warm up the welcome) but the food is inventive and reasonably priced. The *poulet rôti tikka* sandwich with two chutneys marries all the right flavors and textures, as does the shrimpy dog—a shrimp, caper, and pickle mixture served cold in two grilled flatbread buns. Even the asparagus salad, with shaved pecorino and a hard-boiled egg, tastes like an extreme version of itself, like veggies pulled fresh from the garden. McKiernan is especially popular for Saturday brunch.

2485 rue Notre-Dame ouest (near rue Vinet). ✆ **514/759-6677.** Most items cost less than C$13. MC, V. Tues–Fri lunch; Sat brunch; Thurs–Sat dinner (hours vary). Métro: Lionel-Groulx.

9 PICNIC FARE

If you're planning a picnic, bike ride, or simply a meal in, pick up supplies in Vieux-Montréal at any of three shops along rue St-Paul. On the street's west end is **Olive et Gourmando** (p. 92) at no. 351 and, just across the street, **Marché de la Villete** (p. 91) at no. 324. Both sell fresh breads, fine cheeses, sandwiches, salads, and pâtés. On rue St-Paul's east end, a block and a half from Place Jacques-Cartier, is **Chez l'Epicier** (p. 86), at no. 331. It's an ambitious restaurant with a gourmet delicatessen's worth of takeout goodies.

Better still, make a short excursion by bicycle or Métro (the Lionel-Groulx stop) to **Marché Atwater (Atwater Market),** the farmer's market at 138 av. Atwater which is open daily. The long interior shed is bordered by stalls stocked with gleaming produce and flowers. The two-story center section is devoted to vintners, butchers, bakeries, and cheese stores. In the *marché,* **Boulangerie Première Moisson** (✆ 514/932-0328) is filled with the tantalizing aromas of breads and pastries—oh, the pastries!—and has a seating area at which to nibble baguettes or sip a bowl of café au lait. Nearby, **Fromagerie du Marché Atwater** (✆ 514/932-4653) lays out something like 500 cheeses—with hundreds from Québec alone—and also sells pâtés and charcuterie. Marché Atwater is on the Lachine Canal, where you can stroll and find a picnic table.

Exploring Montréal

Montréal is a feast of choices, able to satisfy the desires of physically active and culturally curious visitors. Hike up the city's mountain, Mont Royal, in the middle of the city, cycle for miles beside 19th-century warehouses and locks on the Lachine Canal, take in artworks and ephemera at over 30 museums and as many historic buildings, attend a Canadiens hockey match, party until dawn on rue Crescent and the Main, or soak up the history of 400 years of conquest and immigration. It's all here for the taking.

Getting from hotels to attractions is fairly easy. Montréal has an efficient Métro system, a logical street grid, and wide boulevards that all aid in the largely uncomplicated movement of people from place to place.

If you're planning to check out several museums, consider buying the Montréal Museums Pass (see the "Money Savers" box on p. 103).

For families with children, few cities assure kids of as good a time as this one. There are riverboat rides, the fascinating Biodôme—which replicates four distinct ecosystems—a sprawling amusement park, the Centre des Sciences de Montréal down by the water, and magical circus performances by the many troupes that come through this circus-centric city. We've also flagged attractions that are recommended for children with the (Kids) icon and included an "Especially for Kids" section on p. 115.

Tip: Some museums have good restaurants or cafes. Remember, too, that most museums, though not all, are closed on Mondays.

1 TOP ATTRACTIONS

DOWNTOWN

If this is your first trip to Montréal, consider starting with the downtown walking tour in chapter 9.

Musée des Beaux-Arts ★★★ Montréal's grand Museum of Fine Arts, the city's most prominent museum, was Canada's first building designed specifically for the visual arts. It's made up of several buildings: the original neoclassical pavilion on the north side of Sherbrooke; a striking annex built in 1991 directly across the street; and new in 2011, the adjacent Erskine and American Church, which will be converted into a pavilion of Canadian art. The church, built in 1894, is a designated national historic site. The entire complex will be linked through underground galleries.

The church space will double the museum's exhibition space for Canadian artists, including French-Canadian landscape watercolorist Marc-Aurèle Fortin (1888–1970). It will also be a destination in its own right, with a conversion project restoring its Romanesque Revival architecture and interior ornamentation, which includes 20 stained-glass windows made by Tiffany.

Art on display is dramatically mounted, carefully lit, and diligently explained in both French and English. In addition to Canadian and international contemporary art created

(Tips) **Money Savers**

- **Buy the Montréal Museums Pass.** Good for 3 consecutive days, this pass grants entry to 34 museums and attractions, including most of those mentioned in this chapter. The C$50 pass includes unlimited access to public transportation along with the museums; a C$45 pass covers just the museums. There are no separate rates for seniors or children. The pass is available at all participating museums, many hotels, and the tourist offices at 174 rue Notre-Dame (in Vieux-Montréal) and 1255 rue Peel (downtown). Find out more at www.montrealmuseums.org.
- **Visit Vitrine Culturelle de Montréal for last-minute ticket deals.** The discount ticket office for Montréal cultural events is at 145 rue Ste-Catherine ouest at the Place des Arts. Info at (C) **866/924-5538** or 514/285-4545, or www.vitrineculturelle.com.
- **Flash your AAA card.** Members of the American Automobile Association get the same discounts as members of its Canadian sister organization, the CAA. That includes reduced rates at many museums, hotels, and restaurants (and C$2 off the Montréal Museums Pass).
- **Time your trip to coincide with Montréal Museums Day.** On the last Sunday in May, about 30 museums welcome visitors for free in a citywide open house. Free shuttle buses run between the venues as well.

after 1960, the museum features European painting, sculpture, and decorative art from the Middle Ages to the 19th century. Among the collection's gems are paintings by Hogarth, Tintoretto, Bruegel, El Greco, and portraitist George Romney—and illustrative, if not world-class, works by Renoir, Monet, Picasso, Cézanne, and Rodin.

Temporary exhibitions can be dazzling. A show a few years ago brought the treasures of Catherine the Great, including her spectacular coronation coach, from the Hermitage Museum of Saint Petersburg. An exhibition of Tiffany glass is scheduled for February 11 to May 2, 2010.

The museum's street-level store on the annex (south) side of rue Sherbrooke sells an impressive selection of quality books, games, and folk art. A good restaurant, **Café des Beaux-Arts,** is adjacent.

1339–1380 rue Sherbrooke ouest (at rue Crescent). (C) **514/285-2000.** www.mmfa.qc.ca. Free admission to the permanent collection; donations accepted. Admission to temporary exhibitions C$15 adults, C$10 seniors, C$7.50 students, free for children 12 and younger; C$30 family (1 adult and 3 children 16 and younger, or 2 adults and 2 children 16 and younger); half price for adults Wed 5–8:30pm. AE, MC, V. Tues 11am–5pm; Wed–Fri 11am–9pm; Sat–Sun 10am–5pm. Métro: Guy-Corcordia. Bus: 24.

Musée McCord ★ The permanent exhibition "Simply Montréal: Glimpses of a Unique History" justifies a trip here all on its own. The show steeps visitors in what city life was like over the centuries, and even includes a substantial section about how Montréal handles the massive amounts of snow and ice it receives each year. Associated with McGill University, McCord showcases the eclectic—and, not infrequently, the eccentric—collections of scores of benefactors from the 19th century through today. More than

EXPLORING MONTRÉAL

8

TOP ATTRACTIONS

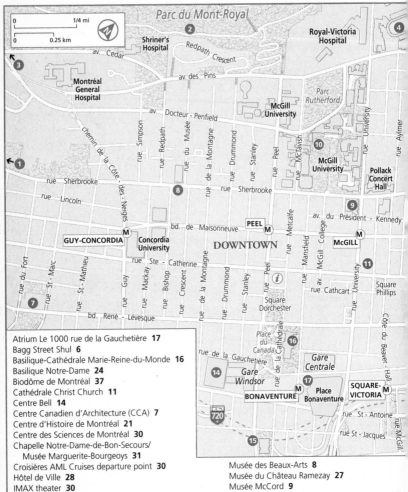

Atrium Le 1000 rue de la Gauchetière **17**
Bagg Street Shul **6**
Basilique-Cathédrale Marie-Reine-du-Monde **16**
Basilique Notre-Dame **24**
Biodôme de Montréal **37**
Cathédrale Christ Church **11**
Centre Bell **14**
Centre Canadien d'Architecture (CCA) **7**
Centre d'Histoire de Montréal **21**
Centre des Sciences de Montréal **30**
Chapelle Notre-Dame-de-Bon-Secours/
    Musée Marguerite-Bourgeoys **31**
Croisières AML Cruises departure point **30**
Hôtel de Ville **28**
IMAX theater **30**
Insectarium de Montréal **35**
Jardin Botanique **34**
L'Oratoire St-Joseph **3**
La Biosphère **18**
Labyrinth Shed 16 **33**
La Ronde Amusement Park **20**
Le Bateau-Mouche departure point **31**
Les Sautes-Moutons departure point **33**
Marché Bonsecours **29**
Montréal Alouettes football team **4**
Musée d'Art Contemporain de Montréal **12**
Musée David M. Stewart **19**
Musée de la Banque de Montréal **23**

Musée des Beaux-Arts **8**
Musée du Château Ramezay **27**
Musée McCord **9**
Musée Redpath **10**
Navette Maritime Shuttle (ferry)
    departure point **32**
Parc du Mont-Royal **2**
Parc La Fontaine **13**
Pavillon de la TOHU **5**
Place Jacques-Cartier **26**
Planétarium de Montréal **15**
Pointe-à-Callière (Montréal Museum of
    Archaeology and History) **22**
Scandinave Les Bains **25**
Segal Centre for Performing Arts **1**
Stade Olympique **36**

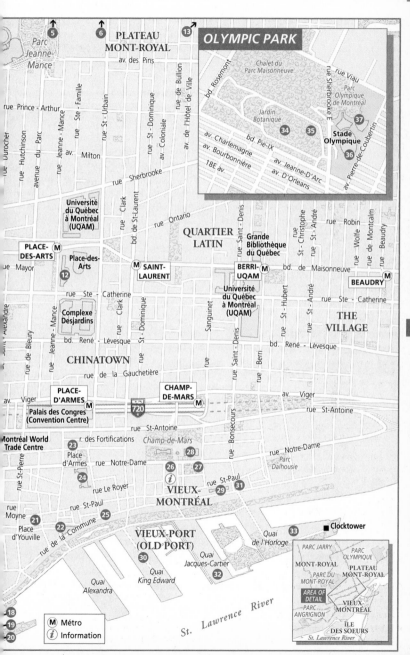

16,600 costumes, 65,000 paintings, and 1.25 million historical photographs documenting Canada's history are rotated in and out of storage to be displayed. A First Nations room is where to see portions of the museum's extensive collection of objects from Canada's native population, including meticulous beadwork, baby carriers, and fishing implements. Exhibits are intelligently mounted, with texts in English and French. There's a small cafe near the front entrance, and a shop that sells Canadian arts and crafts, pottery, and more.

690 rue Sherbrooke ouest (at rue University). ℂ **514/398-7100.** www.mccord-museum.qc.ca. Admission C$13 adults, C$10 seniors, C$7 students, C$5 ages 6–12, free for children 5 and younger; free admission on the first Sat of the month 10am–noon. AE, MC, V. Tues–Fri 10am–6pm; Sat–Sun 10am–5pm. June 24 to Sept 7 and holiday weekends also Mon 10am–5pm. Métro: McGill. Bus: 24.

Parc du Mont-Royal Montréal is named for this 232m (761-ft.) hill that rises at its heart—the "Royal Mountain." Walkers, joggers, cyclists, dog owners, and skaters all use this largest of the city's green spaces throughout the year. In summer, **Lac des Castors (Beaver Lake)** is surrounded by sunbathers and picnickers (no swimming allowed, however). In winter, cross-country skiers and snowshoers follow miles of paths and trails laid out for their use. **Chalet du Mont-Royal** near the crest of the hill is a popular destination, providing a sweeping view of the city from its terrace. Up the hill behind the chalet is the spot where, legend says, Paul de Chomedey, Sieur de Maisonneuve (1612–76), erected a wooden cross after the colony sidestepped the threat of a flood in 1643. The present incarnation of the steel **Croix du Mont-Royal** was installed in 1924 and is lit at night. It usually glows white, though it was red in the 1980s during a march against AIDS and purple in 2005 in recognition of Pope John Paul II's death. See p. 140 for a suggested walking route.

Downtown. ℂ **514/843-8240** for the Maison Smith information center in the park's center. www.lemontroyal.qc.ca. Métro: Mont-Royal. Bus: 11; get off at Lac des Castors (Beaver Lake).

VIEUX-MONTREAL (OLD MONTREAL)

Vieux-Montréal's central plaza is **Place Jacques-Cartier,** the focus of much activity in the warm months. The plaza consists of two repaved streets bracketing a center promenade that slopes down from rue Notre-Dame to Old Port, with venerable stone buildings from the 1700s along both sides. Horse-drawn carriages gather at the plaza's base, and outdoor cafes, street performers, and flower sellers recall a Montréal of a century ago. Locals insist they would never go to a place so overrun by tourists—which makes one wonder why so many of them do, in fact, congregate here. They take the sun and sip sangria on the bordering terraces just as much as visitors do, enjoying the unfolding pageant.

If this is your first trip to Montréal, consider starting with the Vieux-Montréal walking tour in chapter 9 for an overview of the neighborhood and its attractions. The walk leads past most of the sites listed here and can help you get your bearings. For further information about this quarter, go to its official website: **www.vieux.montreal.qc.ca**.

Basilique Notre-Dame ★★★ Breathtaking in the richness of its interior furnishings and big enough to hold 4,000 worshipers, this magnificent structure was designed in 1824 by James O'Donnell, an Irish-American Protestant architect from New York—who was so profoundly moved by the experience that he converted to Catholicism after its completion. The impact is understandable. Of Montréal's hundreds of churches, Notre-Dame's interior is the most stunning, with a wealth of exquisite details, most of it carved from rare woods that have been delicately gilded and painted. O'Donnell, clearly a proponent of the Gothic Revival style, is the only person honored by burial in the crypt.

The main altar was carved from linden wood, the work of Québécois architect Victor Bourgeau. Behind it is the **Chapelle Sacré-Coeur (Sacred Heart Chapel),** much of which was destroyed by an arsonist in 1978; it was rebuilt and rededicated in 1982. The altar displays 32 bronze panels representing birth, life, and death, cast by a Montréal artist named Charles Daudelin. A 10-bell carillon resides in the east tower, while the west tower contains a single massive bell, nicknamed **"Le Gros Bourdon,"** which weighs more than 12 tons and emanates a low, resonant rumble that vibrates right up through your feet.

A sound-and-light show called "Et la lumière fut" ("And then there was light") is presented nightly Tuesday through Saturday.

110 rue Notre-Dame ouest (on Place d'Armes). ✆ **514/842-2925.** www.basiliquenddm.org. Basilica C$7 adults, C$4 ages 7–17, free ages 6 and younger. Includes 20-min. guided tour. Light show C$10 adults, C$9 seniors, C$5 ages 17 and younger. Cash only. Mon–Fri 9am–4pm, Sat 9am–3:30pm, Sun 12:30–3:30pm; light shows Tues–Thurs 6:30pm, Fri 6:30 and 8:30pm, Sat 7 and 8:30pm. Métro: Place d'Armes.

Centre des Sciences de Montréal ★ ⓚ Kids Running the length of a central pier in Vieux-Port (Old Port), this ambitious complex (in English, the Montréal Science Centre) got a big overhaul in 2007. Focusing on science and technology, its attractions include interactive displays, multimedia presentations, and a popular **IMAX theatre** (p. 115). Designed to bring to life the concepts of energy conservation and 21st-century communications, the center's extensive use of computers and electronic visual displays are particularly appealing to youngsters. Indeed, the whole place is designed for ages 9 to 14. Admission fees vary according to the combination of exhibits and movie showings you choose. To avoid long lines, preorder tickets for special exhibits. Several outdoor and indoor cafes sell sandwiches, salads, and sweets.

Vieux-Port, quai King Edward. ✆ **877/496-4724** or 514/496-4724. www.montrealsciencecentre.com. Admission for exhibitions C$12 adults, C$11 seniors and ages 13–17, C$9 ages 4–12, free for children 3 and younger. Movie tickets from C$12 adults, C$11 seniors and ages 13–17, C$9 ages 4–12, free for children 3 and younger. MC, V. Mon–Fri 9am–4pm, Sat–Sun 10am–5pm. Métro: Place d'Armes or Champ-de-Mars.

Pointe-à-Callière (Montréal Museum of Archaeology and History) ★★★ A first visit to Montréal might best begin here. Built on the very site where the original colony (called Pointe-à-Callière) was established in 1642, this modern museum engages visitors in rare, beguiling ways. The triangular new building echoes the Royal Insurance building (1861) that stood here for many years.

Go first to the 16-minute multimedia show in an auditorium that actually stands above exposed ruins of the earlier city. Music and a playful bilingual narration keeps the history slick and painless if a little chamber-of-commerce upbeat. Children 11 and younger may find it a snooze.

Evidence of the area's many inhabitants—from Amerindians to French trappers to Scottish merchants—was unearthed during archaeological digs that took more than a decade. Artifacts are on view in display cases set among the ancient building foundations and burial grounds below street level. Wind your way on the self-guided tour through the subterranean complex until you find yourself in the former customhouse, where there are more exhibits and a well-stocked gift shop.

L'Arrivage Café is open daily for lunch and presents a fine view of Vieux-Montréal and Vieux-Port. Allow 1½ hours to visit this museum, which is wheelchair accessible.

350 Place Royale (at rue de la Commune). ✆ **514/872-9150.** www.pacmuseum.qc.ca. Admission C$14 adults, C$10 seniors, C$8 students, C$6 children 6–12, free for children 5 and younger. Late June–late Aug Mon–Fri 10am–6pm, Sat–Sun 11am–6pm; Sept to mid-June Tues–Fri 10am–5pm, Sat–Sun 11am–5pm. L'Arrivage Café Mon 11:30am–2pm, Tues–Sun 11:30am–3pm. Métro: Place d'Armes.

(Fun Facts) **Cirque du Soleil: Montréal's Hometown Circus**

The whimsical, talented band of artists that became Cirque du Soleil began as street performers in Baie-St-Paul (p. 282), a river town an hour north of Québec City. These stilt-walkers, fire-breathers, and musicians had one pure intention: to entertain. The troupe formally founded as Cirque du Soleil (Circus of the Sun) in 1984 and celebrated its 25th year in 2009.

It has matured into a spectacle like no other. Using human-size gyroscopes, trampoline beds, trapezes suspended from massive chandeliers, and the like (but no animals), Cirque creates worlds that are spooky, sensual, otherworldly, and beautifully ambiguous.

More than 1,000 of the company's acrobats, contortionists, jugglers, clowns, and dancers tour the world. Resident shows are established in Las Vegas and Orlando, Florida. The company's offices are in Montréal in the northern Saint-Michel district, not far beyond the Mile End neighborhood.

And they're not just offices. Cirque has been developing a small campus of buildings in this industrial zone since 1997. All new artists come here to train for a few weeks to a few months and live in residences on-site. The complex has acrobatic training rooms, a dance studio, workshops in which the elaborate costumes and props are made, and a space large enough to erect a circus tent indoors. Some 1,800 are employed at the Montréal facility, including more than 400 who work on costumes alone.

The company doesn't have regular performances in Montréal, alas. For information about when they're coming to town and where else in the world you can find a show, visit **www.cirquedusoleil.com**.

Vieux-Port ★★ (Kids)   Montréal's Old Port was transformed in 1992 from a dreary commercial wharf area into a 2km-long (1¼-mile), 53-hectare (131-acre) promenade and public park with bicycle paths, exhibition halls, and a variety of family activities, including the **Centre des Sciences de Montréal** (see above). It stretches along the waterfront parallel to rue de la Commune from rue McGill to rue Berri.

The area is most active from mid-May through October, when harbor cruises take to the waters and bicycles, in-line skates, and family-friendly quadricycle carts are available to rent. Warm months also bring information booths staffed by bilingual attendants and 50-minute guided tours in the open-sided **La Balade,** a small, motorized tram. **Cirque du Soleil** often sets up its signature blue and yellow tents here in late spring. In winter, things are quieter, but an outdoor ice-skating rink is a big attraction.

At the port's far eastern end, in the last of the old warehouses, is a 1922 clock tower, **La Tour de l'Horloge,** with 192 steps leading past the exposed clockworks to observation decks overlooking the St. Lawrence River (admission is free).

Information booth for the Vieux-Port expanse is at the Centre des Sciences de Montréal on quai King Edward (King Edward Pier). ℂ **800/971-PORT** (971-7678). www.quaysoftheoldport.com. La Balade tram (May–Sept) C$5 adults, C$3.50 seniors (60 and older) and teens (13–17), C$3 children 12 and younger. Métro: Champ-de-Mars, Place d'Armes, or Square Victoria.

ELSEWHERE IN THE CITY

A 20-minute drive east on rue Sherbrooke or an easy Métro ride from downtown is **Olympic Park,** located in a neighborhood called Hochelaga-Maisonneuve. It has four attractions: Stade Olympique (Olympic Stadium), Biodôme de Montréal, Jardin Botanique (Botanical Garden), and Insectarium de Montréal. The first three are described below, and the Insectarium on p. 115. All are walking distance from each other. You could spend a day touring all four sites, and kids will especially love the Biodôme and Insectarium. Combination ticket packages are available, and the Biodôme, Jardin, and Insectarium are all included in the **Montréal Museum Pass** (see the "Money Savers" box on p. 103). Underground parking at the Olympic Stadium is C$12 per day, with additional parking at the Jardin Botanique and Insectarium.

Biodôme de Montréal ★★ (Kids) A terrifically engaging attraction for children of nearly any age, the delightful Biodôme houses replications of four ecosystems: a tropical rainforest, a Laurentian forest, the St. Lawrence marine system, and a polar environment. Visitors walk through each and hear the animals, smell the flora, and, except in the polar region, which is behind glass, feel the changes in temperature. The rainforest area is the most engrossing (the subsequent rooms increasingly less so), so take your time here. It's a kind of "Where's Waldo" challenge to find all the critters, from the capybara, which looks like a large guinea pig, to the golden lion tamarin monkeys that swing on branches only an arm's length away. Only the bats, fish, penguins, and puffins are behind glass. A giant tank in the St. Lawrence area holds Atlantic sturgeon nearly 1.5m (5 ft.) long, while the open-air space features hundreds of shore birds whose shrieks can transport you to the beach. A continual schedule of temporary exhibits and new programs keeps things fresh. The building was originally the velodrome for cycling during the 1976 Olympics. The facility also has a hands-on activity room called Naturalia, a shop, a bistro, and a cafeteria.

4777 av. Pierre-de-Coubertin (next to Stade Olympique). ℂ 514/868-3000. www.biodome.qc.ca. Admission C$16 adults, C$12 seniors and students, C$8 children 5–17, C$2.50 children 2–4. Audio guide C$4. AE, MC, V. Daily 9am–5pm (until 6pm late June–Aug). Closed most Mon Sept–Dec. Métro: Viau.

Jardin Botanique ★★★ Spread across 75 hectares (185 acres), Montréal's Botanical Garden is a fragrant oasis 12 months a year. Ten large exhibition greenhouses each have a theme: one houses orchids; another has tropical food and spice plants, including coffee, cashews, and vanilla; another features rainforest flora. In a special exhibit each spring, live butterflies flutter among the nectar-bearing plants, occasionally landing on visitors. In September, visitors can watch monarch butterflies being tagged and released for their annual migration to Mexico.

Outdoors, spring is when things really kick in: lilacs in May, lilies in June, and roses from mid-June until the first frost. The **Chinese Garden,** a joint project of Montréal and Shanghai, evokes the 14th- to 17th-century era of the Ming Dynasty and was built according to the landscape principles of yin and yang. It incorporates pavilions, inner courtyards, ponds, and plants indigenous to China. A serene **Japanese Garden** fills 2.5 hectares (6 acres) and has a cultural pavilion with an art gallery, a tearoom where ancient ceremonies are performed, a stunning bonsai collection, and a Zen garden.

A small train runs through the gardens from mid-May to October and is included in the entrance fee.

The grounds are also home to the **Insectarium** (p. 115), which displays some of the world's most beautiful and sinister insects (both mounted and live). Exhibits acquaint young and old with honey bees, cockroaches, beetles, and hundreds of other "misunderstood" creatures. *Note:* The Insectarium expects to close for renovations for several months in early 2011.

4101 rue Sherbrooke est (opposite Olympic Stadium). ✆ **514/872-1400.** www.ville.montreal.qc.ca/jardin. Admission includes access to the Insectarium. May 15–Oct 31 C$17 adults, C$13 seniors and students, C$8.25 children 5–17, C$2.50 children 2–4. Rates drop about 15% the rest of the year. AE, MC, V. Jan 1–May 14 Tues–Sun 9am–5pm; May 15–Sept 9 daily 9am–6pm; Sept 10–Oct 31 daily 9am–9pm; Nov 1–Dec 31 Tues–Sun 9am–5pm. No bicycles or dogs. Métro: Pie-IX, and then walk up the hill; or take free shuttle bus from Olympic Park (Métro: Viau).

Stade Olympique Montréal's space-age and controversial Olympic Stadium, the centerpiece of the 1976 Olympic Games, looks like a giant stapler. In truth, it's likely to induce only moderate interest for most visitors. The main event is the 175m (574-ft.) inclined tower, which leans at a 45-degree angle and does duty as an observation deck, with a funicular that whisks passengers to the top in 95 seconds. On a clear day, the deck bestows an expansive view over Montréal and into the neighboring Laurentian mountains, but at C$15, the admission price is as steep as the tower.

The complex includes a stadium that seats up to 56,000 for sporting events and music concerts (it was home to the Montréal Expos before that baseball team relocated to Washington, D.C., in 2005). The Sports Centre houses seven swimming pools open for public swimming and classes, including one deep enough for scuba diving. Thirty-minute guided tours that describe the 1976 Olympic Games and use of the center today are available daily for C$8.

The roof doesn't retract anymore—it never retracted well anyway. That's one reason that what was first known as "the Big O" was scorned as "the Big Woe," then "the Big Owe," after cost overruns led to heavy tax increases.

4141 av. Pierre-de-Coubertin. ✆ **877/997-0919** or 514/252-4141. www.rio.gouv.qc.ca. Tower admission C$15 adults, C$11 seniors and students, C$7.50 ages 5–17. Public swimming scheduled daily, admission C$4.75 adults, C$3.55 children 15 and younger. Tower daily 9am–7pm in summer; until 5pm in winter. Closed mid-Jan to mid-Feb. Métro: Viau.

2 MORE ATTRACTIONS

DOWNTOWN

Basilique-Cathédrale Marie-Reine-du-Monde No one who has seen both will confuse Montréal's "Mary Queen of the World" cathedral with St. Peter's Basilica in Rome, but a scaled-down homage was the intention of Bishop Ignace Bourget, who oversaw its construction after the first Catholic cathedral here burned to the ground in 1852. Construction lasted from 1875 to 1894, its start delayed by the bishop's desire to place it not in Francophone east Montréal but in the heart of the Protestant Anglophone west. Most impressive is the 76m-high (249-ft.) dome, about a third of the size of the original. The statues standing on the roofline represent patron saints of the region, providing a local touch. The interior is less rewarding visually than the exterior, but the high altar is worth a look. Masses are held daily.

1085 rue de la Cathédrale (at rue Mansfield). ✆ **514/866-1661.** www.cathedralecatholiquedemontreal. org. Free admission; donations accepted. Mon–Fri 7:00am–6:15pm; Sat–Sun 7:30am–6:15pm. Métro: Bonaventure.

Cathédrale Christ Church This Anglican cathedral, which is reflected in the shiny exterior of the pink-glassed postmodern Tour KPMG office tower, stands in glorious Gothic contrast to the city's downtown skyscrapers. The building was completed in 1859. The original steeple was too heavy for the structure, so a lighter aluminum version replaced it in 1940. It's sometimes called the "floating cathedral" because of the many tiers of malls and corridors in the underground city beneath it and the way it was elevated during their construction. Choirs sing each Sunday at 10am for Choral Eucharist and at 4pm for Choral Evensong, with the Evensong broadcast live at www.radiovm.com. The church also hosts concerts throughout the year.

635 rue Ste-Catherine ouest (at rue University). ☎ **514/843-6577,** ext. 369 (recorded information about services and concerts). www.montrealcathedral.ca. Free admission; donations accepted. Daily 10am–6pm; services Sun 8am, 10am, and 4pm; weekdays noon and 5:15pm evening prayer. Métro: McGill.

Musée d'Art Contemporain de Montréal Montréal's Museum of Contemporary Art is the country's only museum devoted exclusively to the avant-garde. Its focus is works created since 1939, and much of the permanent collection is by Québécois artists such as Jean-Paul Riopelle and Betty Goodwin. Also represented are international artists Richard Serra, Bruce Nauman, Sam Taylor-Wood, and Nan Goldin. No single style prevails, so expect to see installations, video displays, and examples of pop, op, and abstract expressionism. On Friday Nocturnes—the first Friday of most months—the museum stays open until 9pm with live music, bar service, and tours of the exhibition galleries. A mélange of fun videos are online at www.youtube.com/macmvideos. The museum's glass-walled restaurant, **La Rotonde,** was renovated in 2009 and has a summer dining terrace.

185 rue Ste-Catherine ouest. ☎ **514/847-6226.** www.macm.org. Admission C$8 adults, C$6 seniors, C$4 students, free for children 11 and younger, free to all Wed 6–9pm. Tues–Sun 11am–6pm (until 9pm Wed and Friday Nocturnes). Métro: Place des Arts.

VIEUX-MONTREAL (OLD MONTREAL)

Chapelle Notre-Dame-de-Bon-Secours/Musée Marguerite-Bourgeoys Just to the east of Marché Bonsecours, Notre-Dame-de-Bon-Secours Chapel is called the Sailors' Church because of the special attachment that fishermen and other mariners have to it. Their devotion is manifest in the several ship models hanging from the ceiling inside. There's also an excellent view of the harbor from the church's tower.

The first building, which no longer stands, was the project of an energetic teacher named Marguerite Bourgeoys, and built in 1675. Bourgeoys had come from France to undertake the education of the children of the colonists and, later, the native peoples. She and other teachers founded the Congregation of Notre-Dame, Canada's first nuns' order. The pioneering Bourgeoys was canonized in 1982 as the Canadian church's first female saint and in 2005, for the chapel's 350th birthday, her remains were brought to the church and interred in the left-side altar.

A restored 18th-century crypt under the chapel houses the museum. Part of it is devoted to relating Bourgeoys's life and work, while another section displays artifacts from an archaeological site here, including ruins and materials from the colony's earliest days. An Amerindian fire pit on display dates to 400 B.C.

400 rue St-Paul est (at the foot of rue Bonsecours). ☎ **514/282-8670.** www.marguerite-bourgeoys.com. Free admission to chapel. Museum C$8 adults, C$5 seniors and students, C$4 children ages 6–12, free for children 5 and younger; archaeological site with guide and access to museum C$18 for family. Cash only. May–Oct Tues–Sun 10am–5:30pm; Nov to mid-Jan and Mar–Apr Tues–Sun 11am–3:30pm. Métro: Champ-de-Mars.

Hôtel de Ville City Hall, finished in 1878, is relatively young by Vieux-Montréal standards. It's still in use, with the mayor's office on the main floor. The French Second Empire design makes it look as though it was imported stone by stone from the mother country: Balconies, turrets, and mansard roofs decorate the exterior. The details are particularly visible when the exterior is illuminated at night. The Hall of Honour is made of green marble from Campagna, Italy, and houses Art Deco lamps from Paris and a bronze-and-glass chandelier, also from France, that weighs a metric ton. It was from the balcony above the awning that, in 1967, an ill-mannered Charles de Gaulle, then president of France, proclaimed, "Vive le Québec Libre!"—a gesture that pleased his immediate audience but strained relations with the Canadian government for years.

275 rue Notre-Dame est (at the corner of rue Gosford). ✆ **514/872-0077.** Free admission. Mon–Fri 9am–4pm. One-hour guided tours on weekdays late June–late August. Métro: Champ-de-Mars.

Marché Bonsecours Bonsecours Market is an imposing neoclassical building with a long facade, a colonnaded portico, and a silvery dome. It was built in the mid-1800s—the Doric columns of the portico were cast of iron in England—and first used as the Parliament of United Canada and then as Montréal's City Hall until 1878. The architecture alone makes a brief visit worthwhile. For many years after 1878 it served as the city's central market. Essentially abandoned for much of the 20th century, it was restored in 1964 to house city government offices. Today it houses restaurants, art galleries, and high-end but affordable boutiques featuring Québécois products.

350 rue St-Paul est (at the foot of rue St-Claude). ✆ **514/872-7730.** www.marchebonsecours.qc.ca. Free admission. Daily 10am–6pm (until 9pm during summer). Métro: Champ-de-Mars.

Musée du Château Ramezay ★ **(Kids)** Claude de Ramezay, the colony's 11th governor, built his residence here in 1705. The château became home to the city's royal French governors for almost 4 decades, until Ramezay's heirs sold it to a trading company in 1745. Fifteen years later, British conquerors took it over, and in 1775, an army of American revolutionaries invaded and held Montréal and used the château as their headquarters. For 6 weeks in 1776, Benjamin Franklin spent his days here, trying to persuade the Québécois to rise with the American colonists against British rule (he failed).

After the American interlude, the house was used as a courthouse, a government office building, and headquarters for Laval University before being converted into a museum in 1895. Exhibits about "Natives and the New World," the fur trade, and New France now fill the main floor.

Between October and May, the château invites families to join in on the last Sunday of the month for an old-timey bread-making session using its 18th-century hearth. In the summer, there are workshops in the garden that teach how to make soap and beeswax candles. Dates, details, and additional fees are listed on the website.

Sculpted, formal gardens ringed by a low stone wall evoke 18th-century French *jardins* and provide a soothing respite from the bustle of Place Jacques-Cartier, a few steps away. A cafe, open May 1 through September 30, overlooks the gardens.

In 2008, the Québec tourism office awarded the museum a grand prize for its work.

280 rue Notre-Dame est. ✆ **514/861-3708.** www.chateauramezay.qc.ca. Admission C$9 adults, C$7 seniors, C$6 students, C$4.50 ages 5–17, free for children 4 and younger, C$18 families. MC, V. June to late Nov daily 10am–6pm; late Nov to May Tues–Sun 10am–4:30pm. Métro: Champ-de-Mars.

Scandinave Les Bains ★ Bath complexes are common throughout Scandinavia, but less so in North America. This center, which opened in 2009, aims to bring Euro-style relaxation-through-water to Montréal's locals and guests. Visitors check in and change into bathing suits, and then have the run of the complex for the visit. There's a warm bath the size of a small swimming pool, with jets and a waterfall. There's a steam room thick with eucalyptus oil scent, and a Finnish-style dry sauna. Peppered throughout the hallways are slingback chairs, and one room is set aside just for relaxing or having a drink from the juice bar. The recommended routine is to heat your body for about 15 minutes, cool down in one of the icy rinse stations, and relax for 15 minutes—and then repeat the circuit a few times. Call to reserve a spot. Ask for a time when the fewest people are there; the fewer there are, the more relaxing the experience.

71 rue de la Commune ouest. ☎ **514/288-2009.** www.scandinave.com. Admission C$42. Packages available with massage. Daily 10am–10pm. Métro: Champ-de-Mars.

MONT ROYAL & PLATEAU MONT-ROYAL

To explore these areas, take the walking tours in chapter 9.

L'Oratoire St-Joseph ★ This huge Catholic church—dominating Mont-Royal's north slope—is seen by some as inspiring, by others as forbidding. It's Montréal's highest point, with an enormous dome 97m (318 ft) high. Consecrated as a basilica in 2004, it came into being through the efforts of Brother André, a lay brother in the Holy Cross order who earned a reputation as a healer. By the time he had built a small wooden chapel in 1904 on the mountain, he was said to have performed hundreds of cures. His powers attracted supplicants from great distances, and he performed his work until his death in 1937. In 1982, he was beatified by the pope—a status one step below sainthood—and Brother André's dream of building a shrine to honor St. Joseph, patron saint of Canada, became a completed reality in 1967.

The church is largely Italian Renaissance in style, its giant copper dome recalling the shape of the Duomo in Florence, but of greater size and lesser grace. Inside is a sanctuary and exhibit that displays Brother André's actual heart in a formalin-filled urn. His original wooden chapel, with its tiny bedroom, is on the grounds and open to the public. Two million pilgrims visit annually, many of whom seek intercession from St. Joseph and Brother André by climbing the middle set of 99 steps on their knees. Guided tours are offered in French, English, and five other languages. The 56-bell carillon plays Wednesday to Friday at noon and 3pm and Saturday to Sunday at noon and 2:30pm, all months but February. Also on site is an oratory museum featuring 264 nativity scenes from 111 countries.

A modest 14-room hostel on the grounds is called the **Jean XXIII Pavilion.** A one-bedroom starts at C$50 and includes breakfast.

In 2002, the oratory embarked on a 10-year renovation project to improve overall accessibility for the ever-increasing number of visitors. Most recent completions include an elevator to the basilica and a new vehicle entrance. By 2011 visitors will be allowed unprecedented 360-degree views of Montréal from the basilica's dome.

3800 chemin Queen Mary (on the north slope of Mont-Royal). ☎ **877/672-8647** or 514/733-8211. www.saint-joseph.org. Free admission to most sights, donations requested. Oratory museum C$4 adult, C$3 senior and student, C$2 ages 6–17. Crypt and votive chapel daily 6am–9:30pm; basilica and exhibition on Brother André daily 7am–5:30pm (until 9pm May–Oct), oratory museum open daily 10am–5pm. C$5 suggested donation for parking. Métro: Côtes-des-Neiges or Snowdon. Bus: 165 or 51.

Parc La Fontaine The European-style park in Plateau Mont-Royal is one of the city's oldest and most popular. Illustrating the traditional dual identities of the city's populace, half the park is landscaped in the formal French manner, the other in the more casual English style. A central lake is used for ice-skating in winter, when snowshoe and cross-country trails wind through trees. In summer, these trails become bike paths, and tennis courts become active. An open amphitheater, the **Théâtre de Verdure** (p. 161), features free outdoor theater, music, and tango dancing. The northern end of the park is more pleasant than the southern end (along rue Sherbrooke), which seems to attract a seedier crowd.

Bounded by rue Sherbrooke, rue Rachel, av. Parc LaFontaine, and av. Papineau. ✆ **514/872-4041** for Théâtre, **514/872-3948** for park. Free admission; fee for use of tennis courts. Park open daily 6am–midnight; tennis courts 9am–11pm weekdays, 9am–9pm weekends (✆ 514/872-3626 reservations). Métro: Sherbrooke.

ILE STE-HELENE ★

The small Île Ste-Hélène and adjacent Île Notre-Dame sit in the St. Lawrence River near Vieux-Port's waterfront. Connected by two bridges, they now comprise the recently designated **Parc Jean-Drapeau,** which is almost entirely car-free and accessible by Métro, bicycle, or foot.

La Biosphère (Kids) Not to be confused with the **Biodôme** at Olympic Park (p. 109), this interactive science facility is housed under a geodesic dome designed by Buckminster Fuller to serve as the American Pavilion for Expo 67. A fire destroyed the sphere's acrylic skin in 1976, and for almost 20 years it served no purpose other than as a harbor landmark. In 1995, Environment Canada (www.ec.gc.ca) joined with the city of Montréal to convert the space. The motivation is unabashedly environmentalist, with exhibition areas, a theater, and an amphitheater all devoted to promoting awareness of the St. Lawrence–Great Lakes ecosystem. An interactive walking tour, dubbed GéoTour 67*, uses GPS (Global Positioning System) devices. "Planète Bucky," a permanent exhibit, highlights Fuller's forward-thinking inventions for sustainable development. There's a preaching-to-the-choir quality, but the displays and exhibits are put together thoughtfully and engage and enlighten most visitors, at least for a while.

160 chemin Tour-de-l'Isle (Île Ste-Hélène). ✆ **514/283-5000.** www.biosphere.ec.gc.ca. Admission C$10 adults, C$8 seniors and students 18 and older, free for children 17 and younger. June–Oct daily 10am–6pm; Nov–May Tues–Sun 10am–6pm. Métro: Parc Jean-Drapeau.

Musée David M. Stewart ★ (Kids) This museum was closed for renovation for all of 2009 and will be shut for at least the first half of 2010, with major work scheduled during the 18-month hiatus. Call or check the website for updated information.

The history of the facility is interesting: After the War of 1812, the British prepared for a possible future American invasion of Montréal by building a moated fortress. It's that fortress which now houses the museum. The Duke of Wellington ordered the fort's construction as another link in the chain of defenses along the St. Lawrence River, and it was completed in 1824. It was never involved in armed conflict, and the British garrison left in 1870, after the former Canadian colonies confederated.

In recent years, the low stone barracks and blockhouses have featured staff in period costume performing firing drills, tending campfires, and attempting to recruit visitors into the king's army. The museum owns maps and scientific instruments that helped Europeans explore the New World, military and naval artifacts, and related paraphernalia from the time of French voyager Jacques Cartier (1535) through the end of the colonial period (1763). The fort typically comes to life in July and August with reenactments of military parades and retreats by troupes known as La Compagnie Franche de la Marine and the Olde 78th Fraser Highlanders. (The presence of the French unit is an unhistorical bow to Francophone sensibilities: New France had become English Canada almost 65 years before the fort was erected.)

Vieux-Fort, Île Ste-Hélène. ☎ **514/861-6701.** www.stewart-museum.org. Closed for 18 months of renovation through summer of 2010. Métro: Parc Jean-Drapeau, and then a 10-min. walk. By car: Take the Jacques-Cartier Bridge to the Parc Jean-Drapeau exit, and then follow the signs.

3 ESPECIALLY FOR KIDS

In addition to the three Bs—the **Biodôme** (p. 109), **La Biosphère** (p. 114), and **boat tours** (p. 119)—here are some venues and programs that cater primarily to the under-18 crowd. Also look for other attractions flagged in this chapter with the **Kids** icon.

Atrium Le 1000 **Kids** This indoor ice-skating rink in the heart of downtown offers skating year-round under a glass ceiling. Skate rentals are available on-site, and a food court overlooks the rink. "Tiny Tot Mornings," typically Saturday and Sunday from 10:30 to 11:30am, are reserved for children 12 and younger and their parents. Saturday nights are geared towards adults, with Bermuda-themed parties and DJs.

1000 rue de la Gauchetière ouest, downtown. ☎ **514/395-0555.** www.le1000.com. Admission C$6 adults, C$5 seniors and students, C$4 children 12 and younger. Skate rental C$5.50. MC, V. Daily 11:30am–6pm or later. Métro: Bonaventure.

Fantômes Ghost Walks **Kids** Evenings at 8:30, join with other intrepid souls for a ghost walk of Vieux-Montréal. The 90-minute tour heads down back alleys and to places where gruesome events occurred and actors appear as phantoms to tell about the historical crimes of the city. Because their stories include tales of sorcery, hangings, and being burned and tortured, it's probably too scary for young children.

360 rue St-François-Xavier. ☎ **514/868-0303.** www.fantommontreal.com. Admission C$23 adults, C$19 students, C$14 children 12 and younger. MC, V. Various evenings July through October at 8:30pm; call or go online for exact days. Métro: Place d'Armes.

IMAX Theatre **Kids** Images and special effects are larger than life, visually dazzling, and often vertiginous on this seven-story screen in the **Centre des Sciences de Montréal** (p. 107). The 36,000-watt audio system gives a whole new meaning to surround sound and additional technological upgrades were slated for completion by the end of 2009. Recent films have highlighted the deep waters of the South Pacific and the band U2, in 3D. Running time is usually less than an hour, and about one or two screenings per day are in English. Tickets can be ordered online, with the movie schedule available on the website as well.

Quai King Edward, Vieux-Port. ☎ **877/496-4724** or 514/496-4724. www.montrealsciencecentre.com. Movie tickets from C$12 adults, C$11 seniors and ages 13–17, C$9 ages 4–12, free for children 3 and younger. MC, V. Shows daily 10am–9pm. Métro: Place d'Armes or Champ-de-Mars.

Insectarium de Montréal **Kids** Live exhibits featuring scorpions, tarantulas, honeybees, ants, hissing cockroaches, assassin bugs, and other "misunderstood creatures, which are so often wrongly feared and despised," as its website puts it, are displayed in this two-level structure near the rue Sherbrooke gate of the **Jardin Botanique** (**Botanical Garden;** p. 109). Alongside the live creepy critters are thousands of mounted ones, including butterflies, beetles, scarabs, maggots, locusts, and giraffe weevils. The gift shop sells lollipops with mealworm larva inside. Note: The Insectarium expects to close for renovations for several months in early 2011. Call or check online for updated information.

4581 rue Sherbrooke est. ☎ **514/872-1400.** www.ville.montreal.qc.ca/insectarium. Admission includes access to the Botanical Garden next door. May 15–Oct C$17 adults, C$13 seniors and students, C$8.25

children 5–17, C$2.50 children 2–4, free for children 1 and younger. Rates drop about 20% rest of the year. See p. 103 for information about combination tickets with the Stade Olympique and Biodôme. AE, MC, V. Jan 1–May 14 Tues–Sun 9am–5pm; May 15–Sept 9 daily 9am–6pm; Sept 10–Oct 31 daily 9am–9pm; Nov 1–Dec 31 Tues–Sun 9am–5pm. Métro: Pie-IX or Viau.

Labyrinth Shed 16 (Kids)   From mid-May to the end of October, this gigantic indoor maze at the far eastern end of Vieux-Port entices children to come and explore a mystery, which changes each year. One year, for instance, the maze was set up like the interior of a castle, with a tale of a priceless black diamond family treasure; another year visitors searched throughout the maze for information to open a safe that contained stolen art works. Visitors climb through rope bridges, take staircases to secret corridors, wind through walls of enormous oil drums, and slide down chutes, answering math or logic questions along the way. It takes about 90 minutes to get through. A lot of it is dark, and visitors do some crawling, so be prepared.

Quai de l'Horloge, near the Clock Tower. (C) **514/499-0099.** www.labyrintheduhangar16.com. Admission C$14 ages 18 and over, C$13 seniors and teens 13–17, C$11 children 4–12, free for children 3 and younger. MC, V. June 20–Aug 23 daily 11am–9pm; May 16–June 19 and Aug 24–Oct 9 Sat, Sun and holidays 11:30am–5:30pm. Métro: Champs-de-Mars.

La Ronde Amusement Park (Kids)   Montréal's amusement park, opened as part of Expo 67, the World's Fair, was run for its first 34 years by the city. It was sold to the American-owned Six Flags theme-park empire in 2001. New rides have since been delivered, and like hot sauces, they're categorized by "thrill rating": moderate, mild, or max. There are 13 rides in the "max thrill" category, including Le Vampire, a suspended coaster which has riders experiencing five head-over-heels loops at more than 80kmph (50 mph). Other attractions include a Ferris wheel, acrobatic shows, and plenty of places to eat and drink. An antique carousel, Le Galopant, was built by Belgian artisans in 1885 and was part of the Belgian Pavilion at the 1964 to 1965 New York World's Fair. The Minirail is an elevated train that circles the park. Young children also have ample selection, including the Tchou Tchou Train and *tasses magiques,* in which they sit in one of 12 giant rotating tea cups.

On 11 Saturdays from June to August, La Ronde hosts a huge fireworks competition, **L'International Des Feux Loto-Québec.** Although the pyrotechnics can be enjoyed for free from almost anywhere in the city overlooking the river, tickets can be purchased to watch from the open-air theater here. Call (C) **514/397-2000** or go to www.international desfeuxloto-quebec.com for details.

Parc Jean-Drapeau on Île Ste-Hélène. (C) **514/397-2000.** www.laronde.com. Admission prices by height: C$39 for patrons 1.37m (54 in.) or taller, C$26 for patrons shorter than 1.37m (54 in.) or seniors, free for children 2 and younger. Special rates when purchased online. Parking C$15–C$25. Summer (late June–Aug) daily 11am–9pm (to 11:30pm Sat); spring and fall Sat–Sun 11am–7pm. Closed winter. Métro: Papineau, and then bus no. 169, or Parc Jean-Drapeau, and then bus no. 167.

Planétarium de Montréal (Kids)   A window on the night sky with mythical monsters and magical heroes, Montréal's planetarium is in the heart of the city. Shows under the 20m (66-ft.) dome dazzle and inform kids at the same time. Multimedia presentations change with the season, exploring time and space travel and collisions of celestial bodies. Up to five different shows are screened daily. The special Christmas production, "The Longest Night," plays from November through early January. Shows in English alternate with those in French.

1000 rue St-Jacques ouest (at Peel). (C) **514/872-4530.** www.planetarium.montreal.qc.ca. Admission C$8 adults, C$6 seniors and students, C$4 children 5–17, free for children 4 and younger. AE, MC, V. Hours vary according to show schedule; call or go online for details. Métro: Bonaventure (exit toward rue de la Cathédrale).

4 SPECIAL-INTEREST SIGHTSEEING

Bagg Street Shul   Author Mordecai Richler set most of his books in the working-class Jewish neighborhood of St. Urbain of the 1940s and 1950s (his most famous book is *The Apprenticeship of Duddy Kravitz*). The Bagg Street Shul, also called Temple Solomon or Congregation Beth Shloime, is the heart of this neighborhood and one of the last signs of the Plateau's long history as a Jewish enclave. A replica of the old Eastern European synagogues of Poland and Ukraine, its interior features robin's-egg-blue walls and paintings of the 12 zodiac signs, labeled in Hebrew. It's the city's oldest synagogue in continuous use, but it's been plagued by financial troubles and the need for significant repairs.

3919 rue Clark (at rue Bagg). ℂ **514/288-0561.** Open Saturdays and holidays. Free admission. Métro: Sherbrooke.

Centre Canadien d'Architecture   The understated but handsome Canadian Centre for Architecture (CCA) occupies a city block, joining a contemporary structure with an older building, the 1875 Shaughnessy House. Opened in 1989, this museum has received rave reviews from scholars, critics, and serious architecture buffs. CCA functions as both a study center and a museum, with changing exhibits devoted to the art and history of architecture. Exhibits include architects' sketchbooks, elevation drawings, and photography. The collection is international in scope and encompasses architecture, urban planning, and landscape design. Texts are in French and English. The bookstore has a special section about Canadian architecture with an emphasis on Montréal and Québec City. Podcasts of lectures and conferences that have taken place here are available for free on the CCA website.

A **sculpture garden** that faces the CCA from boulevard René-Lévesque's south side is part of the museum. Designed by Montréal artist/architect Melvin Charney, it's a quiet retreat in the center of downtown.

1920 rue Baile (at rue du Fort). ℂ **514/939-7026.** www.cca.qc.ca. Admission C$10 adults, C$7 seniors, C$5 students, C$3 children 6–12, free for ages 5 and younger and persons with disabilities. Free Thurs after 5:30pm. Wed–Sun 11am–5pm (until 9pm Thurs). Métro: Guy-Concordia.

Centre d'Histoire de Montréal   Built in 1903 as Montréal's central fire station, this redbrick-and-sandstone building on the edge of Vieux-Montréal is now the CHM, which traces the city's development from when it had its first residents, the Amerindians, to the European settlers who arrived in 1642, to the present day. The museum underwent a major renovation in 2009. The permanent exhibit includes memorabilia from the city from 1535 onward, and each year the Centre hosts a Montréal-themed photo competition with the winners' images on display. An exhibit about products made in Montréal runs through March 13, 2011.

335 Place d'Youville (at rue St-Pierre). ℂ **514/872-3207.** www.ville.montreal.qc.ca/chm. Admission C$6 adults, C$5 seniors, C$4 children 6–17 and students, free for children 5 and younger. Jan–late Nov Tues–Sun 10am–5pm; closed Dec. Métro: Square Victoria.

Musée de la Banque de Montréal   Facing the **Basilique Notre-Dame** (p. 106) and Place d'Armes is Montréal's oldest bank building. Architectural features include a classic facade beneath a graceful dome, a carved pediment, and six Corinthian columns. The outside dimensions and appearance remain largely unchanged since the building's completion in 1847. Pop in for 5 minutes to see the teeny one-room museum just off the front hall. It features a replica of the bank's first office, a display showing how to spot

EXPLORING MONTRÉAL

8

SPECIAL-INTEREST SIGHTSEEING

Jewish Montréal

At the turn of the 20th century, Montréal was home to more Jewish persons than any other Canadian city, attracting an especially large Yiddish-speaking population from Eastern Europe. Today Toronto has nearly twice as many Jewish residents, but vestiges of the community's history and ongoing practices remain in Montréal's. Here, places of worship, celebration of Jewish culture through arts, and the so-called bagel and smoked meat wars smolder on, to the delight of local and visiting connoisseurs.

The **Bagg Street Shul** (see above), at the corner of rues Clark and Bagg, began as a two-family residence, was converted to a synagogue in 1920 to 1921 and has been in continuous use ever since. Other synagogues dot the neighborhood but have transitioned as the Jewish community dispersed—one became a French college, another an Evangelical church (though it still houses 10 murals of the history of Jews in Montréal).

Kosher edibles abound. One could start the day with a bagel from either **St-Viateur Bagel & Café,** at 1127 av. Mont-Royal est, or **Fairmont Bagel,** at 74 av. Fairmont ouest in Mile End. Get lunch while traveling back in time at **Wilensky Light Lunch,** 34 rue Fairmount ouest. For dinner, order an unforgettable smoked meat sandwich at **Schwartz's,** 3895 bd. St-Laurent, or opt for a steak at the posh **Moishes,** 3961 bd. St-Laurent. See chapter 7 for restaurant details.

The Snowdon neighborhood in western Montréal is home to the city's contemporary Jewish organizations. The **Jewish Public Library** (© 514/345-2627; www.jewishpubliclibrary.org) boasts the largest circulating collection of Judaica in North America and hosts year-round lectures, cultural events, and concerts. Its archive of more than 17,000 photos of Montréal's Jewish history is in the process of being digitized to be put online. The Library shares a building at 5151 Côte-Ste-Catherine with the **Montréal Holocaust Memorial Centre** (© 514/345-2605; www.mhmc.ca) and two-dozen other Jewish community service agencies. Just across the street at 5170 Côte-Ste-Catherine is the **Segal Centre for Performing Arts** (p. 161), which presents plays in Yiddish.

a forged bill, and a collection of 100-year-old mechanical banks. Take a look at the building's sumptuous interior: It was renovated from 1901 through 1905 by the famed U.S. firm McKim, Mead, and White, and features Ionic and Corinthian columns of Vermont granite and walls of pink marble from Tennessee.

129 rue St-Jacques ouest (at Place d'Armes). © **514/877-6810.** Free admission. Mon–Fri 10am–4pm. Métro: Place d'Armes.

Musée Redpath ⓥ Value   This quirky natural history museum, housed in an 1882 building with a grandly proportioned and richly appointed interior, is on the McGill University campus. The main draws—worth a half-hour visit—are the mummies and coffin that are part of Canada's second-largest collection of Egyptian antiquities, and skeletons of whales and prehistoric beasts. If the unusual name seems slightly familiar, it could be because you've seen it on the wrappings of sugar cubes in many Canadian res- taurants: John Redpath was a 19th-century industrialist who built Canada's first sugar refinery.

859 rue Sherbrooke ouest (rue University). ☎ **514/398-4086.** www.mcgill.ca/redpath. Free admission. Mon–Fri 9am–5pm; Sun 1–5pm. Closed Saturdays, long weekends, and public holidays. Métro: McGill.

Pavillon de la TOHU Adjacent to the Cirque du Soleil training complex on reclaimed industrial land, TOHU is many things, most especially a performance facility that brings small circus companies to its intimate in-the-round theater (p. 159). But it's also a model building for green architecture. It's heated by biogas from a landfill next door and uses an ice bunker for cooling in the summer. Both processes produce zero greenhouse-effect gases and are explained in free brochures. For one weekend in August, TOHU hosts an outdoor fair promoting sustainable food practices. For the rest of the year, it's worth a special trip only if you're an environmental architecture fan. Two guided tours are available with advance reservations by phone: one focuses on TOHU's green technologies, the other on the history of the circus arts. If there's a show playing, build a trip around it.

2345 rue Jarry est (corner of rue d'Iberville, at Autoroute 40). ☎ **888/376-8648** or 514/376-8648. www. tohu.ca. Free to view facility and exhibits; tour admission from C$6 adults, C$4 seniors, students, and children 7–11, free for children 6 and younger. Daily 9am–5pm. Performances from C$22 adults, from C$16 children 12 and younger. 8km (5 miles) from downtown, up rue St-Denis and east on rue Jarry to where it meets Autoroute 40. Métro: Jarry or Iberville and bus no. 94 nord.

5 ORGANIZED TOURS

An introductory guided tour is often the best—or, at least, most efficient—way to begin exploring a new city and can certainly give you a good lay of the land and overview of Montréal's history. Tours take you past many of the attractions listed in this chapter and can give you a better sense of which ones to spend time exploring.

For a complete listing of tour options, check under "Guided Tours" in the *Montréal Official Tourist Guide,* available at the downtown **Infotouriste Centre** at 1255 rue Peel (☎ **877/266-5687** or 514/873-2015; Métro: Peel).

Most land tours leave from the Square Dorchester, right at the tourist office. Most boat tours depart from Vieux-Port (Old Port), at the waterfront bordering Vieux-Montréal. There's parking at the dock, or take the Métro to the Champ-de-Mars or Square Victoria Station and walk toward the river.

BOAT TOURS

Among numerous opportunities for experiencing Montréal and environs by water, here are a few of the most popular:

Le Bateau-Mouche (☎ **800/361-9952** or 514/849-9952; www.bateau-mouche.com) is an air-conditioned, glass-enclosed vessel reminiscent of those on the Seine in Paris. It plies the St. Lawrence River from mid-May to mid-October. Cruises depart for 60-minute excursions at 1:30, 3, and 4:30pm; for a 90-minute cruise at 11:30am; and for a 3½-hour dinner cruise at 7pm. The shallow-draft boat takes passengers on a route inaccessible by traditional vessels, passing under several bridges and providing sweeping views of the city, Mont Royal, and the St. Lawrence and its islands. Daytime snacks are available onboard. The 60-minute tours cost C$23 adults, C$21 students and seniors 65 and

EXPLORING MONTRÉAL

8

ORGANIZED TOURS

older, C$11 children 6 to 16, and are free for children 5 and younger. The 90-minute tour costs C$27 adults, C$25 students and seniors, and C$11 children 6 to 16. Dinner cruises, with meals prepared by the kitchen of Fairmont The Queen Elizabeth, cost from C$89, C$128, or C$152 per person, regardless of age, and reservations are essential (prices higher Saturdays and the evenings of fireworks). The tours depart from the Jacques-Cartier Pier, opposite Place Jacques-Cartier.

Croisières AML Cruises (© 800/563-4643 or 514/842-3871; www.croisieresaml. com) also travels the harbor and the St. Lawrence. Options include a weekend brunch cruise that departs at 11:30am and lasts 1½-hours for C$45 adults, C$42 students and seniors, C$24 children 6 to 16, and free for children 5 and younger. There are also 60- or 90-minute history trips throughout the day, as well as 4-hour Love Boat dinner cruises that depart at 7pm, and 3-hour Latin Fiesta dance parties that leave at midnight. Call or check the website for prices and times. Boats depart from the King Edward Pier, in Vieux-Port.

Croisière Historique sur le Canal de Lachine (© 514/283-6054) is a leisurely Parks Canada trip up the Lachine Canal, which was inaugurated in 1824 so that ships could bypass the Lachine Rapids on the way to the Great Lakes. The canal was reopened for recreational use in 1997 after much renovation. It's lined with 19th-century industrial buildings, many of which are being converted into high-end apartments. The 2-hour guided tours are on a glass-topped *bateau-mouche,* which carries up to 49 passengers. From mid-May to mid-June and early September to mid-October, departures are at 1 and 3:30pm on Saturday, Sunday, and holidays; from late June to early September, departures are at 1 and 3:30pm daily. Phone reservations recommended. Fares are C$18 adults, C$15 children 13 to 17, C$11 children 6 to 12, and free for children 5 and younger. Groups of 18 or more can charter 1-hour or 2-hour tours. Tours departs from a dock near the Marché Atwater farmer's market (Métro: Lionel-Groulx).

Les Descentes sur le St-Laurent (© 800/324-7238 or 514/767-2230; www.rafting montreal.com) also provides hydrojet rides on the white water. This departure point is a little closer to the rapids than the others, so a bit more of an adventure. Rafting and jet-boat options are available for C$40 and C$49 adults, C$34 and C$39 ages 13 to 18, and C$23 and C$29 for children 12 and younger, though kids must be at least 6 years old to go rafting and at least 8 years old to go jet-boating. Open daily from 9am to 5pm. Take the Métro to the Angrignon station and take bus no. 110. Reservations are required.

Les Sautes-Moutons, also known as **Lachine Rapids Tours** (© 514/284-9607; www.jetboatingmontreal.com) provides an exciting—and wet—experience. Its wave-jumper powerboats take on the St. Lawrence River's roiling Lachine Rapids. The stream-lined jet boat makes the 1-hour trip from May to mid-October daily, with departures every 2 hours from 10am to 6pm. It takes a half-hour to get to and from the rapids, which leaves 30 minutes for storming along the 8 to 12 ft. waves. Reservations are required. Plan to arrive 45 minutes early to obtain and don rain gear and a life jacket. Bring a towel and change of clothes, as you almost certainly will get splashed or even soaked. Fares are C$65 adults, C$55 ages 13 to 18, C$45 children 6 to 12, and free for children 5 and younger. The jet boats depart from the Clock Tower Pier (quai de l'Horlage) in Vieux-Port.

The **Navettes Fluviales Maritime Shuttles** (© 514/281-8000; www.navettesmaritimes. com) from Jacques-Cartier Pier in Vieux-Montréal to either Île Ste-Hélène or Longueuil are much milder water voyages, but still offer great views. It's one way to begin or end a picnic outing or extend a bike ride beyond Old Montréal. Both ferries operate from mid-May to mid-October, with daily departures every hour in the high season, and cost C$6 per person. Your ticket stub gets you a discount at an array of partners including the Biosphère and La Ronde amusement park.

LAND TOURS

Gray Line de Montréal (☏ 514/934-1222; www.coachcanada.com) offers commercial guided tours in air-conditioned buses daily year-round. The basic city tour takes 3 hours and costs C$40 for ages 12 and up, C$36 for seniors and students, C$28 for ages 5 to 11, and free for children 4 and younger. Tours depart from 1255 rue Peel in downtown.

Amphi-Bus (☏ 514/849-5181; www.montreal-amphibus-tour.com) is something a little different: It tours Vieux-Montréal much like any other bus—until it waddles into the waters of the harbor for a dramatic finish. Departures are on the hour from 10am until midnight June through September, and at noon, 2, 4, and 6pm in May and October. Fares are C$32 adults, C$29 seniors, C$23 students, C$18 children 4 to 12, and C$10 children 3 and younger. Reservations are required. The bus departs from the intersection of rue de la Commune and bd. St-Laurent.

Montréal's **calèches** (☏ 514/934-6105; www.calechesluckyluc.com) are horse-drawn open carriages whose drivers serve as guides. They operate year-round, and in winter, the horse puffs steam clouds in the cold air as the passengers bundle up in lap rugs. Reserved rides for up to four persons can be arranged from downtown for C$150 per hour and from Vieux-Montréal for C$125 per hour. During summer months, visitors can find the carriages waiting at Place Jacques-Cartier and rue de la Commune, and at Place d'Armes opposite the Notre-Dame Basilica, where a 30-minute ride costs C$45 and an hour costs C$75. All of the guides speak French and English.

WALKING & CYCLING TOURS

Guidatour (☏ 514/844-4021; www.guidatour.qc.ca) developed its walking tour of Vieux-Montréal in collaboration with the Centre d'Histoire de Montréal (p. 117). The 90-minute circuit is conducted in English at 11am and 1:30pm daily in summer, and costs C$18 for adults, C$16 for seniors and students, and C$8.50 for children ages 6 to 12.

Guidatour also offers a 3-hour bicycling tour in conjunction with **ÇaRoule/Montréal on Wheels** that goes from Vieux-Port through the Latin Quarter, to Parc La Fontaine and then west to Parc du Mont-Royal, south through the business district, and back into Vieux-Montréal. The C$49 fee includes rental of a bike, helmet, and lock for the day. Tours are available Thursday and Friday from late June to early September, and Saturday and Sunday mid-May to mid-October. Tours start at 9am at the bike shop at 27 rue de la Commune est in Vieux-Port (also see "Bicycling & In-Line Skating," below). Reservations are required.

6 SPECTATOR SPORTS

Montréalers are as devoted to ice hockey as other Canadians are, with plenty of enthusiasm left over for soccer, U.S.-style football, and the other distinctive national sport, curling. They liked baseball too, but not enough: In 2005, the Montréal Expos, plagued by poor attendance, left for Washington, D.C., where they became the Nationals. (Fun fact: Pioneering black athlete **Jackie Robinson** played for the Montréal Royals in 1946, and there's a sculpture of him outside of Olympic Stadium.)

AUTO RACING

Many in Montréal are still in mourning for the **Grand Prix,** which made its last stop in the city in 2008. The international auto race attracted more than 100,000 people to the city's track (and to hotels and restaurants), and brought in as much as C$100 million in tourism dollars, making it the single biggest tourism event of the year. Formula One, which puts on the race, demanded more money from the government and Tourism Montréal than they were able to offer.

For now, auto race aficionados have to content themselves with **NASCAR** (www.circuit gillesvilleneuve.ca), which comes to Montréal for 2 days in early August, bringing more than 40 top drivers and race cars. One-day general-admission tickets cost C$30 to C$40, with 2-day tickets ranging from C$55 to C$165.

FOOTBALL & SOCCER

What Americans call soccer most of the rest of the world calls football, and there's a big fan base for *that* kind of football in Montréal—not surprising, given the city's wide and varied immigrant population. Montréal doesn't have a team in the Major League Soccer network, but it's been considered as a possible expansion city. The **Montréal Impact** (© 514/328-3668; www.montrealimpact.com) is part of the United Soccer League's First Division and plays at Saputo Stadium, rue 4750 Sherbrooke est, near the Olympic Stadium. Tickets are C$10 to C$40.

Meanwhile, there's also U.S.-style professional football in Canada. The website for the **Montréal Alouettes** (French for "larks") claims, somewhat dubiously, that "Montréal is synonymous with football," citing that "the first recorded game ever played in North America was on the downtown cricket grounds on Oct. 10, 1868." The team does enjoy considerable success, frequently appearing in the Grey Cup, the Canadian Football League's version of the U.S. Super Bowl. The "Als," as they're fondly known, play at McGill University's Percival-Molson Memorial Stadium from June to November. Tickets start at C$25. Details are at © 514/871-2255 and www.montrealalouettes.com.

HOCKEY

The beloved **Montréal Canadiens** play downtown at the Centre Bell arena. The team has won 24 Stanley Cups (the most recent in 1992–93), and the season runs from October to April, with playoffs continuing into June. Tickets are C$25 to C$225. Check www. canadiens.com for schedules and ticketing or call © 877/668-8269 or 514/790-2525.

Popular Canadian Pastimes: Name that Sport!

"With Ontario leading 6 to 4 in the 10th end, Manitoba skip Jennifer Jones prepared for her last shot. Manitoba had three rocks in the house, but Ontario had shot rock and had two guards sitting near one another, high atop the house, toward Jones; another guard sat just outside the rings. Jones was left with one option: She hit and rolled off the lone Ontario stone outside the rings to remove Ontario's shot rock near the button."

So was the verbatim report in *The Globe and Mail* of the Canadian women's championship game in February 2005. Manitoba won, 8 to 6.

The sport? Curling.

The **Rogers Cup** tournament (📞 514/273-1515; www.rogerscup.com) comes each August to the Uniprix Stadium, which is near the De Castelnau and the Jarry Métro stops, with singles and doubles matches. Men's and women's tournaments are played in two different locations, alternating between Montréal and Toronto. The stadium's Centre Court holds more than 11,000. Tickets cost between C$10 and C$158, with up to four matches included. To make the tournament more green, the stadium provides 175 bike-rack slots and 24-hour bike surveillance, free public transit tickets to all spectators, and a downtown shuttle service.

7 OUTDOOR ACTIVITIES

After such long winters, locals pour outdoors to get sun and warm air at every possible opportunity (though there's also lots to do when there's snow on the ground). Even if you come to Montréal without your regular outdoor gear, it's easy to join in.

WARM-WEATHER ACTIVITIES
Bicycling & In-Line Skating

Bicycling and rollerblading are hugely popular in Montréal, and the city helps people indulge these passions: It boasts an expanding network of more than 560km (348 miles) of cycling paths and year-round bike lanes. In warm months, car lanes in heavily biked areas are blocked off with concrete barriers, effectively turning them into two-way lanes for bikers.

If you're serious about cycling, get in touch with the nonprofit biking organization **Vélo Québec** (📞 800/567-8356 or 514/521-8356; www.velo.qc.ca). Vélo (which means bicycle) was behind the development of a 4,000km (2,485-mile) bike network called **Route Verte (Green Route)** that stretches from one end of Québec province to the other. The route was officially inaugurated in summer 2007. The Vélo website has the most up-to-date information on the state of the paths, the Montréal Bike Fest, road races, new bike lanes, and more. It also offers guided tours throughout the province. (*Tip:* Several taxi companies provide bike racks and charge C$3 extra for each bike. See p. 61.)

If you're looking to rent a bike or pair of skates, the shop **ÇaRoule/Montréal on Wheels** (📞 877/866-0633 or 514/866-0633; www.caroulemontreal.com) at 27 rue de la Commune est, the waterfront road bordering Vieux-Port, rents bikes and skates from March to November. Rentals are C$9 per hour and C$30 per day on the weekend. Helmets are included and a deposit is required. The staff will set you up with a map (also downloadable from their website) and likely point you toward the peaceful **Lachine Canal,** a nearly flat 11km (6.8-mile) bicycle path, open year-round (but only maintained by Parks Canada from mid-Apr to the end of Oct), that travels alongside locks and over small bridges. The canal starts just a few blocks away. **Pôles des Rapides,** a nonprofit organization, provides information about the Lachine Canal path and nearby bicycle paths at www.polesdes rapides.com. See p. 121 for information about ÇaRoule's 3-hour guided bike tours.

Also for rent at Vieux-Port in warm months are **quadricycles** (📞 514/849-9953; www.quadricycleintl.com), or "Q-cycles"—four-wheeled bike-buggies that can hold up to six people. You can only ride them along Vieux-Port, and the rental booth is in the heart of the waterfront area, next to the Pavillian Jacques-Cartier. Rentals are by the half-hour and cost C$15 for a three-seater, C$20 for a three-seater with spots for two small children, and C$30 for a six-seater.

In the spring of 2009, the city began rolling out a self-service bicycle rental program called BIXI where users can pick up bikes from designated bike stands in the city and drop them off at other stands, for a small fee. See "Getting Around" in chapter 5 for more information.

Hiking

The most popular hike is to the top of **Mont Royal.** There are a web of options for trekking the small mountain, from using the broad and handsome pedestrian-only **chemin Olmsted** (a bridle path named for Frederick Law Olmsted, the park's landscape architect), to following smaller paths and sets of stairs. The park is well-marked and small enough that you can wander without fear of getting too lost, but our walking tour on p. 140 suggests one place to start and a number of options once you've headed in.

Jogging

There are many possibilities for running. In addition to the areas described above for biking and hiking, consider heading to either of the city's most prominent parks: **Parc La Fontaine** in the Plateau Mont-Royal neighborhood (p. 113), or **Parc Maisonneuve** in the city's east side, adjacent to the **Jardin Botanique** and across the street from **Olympic Park** (p. 109). Both parks are formally landscaped and well used for recreation and relaxation.

Kayaking & Electric Boating

It's fun to rent kayaks, large Rabaska canoes, pedal boats, or small eco-friendly electric boats on the quiet **Lachine Canal,** just to the west of Vieux-Port. **H2O Adventures** (© **877/935-2925** or 514/842-1306; www.h2oadventures.com) won a 2007 *Grand Prix du tourisme Québécois* award for being a standout operation. Their rentals start at C$8 per hour. Two-hour introductory kayak lessons go for C$39 on weekdays, C$45 on weekends. From May to September the shop is open weekdays noon to 9pm and weekends 9am to 9pm. Find it at the **Marché Atwater,** where you can also pick up lunch from the inside *boulangerie* and *fromagerie,* adjacent to the canal. Métro: Lionel-Groulx.

Swimming

On Parc Jean-Drapeau, the island park just across the harbor of Vieux-Port, there are both an outdoor swimming pool complex and a lakeside beach, the Plage des Îles (www.parcjeandrapeau.com). Admission to the beach is C$8 for ages 14 and over, C$4 for ages 6 to 13, and free for children 5 and younger. Métro: Jean-Drapeau.

COLD-WEATHER ACTIVITIES
Cross-Country Skiing

Parc du Mont-Royal has an extensive cross-country course, as do many of the other city parks, though skiers have to supply their own equipment. Just an hour from the city, north in the Laurentides and east in the Cantons de l'Est, there are numerous options for skiing and rentals; see chapter 12 for more information.

Ice-Skating

In the winter, outdoor skating rinks are set up in Vieux-Port, Lac des Castors (Beaver Lake), and other spots around the city; check tourist offices for your best options. One of the most agreeable venues for skating any time of the year is **Atrium Le 1000** (p. 115) in the downtown skyscraper at 1000 rue de la Gauchetière ouest. For one thing, it's indoors and warm. For another, it's surrounded by cafes at which to relax after twirling around the big rink. And yes, it's even open in the summer.

Montréal Strolls

Cities best reveal themselves on foot, and Montréal is one of North America's most pedestrian-friendly locales. There's much to see in the concentrated districts—cobblestoned Vieux-Montréal, downtown and its luxurious "Golden Square Mile," bustling Plateau Mont-Royal, and Mont Royal itself—and in this chapter are strolls that will take you to the best of all of them.

Also listed is a destination walk that gets you to Marché Atwater, a large year-round market. The walk takes you past some of the best antiquing in the city and is a way to take in an interesting area the way locals do.

The city's layout is mostly straightforward and simple to navigate, and the extensive Métro system gets you to and from neighborhoods with ease.

These strolls will give you a taste of what's best about old and new Montréal, and send you off to discover highlights of your own.

WALKING TOUR 1 VIEUX-MONTREAL

START:	Place d'Armes, opposite the Notre-Dame Basilica.
FINISH:	Vieux-Port.
TIME:	2 hours.
BEST TIMES:	Almost any day the weather is decent. Vieux-Montréal is lively and safe day or night. Note, however, that most museums are closed on Monday. On warm weekends and holidays, Montréalers and visitors turn out in full force, enjoying the plazas, the 18th- and 19th-century architecture, and the ambience of the most picturesque part of their city.
WORST TIMES:	Evenings, days that are too cold, and times when museums and historic buildings are closed.

Vieux-Montréal is where the city was born. Its architectural heritage has been substantially preserved, and restored 18th- and 19th-century structures now house shops, boutique hotels, galleries, cafes, bars, and apartments. This tour gives you a lay of the land, passing many of the neighborhood's highlights and some of its best and most atmospheric dining spots.

If you're coming from outside Vieux-Montréal, take the Métro to the Place d'Armes station, which lets off next to the Palais des Congrès, the convention center. Follow the signs up the short hill 2 blocks toward Vieux-Montréal (Old Montréal) and the Place d'Armes. Turn right on rue St-Jacques. On your immediate right, at 119 rue St-Jacques, is the domed, colonnaded:

❶ Banque de Montréal

Montréal's oldest bank building dates from 1847. From 1901 to 1905, American architect Stanford White extended the original building, and in this enlarged space he created a vast chamber with green-marble columns topped with golden capitals. The public is welcome to stop in for a look. Besides being lavishly appointed inside and out, the bank also houses a small **banking museum** (p. 117) which illustrates early operations. It's just off the main lobby to the left and admission is free.

Exiting the bank, cross the street to:

❷ Place d'Armes

The architecture of the buildings that surround this plaza is representative of Montréal's growth: the Sulpician residence of the 17th century (no. 5, below), the Banque de Montréal and Basilique Notre-Dame (no. 6, below) of the 19th century, and the Art Deco Edifice Aldred (no. 4, below), of the 20th century.

The centerpiece of the square is a monument to city founder Paul de Chomedey, Sieur de Maisonneuve (1612–76). These five statues mark the spot where settlers defeated Iroquois warriors in bloody hand-to-hand fighting, with de Maisonneuve himself locked in combat with the Iroquois chief. De Maisonneuve won and lived here another 23 years. The inscription on the monument reads (in French): YOU ARE THE BUCKWHEAT SEED WHICH WILL GROW AND MULTIPLY AND SPREAD THROUGHOUT THE COUNTRY.

The sculptures at the base of the monument represent other prominent citizens of early Montréal: Charles Lemoyne, a farmer; Jeanne Mance, a woman who founded the city's first hospital; Raphael-Lambert Closse, a soldier and the mayor of Ville-Marie; and an unnamed Iroquois brave. Closse is depicted with his dog, Pilote, whose bark once warned the early settlers of an impending Iroquois attack.

Facing the Notre-Dame Basilica from the square, look over to the left. At the corner of St-Jacques is the:

❸ Edifice New York Life

This red-stone Richardson Romanesque building, with a striking wrought-iron door and clock tower, is at 511 Place d'Armes. At all of eight stories, this became Montréal's first skyscraper in 1888, and it was equipped with a technological marvel—an elevator.

Next to it, on the right, stands the 23-story Art Deco:

❹ Edifice Aldred

If this building looks somehow familiar, there's a reason: Built in 1931, it clearly

resembles New York's Empire State Building, also completed that year. The building's original tenant was Aldred and Co. Ltd., a New York–based finance company with other offices in New York, London, and Paris.

From the square, cross rue Notre-Dame, bearing right of the basilica to the:

❺ Vieux Séminaire de St-Sulpice

The city's oldest building is surrounded by equally ancient stone walls. This seminary was erected by Sulpician priests who arrived in Ville-Marie in 1657, 15 years after the colony was founded (the Sulpicians are part of an order founded in Paris in 1641). The clock on the facade dates from 1701 and its gears are made almost entirely of wood. It has been under renovation recently. The seminary is not open to the public.

After a look through the iron gate, head east on rue Notre-Dame to the magnificent Gothic Revival–style:

❻ Basilique Notre-Dame

This brilliantly crafted church was designed in 1824 by James O'Donnell, an Irish Protestant architect living in New York. Transformed by his experience, he converted to Roman Catholicism and is the only person interred here.

The main altar is made from a hand-carved linden tree. Behind it is the Chapel of the Sacred Heart (1982), a perennially popular choice for weddings. The chapel's altar, 32 bronze panels by Montréal artist Charles Daudelin, represents birth, life, and death. Some 4,000 people can attend at a time, and the bell, one of North America's largest, weighs 12 tons. There's a small museum beside the chapel.

Come back at night for a romantic take on the city, when more than a score of buildings in the area, including this one, are illuminated.

See p. 106 for more about the church.

Exiting the basilica, turn right (east) on rue Notre-Dame, crossing rue St-Sulpice. On the north side of rue Notre-Dame is Claude Postel (see p. 90), a great place for sandwiches and pastries. Walk 4 blocks,

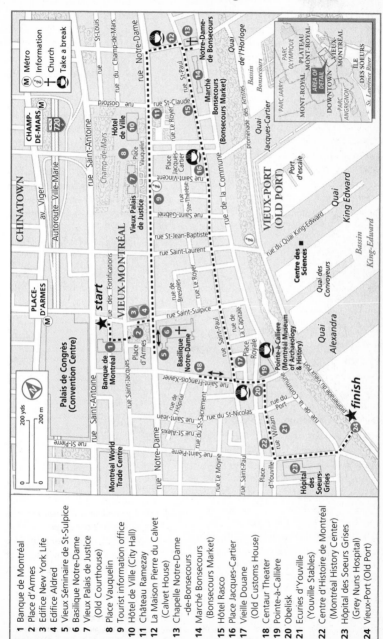

MONTREAL STROLLS

9

VIEUX-MONTRÉAL

1 Banque de Montréal
2 Place d'Armes
3 Edifice New York Life
4 Edifice Aldred
5 Vieux Séminaire de St-Sulpice
6 Basilique Notre-Dame
7 Vieux Palais de Justice (Old Courthouse)
8 Place Vauquelin
9 Tourist information office
10 Hôtel de Ville (City Hall)
11 Château Ramezay
12 La Maison Pierre du Calvet (Calvet House)
13 Chapelle Notre-Dame -de-Bonsecours
14 Marché Bonsecours (Bonsecours Market)
15 Hôtel Rasco
16 Place Jacques-Cartier
17 Vieille Douane (Old Customs House)
18 Centaur Theater
19 Pointe-à-Callière
20 Obelisk
21 Ecuries d'Youville (Youville Stables)
22 Centre d'Histoire de Montréal (Montréal History Center)
23 Hôpital des Soeurs Grises (Grey Nuns Hospital)
24 Vieux-Port (Old Port)

passing chintzy souvenir shops, and then face left to see the:

❼ Vieux Palais de Justice (Old Courthouse)

Most of this structure was built in 1856. The third floor and dome were added in 1891, and the difference between the original structure and the addition can be easily discerned with a close look.

The city's civil cases were tried here until a new courthouse, the Palais de Justice, was built next door in 1978. Civic departments for the city of Montréal are housed in the old courthouse now.

The statue beside the Old Courthouse, called *Homage to Marguerite Bourgeoys,* depicts a teacher and nun and is the work of sculptor Jules LaSalle.

Also on your left, just past the courthouse, is:

❽ Place Vauquelin

This small public square, with a splashing fountain and view of the Champ-de-Mars park, was created in 1858. The statue is of Jean Vauquelin, commander of the French fleet in New France; he stares across rue Notre-Dame at his counterpart, the English admiral Horatio Nelson. The two statues are symbols of Montréal's French and British duality.

On the opposite corner is a small but helpful:

❾ Tourist Information Office

A bilingual staff stands ready to answer questions and hand out useful brochures and maps (daily in warmer months, Wed–Sun in winter). The famed Silver Dollar Saloon, named for the 350 silver dollars that were embedded in its floor, once stood on this site, though it has long since been torn down.

Around the corner, on the right, is the Place Jacques-Cartier, a magnet for citizens and visitors year-round which we will visit later in the stroll. Rising on the other side of rue Notre-Dame, opposite the top of the square, is the impressive, green-capped:

❿ Hôtel de Ville (City Hall)

Built between 1872 and 1878 in the florid French Second Empire style, the edifice is

seen to particular advantage when it is illuminated at night. In 1922, it barely survived a disastrous fire. Only the exterior walls remained, and after substantial rebuilding and the addition of another floor, it reopened in 1926. Take a minute to look inside at the generous use of Italian marble, the Art Deco lamps, and the bronze-and-glass chandelier. The sculptures at the entry are *Woman with a Pail* and *The Sower,* both by Québec sculptor Alfred Laliberté. See p. 112 for more details.

Exiting City Hall, you'll see, across rue Notre-Dame, a small, terraced park with orderly ranks of trees. The statue inside the park honors Montréal's controversial longtime mayor, Jean Drapeau. Next to it is:

⓫ Château Ramezay

Starting in 1706, this was the home of the city's French governors for 4 decades, starting with Claude de Ramezay, before being taken over and used for the same purpose by the British.

In 1775, an army of American rebels invaded and held Montréal, using the house as their headquarters. Benjamin Franklin was sent to try to persuade Montréalers to join the American revolt against British rule, and he stayed in this château. He failed to sway Québec's leaders to join the radical cause.

Today, the house shows off furnishings, oil paintings, costumes, and other objects related to the economic and social activities of the 18th century and the first half of the 19th century. See p. 112 for more about the museum.

Continue in the same direction (east) along rue Notre-Dame. In the far distance, you'll see the Molson beer factory. At rue Bonsecours, turn right. Near the bottom of the street, on the left, is a house with a low maroon roof and an attached stone building on the corner. This is:

⓬ La Maison Pierre du Calvet (Calvet House)

Built in the 18th century and sumptuously restored between 1964 and 1966, this house was inhabited by a fairly well-to-do family in its first years. Pierre du Calvet, believed to be the original owner, was a French Huguenot who supported the American Revolution. Calvet met with Benjamin Franklin here in 1775 and was imprisoned from 1780 to 1783 for supplying money to the Americans. With a characteristic sloped roof meant to discourage snow buildup and raised end walls that serve as firebreaks, the building is constructed of Montréal graystone. It is now a *hostellerie* and **restaurant** with an entrance at no. 405. In 2009 the owner opened the Musée du Bronze on-site as well. Visitors are invited to come in for a look.

> **TAKE A BREAK**
> There is a voluptuously appointed dining room inside the **Hostellerie Pierre du Calvet,** 405 rue Bonsecours, but in the warm months, lunches, dinners, and Sunday brunches are served in a lovely outdoor courtyard that opened to the public in 2007 (before then, it was privately used by the owner). Take a peek to see the greenhouse and songbirds that lead to the stone-walled terrace.

The next street, rue St-Paul, is Montréal's oldest thoroughfare, dating from 1672. The church at this intersection is the small:

⓭ Chapelle Notre-Dame-de-Bon-Secours

Called the Sailors' Church because so many seamen made pilgrimages here to give thanks for being saved at sea, this chapel was founded by Marguerite Bourgeoys, a nun and teacher who was canonized in 1982. Excavations have unearthed foundations of her original 1675 church, although the building has been much altered and the present facade was built in the late 18th century. A **museum** (see p. 111) tells the story of Bourgeoys's life and incorporates the archaeological site.

Climb up to the tower for a view of the port and Old Town.

Head west on rue St-Paul. Just beyond the Sailors' Church is an imposing building with a colonnaded facade and silvery dome, the limestone:

⓮ Marché Bonsecours (Bonsecours Market)

Completed in 1847, this building was used first as the Parliament of United Canada and then as the City Hall, the central market, a music hall, and then the home of the municipality's housing and planning offices. It was restored in 1992 for the city's 350th birthday celebration to house temporary exhibitions and musical performances. It continues to be used for exhibitions, but it's more of a retail center now, with a terrific selection of art shops, clothing boutiques, and sidewalk cafes (p. 112).

When Bonsecours Market was first built, the dome could be seen from everywhere in the city and served as a landmark for seafarers sailing into the harbor. Today it is lit at night.

Continue down rue St-Paul. At no. 281 is the former:

⓯ Hôtel Rasco

An Italian, Francisco Rasco, came to Canada to manage a hotel for the Molson family (of beer-brewing fame) and later became successful with his own hotel on this spot. The 150-room Rasco was the Ritz-Carlton of its day, hosting Charles Dickens and his wife in 1842, when the author was directing his plays at a theater that used to stand across the street. The hotel lives on in legend if not in fact, as it's devoid of much of its original architectural detail and no longer hosts overnight guests. Between 1960 and 1981, the space stood empty, but the city took it over and restored it in 1982. It has contained a succession of eateries on the ground floor and now is home to a standout Mediterranean restaurant called **Version Laurent Godbout** (p. 89).

Continue heading west on rue St-Paul, turning right when you reach:

⓰ Place Jacques-Cartier

Opened as a marketplace in 1804, this is the most appealing of Vieux-Montréal's squares, even with its obviously touristy

MONTRÉAL STROLLS

9

VIEUX-MONTRÉAL

aspects. The square's cobbled cross streets, gentle downhill slope, and ancient buildings set the mood, while outdoor cafes, street entertainers, itinerant artists, and assorted vendors invite lingering in warm weather. Calèches (horse-drawn carriages) depart from both the lower and the upper ends of the square for tours of Vieux-Montréal.

Walk slowly uphill, taking in the old buildings that bracket the plaza (plaques describe some of them in French and English). All these houses were well suited to the rigors of life in the raw young settlement. Their steeply pitched roofs shed the heavy winter snows rather than collapsing under the burden, and small windows with double casements let in light while keeping out wintry breezes. When shuttered, the windows were almost as effective as the heavy stone walls in deflecting hostile arrows or the antics of trappers fresh from raucous evenings in nearby taverns.

At the plaza's northern end stands a monument to Horatio Nelson, hero of Trafalgar, erected in 1809. This monument preceded London's much larger version by several years. After years of vandalism, presumably by Québec separatists, the statue had to be temporarily removed for restoration. The original Nelson is now back in place at the crown of the column.

> ### TAKE A BREAK
> Most of the old buildings in and around the inclined plaza house restaurants and cafes. For a drink or snack during the warm months, try to find a seat in **Le Jardin Nelson** (no. 407), near the bottom of the hill. The courtyard in back often has live jazz, while tables on the terrace overlook the square's activity.

Return to rue St-Paul and continue west. Take time to window-shop the many art galleries that have sprung up alongside the loud souvenir shops on the street. The street numbers will get lower as you approach boulevard St-Laurent, the north-south thoroughfare that divides Montréal into its east and west halves. Numbers will start to rise again as you move onto rue St-Paul ouest (west). At 150 rue St-Paul ouest is the neoclassical:

⑰ Vieille Douane (Old Customs House)

Erected from 1836 to 1838, this building was doubled in size when an extension to the south side was added in 1882; walk around to the building's other side to see how the addition is different. That end of the building faces Place Royale, the first public square in the 17th-century settlement of Ville-Marie. It's where Europeans and Amerindians used to come to trade. The building now houses a **boutique** (p. 156) for the **Pointe-à-Callière museum** (p. 107).

Continue on rue St-Paul to rue St-François-Xavier. Turn right for a short detour; up rue St-François-Xavier, on the right, is the stately:

⑱ Centaur Theatre

The home of Montréal's principal English-language theater is a former stock-exchange building. The Beaux Arts architecture is interesting in that the two entrances are on either side rather than in the center of the facade. American architect George Post, who was also responsible for designing the New York Stock Exchange, designed this building, erected in 1903. It served its original function until 1965, when it was redesigned as a theater with two stages. See p. 161 for theater information.

Return back down rue St-François-Xavier to rue St-Paul.

> ### TAKE A BREAK
> One possibility for lunch or a pick-me-up is the moderately priced **Stash Café** (p. 92) at 200 rue St-Paul ouest at the corner of rue St-François-Xavier. It specializes in Polish fare and opens at 11:30am on weekdays and noon on weekends. Another option is the glass-walled, second-floor **L'Arrivage Café** at the Pointe-à-Callière museum, your next stop. Its lunchtime *table d'hôte* menu starts at C$10.

Continue on rue St-François-Xavier past St-Paul. At the next corner, the gray wedge-shaped building to the left is the:

⑲ Pointe-à-Callière

Known in English as the **Museum of Archaeology and History,** Pointe-à-Callière is packed with artifacts unearthed during more than a decade of excavation at the spot, where the settlement of Ville-Marie was founded in 1642. An underground connection also incorporates the **Old Customs House** you just passed. See p. 107 for more about this top-notch museum.

A fort stood here in 1645. Thirty years later, a château was built on the site for Louis-Hector de Callière, the governor of New France, from whom the museum and triangular square that it's on take their names. At that time, the St. Pierre River separated this piece of land from the mainland. It was made a canal in the 19th century and later filled in.

Proceeding west from Pointe-à-Callière, near rue St-François-Xavier, stands an:

⑳ Obelisk

Commemorating the founding of Ville-Marie on May 18, 1642, the obelisk was erected here in 1893 by the Montréal Historical Society. It bears the names of the city's early pioneers, including French officer Paul Chomedey de Maisonneuve, who landed in Montréal in 1642, and fellow settler Jeanne Mance, who founded North America's first hospital, l'Hôtel-Dieu de Montréal.

Continuing west from the obelisk 2 blocks to 296–316 Place d'Youville, you'll find, on the left, the:

㉑ Ecuries d'Youville (Youville Stables)

Despite the name, the rooms in the iron-gated compound, built in 1825 on land owned by the Gray Nuns, were used mainly as warehouses rather than as horse stables (the actual stables, next door, were made of wood and disappeared long ago). Like much of the waterfront area, the

U-shaped Youville building was run-down and forgotten until the 1960s, when a group of enterprising businesspeople bought and renovated it. Today the compound contains offices and a popular steakhouse, Gibby's. Go through the passage toward the restaurant door for a look at the inner courtyard if the gates are open (they usually are).

Continue another block west to the front door of the brick building on your right, 335 rue St-Pierre and the:

㉒ Centre d'Histoire de Montréal (Montréal History Center)

Built in 1903 as Montréal's central fire station, this building now houses exhibits, including many audiovisual ones, about the city's past and present. Visitors learn about early exploration routes, the fur trade, architecture, public squares, the railroad, and life in Montréal from 1920 to 1950. See p. 117 for details.

Head down rue St-Pierre toward the water. Midway down the block, on the right at no. 138, is the former:

㉓ Hôpital des Soeurs Grises (Grey Nuns Hospital)

The hospital was founded in 1693 by the Charon Brothers to serve the city's poor and homeless. Bankrupt by 1747, it was taken over by Marguerite d'Youville, founder in 1737 of the Sisters of Charity of Montréal, commonly known as the Grey Nuns. It was expanded several times, but by 1871 the Nuns had moved away and portions were demolished to extend rue St-Pierre and make room for commercial buildings. A century later the Grey Nuns returned to live in their original home. From the sidewalk, visitors can see a very cool contemporary sculpture of inscribed bronze strips that cover the surviving chapel walls. The text on the sculpture comes from a letter signed by Louis XIV in 1694, incorporating the hospital. There are three exhibition rooms open to the public, by appointment only (② **514/842-9411**).

From here, continue down rue St-Pierre and cross the main street, rue de la Commune, and then the railroad tracks to this tour's final stop:

㉔ Vieux-Port (Old Port)

Montréal's historic commercial wharves have been reborn as a waterfront park, which, in good weather, is frequented by cyclists, in-line skaters, joggers, walkers, strollers, and lovers. Across the water is the distinctive 158-unit modular housing project **Habitat 67,** built by famed architect Moshe Safdie for the 1967 World's Fair, which Montréal called Expo 67. Safdie's vision was to show what affordable, community housing could be. Today it's a higher-end apartment complex and not open to the public. (Photos are at Safdie's website, www.msafdie.com.)

Walk to your right. The little triangular concrete building you see is the entrance to **Parc des Ecluses (Locks Park),** a canal-side

path where the St. Lawrence River's first locks are located.

From here, you have several options: If the weather's nice, consider entering the Parc des Ecluses to stroll the path along **Lachine Canal.** In an hour or less, you'll arrive at Montréal's colorful **Marché Atwater** (p. 154). If you walk the other direction, you'll take in the busiest section of the waterfront park and end up back at Place Jacques-Cartier.

To get to the subway, walk north along rue McGill to the Square-Victoria Métro station, the staircase to which is marked by an authentic Art Nouveau portal, designed by Hector Guimard for the Paris subway system.

Or, return to the small streets parallel to rue St-Paul, where you'll find more boutiques and one of the highest concentrations of art galleries in Canada.

WALKING TOUR 2   DOWNTOWN

START:	Bonaventure Métro station.
FINISH:	Musée des Beaux-Arts and rue Crescent.
TIME:	1½ hours.
BEST TIMES:	Weekdays in the morning or after 2pm, when the streets hum with big-city vibrancy but aren't *too* busy.
WORST TIMES:	Weekdays from noon to 2pm, when the streets, stores, and restaurants are crowded with businesspeople on lunch-break errands; Monday, when museums are closed; and Sunday, when many stores are closed and the area is nearly deserted.

After a tour of Vieux-Montréal, a look around the commercial heart of the 21st-century city will highlight the ample contrast between these two areas. To see the city at its contemporary best, take the Métro to the Bonaventure stop to start this tour.

After you've emerged from the Métro station, the dramatic skyscraper immediately to the west is:

❶ 1000 rue de la Gauchetière

This newer contribution to downtown Montréal's already memorable skyline is easily identified by its copper-and-blue pyramidal top, which rises to the maximum height permitted by the municipal building code. Inside, past an atrium planted with live trees, is an indoor skating rink (see p. 115).

Walk west on rue de la Gauchetière. Ahead is Le Marriott Château Champlain, whose distinctive facade of half-moon windows inspired its nickname "the Cheese Grater." Turn right on rue de la Cathedrale, heading north. At the next corner, you reach:

❷ Boulevard René-Lévesque

Formerly Dorchester Boulevard, this primary street was renamed in 1988 following the death of René-Lévesque, the Parti Québécois leader who led the movement for Québec independence and the use of the French

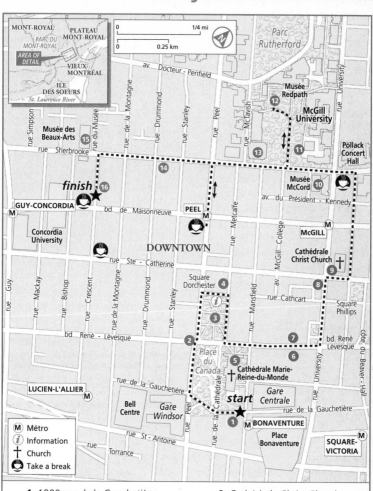

MONTRÉAL STROLLS

9

DOWNTOWN

1 1000 rue de la Gauchetière

2 Boulevard René-Lévesque

3 Square Dorchester

4 Montréal's central tourist office

5 Basilique-Cathédrale Marie-Reine-du-Monde

6 Fairmont The Queen Elizabeth (Le Reine Elizabeth)

7 Place Ville-Marie

8 Rue Ste-Catherine

9 Cathédrale Christ Church

10 Musée McCord

11 McGill University

12 Musée Redpath

13 Site of the Amerindian Hochelaga settlement

14 Maison Alcan

15 Musée des Beaux-Arts (Museum of Fine Arts)

16 Rue Crescent

language. Boulevard René-Lévesque is the city's broadest downtown thoroughfare.

Across bd. René-Lévesque is:

❸ **Square Dorchester**

This is one of downtown's central locations. It's a gathering point for tour buses and horse-drawn calèches, and the square's tall, old trees and benches invite lunchtime brown-baggers. This used to be called Dominion Square, but it was renamed for Baron Dorchester, an early English governor, when the adjacent street, once named for Dorchester, was changed to boulevard René-Lévesque. Along the square's east side is the **Sun Life Insurance building,** built in three stages between 1914 and 1931, and the tallest building in Québec from 1931 until the skyscraper boom of the post–World War II era.

At the north end of the square is:

❹ **Montréal's Central Tourist Office**

The Infotouriste Centre at 1255 rue Peel provides maps and brochures, most of them free for the taking. Visitors can also ask questions of the bilingual attendants, purchase tour tickets, make hotel reservations, or rent a car. Open daily.

On bd. René-Lévesque at the corner of Square Dorchester is the:

❺ **Basilique-Cathédrale Marie-Reine-du-Monde**

Suddenly get the feeling you're in Rome? This cathedral is a copy of St. Peter's Basilica, albeit roughly one-quarter of the size. It was built as the headquarters for Montréal's Roman Catholic bishop. The statue in front is of Bishop Ignace Bourget (1799–1885), the force behind it. See p. 110 for more details.

Continue on bd. René-Lévesque past the cathedral. In the next block, on the right, is:

❻ **Fairmont The Queen Elizabeth (Le Reine Elizabeth)**

Montréal's largest hotel (p. 64) stands above **Gare Centrale,** the main railroad station. There are buses to and from Montréal-Trudeau airport from here. The

Fairmont is where John Lennon and Yoko Ono had their famous weeklong "Bed-in for Peace" in 1969.

On the other side of bd. René-Lévesque, directly across from the hotel, is:

❼ **Place Ville-Marie**

One thing to keep in mind is that the French word "place," or "plaza," sometimes means an outdoor square, such as Place Jacques-Cartier in Vieux- Montréal. Other times, it refers to an indoor building or complex that includes stores and offices. Place Ville-Marie is in the later category. Known as PVM to Montréalers, the glass building was considered a gem of the 1960s urban redevelopment efforts. Its architect? None other than I. M. Pei, who also designed the glass pyramid at the Louvre in Paris. Pei gave the skyscraper a cross-shaped footprint, recalling the cross atop Mont Royal. The complex was completed in 1962.

Continue on bd. René-Lévesque to the end of the block and turn left on rue University. As you walk, look to the top of the skyscraper a few blocks down; this pink, postmodern glass office building is Tour KPMG and was completed in 1987. The two-peaked top is meant to resemble a bishop's mitre, or cap, but many see the ears and mask of a certain DC Comics superhero; see if you can tell which one. In 2 blocks you'll reach:

❽ **Rue Ste-Catherine**

This is one of the city's prime shopping streets, with name brands, local businesses, and department stores. Among them, to the right, is **La Baie**—or "the Bay"—successor to the famous fur-trapping firm Hudson's Bay Co., founded in the 17th century. Also here is **Henry Birks et Fils,** a preeminent jeweler since 1879—the building alone is worth taking in (see "Department Stores," p. 153).

If you're in the mood to shop, stroll west on this main shopping drag. (Be aware that there are adult shops here, too.) To continue the tour, return to this corner and the:

❾ **Cathédrale Christ Church**

Built from 1856 to 1859, this neo-Gothic building is the seat of the Anglican bishop of Montréal. The church garden is modeled on a medieval European cloister. In addition to Sunday's 10am Choral Eucharist and 4pm Choral Evensong, the church has services at noon and 5:15pm weekdays. See p. 111.

Walk east on rue Ste-Catherine to av. Union, where the La Baie department store is. Turn left on av. Union and go north 3 blocks, to rue Sherbrooke. You'll be in front of McGill University's Schulich School of Music.

> **TAKE A BREAK**
> At the corner of Union and Sherbrooke is an outpost of the cheery **Java U** (626 rue Sherbrooke), a local coffee chain that got its start in 1996 at Concordia University. It's a high-design venue with friendly, laid-back staff, serving quiches, salads, wraps, cake, and ice cream from local master purveyor Bilboquet.

Head left (west) on rue Sherbrooke. This is the city's grand boulevard, and the rest of the tour will take you past the former mansions, ritzy hotels, high-end boutiques, and special museums that give it its personality today. One block down on the left is:

⑩ Musée McCord

This museum of Canadian history opened in 1921 and was substantially renovated in 1992. Named for its founder, David Ross McCord (1844–1930), the museum maintains an eclectic collection of photographs, paintings, and First Nations folk art. Its special exhibits make it especially worth a visit. Hours and other details are on p. 103.

Continue west. On your right is:

⑪ McGill University

The gate is usually open to Canada's most prestigious university. It was founded after a bequest from a Scottish-born fur trader, James McGill. The central campus mixes modern concrete and glass structures alongside older stone buildings and is the focal point for the school's 34,000 students.

On campus is the:

⑫ Musée Redpath

Housed in a building dating from 1882, this museum's main draws are the mummies in its Egyptian antiquities collection (p. 118).

Continue on rue Sherbrooke. About 9m (30 ft.) past McGill's front gate, note the large stone on the lawn. This marks the:

⑬ Site of the Amerindian Hochelaga Settlement

Near this spot was the village of Hochelaga, a community of Iroquois who lived and farmed here before the first Europeans arrived. When French explorer Jacques Cartier stepped from his ship onto the land and visited Hochelaga in 1535, he noted that the village had 50 large homes, each housing several families. When the French returned in 1603, the village was empty.

> **TAKE A BREAK**
> Downtown is full of restaurants both fancy and casual. Right in between is **Café Vasco Da Gama** (1472 rue Peel, 1 block south rue Sherbrooke), a sleek, high-ceilinged eatery with a Portuguese feel (the owners also run the esteemed Ferreira Café, p. 81, on the same block). It features big breakfasts, pastries, sandwiches, and tapas.

2 blocks farther down on rue Sherbrooke, at no. 1188, just past rue Stanley, is:

⑭ Maison Alcan

Rue Sherbrooke is the heart of what's known as the "Golden Square Mile." This is where the city's most luxurious residences of the 19th and early 20th centuries were, and where the vast majority of the country's wealthiest citizens lived. (For a period of time, 79 families who lived in this neighborhood controlled 80% of Canada's wealth.) Look across the street at Maison Louis-Joseph Forget at no. 1195 and Maison Reid Wilson at no 1201, both designated historic monuments. Maison Alcan is an example of an office building that has nicely incorporated one of those 19th-century mansions into its late-20th-century facade. Step inside the lobby to see the results over to the right.

Continue on rue Sherbrooke, passing on your left the Holt Renfrew department store, identified on the side of its marquee only as HR. At the corner of rue Crescent is the:

⓯ Musée des Beaux-Arts (Museum of Fine Arts)

This is Canada's oldest museum, and Montréal's most prominent. The modern annex on the left side of rue Sherbrooke was added in 1991 and is connected to the original stately Beaux Arts building (1912) on the right side by an underground tunnel that doubles as a gallery. Both buildings are made of Vermont marble. See p. 102 for details.

There are several options at this point. If you have time to explore the museum, take the opportunity— a visit to the Musée des Beaux-Arts should be part of any trip to Montréal. For high-end boutique shopping, continue on rue Sherbrooke. For drinking or eating, turn left onto:

⓰ Rue Crescent

Welcome to party central. Rue Crescent and nearby streets are the locus of the downtown social and dining district. The area is largely yuppie-Anglo in character, if not necessarily in strict demographics. Crescent's first block is stocked with boutiques and jewelers, but the next 2 blocks are a gumbo of terraced bars and dance clubs, inexpensive pizza joints, and upscale restaurants, all drawing enthusiastic consumers looking to party the afternoon and evening away.

It's hard to imagine that this center of gilded youth was once a run-down slum slated for demolition. Luckily, buyers with good aesthetic sense saw potential in these late-19th-century row houses and brought them back to life.

TAKE A BREAK
Lively spots for food and drink are abundant along rue Crescent. **Thursday's** (no. 1449, in L'Hôtel de la Montagne) is one, if you can find a seat on the balcony.

For a satisfying snack, head to the unassuming Lebanese joint **Boustan** (no. 2020) for a filling *shawarma* sandwich. That's former Canadian Prime Minster Pierre Trudeau's photo at the register; he was a regular.

WALKING TOUR 3   **PLATEAU MONT-ROYAL**

START:	The corner of avenue du Mont-Royal and rue St-Denis.
FINISH:	Square St-Louis or Parc LaFontaine.
TIME:	At least 2 hours, but allow more time if you want to linger in shops, restaurants, or the major park of this intriguing neighborhood.
BEST TIMES:	Monday through Saturday during the day, when shops are open. Most of this area is at its liveliest on Saturday. For barhopping, evenings work well.
WORST TIMES:	Early mornings, when stores and restaurants are closed.

This is essentially a browsing and grazing tour, designed to provide a sampling of the sea of ethnicities that make up Plateau Mont-Royal, north of downtown Montréal and east of Mont-Royal Park. The largely Francophone neighborhood has seen an unprecedented flourishing of restaurants, cafes, clubs, and shops in recent years. It's bounded on the south by rue Sherbrooke, on the north by boulevard St-Joseph (where the Mile End neighborhood begins), on the west by boulevard St-Laurent, and on the east by avenue Papineau. The residential side streets are filled with row houses that are home to students, young professionals, and immigrants old and new. This walk provides a glance into the lives of both established and freshly minted Montréalers and the ways in which they

spend their leisure time. Stores and bistros open and close with considerable frequency **137**
in this neighborhood, so be forewarned that some of the highlights listed below may not
exist when you visit.

To begin, take the Métro to the Mont-Royal station. Turn
left out of the station and walk west on av. du Mont-
Royal to rue St-Denis. Turn left again onto rue St-Denis;
the next 4 blocks are filled with some of the best local
boutique shopping and Francophone dining in the city.
On the left side of the street, at 4481 rue St-Denis, is:

❶ Quai des Brumes

This popular gathering spot for electronic,
rock, jazz, and blues music—and beer—
offers live music on most evenings.

Stroll down rue St-Denis, pausing at shops and cafes
that fill the two stories of the small buildings.
Toward the end of the block, on the other side of the
street, is no. 4380 (but don't cross midstreet; police
give tickets for jaywalking):

❷ Renaud-Bray

A large bookstore with mostly French
stock, it also carries travel guides and lit-
erature in English, as well as CDs, magazines, and newspapers from around the
world. Most of the books are upstairs. It's
open daily from 9am until 10pm.

Continue south on rue St-Denis. On the next block, at
no. 4306, is:

❸ Départ en Mer

This small shop with "antiquitiés marines"
carries model ships, boating clothes, and
shoes.

In the same block, at no. 4268, is:

❹ Jacob

With pop music through the speakers and
a steady stream of locals, this clothing
store is part of the popular Canadian chain
where you'll find inexpensive T-shirts,
denim jackets, and other casual clothes for
the under-30 set.

A little farther, at no. 4246, is:

❺ Zone

Zone is a small Montréal-based chain
(there are two other stores in the city and
one in Québec City) that specializes in
contemporary housewares, sleekly monochromatic and brightly hued.

A little farther still, at no. 4228, is:

❻ Bedo

Another Montréal-based chain, this one has
higher-end men's and women's designer
sportswear, with colorful blouses in the
C$60 range, fun dresses, and well-fit shirts.
This outlet is one of 10 in the city.

At the next intersection, rue Rachel, turn left for a short
diversion off of rue St-Denis. On your left at no. 485 is:

❼ Kanuk

One of Canada's top manufacturers of winter coats and accessories designs, sews, and
sells its wares right here. Kanuk first sold its
heavy parkas primarily to outdoor enthusiasts. Back then, the company wryly notes
on its website, customers had a choice of
royal blue or royal blue. Today, jackets
come in 36 colors and 70 models. The
showroom's fluorescent lighting and mile-
high racks do not suggest luxury, but a
parka can set you back C$600 to C$900.
They're a popular practical necessity—and
a status symbol.

> **TAKE A BREAK**
> If you haven't yet tried *poutine*,
> the national comfort food, by all
> means hop into **La Banquise,** at 995 rue
> Rachel est. The restaurant is practically a
> city landmark, what with its 25 variations
> on *poutine:* the standard french fries with
> gravy and cheese curds are offered with
> add-ons ranging from smoked sausage to
> hot peppers to smoked meat to bacon. It's
> open 24 hours a day, every day.

Just beyond the restaurant is the grand:

❽ Parc La Fontaine

Strolling this park, particularly on a warm
day, is an enormously satisfying way to see
Montréal at play. This northwestern end

of La Fontaine is well used by people (and puppies) of all ages.

In summer, the 2,500-seat **Théâtre de Verdure,** near where rue Duluth runs into the park, becomes an open-air venue for dance, music, theater, and film. In winter, the two ponds are linked and turned into a skating rink (skate rentals available).

There's a bike-rental shop at this corner just before you enter the park, at 1000 rue Rachel est (www. cyclepop.ca). If you're keen to explore the park or head off for a bike ride, consider this tour done. The Sherbrooke Métro will be closest if you leave the park on its west side. To continue the stroll, retrace your steps to go back to rue St-Denis. Turn left and continue south. Among the boutiques still to explore, at 4117 rue St-Denis, is:

9 Artéfact Montréal
Québécois designers sell clothing and paintings at this bright little boutique, where a slip of a summer dress runs about C$250.

After that, find no. 4107:

10 Kaliyana
More women's clothes from a Canadian designer: This shop's natural-fiber outfits are flowing, angular, and border on being avant-garde—think Asian-influenced Eileen Fisher. It also stocks contemporary footwear including Arche from France and Trippen from Germany.

At 4077 rue St-Denis, you'll come upon:

11 Senteurs de Provence
One of a small chain, this store displays hand-painted pottery and printed linens, as well as soaps, shower gels, and lotions of high order, all from France.

At no. 4067, take a whiff of:

12 Lush
On the ground floor of one of the street's prettiest Queen Anne Victorian row houses, Lush sells soaps presented and wrapped as if they were aromatic, bubble-gum-colored hunks of cheese.

At the next corner is rue Duluth. Turn right here to get a taste of:

13 Rue Duluth
This street is dotted with an ever-changing collection of Greek, Portuguese, Italian, North African, Malaysian, and Vietnamese eateries. Many of the restaurants state that you can *apportez votre vin* (bring your own wine). There are also several small antiques shops.

Continue along rue Duluth until bd. St-Laurent, the north-south thoroughfare that divides Montréal into its east and west sides. Turn left.

14 Boulevard St-Laurent
St-Laurent is so prominent in Montréal's cultural history that it's known to Anglophones, Francophones, and Allophones (people whose primary language is neither English nor French) alike simply as "the Main." Traditionally a beachhead for immigrants to the city, St-Laurent has become a street of chic bistros and clubs. The late-night section runs for several miles, roughly from rue Laurier in the north all the way down to rue Sherbrooke in the south. The bistro and club boom was fueled by low rent prices and the large number of industrial lofts in this area, a legacy of St-Laurent's heyday as a garment-manufacturing center. Today, these cavernous spaces are places for the city's hipsters, professionals, artists, and guests to eat and play. Many spots have the life spans of fireflies, but some pound on for years.

At 3895 bd. St-Laurent, you'll find:

15 Schwartz's
The language police insisted on the exterior sign with the French mouthful CHEZ SCHWARZ CHARCUTERIE HEBRAIQUE DE MONTREAL, but everyone just calls it Schwartz's (p. 95). This narrow, no-frills Hebrew deli might appear completely unassuming, but it serves smoked meat against which all other smoked meats must be measured. Don't forget a side of fries and a couple of garlicky pickles.

MONTRÉAL STROLLS

9

PLATEAU MONT-ROYAL

1 Quai des Brumes
2 Renaud-Bray
3 Départ en Mer
4 Jacob
5 Zone
6 Bedo
7 Kanuk
8 Parc La Fontaine
9 Artéfact
10 Kaliyana
11 Senteurs de Provence
12 Lush
13 Rue Duluth
14 Boulevard St-Laurent
15 Schwartz's
16 La Vieille Europe
17 Rue Prince-Arthur
18 Square St-Louis

Next, a few steps along at no. 3855, is:

⑯ La Vieille Europe
An old-Europe deli that sells aromatic coffee beans from around the world, sausages and meats, cheeses, cooking utensils, and other gourmet fare. Stock up here if you're thinking of having a picnic in the next day or two.

Continue down bd. St-Laurent 2 more blocks and turn left (east) onto:

⑰ Rue Prince-Arthur
Named after Queen Victoria's third son, who was governor-general of Canada from 1911 to 1916, this pedestrian street is filled with bars and restaurants that add more to the area's liveliness than to the city's gastronomic reputation. The older establishments go by such names as La Cabane Grecque, La Caverne Grec, Casa Grecque—no doubt you will discern an emerging theme—but the Greek stalwarts

are being challenged by Latino and Asian newcomers. Their owners vie for customers constantly, with such gimmicks as two-for-one drinks and dueling *tables d'hôte*. Tables and chairs are set out along the sides of the street, and in warm weather, street performers, vendors, and caricaturists also compete for tourist dollars.

Five short blocks later, rue Prince-Arthur ends at:

⑱ Square St-Louis
This public garden plaza is framed by attractive row houses erected for well-to-do Francophones in the late 19th and early 20th centuries. People stretch out on the grass to take in the sun, or sit bundled on benches willing March away (there often are a few harmless derelicts among them). The square ends at rue St-Denis.

To pick up the Métro, cross rue St-Denis and walk east on rue des Malines. The Sherbrooke station is just ahead at the corner of rue Berri.

WALKING TOUR 4	PARC DU MONT-ROYAL

START:	At the corner of rue Peel and av. des Pins.
FINISH:	At the cross on top of the mountain (la Croix du Mont-Royal).
TIME:	1 hour to ascend to the Chalet du Mont-Royal and its lookout over the city and come back down by the fastest route; 3 hours to take the more leisurely chemin Olmstead route and see all the sites listed below. It's easy to leave out some sites to truncate the walk.
BEST TIMES:	Spring, summer, and autumn mornings.
WORST TIMES:	During the high heat of midday in summer, or in winter, when snow and slush make a sleigh ride to the top of the mountain much more enticing than a hike.

Join the locals: Assuming a reasonable measure of physical fitness, the best way to explore the jewel that is Parc du Mont-Royal is simply to walk up it from downtown. It's called a mountain but is more like a very large hill. A broad pedestrian-only road and smaller footpaths form a web of options for strollers, joggers, cyclists, and in-line skaters of all ages. Anyone in search of a little greenery and space heads here in warm weather, while in winter, cross-country skiers follow miles of paths and snowshoers tramp along trails laid out especially for them.

The 200-hectare (494-acre) urban park was created in 1876 by American landscape architect Frederick Law Olmsted, who also designed Central Park in New York City and parks in Philadelphia, Boston, and Chicago (although in the end, relatively little of Olmsted's full design for Mont Royal actually came into being). If you're carrying a PDA or a phone with Internet access, you can pull up a terrific interactive map at **www.lemontroyal.qc.ca/carte/en/index.sn**. You can also download podcasts for guided audio-video walks at the same URL.

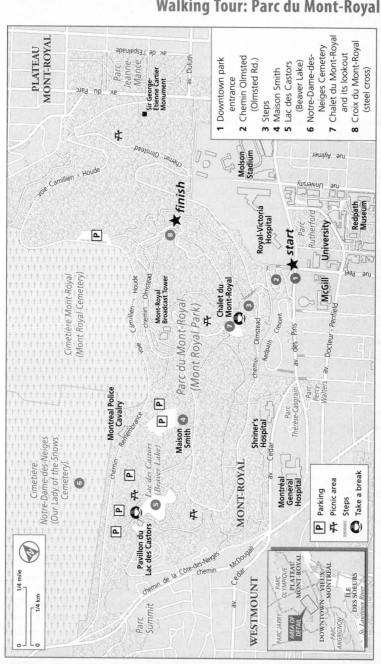

1 Downtown park entrance
2 Chemin Olmsted (Olmsted Rd.)
3 Steps
4 Maison Smith
5 Lac des Castors (Beaver Lake)
6 Notre-Dame-des-Neiges Cemetery
7 Chalet du Mont-Royal and its lookout
8 Croix du Mont-Royal (steel cross)

MONTREAL STROLLS

9

PARC DU MONT-ROYAL

Destination: Antique Alley & Marché Atwater

This is a great walk to take if you 1) are in Vieux-Montréal and want to get outside the tourist orbit into a nearby interesting neighborhood; 2) like antiques shops; 3) are looking for a stroll that concludes (preferably at lunchtime) at one of the city's great farmers' markets.

The walk itself is simple: Start in Vieux-Montréal on rue Notre-Dame and head west. Stay on rue Notre-Dame. About an hour later, if you don't make many stops, you'll reach **Marché Atwater,** a farmer's market that in summer is lined with stalls and stalls of fresh fruit, vegetables, flowers, and snacks, as well as cheese and meat shops, cafes, and food stores that stay open year-round. From rue McGill, the street at the western side of Vieux-Montréal, the walk is about 3km (2 miles). There is a subway stop near the market for your return.

You first come upon a tangle of highways, where the downtown skyline is displayed in a great expanse. After that are some of the city's newer (and then older) condominium complexes.

After about 20 minutes, at rue Guy, the gentrified "Antique Alley" begins. Little shops door to door on the next few streets are chockablock with every kind of high- and low-end antique under the sun. Vegetarians will also want to note **Bonnys,** at no. 1748 (℡ **514/931-4136**), where options can include lasagna with tofu ricotta or black bean chili with quinoa and sweet potato. It's open weekdays 11am to 9pm, and Saturdays noon to 8pm.

Milord Antiques (℡ **514/933-2433;** www.milordantiques.com) at no. 1870 specializes in classically designed European furniture from the 18th and 19th centuries and features a notable collection of marble mantles. Pop in and grab a copy of the *Antiques Art Galleries* guidebook for free—it prints ads for many of the shops on this street. A few doors down, at no. 1896, is **L'Ecuyer Antiques** (℡ **514/932-8461**) which sells vintage suitcases, canes, and other goodies.

The antiquing stops for a few blocks but picks up again at rue Vinet. On this same block are some of the city's culinary highlights. At no. 2491 is the

Start at the corner of rue Peel and av. des Pins, at the:

❶ Downtown Park Entrance

Note that this entrance has been under construction; normally a map at the site helps to set bearings. From here, it's possible to reach the top of this small mountain by a variety of routes. Hearty souls can choose the quickest and most strenuous approach—taking the steepest sets of stairs at every opportunity, which go directly to the Chalet du Mont-Royal and its lookout at the top (see no. 7). Those who prefer to take their time and gain

altitude slowly can use the switchback bridle path. Or mix and match the options as you go along. Don't be too worried about getting lost; the park is small enough that it's easy to regain your sense of direction no matter which way you head.

Head up either footpath from the entrance (the paths are not particularly well maintained here, but improve the further up you go). You'll soon reach the broad bridle path:

❷ Chemin Olmsted (Olmsted Road)

Frederick Law Olmsted designed this road, which is closed to automobiles, at a seafood-and-meat neighborhood joint **Joe Beef** (© 514/935-6504) and two new adjacent operations run by the same folks: **Liverpool House** (no. 2501), an Italian gastropub, and the **McKiernan** luncheonette and wine bar (no. 2485). See p. 101 for restaurant info. Graphic-design fans will appreciate the old-fashioned type used by all three properties with the oversight of typographer Glenn Goluska.

In the next block, **itsi bitsi,** at no. 2621 (© 514/509-3926; www.itsi-bitsi.com) sells designer cupcakes and gelato, in flavors like *mojito* and chocolate-wasabi. You can get a killer cup of coffee at no. 2695, **Toi et Moi Café** (© 514/788-9599; www.toimoicafe.com), or an egg breakfast, at no. 2745 **Quoi de N'Oeuf** (© 514/931-3999). Or just to save your appetite for the grand finale…

Montréal has **Marché Atwater,** at 138 av. Atwater (near the corner of rue Notre-Dame), www.marche-atwater.com, the way Barcelona has its Boqueria market and Venice has the Rialto fish market. The Atwater market has been in business since 1933 and is housed in an Art Deco–style brick tower building.

One of the must-sees is **Première-Moisson** (© 514/932-0328; www.premieremoisson.com). It uses wheat flour made from wheat grown in Québec, but even without the local angle it's easy to be drawn into the bakery's orbit, with its cases of pastries and cakes. Look for the Piquant Truffé, a many-peaked concoction dusted with chocolate. In the rest of the market, more than a dozen butchers and cheese shops do business alongside boutiques selling gourmet packaged goods, *bonbons au miel* (honey drops), and high-end condiments. Small Parisian-style tables are peppered throughout the complex. Even the pizza is worth traveling for, piled high with fresh mozzarella and veggies. In the warm months, the market is flush with fresh fruit and vegetables.

The Lionel-Groulx Métro stop is only 3 blocks away, north on rue Atwater. The paths of the Lachine Canal are just a few blocks south, where kayak and pedal boat rentals are available in summer (p. 124).

gradual grade for horse-drawn carriages. Horses could pull their loads up the hill at a steady pace, and on the way down would not be pushed from behind by the weight of the carriage.

Early on, the road passes some beautiful stone houses off Redpath Circle, to the left. If you want to bypass some of the switchbacks, use any of a number of paths for a shortcut—but stay only on established trails to prevent erosion.

After about the fourth switchback, you'll reach an intersection with the option to go left or right. Turn left. Following this shaded, pleasant road in the woods will get you to Maison Smith (see no. 4) in about 45 minutes.

Another option is to take the:
❸ **Stairs**
There are numerous sets of stairs through the woods that let you bypass chemin Olmstead's broad switchbacks. These steps get walkers to the Chalet du Mont-Royal and its lookout (see no. 7) more quickly.

Fair warning: The last 100 or so steps go almost straight up. On the plus side, you'll get to share sympathetic smiles with strangers. Taking the steps bypasses sites no. 4, 5, and 6.

If you're taking chemin Olmsted, you eventually arrive at:

❹ Maison Smith

Built in 1858, this structure has been used as a park rangers' station and park police headquarters. Today, it's a year-round information center with a small exhibit about the park and a gift shop. **Café Smith,** a terrace restaurant, offers soups, sandwiches, beverages, and sweets.

From Maison Smith, walk through the field of sculptures, away from the radio tower, until you reach:

❺ Lac des Castors (Beaver Lake)

This lake's name refers to the once-profitable fur industry, not to the actual presence of the long-gone animals. In summer, it's surrounded by sunbathers and picnickers, and you can rent a paddleboat. In the winter it becomes an ice skater's paradise and, after the snow, a cross-country ski retreat.

TAKE A BREAK
Le Pavillon (☏ 514/849-2002) is a French restaurant that looks out on Beaver Lake. Run by the Holder brothers (who are behind the popular **Holder** restaurant in Vieux-Montréal), it features lobster bisque, duck confit salad, and steak. There's also a more modest cafeteria on-site, an area for picnicking, and a rental office with skis, snowshoes, and skates.

Walk across the road behind the pavilion, called chemin de la Remembrance (Remembrance Rd.), to enter:

❻ Notre-Dame-des-Neiges Cemetery

This is the city's predominantly Catholic cemetery, and from here you can visit the adjacent Protestant Mount Royal graveyard. Behind it (to the north), if you're up for a longer walk, is the small adjoining Jewish and Spanish-Portuguese cemetery.

Notre-Dame-des-Neiges Cemetery reveals much about Montréal's ethnic mix: Headstones, some with likenesses in photos or tiles, are engraved with surnames as diverse as Zagorska, Skwyrska, De Ciccio, Sen, Lavoie, O'Neill, Hammerschmid, Fernandez, Müller, Haddad, and Boudreault.

If you've had enough walking, find a no. 11 bus on chemin de la Remembrance that heads east toward the Guy Métro station. To continue the tour, head back to Maison Smith and follow the signs on the main path for:

❼ Chalet du Mont-Royal & Its Lookout

The front terrace here offers the most popular panoramic view of the city and the river. The chalet itself was constructed from 1931 to 1932 and has been used over the years for receptions, concerts, and various other events. Inside the chalet, take a look at the 17 paintings hanging just below the ceiling, starting to the right of the door that leads into the snack bar. They relate the region's history and the story of the French explorations of North America. In winter, there's a warming room for skiers.

TAKE A BREAK
The **Chalet du Mont-Royal** is usually open from 9am to 8pm daily and has vending machines with beverages and light snacks. Heed the signs that ask patrons to refrain from feeding the squirrels, no matter how adorably they're begging.

Facing the chalet from the terrace, locate the path running off to the right, marked by a sign that says croix. **Follow it for about 10 minutes to the giant:**

❽ Croix du Mont-Royal

Legend has it that Paul de Chomedey, Sieur de Maisonneuve (1612–76), erected a wooden cross here in 1643 after the young colony survived a flood threat. The present incarnation of the Croix du Mont-Royal, installed in 1924, is lit at night and visible from all over the city.

Beside the cross is a plaque marking where a time capsule was interred in August 1992, during Montréal's 350th-birthday celebration. Some 12,000 children ages 6 to 12 filled the capsule with messages and drawings depicting their visions for the city in the year 2142, when Montréal will be 500 years old and the capsule will be opened.

To return to downtown Montréal, go back along the path to the chalet terrace. On the left, just before the terrace, is another path. It leads to the staircase described in no. 3 and descends to where the tour began. The walk down by this route takes about 15 minutes. The no. 11 bus also runs from the summit to the Mont-Royal Métro, and there are buses at Beaver Lake and along chemin de la Remembrance.

10

Montréal Shopping

You can shop in Montréal until your feet swell and your eyes cross. Whether you view shopping as a focus of your travels or simply as a diversion, you won't be disappointed. Among natives, shopping ranks right up there with dining out as a prime activity. Most Montréalers are of French ancestry, after all, and seem to believe that impeccable taste bubbles through the Gallic gene pool. The city has produced a thriving fashion industry, from couture to ready-to-wear, with a history that reaches back to the earliest trade in furs and leather. More than 1,700 shops populate the underground city alone, and many more than that are at street level and above. It is unlikely that any reasonable consumer need—or even outlandish fantasy—cannot be met here.

1 THE SHOPPING SCENE

When you're making purchases with a credit card, the charges are automatically converted at the going bank rate before appearing on your monthly statement. In most cases, this is the best deal of all for visitors. Visa and MasterCard are the most popular credit cards in this part of Canada. Many shops accept American Express. Discover is accepted less frequently.

Most stores are open from 9 or 10am to 6pm Monday through Wednesday, to 9pm on Thursday and Friday, and to 5pm on Saturday. Many stores are now also open on Sunday from noon to 5pm. Since November 2008, stores in downtown Montréal have been able to stay open until 8pm on Saturdays and Sundays, an 18-month change in law that's part of a government-sanctioned pilot project to stimulate tourism.

The Visitor Rebate Program, which used to allow nonresident visitors to apply for a tax rebate on items purchased in Québec, was eliminated in April 2007.

THE BEST BUYS

While not cheap, **Canadian Inuit sculptures** and 19th- to early-20th-century **country furniture** are handsome and authentic. Less expensive crafts than the intensely collected Inuit works are also available, including quilts, drawings, and carvings by Amerindian and other folk artists.

The province's daring **high fashion** designers produce appealing clothing at prices that are often reasonable. And while demand has diminished somewhat, superbly constructed **furs and leather goods** that recall Montréal's long history as part of the fur trade remain high-ticket items.

Ice cider *(cidre de glace)* and **ice wines** made in Québec province from apples and grapes left on trees and vines after the first frost are unique products to bring home. They're sold in duty-free shops at the border in addition to the stores listed at the end of this chapter.

Most international clothing items, including those by such big names as Burberry and Ralph Lauren, cost approximately what they would in other cities around the world.

THE BEST SHOPPING AREAS

In downtown, **rue Sherbrooke** is a major shopping street, with international and domestic designers, luxury shops, art galleries, and the Holt Renfrew department store.

Also downtown, **rue Ste-Catherine** is home to the city's top department stores and is the heart of midpriced shopping—it's the central commercial artery. From the cross street rue Aylmer, where the department store **La Baie** is located, traveling west to rue Mackay, Ste-Catherine offers a 12-block stretch of stores that includes jeweler **Henry Birks,** Tommy Hilfiger, Old Navy, **SAQ Signature,** Kiehl's, Banana Republic, **Simons, Mango,** HMV, **Roots,** Guess, H&M, Foot Locker, Jacob, Adidas, Benetton, **Ogilvy,** Apple, and Steve Madden—to name a sampling (shops in bold are discussed later in this chapter). Note that Ste-Catherine also has a smattering of adult strip clubs and sex shops right along side the family-friendly fare (there's a gigantic neon sign announcing Club Super Sexe, for instance). For better or for worse, the mixed use of the street is a Montréal signature.

Rue Peel, which crosses rue Ste-Catherine in about the middle of the shopping stretch noted above, is known for its men's fashions.

In Vieux-Montréal, the western end of **rue St-Paul** has an ever-growing number of art galleries, clothing boutiques, and jewelry shops. **Marché Bonsecours** on the eastern end of the same street is home to regular contemporary art exhibitions as well as boutiques selling high-end Québec-made crafts and clothing.

In Plateau Mont-Royal, **rue St-Denis** north of Sherbrooke has blocks of shops filled with fun, funky items; see p. 136 for a recommended stroll on St-Denis. **Boulevard St-Laurent** sells everything from budget practicalities to off-the-wall handmade fashions. And further north, **avenue Laurier,** between boulevard St-Laurent and avenue de l'Epée, is where to head for French boutiques, furniture and accessories shops, and products from the ateliers of young Québécois designers.

SHOPPING COMPLEXES & THE UNDERGROUND CITY

A unique shopping opportunity in Montréal is the **underground city,** also known, somewhat less dramatically, as the underground pedestrian network, and known officially as RESO. It's a warren of passageways connecting more than 1,700 shops in 10 shopping malls that have levels both above and below street level (p. 56). Typical is the **Complexe Desjardins** (© 514/845-4636; www.complexedesjardins.com), a downtown mall with entrances at street level and underground, bounded by rues Ste-Catherine, St-Urbain, and Jeanne-Mance and boulevard René-Lévesque. It has waterfalls and fountains, trees and hanging vines, music, lanes of shops going off in every direction, and elevators whisking people up to one of the three tall office towers.

Another intriguing hub is **Les Cours Mont-Royal** at 1455 rue Peel (© 514/842-7777; www.lcmr.ca), which also has entrances both at street level and underground. It feels like a regular mall on the "Métro level," where food courts, shoe shines, and scarf kiosks begin to repeat, but upstairs you'll find shops suitable for outfitting indie rock bands, at least ones that have sold (many) albums. Here C$300 jeans are *de rigueur* at independently-owned boutiques, sunglasses are worn indoors, and a giant chandelier harkens back to the building's former life as the Mont Royal Hotel.

Shoppers are likely to end up at some point in **Place Ville-Marie,** opposite Fairmont The Queen Elizabeth hotel, between boulevard René-Lévesque and Cathcart (© 514/861-9393; www.placevillemarie.com). This was Montréal's first major post–World War II shopping complex and is known locally as "PVM." It has some 80 boutiques and eateries.

A plaque honoring Vincent Ponte, who designed the underground city and died in 2006, is on the PVM esplanade.

The Montréal tourist office's *Official Tourist Guide,* available at tourist offices (p. 52), contains a map of the underground city. It can be difficult (but fun!) to navigate, as maps, signage, and even numbering of levels can differ from one section to the next. To retreat underground, ask for directions to the "Métro level" or look for blue signs with a white arrow pointing down. On occasion, you'll see signs marked RESO which indicate you are headed *souterrain.* Some complexes, including **Eaton Centre** (© **514/282-6792;** www.centreeatondemontreal.com), a central artery of the underground, have information desks and printed maps. The main thing to remember is that when you enter a street-level shopping emporium downtown, it's likely that you'll be able to head to a lower level and connect to the tunnels and shopping hallways that lead to another set of stores. It's also likely that the best way to reorient is by surfacing and using actual street signs and a city map.

2 SHOPPING FROM A TO Z

ANTIQUES

Some of the city's quirkier antiques shops have disappeared in recent years, thanks, in part, to eBay. But there are still tempting shops along **"Antique Alley,"** as it's nicknamed, on rue Notre-Dame west of Vieux-Montréal. They're especially concentrated between rue Guy and avenue Atwater. See p. 142 in chapter 9 for directions for an easy stroll to the area.

Antiques can also be found downtown along rue Sherbrooke near the Musée des Beaux-Arts, on the little side streets near the museum, and in the Village (the gay neighborhood described on p. 55) on rue Amherst.

ARTS, CRAFTS & GALLERIES

Some of Montréal's best crafts stores are in museums. See p. 155 for a listing of museum stores.

Atelier Entre-Peaux This company specializes in lightweight bags made from recycled billboards—all products, in fact, are produced from 75% to 95% recycled material, earning the business a spot on Recyc-Québec, the official government recycling industry website. The company is also officially appointed by the city of Montréal to transform all the banners posted on the city's street lamps. The bags are super-cool looking, too. Bike bags run about C$69 and can be found at **Galerie Zone Orange** (see below), the **Musée d'Art Contemporain Boutique** (p. 155, later), or the company website: www.entre-peaux-ecodesign.com.

Galerie Le Chariot Galleries that feature Inuit art are found throughout the city, but few are as accessibly located as Le Chariot, whose showroom is directly on the Place Jacques-Cartier, in the heart of Vieux-Montréal. Here shoppers can find handmade pieces by Inuk artists from Cape Dorset, Lake Harbour, and Baffin Island—carved bears, seals, owls, and tableaus of mothers and children. Pieces range in price from about C$150 to C$25,000 and are certified by the Canadian government. Think of it as a museum where you can buy the art. 446 Place Jacques-Cartier (in the center of the plaza), Vieux-Montréal. ©514/875-4994. www.galerielechariot.com.

Galerie Zone Orange   Angry sock monkeys, creative jewelry, and colorful ceramics from 30 regional artists are on display at the small Zone Orange, which also has a teeny espresso bar in its center. Perhaps the coolest products are the lightweight bags made from recycled billboards and street lamp banners by the eco-focused Atelier Entre-Peaux, a Montréal company; its bike bags run about C$69. 410 rue St-Pierre (near rue St-Paul), Vieux-Montréal. ℭ **514/510-5809.** www.galeriezoneorange.com.

Guilde Canadienne des Métiers d'Art ★   In English, it's called the Canadian Guild of Crafts. A small but choice collection of items is displayed in a meticulously arranged gallery setting. Among the objects are blown glass, silk paintings, pewter, tapestries, wooden bowls, and ceramics. The store is particularly strong in avant-garde jewelry and Inuk sculpture. A small carving might be had for C$100 to C$300, while larger, more important pieces go for hundreds, and even thousands, more. 1460 rue Sherbrooke ouest (near rue Mackay), downtown. ℭ **866/477-6091.** www.canadianguild.com.

La Guilde Graphique   Contemporary artists are represented here, working with a variety of media and techniques, but primarily producing works on paper, including drawings, serigraphs, etchings, lithographs, and woodcut prints. 9 rue St-Paul ouest (at bd. St-Laurent), Vieux-Montréal. ℭ **514/844-3438.** www.guildegraphique.com.

L'Empreinte   This is a *coopérative artisane* (a craftspersons' collective). The ceramics, textiles, glassware, and other items on sale often occupy that vaguely defined territory between art and craft. Quality is uneven but usually tips toward the high end. 272 rue St-Paul est (next to Marché Bonsecours), Vieux-Montréal. ℭ **877/861-4427.** www.lempreinte coop.com.

Les Artisans du Meuble Québécois   A mix of crafts, jewelry, and other objects makes this an intriguing stop in Vieux-Montréal. Among the possibilities are handmade clothing and accessories for women, greeting cards, woven goods, and items for the home. 88 rue St-Paul est (near Place Jacques-Cartier), Vieux-Montréal. ℭ **514/866-1836.**

Salon des Métiers d'Art du Québec   Since the 1950s, the salon has brought together masses of artisans into one space for the Christmas season. Some 450 exhibitors sell original, handmade, and exclusive creations for gift-givers, and nearly 200,000 people visit each year. It takes place daily for about 2 weeks in mid-December. Place Bonaventure, downtown. No phone number. www.salondesmetiersdart.com.

Yves Laroche Galerie d'Art   High art meets punk rock and comic-book culture. The large paintings and prints on display here include works by Shepard Fairey, the American artist who designed both the beautiful Obama graphic that became the signature image of the 2008 U.S. presidential campaign and the obnoxiously ubiquitous OBEY stickers, which are posted illegally all over the U.S. Also on display are works by Kathie Olivas and Brandt Peters, who depict grim-faced doll figures in horror-show-meets-Looney-Tunes situations. The store sells graphic novels and collectible figurines as well. Its blog-style website is engaging. 4 rue St-Paul est (at bd. St-Laurent), Viuex-Montréal. ℭ **514/393-1999.** www.yveslaroche.com.

BATH & BODY

Spa Dr. Hauschka   High-end pampering and getting "in touch with your inner beauty" is the goal of this chichi spa in a rue Sherbrooke brownstone. On-site treatments include facials, lavender baths, volcanic mud baths, and more. You can also buy the Dr. Hauschka products to indulge at home. 1444 rue Sherbrooke ouest (at rue Redpath), downtown. ℭ **514/286-1444.** www.spadrhauschka.com.

BOOKS

As is the case with arts and crafts, some of Montréal's best bookstores are in the city's museums.

Canadian Centre for Architecture Bookstore A comprehensive selection of books about architecture, with an emphasis on Montréal in particular and Canada in general. Volumes are also available on landscape and garden history, photography, preservation, conservation, design, and city planning. 1920 rue Baile (at rue du Fort), downtown. ✆ 514/939-7028. www.cca.qc.ca/bookstore.

Chapters The flagship store of a chain with many branches is the result of a merger between Smithbooks and Coles booksellers. Thousands of titles are available in French and English. 1171 rue Ste-Catherine ouest (at rue Stanley), downtown. ✆ 514/849-8825. www.chapters.indigo.ca.

Indigo Livres, Musique & Café Occupying a street-level space in the Place Montréal Trust, this very complete sister store to Chapters (see above) sells music, books, magazines, and gifts, and operates a cafe upstairs. 1500 av. McGill College (at rue Ste-Catherine), downtown. ✆ 514/281-5549. www.chapters.indigo.ca.

Paragraphe This long storefront is popular with students from the McGill campus, which is a block away. The store hosts frequent author readings. 2220 av. McGill College (south of rue Sherbrooke). ✆ 514/845-5811. www.paragraphbooks.com.

Renaud-Bray Kids For those who know French or want to brush up, this two-level bookstore with a primarily French-language stock is a valuable resource. It also sells tapes, DVDs, CDs, and newspapers and magazines from all over the world. Most English-language books are on the upper floor. There's a large children's section, too. 4380 rue St-Denis (at rue Marie-Anne), Plateau Mont-Royal. ✆ 514/844-2587. www.renaud-bray.com.

CLOTHING
For Men

Eccetera & Co. Favoring ready-to-wear attire from such higher-end manufacturers as Baldessarini and Canali, this store lays out its stock in a soothing setting with personalized service. As it says on the door: GOOD CLOTHES OPEN ALL DOORS. 2021 rue Peel (near bd. de Maisonneuve), downtown. ✆ 514/845-9181. www.eccetera.ca.

Harry Rosen ★ For more than 50 years, this well-known retailer of designer suits and accessories has been making men look good in Armani, Dolce & Gabbana, and its own Harry Rosen Made in Italy line. The store's website features a nifty timeline of the shop's evolution from Toronto made-to-measure store to national leader in men's fashion. Les Cours Mont-Royal, 1455 rue Peel (at bd. de Maisonneuve), downtown. ✆ 514/284-3315. www.harryrosen.com.

L'Uomo Montréal ★ A top men's clothing boutique founded in 1980, L'Uomo mostly deals in Italian and other European menswear by such forward-thinking designers as Ermenegildo Zegna, Kiton, Prada, Avon Celli, and Borrelli. 1452 rue Peel (near rue Ste-Catherine), downtown. ✆ 514/844-1008. www.luomo-montreal.com.

For Women

Montréal Fashion Week happens every March. The 2009 event took place at the Marché Bonsecours and featured 20 Canadian designers including **Harricana** (p. 151); photos and links are online at www.montrealfashionweek.ca. The **Montréal Fashion &**

Design Festival happens on avenue de McGill College each June; see www.festivalmode design.com.

Aime Com Moi If you're heading north to the hipster bar Bílý Kůň (p. 168), build in time to stroll avenue du Mont-Royal, which is chock-full of new and used clothing. Among the shops is this one, which features fabulously funky dresses by Québécois designers. 150 av. du Mont-Royal est (3 blocks from bd. St-Laurent), Plateau Mont-Royal. ✆ 514/982-0088.

Ambre Cocktail dresses and casual wear made of linen, rayon, and cotton are featured in this small, centrally located shop. Shoppers might also find bold accessories to go with the clothes. 201 rue St-Paul ouest (at rue St-François-Xavier), Vieux-Montréal. ✆ 514/982-0325.

Artéfact Montréal Sold here are moderate to expensive articles of clothing by up-and-coming Québécois designers and artists. 4117 rue St-Denis (near rue Rachel), Plateau Mont-Royal. ✆ 514/842-2780.

Collection Méli Mélo (Finds) This shop used to feature furniture from sub-Saharan Africa. There's still some of that, but a shift in spring 2007 brought a new concentration: women's fashion by Montréal's chic designers, including Anastasia Lomonava. 205 rue St-Paul ouest (at rue St-François-Xavier), Vieux-Montréal. ✆ 514/285-5585. www.collectionmeli melo.com.

Fourrures Dubarry Furs Inc. Coats and capes in fur, shearling, cashmere, and leather, along with hats, earmuffs, purses, and scarves, are all on display at the family-run, high-end Dubarry Furs. 206 rue St-Paul ouest (at rue St-François-Xavier), Vieux-Montréal. ✆ 514/844-7483. www.dubarryfurs.com.

Giorgio Femme Ursula B Montréal's malls are peppered with boutiques featuring cutting-edge fashion from around the world, and Ursula B is one of the top options. Among the collections on the racks are Dolce & Gabbana, Malo, and Giambattista Valli. Les Cours Mont-Royal, 1455 rue Peel (at bd. de Maisonneuve), downtown. ✆ 514/282-0294. www.ursulab.com.

Harricana ★ One designer taking a unique cue from the city's long history with the fur trade is Mariouche Gagné, who was born on Île d'Orléans near Québec City in 1971. Her company recycles old fur into funky patchwork garments and uses the slogan "Made from your mother's old coat." A leader in the so-called ecoluxe movement, Gagné also recycles silk scarves, turning them into tops and skirts. Her boutique is close to the Marché Atwater (p. 154) and the Lionel-Groulx Métro station. 3000 rue St-Antoine ouest (at av. Atwater), west of Vieux-Montréal. ✆ 877/894-9919 or 514/287-6517. www.harricana.qc.ca.

Kaliyana ★ Vaguely Japanese and certainly minimalist, the free-flowing garments sold here are largely asymmetrical separates. Made by a Canadian designer, they come in muted tones of solid colors. Ask for "the kit" and you'll get six of Kaliyana's most popular pieces, apt foundation for a new wardrobe. Simple complementary necklaces and comfy but über-cool shoes available, too. 4107 rue St-Denis (near rue Rachel), Plateau Mont-Royal. ✆ 514/844-0633. www.kaliyana.com.

La Cache Clothes designed by Montréal-born April Cornell, with flowers, leaves, and birds as the recurring motifs, are among the offerings of this small Canadian chain. 1051 bd. Laurier ouest (2 blocks west of av. du Parc), Plateau Mont-Royal. ✆ 514/273-9700. www.lacache.ca.

Mango This was the first downtown outlet of an ever-growing Spanish-owned international chain. Much of its merchandise consists of upmarket jeans and tees. The dressier separates intrigue with quiet tones and jazzy cuts—very Euro. 1000 rue Ste-Catherine ouest (at rue Metcalfe), downtown. ✆ 514/397-2323. www.mango.com.

Moov Design Yoga enthusiasts seek out Moov's comfortable active wear. Even more intriguing is the option of having a bathing suit made-to-order within Montréal city limits. Customers choose the style and fabric that most complements their silhouette. 4148 bd. St-Laurent (near rue Rachel), Plateau Mont-Royal. ✆ 514/658-9912. www.moovdesign.com.

Tag Cuir (Finds) You have to check this out: Suede jeans that are washable! These Skotts brand pants (www.skotts.com) are made in Canada, of course, and are super-warm on icy days. Also on display in this small *cuir* (leather) shop are bomber jackets and other leather items. 1325 rue Ste-Catherine ouest (at rue Crescent), downtown. ✆ 514/499-1180.

For Men & Women

Montréal's fur-trading past buttresses the many wholesale and retail furriers, which maintain outlets downtown and in Plateau Mont-Royal. Fur shops are particularly concentrated on the "fur row" of **rue Mayor,** downtown between rue de Bleury and rue City Councillors.

Club Monaco Awareness of this expanding international chain is growing, as is appreciation of its minimalist, largely monochromatic garments for men and women, along with silver jewelry, eyewear, and cosmetics. Think Prada but more affordable, with a helpful young staff. In Les Cours Mont-Royal shopping complex, 1455 rue Peel (north of rue Ste-Catherine), downtown. ✆ 514/499-0959. www.clubmonaco.com.

Crocs The pillowy, marshmallowy, bright-colored foam clog originated in Québec (who knew?) and was acquired by the American Crocs company in 2004, although these days they're more likely to be manufactured in Mexico or China. The company has branched into more normal-looking (read: less childlike) shoes, and opened a store in the heart of downtown in 2008. 1382 rue Ste-Catherine ouest (near rue Crescent), downtown. ✆ 514/750-9796. www.crocs.ca.

Henri Henri As the porkpie makes a comeback, so may Henri Henri, a Montréal haberdasher since 1932. Step in and be outfitted with a classic Stetson or any number of styles that come in wool, felt, fur, leather, suede, cotton, or straw. Wondering how you look? Three-way oak mirrors abound, or the gentleman behind the counter will give you his honest assessment. Shop includes a hint of a woman's section and accessories like umbrellas with hardwood handles. 189 rue Ste-Catherine est (at Hôtel-de-Ville), downtown. ✆ 514/845-7995. www.henrihenri.ca.

Kanuk ★ One of the top Canadian manufacturers of high-end winter jackets makes its clothes right in Montréal and has a warehouse-like factory store in the heart of Plateau Mont-Royal. Like L.L.Bean in the U.S., Kanuk's first customers for the heavy parkas were outdoor enthusiasts. Today, its clientele includes the general public. The jackets aren't cheap—the heavy-duty ones cost upwards of C$600—but they're extremely popular. The more modestly priced winter caps make nice (and cozy) souvenirs. Look, too, for end-of-season sales. 485 rue Rachel est (near rue St-Denis), Plateau Mont-Royal. ✆ 514/284-4494. www.kanuk.com.

Roots This Canadian company has churned out stylish casual wear for the masses since 1973. It has a three-floor store here, in addition to other locations throughout Canada. Along with clothing, the store sells leather bags and briefcases and home accessories. 1035 rue Ste-Catherine ouest (at rue Peel), downtown. ✆ 514/845-7995. www.roots.com.

DEPARTMENT STORES

Montréal's major downtown shopping emporia stretch along rue Ste-Catherine from avenue Union westward to rue Guy. Most of the big department stores here were founded when Scottish, Irish, and English families dominated the city's mercantile class, so most of their names are identifiably English, albeit shorn of their apostrophes. The principal exception is La Baie, French for "the Bay," itself a shortened reference to an earlier name, the Hudson's Bay Company.

Henry Birks et Fils ★   Across from Christ Church Cathedral at the corner of rue Ste-Catherine stands Henry Birks et Fils, a highly regarded jeweler since 1879. This beautiful old store has marble pillars and an ornamental ceiling, and is a living part of Montréal's Victorian heritage. The expensive products on display go beyond jewelry to encompass pens, desk accessories, watches, belts, glassware, and china. 1240 Phillips Square (at rue Ste-Catherine), downtown. © 514/397-2511. www.birks.com.

Holt Renfrew ★   One of the best known department stores in the city began as a furrier in 1837 and is now a showcase for the best in international style. A young Montréal clothier recently praised it as hip for "both grandmother and granddaughter." Wares are displayed in miniboutiques and focus on fashion for men and women. Brands, including Hermès, Armani, Stuart Weitzman, Stella McCartney, and Eileen Fisher, are displayed with a tastefulness bordering on solemnity. The marquee outside reads HR. 1300 rue Sherbrooke ouest (at rue de la Montagne), downtown. © 514/842-5111. www.holtrenfrew.com.

La Baie ★   No retailer has an older or more celebrated pedigree than the Hudson's Bay Company, whose name was shortened to "the Bay" and then transformed into "La Baie" by Québec language laws that decreed French the lingua franca. The company was incorporated in Canada in 1670. Its main store focuses on clothing, but also offers crystal, china, Inuit carvings, and its famous Hudson's Bay "point blanket." The company is the official outfitter of the Canadian Olympic teams in 2010 and 2012. 585 rue Ste-Catherine ouest (near rue Aylmer), downtown. © 514/281-4422. www.hbc.com.

Ogilvy ★★   This most vibrant of a classy breed of department store that appears to be fading from the scene was established in 1866 and at this location since 1912. A bagpiper still announces the noon hour (a favorite sight for tourists), and special events, glowing chandeliers, and wide aisles enhance the shopping experience. Ogilvy has always had a reputation for quality merchandise and now contains more than 60 boutiques, including Louis Vuitton, Anne Klein, and Burberry. It's also known for its eagerly awaited Christmas windows. The basement-level **Café Romy** sells quality sandwiches, salads, and desserts. 1307 rue Ste-Catherine ouest (at rue de la Montagne), downtown. © 514/842-7711. www.ogilvycanada.com.

Simons (Finds)   This branch was the first expansion for Québec City's long-established family-owned department store. A must-see for teen shoppers, Simons takes the labels-within-a-store approach now popular at trendy but affordable chains such as H&M or Forever 21, and throws in a few cutting-edge designers for inspiration. Most Montréalers had never heard of it, but that changed fast given the fairly priced fashions. 977 rue Ste-Catherine ouest (at rue Mansfield), downtown. © 514/282-1840. www.simons.ca.

EDIBLES

The food markets described in "Picnic Fare" at the end of chapter 7 carry abundant assortments of cheeses, wines, and packaged food products that can serve as gifts or delicious reminders of your visit when you get home.

Canadian Maple Delights (Kids) Everything maple-y is presented here by a consortium of Québec producers: pastries, gift baskets, truffles, and, of course, every grade of syrup. A wee little cafe serves sweets and gelato; on nearly any day, a cone of maple-raspberry gelato is a good thing. 84 rue St-Paul est (near Place Jacques-Cartier), Vieux-Montréal. © 514/765-3456. www.mapledelights.com.

La Vieille Europe In this compact storehouse of culinary sights and smells, you can choose from wheels of pungent cheeses, garlands of sausages, pâtés, *jamón ibérico,* cashews, honey, fresh peanut butter, and dried fruits. Coffee beans are roasted in the back, adding to the mixture of maddening aromas. 3855 bd. St-Laurent (north of rue Roy), Plateau Mont-Royal. © 514/842-5773.

Les Chocolats de Chloé (Finds) If you approach chocolate the way certain aficionados approach wine or cheese—that is, on the lookout for the best of the best—then the teeny Chocolats de Chloé will bring great delight. Chocolates are made on-site, and tastes can be had for C$1.65. Especially adorable at Easter: a hollow chocolate fish filled with three little chocolate fishes. Owner Chloé Gervais-Fredette moved the shop from its original locale on rue Roy to the cobblestoned rue Duluth near the restaurant Au Pied de Cochon (p. 93) in late 2008. 546 rue Duluth est (near rue St-Hubert), Plateau Mont-Royal. © 514/849-5550. www.leschocolatsdechloe.com.

Les Glaceurs We can probably all agree that the rise in cupcake shops is one of the greatest phenomena of the early 21st century. Day trippers in Vieux-Montréal may end up making repeated visits to this cheery cafe with pink and lime green walls, where cupcakes go for C$3 in flavors that include coconut, key lime, strawberry, and *choco-menthe*. The shop also sells sandwiches and ice cream from Montréal favorite Bilboquet (p. 98). 453 rue St-Sulpice (across from Basilique Notre-Dame), Vieux-Montréal. © 514/504-1469.

Marché Atwater ★ The Atwater market, west of Vieux-Montréal, is an indoor-outdoor farmer's market that's open daily. French in flavor, it features fresh fruits, vegetables, and flowers, *boulangeries* and *fromageries,* and shops with easy-to-travel-with food. There are also specialty boutiques like Chocolats Geneviève Grandbois. You can walk to the market from Vieux-Montréal by heading down rue Notre-Dame, where you'll pass Antique Alley (about 45 min.; p. 142), or take the Métro to Lionel-Groulx. 138 av. Atwater (at rue Notre-Dame ouest), west of Vieux-Montréal. © 514/937-7754. www.marchespublicsmtl.com.

Mycoboutique Mushrooms, in every shape and form: fresh, dried, frozen, made into truffle oil, and folded into gelato (really). There are also books and housewares with mushroom motifs. The shop runs mushroom foraging events, too (in French only). 16 rue Rachel est (at bd. St-Laurent), Plateau Mont-Royal. © 514/223-6977. www.mycoboutique.ca.

Suite 88 Chocolatier More fancy chocolates. These are displayed in cases like fine jewelry, and flavors include jalapeño, chili-cayenne, ouzo, sake, and *mojito*. Small bars start at C$3.25. There's a cafe, too, with gelato, and on cold days be sure to try the hot chocolate—made with cayenne. 3957 rue St-Denis (near rue Roy), Plateau Mont-Royal. © 514/844-3488. www.suite88.com.

HOME DESIGN & HOUSEWARES

Also see "Arts, Crafts & Galleries," earlier in this chapter, and "Department Stores," above.

Arthur Quentin ★ Doling out household products of quiet taste and discernment for more than 25 years, this St-Denis stalwart sells tableware, kitchen gadgets, and home decor. That means lamps and Limoges china, terrines and tea towels, and cake molds and copper pots. Clay jugs for making vinegar? *Naturellement.* 3960 rue St-Denis (south of av. Duluth), Plateau Mont-Royal. © 514/843-7513. www.arthurquentin.com.

Bleu Nuit A sister store to Arthur Quentin, above, Bleu Nuit is *the* place to go for natural fiber bedding, super-soft nightwear, and swank soaps. The store does a good job positioning itself as the place for women (and men!) to register to build a classic trousseau of linens for the kitchen and bedroom. 3913 rue St-Denis (south of av. Duluth), Plateau Mont-Royal. © 514/843-5702. www.bleunuit.ca.

Les Touilleurs Kitchenware of the highest order is sold here, meticulously arranged like museum pieces in a minimalist setting (the shop earned design honors shortly after it opened). Stock includes only superior versions of cooking essentials, including small appliances that strike high new standards. Now it has doubled its size, incorporating a full kitchen where **cooking classes** are conducted by local chefs, often though, only in French. 152 rue Laurier ouest (near rue St-Urbain), Mile End. © 514/278-0008. www.lestouilleurs.com.

Option D Option D sells high-end housewares, candy-colored and steel, in the heart of Old Town. Brands include Alessi, Iittala, Alexandre Turpault, and Bodum. 50 rue St-Paul ouest (near rue St-Sulpice), Vieux-Montréal. © 514/842-7117. www.optiond.ca.

12° en Cave This store is dedicated to the good life, with an emphasis on the passions of wine aficionados. Reidel crystal and a variety of mostly high-end wine-related paraphernalia are for sale. Especially notable is a glass designed to heighten the tasting experience, with an indentation for thumb and forefinger. They also sell a nearly unbreakable wine glass made with titanium by Schott Zwiesel, starting at C$16; a salesperson tapped a goblet right on the metal shelf to demonstrate. 367 rue St-Paul est (opposite Marché Bonsecours), Vieux-Montréal. © 514/866-5722. www.12encave.com.

JEWELRY & ACCESSORIES

Also see "Arts, Crafts & Galleries," earlier in this chapter.

Château D'Ivoire When you absolutely, positively have to buy a Rolex *right now,* this store carries jewelry and watches from that brand plus other top luxury names: Raymond Weil, Omega, Cartier, Piaget, et al. 2020 rue de la Montagne (at bd. de Maisonneuve), downtown. © 514/845-4651. www.chateaudivoire.com.

Clio Blue, Paris This little rue Peel shop of the Paris-based international chain features spare displays in a narrow modernist storefront (the store is a design-competition winner). Custom jewelry tastefully incorporates Middle Eastern and South Asian motifs, often with carefully spaced semiprecious stones on silver strands and more festively designed bracelets. A sister store, **bleu comme le ciel,** is just down the block at no. 2000 and stocks costume jewelry that's worth a visit for women looking to shake up their image. 1468 rue Peel (near bd. de Maisonneuve), downtown. © 514/281-3112. www.clioblue.com.

MUSEUM STORES

Musée d'Art Contemporain Boutique The contemporary art museum's boutique sells the usual, including poster-size reproductions of paintings and prints. Added to the mix are tasteful design pieces and unusual gifts, including the bags made from recycled billboards by local company Atelier Entre-Peaux (p. 148). The museum's bookstore has a wide selection, in both French and English, of monographs about Canadian and international artists since the 1950s. 185 rue Ste-Catherine ouest (at rue Jeanne-Mance), downtown. © 514/847-6903. www.macm.org.

Musée des Beaux-Arts Boutique ★ An unusually large and impressive shop (which goes by the name M Boutique) that sells everything from folk art to furniture. The expected art-related postcards and prints are at hand, along with ties, watches, scarves, address books, toys, games, clocks, jewelry, and Inuit crafts, with special focus on work by Québec artisans. The boutique is also online in case you're looking for gifts after you've left the city. 1390 rue Sherbrooke ouest (at rue Crescent), downtown. ☏ 514/285-1600. www.mbam.qc.ca.

Musée McCord Boutique Part of an expanded museum that relates the province's history, this shop stocks a small, carefully chosen selection of Native and Canadian arts and crafts, china, rustic pottery, books with an emphasis on history, jewelry, and clothing, including moccasins. There's also a nice cafe inside the museum. 690 rue Sherbrooke ouest (at rue Victoria), downtown. ☏ 514/398-7100 ext. 274. www.mccord-museum.qc.ca.

Pointe-à-Callière Gift Shop Located in the Old Customs House at the end of the Museum of Archaeology and History's underground tour (and with a separate entrance on rue St-Paul), this boutique sells collectibles for the home, gift items, paper products, souvenirs, toys, and books (in French). Particularly nice are the maple spoons and spatulas made by Québec artist Tom Littledeer. 150 rue St-Paul ouest (at Place Royale), Vieux-Montréal. ☏ 514/872-9149. www.pacmusee.qc.ca.

MUSIC

Archambault Musique A premier spot to search out French-Canadian CDs as well as discs by the Montréal Symphony Orchestra, I Musici, and others. Many of the recordings can be difficult to get outside of Québec, so stock up here. 500 rue Ste-Catherine est (at rue Berri), downtown. ☏ 514/849-6201. www.archambault.ca.

Inbeat The decor is plain, but the stock includes CDs and vinyl that just aren't available elsewhere—deep house, techno, nu rave—with albums and singles that don't even fit *those* categories. 3814 bd. St-Laurent (near rue Roy), Plateau Mont-Royal. ☏ 514/499-2063. www.inbeatstore.com.

WINES & SPIRITS

The food markets described in "Picnic Fare" at the end of chapter 7 carry a good variety of wines, which are also sold in supermarkets and convenience stores. Beer is also available in these venues.

Liquor and other spirits, on the other hand, can only be sold in stores operated by the provincial **Société des Alcools du Québec (SAQ).** Though it was once as bureaucratic as most state-run agencies, successful upgrade efforts have made its stores more inviting and given differently named stores different personalities. The SAQ website, www.saq. com, provides a wealth of information about Québec wines and area outlets.

One of the largest outlets is the downtown **SAQ Selection** at 440 bd. de Maisonneuve ouest (☏ 514/873-2274), a veritable supermarket of wines and liquors with thousands of labels. Prices run from C$10 to way, way up for Bordeaux vintages. The downtown **SAQ Signature** at 677 Ste-Catherine ouest in the Complexe Les Ailes (☏ 888/454-7007 or 514/282-9445) is one of SAQ's boutique shops, featuring a smaller selection of rarer wines and fine liquors.

Bring your own carry bag when you visit a SAQ store: in early 2009 the shops eliminated single-use plastic and paper bags. If you don't have one, you'll have to buy a reusable bag for C75¢ to C$4, depending on the size.

Look for the VQA logo (Vintners Quality Alliance), which is given to wines that meet the state's quality standards.

Québec's unique **ice cider** *(cidre de glace),* made from apples left on trees after the first frost, can be purchased in duty-free shops at the border in addition to the stores listed above. One top producer is **Domaine Pinnacle** (℡ **450/298-1226;** www.icecider. com), based about an hour and a half from the city. It's a regular gold medalist in international competitions.

Montréal After Dark

Montréal's reputation for efferves-
cent nightlife reaches back to the Roaring
Twenties—specifically to the 13-year Prohibition in the U.S. from 1920 to 1933.
Americans streamed into Montréal for
relief from alcohol deprivation (while
Canadian distillers and brewers made fortunes). Montréal already enjoyed a sophisticated and slightly naughty reputation as
the Paris of North America, which added
to the allure.

Nearly a century later, clubbing and
barhopping remain popular activities,
with nightspots open until 3am—much
later hours than in many Canadian cities
which still heed Calvinist notions of pro-
priety and early bedtimes.

Nocturnal pursuits are often as cultural
as they are social. The city boasts its own
outstanding symphony, dozens of French-
and English-language theater companies,
and the incomparable Cirque du Soleil.
It's also on the standard concert circuit
that includes Chicago and New York, so
internationally known entertainers, music
groups, and dance companies pass through
frequently.

A decidedly French enthusiasm for
film, as well as the city's reputation as a
movie-production center, ensures support
for film festivals and screenings of offbeat
and independent movies.

A ticket office for Montréal cultural
events is centrally located at the Place des
Arts. **Vitrine Culturelle de Montréal
(Cultural Window of Montréal; © 866/
924-5538** or 514/285-4545; www.vitrine
culturelle.com) is at 145 rue Ste-Catherine
ouest and sells last-minute deals as well as
full-price tickets.

In summer, the city is awash in festivals.
Many are listed in the "Calendar of
Events" in chapter 3.

Concentrations of pubs and discos
underscore the city's linguistic dichotomy.
While there's much crossover, the parallel
blocks of **rue Crescent, rue Bishop,** and
rue de la Montagne north of rue Ste-
Catherine have a pronounced Anglophone
(English-speaking) character, while Francophones (French speakers) dominate the
Quartier Latin, with college-age patrons
most evident along the lower reaches of rue
St-Denis. Their yuppie elders gravitate to
the nightspots of the slightly more uptown
blocks of the same street. **Vieux-Montréal,**
especially along rue St-Paul, has a more
universal quality, and many of its bars and
clubs showcase live jazz, blues, and folk
music. In **Plateau Mont-Royal,** boulevard
St-Laurent, parallel to St-Denis and known
locally as "the Main," has become a miles-
long haven of hip restaurants and clubs,
roughly from rue Sherbrooke up to rue
Laurier. It's a good place to wind up in the
wee hours, as there's always someplace with
the welcome mat still out, even after the
official 3am closings.

Most bars and clubs don't charge cover,
and when they do, it's rarely more than
C$10.

Beer is usually in the C$4 to C$7 range,
while cocktails typically cost C$7 to C$12.
Belle Gueule Rousse is a good amber lager
made in Montréal by the Les Brasseurs RJ
company and on tap in many venues. On
Thursdays from 5pm to 7pm, nearly every
bar and restaurant offers some sort of
happy-hour special.

Smoking has been banned in bars and
restaurants since 2006.

Tips **Finding Out What's On**

For details about performances or special events when you're in town, pick up a free copy of *Montréal Scope* (www.montrealscope.com), a monthly ads-and-events booklet usually available in hotel lobbies; the free weekly papers *Mirror* (www.montrealmirror.com) and *Hour* (www.hour.ca), both in English; or *Voir* (www.voir.ca) and *Ici* (www.icimontreal.com), both in French, available all over town. Also in French is the free monthly *Nightlife* magazine (www.nightlife magazine.ca), which is also available in English online. *Fugues* (www.fugues.com) provides news and views of gay and lesbian events, clubs, restaurants, and activities. One particularly fun blog about city happenings is **Midnight Poutine** (www.midnightpoutine.ca), a self-described "delicious high-fat source of rants, raves and musings." Extensive listings of mainstream cultural and entertainment events are posted at **www.canada.com** and **www.montrealplus.ca.**

1 THE PERFORMING ARTS

CIRCUS

The extraordinary circus company **Cirque du Soleil** (p. 108) is based in Montréal. Each show is a celebration of pure skill and nothing less than magical, with acrobats, clowns, trapeze artists, and people costumed to look like creatures not of this world—iguanas crossed with goblins, or peacocks born of trolls. Cirque performs internationally, with as many as 19 shows simultaneously. Although there isn't a permanent show in Montréal, the troupe often comes to town in the summer (in 2009, it set up in Vieux-Port from late Apr–late July). Check **www.cirquedusoleil.com** for the schedule.

Pavillon de la TOHU (Value) Adjacent to Cirque du Soleil's training complex and company offices, TOHU is a performance space devoted to the circus arts. Acrobats and performers from Québec's Productions à Trois Têtes and the Imperial Acrobats of China have performed here, and the annual June shows by students of the National Circus School present many of the top rising stars. TOHU features an intimate in-the-round hall done up like an old-fashioned circus tent, and an exhibit space displays more than 100 circus artifacts. The entire venue was built with recycled pieces of an amusement-park bumper-car ride and wood from a dismantled railroad. The facility is in the lower-income Saint-Michel district well north of downtown, and accessible by Métro and bus as well as taxi. 2345 rue Jarry est (corner of rue d'Iberville, at Autoroute 40). ℂ **888/376-8648** or 514/376-8648. www.tohu.ca. Free to view facility and exhibits; tour admission from C$6 adults; C$4 seniors, students, and children 7–11; free for children 6 and younger. Daily 9am–5pm. Performances from C$22 adults, from C$16 children 12 and younger. 8km (5 miles) from downtown, up rue St-Denis and east on rue Jarry to where it meets Autoroute 40. Métro: Jarry or Iberville and bus 94 nord.

CLASSICAL MUSIC & OPERA

L'Opéra de Montréal ★★★ Founded in 1980, this outstanding opera company mounts six productions per year in Montréal, with artists from Québec and abroad participating in such shows as Mozart's *The Magic Flute*, Jules Massenet's *Cendrillon*, and Puccini's *Tosca*. Video translations are provided from the original languages into French and English. Performances are held from September to June at Place des Arts. Place des Arts, 175 rue Ste-Catherine ouest (main entrance), downtown. (℃) 514/985-2258 for tickets. www.operademontreal.com. Tickets from C$46. Métro: Place des Arts.

L'Orchestre Symphonique de Montréal (OSM) ★★ Kent Nagano was brought on as music director in 2005 and has focused this world-famous orchestra's repertoire on programs featuring works by Beethoven, Bach, Brahms, Mahler, and Messiaen. The orchestra performs at Place des Arts, occasionally at the Notre-Dame Basilica, and offers a few free concerts in regional parks each summer. Place des Arts, 175 rue Ste-Catherine ouest (main entrance), downtown. (℃) 514/842-9951 for tickets. www.osm.ca. Tickets from C$25; discounts available for people under 30. Métro: Place des Arts.

Orchestre Métropolitain du Grand Montréal This orchestra performs during its regular season at Place des Arts. Its 2010 schedule includes an assorted program *Airs de jeunesse*, and Mahler's Symphony No. 8. In summer, this talented group presents free outdoor concerts at Théâtre de Verdure in Parc La Fontaine. Place des Arts, 175 rue Ste-Catherine ouest (main entrance), downtown. (℃) 866/842-2112 or 514/842-2112. www.orchestre metropolitain.com. Tickets from C$25. Métro: Place des Arts.

CONCERT HALLS & AUDITORIUMS

Montréal has a score of venues. Check newspapers, magazines, and websites to find out who's playing where.

Centre Bell Seating up to 22,500, Centre Bell is the home of the Montréal Canadiens hockey team and host to the biggest international rock and pop stars traveling through the city, including Montréal native Céline Dion, Beyoncé, and Coldplay, as well as Disney On Ice. Check the website for information about guided tours. 1260 rue de la Gauchetière ouest, downtown. (℃) 800/663-6786 or 514/989-2841. www.centrebell.ca. Métro: Bonaventure.

Métropolis After starting life as a skating rink in 1884, the Métropolis is now a prime showplace for traveling rock groups, especially for bands on the way up or retracing their steps down. It has recently hosted Beirut, Estelle, Kool and the Gang, and the "Ethnic Heroes of Comedy" comedy tour. There's also a small attached lounge, **Le Savoy.** 59 rue Ste-Catherine est, downtown. (℃) 514/844-3500. www.montrealmetropolis.ca/metropolis. Métro: St-Laurent or Berri-UQAM.

Place des Arts ★★ Since 1992, Place des Arts has been the city's central entertainment complex, presenting performances of musical concerts, opera, dance, and theater in five halls: **Salle Wilfrid-Pelletier** (2,990 seats), where l'Orchestre Symphonique de Montréal (see above) and Les Grands Ballets Canadiens (p. 161) often perform; **Théâtre Maisonneuve** (1,458 seats), where the Orchestre Métropolitain du Grand Montréal (see above) performs; **Théâtre Jean-Duceppe** (765 seats); **Cinquième Salle** (417 seats); and the small **Studio-Théâtre Stella Artois** (138 seats). Portions of the city's many arts festivals are staged in the halls and outdoor plaza here, as are traveling productions of Broadway shows. *Note:* In 2010, portions of the Place des Arts plaza are under construction. Consult the web for current parking and building entrance news. Place des Arts, 175 rue Ste-Catherine ouest (ticket office), downtown. (℃) 866/842-2112 or 514/842-2112 for information and tickets. www.pda.qc.ca. Métro: Place des Arts.

Pollack Concert Hall In a landmark building dating from 1899 and fronted by a statue of Queen Victoria, this McGill University venue is in nearly constant use, especially during the school year with concerts and recitals by university students and music faculty. Recordings of some concerts are available on the university's label, McGill Records. Concerts are also given in the campus's smaller **Redpath Hall,** 861 Sherbrooke St. ouest (✆ **514/398-4547**). On the McGill University campus, 555 rue Sherbrooke ouest, downtown. ✆ 514/398-4547. www.music.mcgill.ca. Performances are usually free. Métro: McGill.

Théâtre de Outremont Opened in 1929, the Outremont started a new life in 2001, with a larger stage and terraced seating. Its calendar incorporates all manner of French-language music, comedy, theater, and film, but non-Francophones will enjoy the dance shows, especially performances during the Montréal International Festival of Tango. 1248 av. Bernard ouest (at av. Champagneur), Mile End. ✆ 514/495-9944. www.theatreoutremont.ca/outremont. Métro: Outremont.

Théâtre de Verdure (Value) Tango nights in July are especially popular at this open-air theater nestled in a popular park in Plateau Mont-Royal. Everything is free: music, dance, and theater, often with well-known artists and performers. Many in the audience pack picnics. Performances are held from June to August; check with the tourism office (p. 52) for days and times. Parc La Fontaine, Plateau Mont-Royal. ✆ 514/872-4041. Métro: Sherbrooke.

Théâtre St-Denis Recently refurbished, this theater complex in the heart of the Latin Quarter hosts a variety of shows by the likes of Norah Jones and Alice Cooper, as well as segments of the Juste pour Rire (Just for Laughs) comedy festival in July. One hall seats 2,218 and the other fits 933. 1594 rue St-Denis (at Emery), Quartier Latin. ✆ 514/849-4211. www.theatrestdenis.com. Métro: Berri-UQAM.

DANCE

Montréal hosts frequent appearances by notable dancers and troupes from other parts of Canada and the world—among them Hofesh Shechter Company, Balé de Rua, and Toronto's Le Ballet National du Canada—and has accomplished resident companies as well.

Les Grands Ballets Canadiens ★★ This prestigious touring company, performing both a classical and a modern repertoire, has developed a following far beyond national borders in its 50-plus years (it was founded in 1957). In the process, it has brought prominence to many gifted Canadian choreographers and composers. The troupe's production of *The Nutcracker* is always a big event each winter. Performances are held October through May. Place des Arts, 175 rue Ste-Catherine ouest (main entrance), downtown. ✆ 514/842-2112. www.grandsballets.qc.ca. Tickets from C$26. Métro: Place des Arts.

THEATER

Centaur Theatre The city's principal English-language theater is housed in a former stock-exchange building (1903). Presented here are a mix of classics, foreign adaptations, and works by Canadian playwrights. It was here that famed playwright Michel Tremblay's *Forever Yours, Marie-Lou* received its first English-language staging in 2008. Shakespeare's The Comedy of Errors and a drama about former Canadian Prime Minister Pierre Elliott Trudeau are slated for 2010. 453 rue St-François-Xavier (near rue Notre-Dame), Vieux-Montréal. ✆ 514/288-3161. www.centaurtheatre.com. Tickets from C$33. Métro: Place d'Armes.

Segal Centre for Performing Arts at the Saidye From about 1900 to 1930, Yiddish was Montréal's third most common language. That status has since been usurped by any number of languages, but its dominance lives on here. The Centre presents theater performed in both Yiddish and English and is one of the few North American theaters that still presents plays in Yiddish. Recent productions have included Willy Russell's Educating Rita and the Dora Wasserman Yiddish Theatre's production of Pirates of Penzance. Note that the venue is at a considerable distance from downtown. 5170 Côte-Ste-Catherine (near bd. Décarie), Plateau Mont-Royal. © **514/739-7944.** www.saidyebronfman. org. Tickets from C$35. Métro: Côte-Ste-Catherine or Snowdon. Bus: 129 or 17.

2 MUSIC & DANCE CLUBS

A note to clubbers: This city is *serious* about going out. Regular bars stay open until 3am and still others keep the fire burning after-hours. Popular clubs can be exclusive—waiting in line is an unfortunate reality, and dress codes are observed. You can increase your chances for entry at the most exclusive spots by making advance reservations or guaranteeing a table by "buying a bottle." Young clubbers avoid cover charges and lines by registering with **www.montrealguestlist.com**. Once on the list you may have to arrive early, or within a small window of time.

A note to walkers: Montréal is one of the safest cities to visit, but the area just north of Vieux-Montréal and the convention center, and south of rue Sherbrooke, has a pocket of streets that are nearly deserted at night. You may want to take a cab or the Métro when traveling through this area after dark.

DOWNTOWN/RUE CRESCENT

Hard Rock Cafe   No surprises here, not with all of its clones scattered around the world. This outpost in the heart of the rue Crescent party strip gets crowded at lunch and on weekend evenings, and its terrace is a boozy party land. Open Sunday through Thursday from 11am to 11pm, Friday and Saturday 11am to midnight, with a big dance floor that's hopping in the evenings. 1458 rue Crescent (near bd. de Maisonneuve). © **514/987-1420.** www.hardrock.com. Métro: Guy-Concordia.

Hurley's Irish Pub   In front is a street-level terrace, and there are several semi-subterranean rooms in back. Celtic instrumentalists perform nightly, usually starting around 9:30pm. There are 19 beers on tap and more than 40 single-malt whiskeys to choose from. 1225 rue Crescent (at rue Ste-Catherine), downtown. © **514/861-4111.** www.hurleysirish pub.com. Métro: Guy-Concordia.

Maison de Jazz ★   Right downtown, this New Orleans–style jazz venue has been on the scene for decades. Lovers of barbecued ribs and jazz, most of them well past the bloom of youth, arrive early to fill the room, which is decorated in mock Art Nouveau style with tiered levels. Live music starts around 8pm most nights and continues until closing time. The ribs are okay and the jazz is of the swinging mainstream variety, with occasional digressions into more esoteric forms. 2060 rue Aylmer (south of rue Sherbrooke). © **514/842-8656.** www.houseofjazz.ca. Cover C$5. Métro: McGill.

Newtown   A tri-level club in the white-hot center of rue Crescent nightlife, Newtown is still a sought-after destination (it changed ownership in 2008). The square bar in the middle of the main barroom is a friendly place, even if you're on your own. One option on the martini menu is the Berlin—made with gin, lime juice, and cane sugar syrup. On the sweeter side is the French Kiss with vodka, *framboise* liquor, and pineapple and lime juices. There's a disco in the basement, a restaurant one floor up, and, most prominently, a rooftop terrace in summer. The bar and restaurant are open daily, the disco Friday and Saturday. 1476 rue Crescent (at de Maisonneuve), downtown. ℂ **514/284-6555**. www.lenewtown. com. Métro: Peel.

Time Supper Club Though food is served, it isn't the prime attraction—after dinner, Time's fabulous crowd gets up from the tables and works off the calories to rock, house, and hip-hop that thumps on until closing at 3am. The waitstaff is startlingly sexy. Dress well, look good, and approach the door with confidence. The club is in a dreary industrial neighborhood south of the downtown core, so you might want to arrive by car or taxi. 997 rue St-Jacques ouest (near rue Peel), downtown. ℂ **514/392-9292**. www.timesupper club.com. Métro: Bonaventure.

Upstairs Jazz Bar & Grill ★ The Upstairs Jazz Bar, decidedly *down* a few steps from the street, has been hosting live jazz music nightly for years. Big names are infrequent, but the groups are more than competent. Sets begin as early as 7:30pm. Decor includes record-album covers and fish tanks. Pretty good food ranges from bar snacks to more substantial meals, including *table d'hôte* offerings. Most patrons are edging toward their middle years. 1254 rue Mackay (near rue Ste-Catherine). ℂ **514/931-6808**. www.upstairsjazz. com. Reservations recommended. Cover usually btw. C$5 and C$30. Métro: Guy-Concordia.

VIEUX-MONTREAL

Le Deux Pierrots ★ This is perhaps the best-known of Montréal's *boîtes-à-chansons* (song clubs), but its more visible personality these days is as a sports bar. The athletic-style posters are certainly what you'll see when you walk by, and that's how the operation appears to make most of its money. But on Friday and Saturday nights, an intimate French-style cabaret still brings in singers who interact animatedly, and often bilingually, with the crowd. Arrive by 9pm or make a reservation, tables fill fast. 104 rue St-Paul est (west of place Jacques-Cartier). ℂ **514/861-1270**. www.lespierrots.com. Métro: Place d'Armes.

Modavie Set aside an evening for dinner with jazz at this popular Vieux-Montréal bistro (p. 89) and wine bar. Music is usually mainstream jazz by duos or trios, and there's no fee for the show. In addition to tables, there are about a dozen seats at a handsome horseshoe-shaped bar just inside the door. Choose from 10 scotches; a long wine list; and some 30 cognacs, grappas, and ports. It's a friendly place and the food is good, too. 1 rue St-Paul ouest (corner of rue St-Laurent). ℂ **514/287-9582**. www.modavie.com. Métro: Place d'Armes.

PLATEAU MONT-ROYAL

Buonanotte It's a high-end, expensive Italian restaurant, but many head to Buon-anotte just for a drink. Its reputation comes as much from being a nightspot for the fabulous and the celebrated as anything else, and it attracts people with serious money to spend. It can be crowded, and if you're not a regular you might get shut out if you show up after 11pm. 3518 bd. St-Laurent (near rue Sherbrooke). ℂ **514/848-0644**. www.buonanotte. com. Métro: St-Laurent.

Casa del Popolo This is the heart of the Montréal indie music scene. Set in a scruffy storefront, Casa del Popolo serves vegetarian food, operates a laid-back bar, and has a small first-floor stage. Across the street, a sister performance space, **La Sala Rosa,** is a bigger venue and has a full calendar of interesting rock, experimental, and jazz music. The attached **Sala Rosa Restaurant** is a hearty Spanish restaurant with a big card of tapas and paella and, every Thursday, live flamenco music with dancing and singing—be

(Moments) **Late Night Montréal, when the Street Festivals Subside**

Montréal closes streets to car traffic with the blink of an eye for music festivals, sidewalk sales, street fairs, and everything in between. One recent June night, we walked the Main—boulevard St-Laurent—from av. du Mont-Royal in the north to rue Sherbrooke in the south, at 1am. Normally a busy, main thoroughfare, the road had become pedestrian-only because of the afternoon fair earlier that day. Most of the food vendors were packed up, although a few were still selling the last of their food—crepes and strawberries from one, meat on a stick from another. On every block, bars and restaurants had set up impromptu outdoor cafes jutting into the street, and most were thick with people drinking, chatting, and flirting. Some of the thumping music clubs had lines out the door and bouncers manning velvet ropes. Bicyclists slalomed through the walkers. On the northern end of the street, the attire was more casual, more T-shirt than high fashion. Closer to rue Sherbrooke, there was a sharp spike in the number of men dressed in all-black suits and women teetering in superhigh heels and wrapped in teeny, tight dresses. The crowds were French speaking, English speaking, Spanish speaking, black, white, brown, dressed up, dressed down. It was a snapshot of the hodgepodge that is this city's nightlife, all in 8 blocks.

advised to reserve your spot a week or more in advance. 4873 and 4848 bd. St-Laurent (near bd. St-Joseph). 🕐 **514/284-3804.** www.casadelpopolo.com. Cover C$6–C$15. Métro: Laurier.

Club Balattou   This club on the Main is a premiere venue for seeing African music and performers from the West Indies and Latin America. An infectious, sensual beat issues from it, a happy variation from the prevailing grunge and dance music of mainstream clubs. 4372 bd. St-Laurent (at rue Marie-Anne). 🕐 **514/845-5447.** www.lucubrium.com/balattou. Cover C$5–C$20. Métro: Mont-Royal.

Le Divan Orange   A hopping club with a good, hipster vibe, bands and combos here include indie rock, jazz, country, and traditional North African. There are also events best described as performance art. Shows start around 9:30pm. Open every night. 4234 bd. St-Laurent (near rue Rachel). 🕐 **514/840-9090.** www.ledivanorange.org. Cover C$5–C$10. Métro: Mont-Royal.

Les Bobards   There's music here every night (except some Mondays) in a wide variety of forms—swing, jazz, blues, salsa, sync-pop, and Brazilian. Live shows start around 9pm. Foosball and billiards can fill the time until then. 4328 bd. St-Laurent (at rue Marie-Anne). 🕐 **514/987-1174.** www.lesbobards.qc.ca. Cover C$5–C$10. Métro: Mont-Royal.

Orchid   Wonder where Montréal's young, black, and fabulous crowd is? Their hands-down choice is the Orchid nightclub, and the line to get in here is as big as any on the Main. The demographic: fine young professionals and college kids dressed to impress. The R&B and hip-hop start up around 10pm. Ladies drink for free until midnight on Friday. Photos are posted regularly on the club's zippy website. 3556 bd. St-Laurent (1 block north of rue Sherbrooke). 🕐 **514/848-6398.** www.orchidnightclub.com. Métro: Sherbrooke.

Cabaret Mado The glint of the sequins can be blinding! Inspired by 1920s cabaret theater, this determinedly trendy place in the Village has nightly performances and a dance floor and is considered a premiere venue these days. Friday and Saturday feature festive drag shows, which, on a given night, may honor the likes of Tina Turner or Céline Dion. Look for the pink-haired drag queen on the retro marquee. 1115 rue Ste-Catherine est (near rue Amherst). © 514/525-7566. www.mado.qc.ca. Cover C$5–C$10. Métro: Beaudry.

Club Opera One of the hottest dance clubs in the city, attracting the thin, the tanned, and the well-turned out. The club has an elegant ambiance and international DJs spinning nearly every evening. 32 rue Ste-Catherine (at bd. St-Laurent), Quartier Latin. © 514/842-2836. www.operamtl.com. Tickets from C$15. Métro: St-Laurent.

Club Soda This long-established rock club in a seedy part of the Latin Quarter remains one of the prime destinations for performers just below the star level—Queensryche, Mara Tremblay, and Pauly Shore have all come through recently—and also hosts several of the city's comedy festivals and acts for the annual jazz festival. 1225 bd. St-Laurent (at rue Ste-Catherine), Quartier Latin. © 514/286-1010. www.clubsoda.ca. Tickets from C$22. Métro: St-Laurent.

Gotha Salon Bar Lounge For a quieter venue in the Village, the cozy Gotha lounge has a fireplace and live piano on Sunday nights, and attracts a mixed gay/ straight crowd. Try the honey wine, a digestive that's made in Canada, or the signature Le Gotha martini, with vodka, triple sec, white cranberry juice, and lime. It's at street level below the **Aubergell Bed & Breakfast** (www.aubergell.com) on rue Amherst, a road chockablock with antiques shops sporting vintage and collectible goodies from the 1930s to 1980s. 1641 rue Amherst. © 514/ 526-1270. Métro: Beaudry.

Les Foufounes Electriques From the outside, this Latin Quarter club looks like something out of a *Mad Max* movie, with a spider the size of a Smart Car hanging over the front gate. Inside, it's a multilevel rock club that features hard-core and disco-punk bands and DJs. If you're within 2 blocks, you'll hear it. Open daily to 3am. 87 Ste-Catherine est (near bd. St-Laurent). © 514/844-5539. www.foufounes.qc.ca. Métro: St-Laurent.

Sky Club & Pub ★ A complex that includes drag performances in the cabaret room, a pub serving dinner daily from 4 to 9pm, a hip-hop room, a spacious dance floor that's often set to house music, and a popular roof terrace, Sky is thought by many to be the city's hottest spot for the gay, young, and fabulous. It's got spiffy decor and pounding music. 1474 rue Ste-Catherine est (near rue Plessis). © 514/529-6969. www.complexesky.com. Métro: Beaudry.

Stéréo Passionate devotees have been known to tattoo the club's audio-wave logo on their bodies. But a 2008 fire crippled and closed this hyperhip, after-hours disco that wouldn't rev up until 3am and then roared until noon. Club kids, drag queens, hipsters, and students gay and straight all anxiously awaited a 2009 grand re-opening that promised an even BIGGER sound system. You'll have to keep tabs online to know for sure that it's back in business. 858 rue Ste-Catherine est (near rue Berri). No phone. www.stereonightclub.net. Métro: Berri-UQAM.

Unity The former dance club Unity II was one of the biggest and most popular gay discos in town before it was severely damaged in an April 2006 fire. It reopened as Club Unity Montréal a few months later (now known again just as Unity) and once more draws well-dressed, friendly, mixed crowds. The large outdoor roof terrace is especially popular. 1171 rue Ste-Catherine est (at Montcalm). ✆ **514/523-2777.** www.clubunitymontreal. com. Métro: Beaudry.

OUTER DISTRICTS

Piknic Electronik   From May to October on sunny Sunday afternoons a DJ starts spinning or live acts amp up and the electronica begins at Parc Jean-Drapeau. Hipster kids, families, and dancing queens who just didn't get enough Saturday night gather and shake it outdoors under the Alexander Calder sculpture, *Man and His World,* located on the Belvedere on the north shore of Île Sainte-Hélène, facing the river. Piknik Electronik also sets up shop in other locales for city events. While the group's website is in French only, Parc Jean-Drapeau offers info in English at www.parcjeandrapeau.com. Belvedere in Parc Jean-Drapeau (Île Ste-Hélène). No phone. www.piknicelectronik.com. Admission C$10 adults, free for children 12 and younger. Sundays May–Oct. Métro: Jean-Drapeau.

3 BARS

There are four main drags to keep in mind for a night on the town. Downtown's **rue Crescent** hums with activity from late afternoon until far into the evening, especially on summer weekend nights, when the street swarms with people careening from bar to restaurant to club. In the Plateau Mont-Royal neighborhood, **boulevard St-Laurent,** or the Main, as it's known, has blocks and blocks of bars and clubs, most with a distinctive French personality, as opposed to rue Crescent's Anglo flavor. In Vieux-Montréal, **rue St-Paul** west of Place Jacques-Cartier falls somewhere in the middle on the Anglophone-Francophone spectrum. And in the Village, **rue Catherine** closes in summer to cars and becomes flush with people as the cafes and bars that line the street build temporary terraces that fill in the afternoons and evenings.

   In most cases, bars tend to open around 11:30am and stay open until 2am or 3am. Many of them have *heures joyeuses* (happy hours) from as early as 3pm to as late as 9pm, but usually for a shorter period within those hours. You'll see signs that read BIERES EN FUT, which means "beer on draft."

DOWNTOWN/RUE CRESCENT

Brutopia ★   This pub pulls endless pints of its own microbrews, which might include maple cream, IPA, or java stout on a given day. With several rooms on three levels, a terrace in back, and a street-side balcony, it draws a mix of ages, students with laptops, and old friends just hanging out. Unlike other spots on rue Crescent, where the sound levels can be deafening, here you can actually have a conversation. The snacking menu spans the globe. Bands perform, too, with an open-mic night on Sunday. 1219 rue Crescent (north of bd. René-Lévesque). ✆ **514/393-9277.** www.brutopia.net. Métro: Lucien L'Allier.

Le Cabaret   In L'Hôtel de la Montagne (p. 69) and within sight of the hotel's trademark lobby fountain with its nude bronze sprite sporting stained-glass wings, this appealing piano bar draws a crowd of youngish to middle-aged professionals after 5:30pm. In summer, the hotel's **La Terrasse Magnétic** on the roof offers meals, drinks, dancing, and use of the outdoor pool until 3am. 1430 rue de la Montagne (north of rue Ste-Catherine). ✆ **514/288-5656.** www.hoteldelamontagne.com. Métro: Guy-Concordia.

Le Tour de Ville   Memorable and breathtaking. We're talking about the view, that is, from Montréal's only revolving restaurant and bar (the bar part doesn't revolve, but you still get a great view). The best time to go is when the sun is setting and the city lights are beginning to blink on. Open Tuesday through Saturday from 5:30pm to 11pm, and on Sunday for brunch at two seatings: 10:30am to 12:30pm and 1pm to 3pm. In the Delta Centre-Ville Hôtel, 777 rue University. © 514/879-4777 for reservations. Métro: Square Victoria.

Pullman   This sleek wine bar offers either 2- or 4-ounce pours, so there is room for adventure. A competent tapas menu with standards like charcuterie and grilled cheese bedazzled with port are prepared with the precision of a sushi chef. The smartly designed multilevel space creates pockets of ambience, from cozy corners to tables drenched in natural light. Open Tuesday through Saturday from 4:30pm to 1am. 3424 av. du Parc (north of Sherbrooke). © 514/288-7779. www.pullman-mtl.com. Métro: Place des Arts.

Sir Winston Churchill Pub ★   The three levels of bars and cafes here are rue Crescent landmarks, and the New Orleans–style sidewalk and first-floor terraces (open in warm months) make perfect vantage points from which to check out the pedestrian traffic. Inside and down the stairs, the pub, with English ales on tap, attempts to imitate a British public house and gets a mixed crowd of young professionals. Open daily to 3am, with DJs every day. 1459 rue Crescent (near rue Ste-Catherine). © 514/288-3814. www.swcpc. com. Métro: Guy-Concordia.

Thursday's   A prime watering hole for Montréal's young, professional set. The pubby bar spills out onto a terrace that hangs over the street, and there's a glittery disco in back. Voted "Best Pick-Up Spot" by the *Montréal Mirror* in 2009 (and 2008 and 2007), Thursday's "gets more people laid than Craigslist," as the *Mirror* puts it. In L'Hôtel de la Montagne, 1430 rue de la Montagne (north of rue Ste-Catherine). © 514/288-5656. www.hoteldela montagne.com. Métro: Guy-Concordia.

W Hotel   With its Plateau Lounge, W Bartini, and Wunderbar open daily until 3am, W attracts some of the best-looking partiers in town. 901 Victoria Square (at rue McGill). © 514/395-3100. Métro: Square-Victoria.

VIEUX-MONTREAL

Aszú (Finds)   This classy wine bar features hundreds of labels. Better still, on any given night, some 50 of them are available by the glass. A menu of tuna tartar, Québécois guinea fowl, wild boar chop, and the like provides accompaniment to the main event. With room for about 30 people at the bar, 40 at inside tables, and 75 on an attractive side terrace, this is a cozy find. Open Tuesday through Saturday for lunch and dinner. Call to confirm for seasonal additions or closures. 212 rue Notre-Dame ouest (at rue St-François-Xavier). © 514/845-5436. www.aszu.ca. Métro: Place d'Armes.

Le Jardin Nelson   In the summer, the outdoor dining options that line Place Jacques Cartier are tempting, but touristy. Le Jardin Nelson has a people-watching porch adjacent to the plaza, but you're better off tucking into its tree-shaded garden court, which sits behind a stone building dating from 1812. A pleasant hour or two can be spent listening to live jazz, played every afternoon and evening. Food takes second place, but the kitchen does well with its pizzas and crepes, with crepe options both sweet and savory (including lobster). There are heaters outdoors to cut the chill, and a few indoor tables indoors, too. When the weather's nice, it's open until 2am. Closed November through mid-April. 407 Place Jacques-Cartier (at rue St-Paul). © **514/861-5731.** www.jardinnelson.com. Métro: Place d'Armes or Champ-de-Mars.

Óra This has been a bright spot in Vieux-Montréal since its opening in 2007. With white leatherlike walls and banquettes, a neon pink glow from recessed spots in the ceiling, and a serious sound system with a corner DJ booth, Óra is a restaurant with good food, good drinks, and—as the evening wears on—a trendy, well-clad crowd. 394 rue St-Jacques (near rue St-Pierre). © **514/848-0202.** Métro: Square-Victoria.

Suite 701 When Le Place d'Armes Hôtel (p. 74) converted its old lobby and wine bar into a spiffy lounge, yuppies got the word fast. The so-called *cinq-à-sept* (5 to 7) afterwork crowd fills the space evenings, especially on Thursdays. Upscale bar food comes from the same kitchen as the restaurant's high-end operation, **Aix Cuisine du Terroir** (p. 86). At the corner of rue St-Jacques and Côte de la Place d'Armes. © **514/904-1201.** Métro: Place d'Armes.

PLATEAU MONT-ROYAL & MILE END

Bifteck A grungy crowd aging from barely legal (18) to early 30s holds court at this perennially popular bar. Most quaff beer by the pitcher, but attention is also given to shooters, including classy evergreens such as the Kamikaze and the Windex. Late at night, it's one of the Main's most packed bars. 3702 bd. St-Laurent (near rue Prince Arthur). © **514/844-6211.** Métro: Sherbrooke.

Bílý Kůň Pronounced "Billy Coon," this popular bar is a bit of Prague right in Montréal, from the avant-garde decor (mounted ostrich heads ring the room) to the full line of Czech beers, local microbrews, and dozen-plus scotches. Martini specials include the Absinthe Aux Pommes. Students and professionals jam in for the relaxed candle-lit atmosphere, which includes twirling ceiling fans and picture windows that open to the street. There's live jazz from 6 to 8pm daily and DJs spinning upbeat pop most nights from 8pm to 3am. Get here early to do a little shopping in the hipster boutiques along the street. 354 av. Mont-Royal est (near rue St-Denis). © **514/845-5392.** www.bilykun.com. Métro: Mont-Royal.

Champs Montréalers are no less enthusiastic about sports, especially hockey, than other Canadians, and fans both avid and casual drop by this three-story sports emporium to catch up with their teams and hoist a few. Games from around the world are fed to walls of TVs; more than a dozen athletic events might be showing at any given time. Food is what you'd expect—burgers, steaks, and such. 3956 bd. St-Laurent (near rue Duluth). © **514/987-6444.** Métro: Sherbrooke.

Chesterfield Bar à Vin Stop in to Chesterfield for a nice glass of wine and you could find yourself veering off the nibbles menu and dining instead on lobsters and a crisp whole bottle of vino, in perfect complement to one another. In warmer months the windows open to rue Rachel and the scene heats up further with on again, off again DJs. It opened in fall 2008 and is owned by four young Montréalers. 451 rue Rachel est (near rue St-Denis). © **514/544-5316.** www.chesterfieldmtl.com. Métro: Mont-Royal.

Dieu Du Ciel ★ Tucked into a corner building on rue Laurier, this neighborhood artisanal brewpub offers an alternating selection of some dozen beers, including house brews and exotic imports. The place buzzes even midweek. With good conversation and some friends to sample the array, what more do you need? If it's guidance on where to begin, how about starting with the Première Communion (First Communion), a Scottish ale; moving on to the Rosée d'Hibiscus, which is less sweet than feared; and finishing with the Rigor Mortis ABT. Dieu du Ciel beers are also bottled and sold throughout the province. 29 rue Laurier ouest (near St. Laurent). ℂ **514/490-9555.** www.dieuduciel.com. Métro: Laurier.

Koko One of *the* chic bars of the city. Koko is a prime reason to visit, if not stay at, the Opus Hotel (which took over the Hôtel Godin in 2007). The bar includes a spectacular terrace and an Asian-influenced menu, and it's open until 1am Sunday through Wednesday and 3am Thursday through Saturday. As befits its positioning as a premier venue for urban glamour, a bouncer often stands watch at the door. Try the C$12 Wilde Child cocktail, with Prosecco and candied wild hibiscus flower. 8 rue Sherbrooke ouest (at bd. St-Laurent). ℂ **514/657-5656.** www.kokomontreal.com. Métro: Saint-Laurent.

Laïka Amid the plethora of St-Laurent watering stops, this bright little *boîte* offers tasty sandwiches and tapas and a popular Sunday brunch. DJs spin house, funk, electronica, and whatnot from midevening until 3am for a mostly 18- to 35-year-old crowd. Très cool. 4040 bd. St-Laurent (near rue Duluth). ℂ **514/842-8088.** www.laikamontreal.com. Métro: Sherbrooke.

Le Pistol Get here early, because this spot on the Main gets packed in no time. Catering to the post-collegiate T-shirt-and-jeans crowd, Pistol offers ample attractions, including high-definition plasma TVs showing hockey, and tasty food, including sandwiches named for Bond flicks—Goldfinger, Moonraker, and so on. Music moves from jazz to house to rock. The ground-floor front is open in decent weather. Drinks and eats are mostly less than C$10. 3723 bd. St-Laurent (near rue Prince Arthur). ℂ **514/847-2222.** Métro: Sherbrooke.

Whisky Café Those who enjoy scotch, particularly single-malts like Laphraoig and Glenfiddich, will find more than 150 different labels to sample at this handsome bar. Newbies can try a *degustation* by region or brand, as each of three pours comes with a description of aroma and taste. Side dishes of nuts and cheese are as simple and sophisticated as the decor—wood-framed leather chairs surround handmade tiled tables or you can grab a cozy booth. Another decorative triumph: The men's urinal has a waterfall acting as the *pissoir*. Attached is a separate cigar lounge with leather armchairs and Cubans. 5800 bd. St-Laurent (at rue Bernard). ℂ **514/278-2646.** Métro: Laurier.

4 MORE ENTERTAINMENT

GAMBLING & CABARET

The **Casino de Montréal** (ℂ **800/665-2274** or 514/392-2746; www.casinosduquebec. com), Québec's first, is housed in recycled space: The complex reuses what were the French and Québec pavilions during Expo 67. Asymmetrical and groovy, the buildings provide a dramatic setting for games of chance. Four floors contain more than 120 game tables, including roulette, craps, blackjack, baccarat, and varieties of poker, and there are more than 3,200 slot machines. Admission is restricted to persons 18 and over.

It has four restaurants, and the elegant **Nuances** (p. 99) is one of the top restaurants in the city. There are also live dinner shows most evenings at the **Cabaret du Casino** (ℂ **800/361-4595** or 514/790-1245).

No alcoholic beverages are served in the gambling areas, and patrons must be at least 18 years old and dressed neatly (the full dress code is posted online). The casino is entirely smoke-free, though it offers outside smoking areas. It's open 24 hours a day, 7 days a week, with overnight packages available at nearby hotels.

The casino is on Parc Jean-Drapeau. You can drive there or take the Métro to the Parc Jean-Drapeau stop and then walk or take the casino shuttle bus (no. 167, labeled CASINO). From June through October, a free shuttle bus *(navette)* leaves on the hour from the downtown Infotouriste Centre at 1001 rue du Square Dorchester (it makes other stops downtown, too). Shuttles depart from the Infotouriste Centre starting at 10am and ending at 7pm; the last shuttle leaves the casino for downtown at 7:45 pm. Call ✆ **514/ 392-2746** with questions.

CINEMA

In Montréal, English-language films are usually presented with French subtitles. However, when the initials "VF" (for *version française*) follow the title of a non-Francophone movie, it means that the movie has been dubbed into French. Policies vary regarding English subtitles on non-English-language films, so ask at the box office. Admission to films is usually about C$10 for adults, and less for students, seniors, and children. There are usually special afternoon rates for matinees.

The **Ex-Centris** has long been a cutting edge Plateau Mont-Royal independent film venue but began transitioning its programming at 3530 bd. St-Laurent in late 2009. The new iteration (redubbed eXcentris, **www.excentris.com**) promises to be an "iconic new media complex" that features "music, theater, poetry, visual arts and dance, in an ambiance of fine food and drink, seductive design, and seamless technology." To find out what's on deck, call the box office at ✆ **514/847-2206.**

Another long-standing programmer of independent cinema, **Cinéma Parallèle** (www. cinemaparallele.ca) is in the process of relocating to a new complex at the corner of boulevards de Maisonneuve and St-Laurent. Visit the website for a status report on programming.

The National Film Board (NFB) of Canada operates **CineRobotheque** at 1564 rue St-Denis (✆ **514/496-6887;** www.nfb.ca). The first floor houses the NFB film library—a high-tech screening center where visitors can browse a multimedia catalog and then watch a film at a personal viewing station. The second floor features screenings of classic Canadian and international films, or films showing as part of festivals, primarily in English and French.

The **Cinémathèque Québécoise** (✆ **514/842-9763;** www.cinematheque.qc.ca) calls itself "Montréal's Museum of the Moving Image." Its mission is to preserve and document film and television heritage, particularly that of Québec and Canada. In addition to housing archives of films, photographs, and equipment, the Cinémathèque screens exhibits and retrospectives at 335 bd. de Maisonneuve est.

Imposing, fantastically huge images confront viewers of the seven-story **IMAX Theatre** screen in the Centre des Sciences de Montréal (Montréal Science Centre; ✆ **877/ 496-4724** or 514/496-4724; www.montrealsciencecentre.com). Many of the films are suitable for the entire family. See "Especially for Kids," in chapter 8.

When movie-going in Québec, remember to check what language the films are in and if they're subtitled.

COMEDY

The once red-hot market for comedy clubs across North America may have cooled off in many places, but it lives on in Montréal, mostly because the city is the home to the highly regarded **Juste pour Rire (Just for Laughs) Festival** (© 888/244-3155; www.hahaha. com) every summer. (Those who have so far avoided the comedy-club experience should know that profanity, bathroom humor, and ethnic slurs are common fodder. To avoid becoming the object of comedians' barbs, sit well back from the stage.) Check before buying tickets whether the show you're interested in is in French or English.

There's a full array of comedy at **Comedyworks,** a long-running club at 1238 rue Bishop (© **514/398-9661;** www.comedyworksmontreal.com). Monday is open-mic night, Tuesday and Wednesday are improv nights (a comedy troupe works off the audience's suggestions), and Thursday through Saturday nights feature international headliners. No food is served, just drinks. Reservations are recommended, especially on Friday, when it may be necessary to arrive early to secure a seat. Shows are in English and happen nightly at 8:30pm, with additional shows at 11pm on Friday and Saturday.

Side Trips from Montréal

You don't have to travel far from Montréal to reach mountains, parks, or bike trails. In fact, enjoyable touring regions are a mere 30-minute drive from the city.

The **Laurentians** (to the north) and the **Cantons-de-l'Est** (to the southeast) both are developed with year-round vacation retreats, with skiing in winter, biking and boating in summer, maple-sugaring in spring, and vineyard-touring and leaf-peeping in fall.

The pearl of the Laurentians (also called the Laurentides) is **Mont-Tremblant,** eastern Canada's highest peak and a winter mecca for skiers and snowboarders from all over North America. Development has been particularly heavy in the resort town here.

The region has dozens of other ski centers, too, with scores of trails at every level of difficulty, and many are less than an hour from Montréal. The area loses none of its charm in summer (and in fact gains some with thinned-out traffic). That's when ski resorts turn into attractive, green mountain properties close to

biking, fishing, and golfing. It's even possible to participate in cattle roundups.

The bucolic Cantons-de-l'Est were known as the Eastern Townships when they were a haven for English Loyalists and their descendants, and some Anglophones still refer to the region by that name by today. It's blessed with memorable country inns, former homes of early 1900s aristocracy, and the beautiful Lake Massawippi. As with the Laurentians, many of the same trails developed for winter sports are used for parallel activities in summer. The mountain of **Bromont,** for example, known in the winter for its skiing, has marked paths for mountain biking, and **Mont-Orford Park** is the focal point for hiking trails linking six regional parks. Rock climbing, whitewater kayaking, sailing, and fishing are additional options, with equipment readily available for rent.

Because the people of both regions rely heavily on tourism for their livelihoods, knowledge of at least rudimentary English is widespread, even outside such obvious places as hotels and restaurants.

1 NORTH INTO THE LAURENTIANS (LAURENTIDES)

55–129km (34–80 miles) N of Montréal

Don't expect spiked peaks or high, ragged ridges. The Laurentian Shield's rolling hills and rounded mountains are among the world's oldest, worn down by wind and water over eons. They average between 300m and 520m (984 ft.–1,706 ft.) in height, with the highest being Mont-Tremblant, at 968m (3,176 ft.). In the lower area, closer to Montréal, the terrain resembles a rumpled quilt, its folds and hollows cupping a multitude of lakes large and small. Farther north, the summits are higher and craggier, with patches of snow persisting well into spring. These are not the Alps or the Rockies, but they're welcoming and embracing.

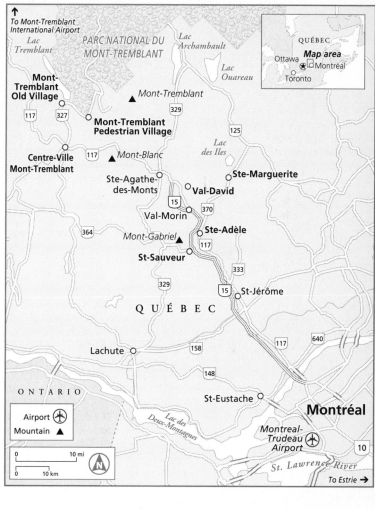

Half a century ago, the first ski schools, rope tows, and trails began to appear. Today, there are 14 ski centers within a 64km (40-mile) radius, and cross-country skiing has as enthusiastic a following as downhill. Sprawling resorts and modest lodges and inns are packed in winter with skiers, some of them through April. Trails for those with advanced skills typically have short pitches and challenging moguls, with broad, hard-packed avenues for beginners and the less experienced. Skiers can usually expect reliable snow from early December to mid-April. In 2008, the area enjoyed record snow falls.

But skiing is only half the story. As transportation improved, people took advantage of the obvious warm-weather opportunities for watersports, golf (courses in the area now total more than 30), tennis, mountain biking, hiking, and the like. Before long, the region gained a sometimes-deserved reputation for fine dining and a convivial atmosphere.

Bird-watchers of both intense and casual bent can be fully occupied. Loon lovers, in particular, know that the lakes of Québec province's mountains are home to the native waterfowl that gives its name to the dollar coin. Excellent divers and swimmers, the birds are unable to walk on land, which makes nesting a trial. They're identified by a distinctive call that might be described as an extended, mournful giggle.

At any time of year, a visit to any of the villages or resorts in the Laurentians is likely to yield pleasant memories. The busiest times are February and March for skiing, July and August for summer vacation, and during the Christmas-to-New Year's holiday period.

In March and April, the maple trees are tapped, and *cabanes à sucre* (sugar shacks) open up everywhere, some selling just maple syrup and candies, others serving full meals and even staging entertainment. May is often characterized by warm days, cool nights, and just enough people that the streets don't seem deserted. September is the same way, and in the last 2 weeks of that month, the leaves put on a stunning show of autumnal color.

In May and June, it must be said, the indigenous black flies and mosquitoes can seem as big and as ill-tempered as buzzards, so be prepared. And some of the resorts, inns, and lodges close down for a couple of weeks in spring and fall, so be sure to check ahead if you're traveling during that time.

Prices can be difficult to pin down. The large resorts have so many types of rooms, suites, cottages, meal plans, discounts, and packages that you may need a travel agent to pick through the thicket of options. Prices listed for hotels in this chapter are the rack rate for double occupancy during the busy skiing and summer-vacation months, unless otherwise noted. At other times of the year, reservations are easier to get and prices for virtually everything are lower. Most hotels and resorts offer package deals with meals or activities, so consult their websites for options. Many also offer discounts to AAA members.

Remember that Montréalers fill the highways when they "go up north" on weekends, particularly during the top skiing months, so make reservations early if that's when you'll be traveling.

See p. 62 for general information about hotel rates and the Frommer's star rating system.

ESSENTIALS
Getting There
BY CAR The fast and scenic **Autoroute des Laurentides,** also known as **Autoroute 15,** goes straight from Montréal to the Laurentians. Leaving Montréal, you just follow the signs to St-Jérôme. The exit numbers represent the distance in kilometers that the village lies from Montréal.

Though the pace of development is quickening, flanking the highway with water parks, condos, and chain restaurants, this is still a pretty drive once you're out of the clutches of the tangle of expressways surrounding Montréal and past St-Jérôme. You'll quickly get a sweeping, panoramic introduction to the area, from lower Laurentians' rolling hills and forests to the mountain drama of the upper range.

Those with the time to meander can exit at St-Jérôme and pick up the older, parallel **Route 117,** which plays tag with the autoroute all the way to Ste-Agathe-des-Monts. Many of the region's more appealing towns are along or near this route. (Beware in winter, however, when parts of Rte. 117 can become riddled with potholes large enough to seriously damage your car. The extreme weather does a job on the state of the roads.) North of Ste-Agathe, the autoroute ends and Route 117 becomes the major artery for the region. It continues well past Mont-Tremblant and deep into Québec's north country, finally ending at the Ontario border hundreds of miles from Montréal.

Québec's equivalent of the highway patrol, Sûreté de Québec, maintains a presence along the stretch of Autoroute 15 between St-Faustin and Ste-Adèle. While enforcement of speed limits is loose, if you're pulled over, remember that radar detectors are illegal in the province (even if they're not turned on) and can be confiscated.

BY PLANE **Mont-Tremblant International Airport** (airport code YTM; ✆ **819/275-9099**; www.mtia.ca), 39km (24 miles) northwest of Mont-Tremblant, began receiving direct flights from Newark, New Jersey, in 2007 (Continental Airlines; winter months only). It also gets direct flights from Toronto. Car rentals are available from Hertz and Budget by reservation only. An airport shuttle bus delivers guests directly to 16 hotels in Mont-Tremblant and the ski mountain, and taxis are available. The ride takes about 40 minutes.

Aéroport International Pierre-Elliott-Trudeau de Montréal (airport code YUL; ✆ **800/465-1213** or 514/394-7377; www.admtl.com), known more commonly as **Montréal-Trudeau Airport,** is 30 to 60 minutes from the Laurentians, depending on how far north you're headed. **Skyport** (✆ **800/471-1155** or 514/631-1155; www.skyportinternational.com) runs a shuttle to Mont-Tremblant from mid-December to mid-April and from mid-May to mid-October by reservation. There are also taxis and limousines that will take you to any Laurentian hideaway—for a price. Ask about the best options when making accommodations reservations.

BY BUS From Montréal, **Galland** buses (✆ **514/333-9555;** www.galland-bus.com) depart from **Station Centrale D'autobus,** 505 bd. de Maisonneuve est, stopping in the larger Laurentian towns, including Ste-Sauveur, Ste-Adèle, and Mont-Tremblant. The ride to Mont-Tremblant takes just less than 3 hours.

Another option is the nonprofit **Allo Stop,** an alternative program that coordinates rideshares to help reduce the numbers of cars on the road. Travelers help pay for gas. Call ✆ **514/985-3032** for the Montréal office or visit www.allostopmontreal.com.

Visitor Information

Tourist offices are plentiful throughout the Laurentians. Look for the blue "?" signs along the highways or in towns. Closed offices are marked with a sign that reads FERME. For an orientation to the entire region, stop in at the major information center, well marked from the highway, at exit 51 off Autoroute 15. It shares a building with a 24-hour McDonald's, and there's a gas station next door. Called **Tourisme Laurentides** (✆ **800/561-6673** or 450/224-7007; www.laurentides.com), it has racks of brochures and a helpful staff that can, for no charge, make reservations for lodging throughout the Laurentides. It's open daily from 8:30am to 5pm (until 6pm on Fri) and from late-June through September daily from 8:30am to 8:30pm.

Tips **On the Road: A Quick Guide**

Canada is on the metric system, so distances are measured in kilometers (1 kilometer = .62 miles). Many U.S. cars have a secondary speedometer that gives speed in kilometers. The maximum posted speed limit on most highways is 100kmph (62 mph).

At gas stations, *avec service* means full-service, and *libre service* means self-service. The directions on the pump are usually in French and English, especially at name-brand stations. Gas is sold by the liter, and 3.78 liters equals 1 gallon. It's slightly more expensive by U.S. standards, with recent prices of C93¢ per liter, translating to about US$3.52 per gallon, but will not raise the eyebrows of travelers from countries where gas is much more costly.

Road signs are always in French; ARRET means stop, DEMI TOUR means U-turn.

ST-SAUVEUR

Only 60km (37 miles) north of Montréal, the village of St-Sauveur (pop. 8,470) can easily be a day trip. The area is flush with outlet malls and the carloads of shoppers they attract, but a few blocks farther north, the older village square is dominated by a handsome church, and the streets around it bustle with a less frenzied activity for much of the year. Be prepared to have difficulty finding a parking place in season (try the large lot behind the church). Dining and snacking on everything from crepes to hot dogs are big activities here, evidenced by the many beckoning cafes. In summer, there's a tourist kiosk on the square.

In summer, **Parc Aquatique du Mont St-Sauveur,** 350 av. St-Denis (© **450/227-4671;** www.parcaquatique.com), Canada's largest water park, features rafting, a wave pool, a tidal-wave river, a three-level spa pool, and slides, including one you ride a chairlift to get to the top of and ride down in a tube. Full-day admission is C$35 for ages 13 and older, C$28 for ages 6 to 12, C$17 for ages 3 to 5, and free for 2 and younger. Half-day, nights, and family admissions also available.

Ten days in early August are dedicated to St-Sauveur's annual **Festival des Arts** (© **450/227-0427;** www.fass.ca), with an emphasis on music and dance, including jazz and chamber concerts and ballet troupes. The schedule always includes a number of free events.

Where to Stay & Dine

If the idea of a picnic appeals—and in this town of ordinary restaurants, it well might—drive west on the main street, rue Principale, to **Chez Bernard,** 411 rue Principale (© **450/240-0000;** www.chezbernard.com). Inside the pretty little house behind the iron fence, you'll find a store selling fragrant cheeses, crusty breads, wines, savory tarts, pâtés, sausages, smoked meats, and a variety of prepared meals. There are three small tables. Prices range from C$4 to C$17. The store opens daily at 10am.

Le Petit Clocher At the end of a residential cul-de-sac at the top of a hill, tucked in the woods and looking out to the mountains in the distance, this converted monastery is an intriguing B&B. The decor is a riot of styles: English country-cottage braided rugs, wood roosters, medieval tapestries, and knights' armor. Each room has a French-Catholic theme (La Chapelle, La Divine), and La Cardinale features a red double whirlpool in the bedroom corner. In winter, the antique piano in the main room gets covered with miniature houses to make a multi-leveled village tableau. All rooms but one look out at the mountains, and the last faces the woods where deer wander by. Have a light dinner to take full advantage of the opulent breakfast: fresh croissants, French cheeses, quiche, just-tapped maple water, and individual soufflés. This could be the best breakfast in all the Laurentians.

216 av. de l'Eglise, St-Sauveur, PQ J0R 1R7. $\textcircled{C}$ **450/227-7576.** Fax 450/227-6662. www.bbcanada.com/lepetitclocher. 7 units. C$185–C$215 double. Rates include huge breakfast. Packages available. AE, MC, V. Exit 60 from Autoroute 15, left at the traffic light (Rte. 364 W), right on chemin de la Gare, right on rue Principale, left on av. de l'Eglise. Watch for sign after 1km ($^2/_3$ mile) and turn left up driveway. Inquire before bringing children. **Amenities:** Outdoor hot tub. *In room:* A/C, TV, hair dryer, Wi-Fi (free).

Manoir Saint-Sauveur Just minutes off the autoroute and in the heart of the outlet shopping frenzy, Manoir Saint-Sauveur offers a monster outdoor pool and a comprehensive roster of four-season activities. The on-site spa, **Le Spa du Manoir,** specializes in body treatments and massage therapy. Rooms are spacious and comfortable, blandly modern with light-wood furnishings that hint vaguely of 19th-century Gallic inspirations. Units in the condo section have kitchenettes. The main building, with its many dormers, is easily spotted from the road. Like most properties in the region, the front desk adjusts prices up or down according to season, demand, and occupancy rate on any given night, so ask if they have anything less expensive when you book or arrive.

246 chemin du Lac Millette, St-Sauveur, PQ J0R 1R3. $\textcircled{C}$ **800/361-0505** or 450/227-1811. Fax 450/227-8512. www.manoir-saint-sauveur.com. 280 units. C$149–C$289 double; C$239–C$459 suite. Children 17 and younger stay free in parent's room. Packages available. AE, MC, V. Indoor parking C$10, outdoor parking free. Take exit 60 off Autoroute 15. **Amenities:** 2 restaurants; bar; babysitting; large indoor and outdoor pools; substantial health club; room service; spa; tennis courts. *In room:* A/C, TV, hair dryer, Wi-Fi (C$11 per day).

STE-ADELE & MONT GABRIEL

In winter, the ski mountain of **Mont Gabriel** is a popular destination (for information, see Hôtel Mont Gabriel, below). To get there, follow Autoroute 15 to exit 64 and turn right at the stop sign. In addition to offering downhill skiing, the mountain is wrapped in cross-country trails that range through the surrounding countryside.

The adjacent village, Ste-Adèle (pop. 10,835), only 67km (42 miles) north of Montréal, is a near-metropolis compared to the other Laurentian villages. What makes it seem big are its services: police, doctors, ambulances, a shopping center, cinemas, art galleries, and a larger collection of places to stay and dine. As rue Morin mounts the hill to Lac Rond, Ste-Adèle's resort lake, it's easy to see why the town is divided into a lower part *(en bas)* and an upper part *(en haut).*

To get to the village, either take Route 117, which swings directly into its main street, boulevard Ste-Adèle, or get off Autoroute 15 at exit 67.

Exploring Ste-Adèle

Ste-Adèle's main street, **rue Valiquette,** is a busy one-way thoroughfare lined with cafes, galleries, and bakeries. Locals favor **Au Bistro Le Monde** at 1049 rue Valiquette ($\textcircled{C}$ **450/229-3131**) for its relaxed atmosphere and consistently good game dishes such as the C$26 bison medallions. Friendly staff will help you choose a bottle from the affordable wine list. Summer meals are served alfresco.

Lac Rond is the center of summer activities. Canoes, sailboats, and *pédalos* (pedal-powered watercraft), which can be rented from several docks, glide over the placid surface, while swimmers splash and play near shore-side beaches.

Where to Stay & Dine

Hôtel Le Chantecler ★ (Kids (Value Sprawled across steep slopes cupping Lac Rond, this resort draws families in both summer and winter. Housing is comprised of two- and three-story stone buildings, their roofs bristling with steeples and dormers. The hotel operates a ski mountain, about 15 minutes away by car or hotel shuttle, with discounts for guests. Cross-country skiing and ice-skating are available. Warm weather brings the possibilities of windsurfing and boating on the lake, as well as rounds on two golf courses. Parents can enjoy a seaweed or mud body wrap while kids explore the arcade. Rooms renovated in 2006 have pine furniture. Most also have air-conditioning and many have whirlpools. A buffet breakfast is served in a dining room overlooking the lake.

1474 chemin Chantecler, Ste-Adèle, PQ J8B 1A2. ℂ 888/916-1616. www.lechantecler.com. 215 units. $108–$138 double; C$165–C$269 suite. Children 17 and younger stay free in parent's room. Packages and meal plans available. AE, DC, DISC, MC, V. Free parking. Take exit 67 off Autoroute 15, turn left at the 4th traffic light onto rue Morin, and then turn right at the top of the hill onto chemin Chantecler. **Amenities:** Restaurant; bar; babysitting; badminton; bike rental; golf; health club and spa w/squash and racquetball; hiking trails; horseback riding; pool (indoor); lake beach; room service; tennis courts (6 lit); whirlpool and saunas; watersports equipment. *In room:* A/C, TV, hair dryer, Wi-Fi (free).

Hôtel Mont Gabriel ★ (Kids Perched high atop Mont Gabriel and looking like the rambling log cottages of the turn-of-the-20th-century wealthy, this kid-friendly resort is set on a 480-hectare (1,186-acre) forest estate and features golf and tennis programs in summer and ski and spa packages in winter. The hotel is a ski-in-ski-out facility with more than half the trails open for night-skiing. The spacious rooms in the Tyrol section were renovated in 2006 and are the most modern and desirable, and many provide views of the surrounding hills. One luxury suite and two chalets offer the option for more space still and wheelchair accessible rooms are available. Dog sledding and snowmobiling are possible in-season. The hotel is only 45 minutes from Montréal's Trudeau Airport.

1699 chemin Mont-Gabriel, Ste-Adèle, PQ J8B 1A5. ℂ 800/668-5253 or 450/229-3547. Fax 450/229-7034. www.montgabriel.com. 128 units. C$99–C$199 double. Children 16 and younger stay free in parent's room. Meal plans and packages available. AE, MC, V. Free parking. Take exit 64 from Autoroute 15. **Amenities:** Restaurant; bar; babysitting; 18-hole golf course; health club and spa; pools (heated indoor and outdoor); sauna; tennis courts (6 lit, clay) and tennis instruction; whirlpools (indoor and outdoor); alpine skiing on-site. *In room:* A/C, TV, hair dryer, Wi-Fi (C$10 per day).

L'Eau à la Bouche ★ The owners leave no doubt as to where their priorities lie. While the hotel, directly on busy Route 117, is entirely satisfactory, the restaurant is their beloved baby and has the glowing reviews to prove it. False modesty isn't a factor—*l'eau à la bouche* means "mouthwatering"—and the kitchen uses native ingredients with nouvelle presentations. Full advantage is taken of seasonal products, as with one summer starter of a poached half lobster with chanterelles and gathered wild vegetables. Desserts are impressive, and the cheese plate—pungent nubbins delivered with warm baguette slices—is truly special. Everything is pricey: the C$150 discovery menu that includes wine pairings, the *table d'hôte* for C$75, the à la carte main courses for C$40 and up. The hotel boasts a spa with massage rooms and a pretty outdoor hot tub and small waterfall, which nonguests can visit for C$40.

3003 bd. Ste-Adèle (Rte. 117), Ste-Adèle, PQ J8B 2N6. ℂ 888/828-2991 or 450/229-2991. Fax 450/229-7573. www.leaualabouche.com. 17 units. C$185–C$225 double; C$205–C$325 for renovated rooms and

(Tips) Biker's Paradise: The 4,000km Route Verte

Québec is bike crazy, and it's got the goods to justify it. In summer 2007, the province officially inaugurated the new **Route Verte (Green Route),** a 4,000km (2,485-mile) bike network that stretches from one end of the province to the other linking all regions and cities. The idea started in 1995 and is modeled on the Rails-to-Trails program in the U.S. and cycling routes in Denmark, Great Britain, and along the Danube and Rhine rivers. It was initiated by the nonprofit biking organization Vélo Québec with support from the Québec Ministry of Transportation. Route Verte won the prestigious Prix Ulysse, one of the grand prizes given annually by the Québec tourist office, right out of the gate. The National Geographic Society went on to declare it one of the 10 best bicycle routes in the world.

Included in the network is the popular **P'tit Train du Nord** bike trail through the Laurentians to Mont-Tremblant and beyond. It's built on a former railway track and passes through the villages of Ste-Adèle, Val David, and Ste-Agathe-des-Monts. Cyclists can get food and bike repairs at renovated railway stations along the way and hop on for a day trip or a longer tour. The trail is free to ride on.

The Route Verte website **(www.routeverte.com)** provides maps of all the paths by region, with an "Accommodations" link that lists places to rent bikes as well as B&Bs, campsites, and hotels that are especially focused on serving bikers. Accredited accommodations display a BIENVENUE CYCLISTES! sticker or sign and provide a covered and locked place for overnight bicycle storage, access to high-carb meals with lots of fruits and veggies, a bike pump and tools, and information about where to make repairs nearby. The guidebook Cycling in Québec: Official Guide to Bicycling on Québec's Route Verte can be ordered from the site.

Also look for the free Official Tourist Guide to the Laurentians, published by the regional tourist office (www.laurentides.com); it always has a big section on biking. And if you decide to plan a big trip, keep in mind Transport du Parc Linéaire (✆ **888/686-1323** or 450/569-5596; www.transportduparclineaire.com), which provides baggage transport from inn to inn.

suites. Packages and meal plans available. AE, DC, MC, V. Free parking. **Amenities:** Restaurant; cafe; babysitting; pool (outdoor); room service; spa with sauna, steam room, cold and hot pool. In room: A/C, TV, hair dryer, Wi-Fi.

STE-MARGUERITE-DU-LAC-MASSON

Ste-Marguerite (pop. 2,581), about 12 km (7½ miles) east of Autoroute 15, is alongside the large Lac Masson and home to **Bistro à Champlain,** one of the region's prime restaurants (see below). To get there, take exit 69 off of Autoroute 15 onto Route 370. Or, if you're driving from Ste-Adèle, look for a street heading northeast named chemin Pierre-Péladeau (which is Rte. 370). It becomes a narrow road that crosses the 9m-wide (30-ft.) Rivière du Nord and then winds through evergreen forests past upscale vacation homes. The road dead-ends at the lake, with the restaurant at the intersection.

In summer, information about the area is available from Pavillon du Parc, a kiosk alongside Lac Masson and across from the restaurant.

Where to Dine

Bistro à Champlain ★ FRENCH   On Lac Masson's shore is one of the most honored restaurants in the Laurentians. The 35,000-bottle cellar is the reason most people make gastronomic pilgrimages here from Montréal. In fact, it can be fairly said that the tail wags the dog—this is a place to have some food with your wine. The vintage list is as thick as the A-to-D volume of an encyclopedia and is posted as a 120-page PDF on the restaurant's website. Everyone is invited to visit the cellar. If you're feeling giddy, try a 2-ounce pour of Château d'Yquem with a serving of seared duck foie gras for C$70. It goes without saying that waiters are readily equipped to discuss even the humblest bottles at length. The 1864 building used to be a general store, and it retains the exposed beams and original cash register. Abstract paintings and prints by prominent artists including Jean-Paul Riopelle adorn the rough-hewn board walls.

75 chemin Masson, Ste-Marguerite-du-Lac-Masson. © **450/228-4988.** www.bistroachamplain.com. Reservations recommended. Main courses C$18–C$43; *table d'hôte* C$46; *menu degustation* C$85. AE, MC, V. Summer Tues–Sun from 6pm; winter Thurs–Sat from 6pm but call to confirm.

VAL-DAVID

At exit 76 of Autoroute 15 (and also along Rte. 117) is Val-David, the region's faintly bohemian enclave (pop. 4,284). About 80km (50 miles) north of Montréal, it conjures up images of cabin hideaways set among hills rearing above ponds and lakes, and creeks tumbling through fragrant forests.

The **tourist office** is on the main street at 2579 rue de l'Église (© **888/322-7030** ext. 235, or 819/322-2900 ext. 235; www.valdavid.com). Another possibility for assistance is **Centre d'Exposition de Val-David,** a cultural center that mounts art exhibits in a two-story wooden building at 2495 rue de l'Église (© **819/322-7474;** www.culture.val-david.qc.ca).

Note that this far north into the Laurentians, the telephone area code changes to 819.

Exploring Val-David

Val-David is small, so park anywhere and meander at leisure. There are many artist studios, and the village sponsors a huge **ceramic art festival** (© **819/322-6868;** www.1001pots.com) from mid-July to mid-August that it claims is "the largest exhibition of ceramics in North America." Sculptors and ceramicists, along with painters, jewelers, pewter smiths, and other craftspeople display their work, and there are concerts and other outdoor activities. There are pottery workshops for children every Saturday and Sunday; reserve a spot online.

Also look for the organic **farmer's market** every Saturday morning from late June to late September on rue de l'Académie (opposite the church).

Val-David is one of the villages along the bike path called **Parc Linéaire le P'Tit Train du Nord,** built on a former railroad track (see "Biker's Paradise: The 4,000km Route Verte," above). Rock-climbing enthusiasts flock to the nearby Dufresne Regional Park to explore its more than 500 rated routes. For a relaxing picnic, get fixings at the **Metro Supermarket** across from the tourist office. Then turn left onto the bike path just around the corner from the tourist office. Walk 5 minutes to the North River and the teeny **Parc des Amoureux.** There are plenty of benches (and some parking spaces). Look for the sign that says SITE PITTORESQUE.

Au Petit Poucet ★ (Finds) QUEBECOIS   If you crave a Québec of hunting cabins and hearty sugar shack cuisine, look no further than the pig's knuckles, pea soup, and maple-smoked ham at Au Petit Poucet, marked by a sign with a dangling pig and a young boy with giant boots and a knapsack on a stick, off Route 117 (south of Val-David). A floor-to-ceiling fireplace anchors the interior, rebuilt in 2007 after a devastating fire. Stuffed raccoons keep watchful eyes over diners who fill the room even on midwinter weekdays. Stave off winter chills with an *érableccino* (espresso, maple syrup, and hot milk topped with a mountain of frothed milk and a sprinkling of maple sugar) or opt for the any-season main course of *tourtière* (meat pie), best sampled with its traditional side of tomato chutney. If there's no time to dine, products can be purchased in the restaurant's shop.

1030 Rte. 117, Val-David. ⓒ **888/334-2246** or 819/322-2246. www.aupetitpoucet.com. Main courses C$7–C$17. AE, MC, V. Daily 6:30am–4pm.

STE-AGATHE-DES-MONTS

With a population of 10,077, Ste-Agathe-des-Monts, 103km (64 miles) north of Montréal, has as its main thoroughfare **rue Principale,** which is lined with shops, restaurants, and cafes. The town marks the end of Autoroute 15.

Exit from the autoroute and follow the signs for CENTRE-VILLE and then QUAI MUNIC-IPAL. The town dock on the lake, **Lac des Sables,** and the pretty **waterfront park** make Ste-Agathe a good place to pause in warm months. If you like, rent a bicycle from **Intersport Jacque Champoux,** 74 rue St-Vincent (ⓒ **800/667-3480** or 819/326-3480; www.jacque-champoux.ca), for the 5km (3-mile) ride around the lake. Lake cruises, beaches, and watercraft rentals seduce many visitors into lingering for days.

In the heart of the village, stop off for a casual breakfast or lunch at the sunlit **Au Petit Creux,** 84 rue Principale (ⓒ **819/326-7055**), where the fresh-pressed juices and simple but tasty sandwiches will fill that hankering for a snack, just as the restaurant's name suggests. (*Avoir un petit creux* is a French idiom that means something like, "I have the munchies.") If in fact you do, be sure to also check out desserts made on the premises displayed in the case midway through the narrow cafe.

Croisières Alouette (ⓒ **819/326-3656;** www.croisierealouette.com) offers 50-minute lake cruises that depart from the dock at the foot of rue Principale from late-May to late-October. A running commentary explains the sights (in English and/or French, with Spanish and Italian available upon request) and provides information about the water-skiing competitions and windsurfing that Ste-Agathe and the Lac des Sables are famous for. The Alouette cruise costs C$14 for adults, C$12 for seniors 60 and older, C$5 for children 6 to 15, and is free for children 5 and younger.

VILLE DE MONT-TREMBLANT

The Mont-Tremblant area is a kind of Aspen-meets-Disneyland. It's beautiful country, with great skiing and an ever-expanding resort village on the slope—a prime destination in the province in all four seasons.

In 2005, the villages of St-Jovite and Mont-Tremblant and the pedestrian area at the base of the mountain, which had all been independent, combined to become the single entity called Ville de Mont-Tremblant. Note that many maps, hotels, and residents still refer to the areas as distinct "sectors," which can cause some confusion.

In fact, the abundant use of the name "Tremblant" makes things difficult to keep straight. Here's a primer: There is Mont-Tremblant, the mountain. At the base of its slope is Tremblant, a growing resort village of hotels, restaurants, and shops sometimes called Mont-Tremblant Station or "the pedestrian village" (see "Mont-Tremblant's Pedestrian Village," p. 189). Just adjacent to the pedestrian village is Lac (Lake) Tremblant. About 5km (3 miles) northwest of the resort is a small village which long ago was the region's center and which is now known as the old village of Mont-Tremblant. A cute commercial district about 12km (7½ miles) south of the mountain that used to be called St-Jovite is now called Centre-Ville (Downtown) Mont-Tremblant. Oh, and don't forget the large national park: Parc National du Mont-Tremblant.

Clear as mud?

Getting There

There are two exits from the main roadway, Route 117. The first is exit 122, labeled MONT-TREMBLANT CENTRE-VILLE. Watch closely: Last time we visited, it was marked with an inconspicuous sign directing cars to bear right off the highway onto the small rue de St-Jovite. If you miss it, turn into the gas stations on the right directly after the turnoff and pass through them onto the smaller road.

This exit takes visitors through Centre-Ville Mont-Tremblant, formerly the village of St-Jovite, a pleasant community with most of the expected services. The main street, rue de St-Jovite, is lined with cafes and shops, including the women's clothing boutique **Mode Plus** (no. 813), the folk-art and country-antiques store **Le Coq Rouge** (no. 821), and the restaurant **Antipasto** (no. 855; p. 190). From the center of town, Route 327 heads to the mountain.

The second exit from Route 117 bypasses Centre-Ville and goes directly to the mountain and most of the properties listed here. Take exit 119 to Montée Ryan and follow the blue signs for 10km (6¼ miles). Also watch for signs with the resort's logo, which turns the "A" in "Tremblant" into a graphic of a ski mountain.

Mont-Tremblant International Airport (airport code YTM; © **819/275-9099**; www.mtia.ca) is 24 miles north of the mountain. See p. 175 for more information.

Visitor Information

Tourist information, including maps of local ski trails, is available at © **877/425-2434** or 819/425-2434 and two **Visitor Information Centres:** one in Centre-Ville Mont-Tremblant at 48 chemin de Brébeuf (© **819/425-3300**), open daily 9am to 5pm, and another closer to the ski mountain, at 5080 Montée Ryan (© **819/425-2434**), open daily 9am to 5pm.

You can also check **www.tourismemonttremblant.com**, an official tourism site, and **www.tremblant.ca**, the Mont-Tremblant ski resort's website.

Skiing, Watersports & More

Mont-Tremblant, the mountain, is the highest peak in the Laurentians at 968m (3,176 ft.). In 1894, the provincial government began setting aside land for a government forest preserve, establishing Parc Mont-Tremblant. The foresight of this early conservation effort has afforded outdoor enjoyment to hikers, skiers, and four-season vacationers ever since: The park is the largest in the province, at 1,510 sq. km (583 sq. miles). It has 400 lakes and 6 rivers, along with 196 bird species and a forest primarily of sugar maple and yellow birch as far as the eye can see. The mountain's name comes from a legend of the area's first inhabitants: Amerindians named the peak after the god Manitou and say that when humans disturbed nature in any way, Manitou became enraged and made the great mountain tremble—*montagne tremblante.*

The **Mont-Tremblant ski resort** (www.tremblant.ca) draws the biggest downhill crowds in the Laurentians and is repeatedly ranked as the top resort in eastern North America by *Ski Magazine*. Founded in 1939 by a Philadelphia millionaire named Joe Ryan, it's one of the oldest in North America. It pioneered creating trails on both sides of a mountain and was the second mountain in the world to install a chairlift. The vertical drop is 645m (2,116 ft.).

When the snow is deep, skiers here like to follow the sun around the mountain, making the run down slopes with an eastern exposure in the morning and down the western-facing ones in the afternoon. There are higher mountains with longer runs and steeper pitches, but something about Mont-Tremblant compels people to return time and again.

Today, the resort has snowmaking capability to cover almost three-quarters of its skiable terrain (255 hectares/631 acres). Of its 94 downhill runs and trails, half are expert terrain, about a third are intermediate, and the rest beginner. The longest trail, Nansen, is 6km (almost 4 miles).

There is plenty of **cross-country** action on nearby trails. The adjacent **Parc National du Mont-Tremblant** boasts 10 loops (53km/33 miles) of groomed track in the Diable sector; as of winter 2009-2010, the Pimbina sector is designated exclusively to snowshoeing and backcountry skiing. Visit www.sepaq.com to locate visitor centers and information kiosks or to check availability of the sector's five new yurts, which sleep four in any season. Many enthusiasts maintain that some of the best cross-country trails are on the grounds of **Domaine Saint-Bernard,** formerly a congregation of the Brothers of Christian Instruction, 545 chemin St-Bernard (© **819/425-3588;** www.domainesaint bernard.org).

Curling, ice climbing, ice skating, dogsledding, tubing, or acrobranche—a series of zip lines that allow you to swing from tree to tree at heights exceeding 22m (75 ft.)—are also available in the Mont-Tremblant region. For a truly unique aerial view, try acrobranche at night; make reservations through the **Tremblant Activity Center** (© **819/681-4848;** www.tremblantactivities.com).

In warm weather, watersports are almost as popular as the ski slopes are in winter, thanks to the opportunities surrounding the base of Mont-Tremblant. They include Lac Tremblant, a gorgeous stretch of lake, and another dozen lakes, as well as rivers and streams. From June until October, **Croisières Mont-Tremblant,** 2810 chemin du Village (© **819/425-1045;** www.croisierestremblant.com), offers a 70-minute narrated cruise of Lac Tremblant, focusing on its history, nature, and legends. Fares are C$18 for adults, C$15 for seniors, C$5 for children ages 6 to 15, and free for children 5 and younger.

Other summer options include **golf** at the renowned **Le Diable** and **Le Géant** courses, as well as tennis, boating, swimming, biking, and hiking.

There are some well-regarded cultural offerings here, too. The **Tremblant International Blues Festival** (www.tremblantblues.com), which celebrated its 15th year in 2008, hosts up to 150 free shows for 10 days in July with artists such as Jonas, Buckwheat Zydeco, Keb'Mo, Ana Popovic, and Pinetar Perkins. Five stages are set up throughout the pedestrian village. Despite being named the 2008 cultural event of the year by the Mont-Tremblant Chamber of Commerce, the **Tremblant Film Festival** (www.tremblantfilm festival.org) took a year off in 2009 for economic reasons but plans to resume for 5 days in June 2010.

A new summer diversion is the downhill dry-land alpine **luge run** right at the pedestrian village. The engineless sleds are gravity-propelled, reaching speeds of up to 48kmph (30 mph), if you so choose (it's easy to go down as a slowpoke, too). Rides are priced by

(Tips) **With Apologies to Monty Python: "SPA, spa, spa, spa . . ."**

Spas are big business around here: They're probably the most popular new features at hotels, especially in the Mont-Tremblant area, where people are looking for other things to do (and new ways to pamper themselves) beyond dropping a lot of money on skiing.

At some hotels, innkeepers might say they have a "spa" on-site when what they've got is an outdoor hot tub. What we're talking about here, though (and what we mean in the hotel listings when we say a facility has a spa), is a complex that features therapeutic services, particularly ones that involve water.

The spa industry, it turns out, has some clear definitions of what constitutes a spa. In the Québec province, the organization **Spas Relais Santé** (www.spas relaissante.com) distinguishes between *day spas,* which offer massages and *estétique* services such as facials and pedicures; *destination spas,* which often involve overnight stays and healthy cuisine; and *Nordic spas,* which are built around a natural water source and include outdoor and indoor spaces.

If you've never experienced a European-style Nordic spa before, try to set aside 3 hours for a visit to **Le Scandinave Spa,** at 4280 Montée Ryan, Mont-Tremblant (© **888/537-2263** or 891/425-5524; www.scandinave.com). It's a tranquil complex of small buildings tucked among evergreen trees on the Diable River shore and is as chic as it is rustic. For C$43 weekdays or C$45 weekends, visitors (18 and older only) have run of the facility. Options include outdoor hot tubs designed to look like natural pools (one is set under a man-made waterfall); a Norwegian steam bath thick with eucalyptus scent; indoor relaxation areas with super-comfortable, low-slung chairs; and the river itself, which the heartiest of folk dip into even on frigid days. (A heat lamp keeps a small square of river open even through the iciest part of winter.) The idea is to move from hot to cold to hot, which supposedly purges toxins and invigorates your skin. Bathing suits are required, and men and women share all spaces except the changing rooms. For extra fees, massages and yoga classes are offered.

Couples, mothers and daughters, groups of friends, and folks on their own all come to "take the waters." The spa is year-round, and few activities are more relaxing than being in a warm outdoor pool as snow falls, the sun sets, and the temperature plummets. (That stroll back to the locker room is another story, though, especially with bare feet.)

In the Mont-Tremblant region, many hotels have on-site spas. Fairmont Tremblant houses one of eight **Amerispas** in the province (© **819/681-7680;** www.amerispa.ca), which offers rain massages, ice cider body wraps, and aromatherapy, and at Hôtel du Lac's **Spa-sur-le-Lac** (© **819/425-2731;** www.hoteldulac.ca), you can try the "chocolate package"—a truffle bath, exfoliation with Dead Sea salts, a chocolate body wrap, and a back massage with vanilla oil.

number of descents, starting at C$12 for adults. Pee-wees start at C$2. The village has **185** other games and attractions that can keep visitors occupied for days.

There's also the opportunity to participate in a real **cattle roundup.** The adventure lasts 5 hours and takes place at **Ranch Mont-Tremblant** (© 819/326-7654; www. ranch-mont-tremblant.qc.ca), 40 minutes from the mountain. Cost is C$150. Teens and young adults tend to love it.

No matter the season, the lucky (or brave) can hold 'em or fold 'em at **Casino de Mont-Tremblant** (© 800/665-2274 or 514/499-5180; www.casinosduquebec.com/ mont-tremblant), which opened its doors in summer 2009. Table games include poker, baccarat, blackjack, craps, and roulette, not to be outdone by 400 slot machines. Admittance is free but restricted to persons over 18. Open Sunday to Wednesday 11am to 1am and Thursday to Saturday 11am to 3am. Wheelchairs are available on loan free of charge. Located on Versant Soleil and connected to the pedestrian village by a new gondola, getting there may be half the fun—unless of course, you win big.

Where to Stay

There are abundant options for housing in the area. In addition to the listings below, **B&Bs** are listed at **www.bbtremblant.com.** For **camping** options within the national park, visit **www.parcsquebec.com.** Also see the sidebar "Mont-Tremblant's Pedestrian Village," on p. 189.

Of the accommodations listed below, the following are in or just adjacent to the pedestrian village: Ermitage du Lac, Fairmont Tremblant, Homewood Suites by Hilton, and Quintessence. Also, Auberge La Porte Rouge and Hôtel Mont-Tremblant are located in the old village, and the following are a short driving distance from both the pedestrian village and the old village: Château Beauvallon, Hôtel du Lac, Le Grand Lodge, and Wyndham Cap Tremblant.

Past visitors to the area may recall **Gray Rocks,** a 102-year-old Mont-Tremblant resort with its own ski mountain and ski school. In 2009 the resort closed all but its two golf courses, La Belle and La Bête (© 800/567-6744 or 819/425-2772; www.golflabelleet labete.com).

Auberge La Porte Rouge (Value) This unusual motel-inn, run by a third-generation owner, is located in the old village of Mont-Tremblant, on a public beach. Wake to a view of Lake Mercier through your picture window (every unit has one), or take in the vista from a little balcony. Some rooms have both fireplaces and whirlpool tubs. There is a terrace facing the lake and a small cocktail lounge. Rooms accommodate two to three people, while cottages have space for 10. Rowboats, canoes, and pedal boats are all available, and the motel is directly on the regional bike and cross-country ski linear park, Le P'tit Train du Nord.

1874 chemin du Village, Mont-Tremblant. PQ J8E 1K4. © 800/665-3505 or 819/425-3505. Fax 819/425-6700. www.aubergelaporterouge.com. 26 units. C$174–C$224 double. Rates include dinner and breakfast. Packages available. C$30 for children 6 to 17; children 5 and younger stay free. AE, MC, V. **Amenities:** Restaurant; bike rental; pool (heated outdoor); watersports equipment. *In room:* A/C, TV, hair dryer, Wi-Fi (free).

Château Beauvallon ★★ (Kids) (Value) Since opening in 2005, Château Beauvallon has become the region's premiere property for families who want to stay off the mountain. A member of Small Luxury Hotels of the World, the 70-suite, three-story hotel has positioned itself as an affordable luxury retreat for seasoned travelers, and it delivers with a relaxed elegance. Every suite has two bathrooms, a small bedroom with a plush

California-king-size bed, a queen-size Murphy bed, a pullout couch, a balcony, a gas fireplace, a 32-inch high-definition flatscreen TV (with a smaller TV in the bedroom), and an equipped kitchenette. All rooms face the pool or the lake behind the property, which sits between two holes on La Diable golf course. A large central fireplace lounge provides a warm gathering place, and the staff is friendly and competent. Both hotel and restaurant adhere to eco-friendly guidelines set by regional and national associations.

6385 Montée Ryan, Mont-Tremblant, PQ J8E 1S5. ✆ **888/681-6611** or 819/681-6611. Fax 819/681-1941. www.chateaubeauvallon.com. 70 units. C$179–C$239 1-bedroom suite. Packages available. AE, DC, MC, V. Free self-parking. Dogs under 20lb. accepted for fee. **Amenities:** Restaurant; bar; babysitting; children's programs (high-season); concierge; exercise room; golf adjacent; hot tub (all-year outdoor); 2 pools (outdoor heated pool w/terrace, indoor heated); room service; putting green. In room: A/C, TV, DVD on request, hair dryer, kitchenette, MP3 docking station, Wi-Fi (free).

Ermitage du Lac (Kids) Convenient to the ski mountain and the pedestrian village without being directly upon either, this boutique hotel offers a little more peace and quiet than larger properties closer to the action. It's also agreeably close to Parc Plage, the beach on Lac Tremblant, which makes for an enjoyable summer stay. All units are large studios or one- to three-bedroom suites, with kitchenettes or full kitchens equipped with oven ranges, microwaves, unstocked fridges, and necessary cookware and crockery (not all have dishwashers, though). Most have fireplaces and balconies, too. There is a secure underground parking garage.

150 chemin du Curé-Deslauriers, Mont-Tremblant, PQ J8E 1C9. ✆ **800/461-8711** or 819/681-2222. Fax 819/681-2223. www.tremblant.ca. 69 units. C$225 double; from C$299 suite. Rates include breakfast. Packages available. Children 17 and younger stay free in parent's room. AE, MC, V. Self-parking C$10. **Amenities:** Breakfast room; children's activity room; concierge; exercise room; hot tub (outdoor, year-round); pool (outdoor, in summer); locker area for skis. In room: A/C, TV, CD player, hair dryer, kitchenette or kitchen, Wi-Fi (C$10 per day).

Fairmont Tremblant ★★ (Kids) The high-end resort for families who want to stay directly on the mountain was built in 1996, and a renovation of its slope-side bar and restaurant was to be completed by 2010. The luxury property stands on a crest above the pedestrian village, as befits its stature among the Tremblant hostelries. Thirteen levels of rooms include the appealing Fairmont View, which overlooks the ski runs and the fairy-tale resort, and Fairmont Gold, which offers access to a private lounge. Families can take advantage of arts-and-crafts programs, year-round outdoor and indoor pools, the 38-person outdoor Jacuzzi, and ski-in-ski-out accessibility to the chairlifts. Couples looking for a quiet break or the attention to detail normally paid at a Fairmont may want to avoid school vacation weeks. An on-site **Amerispa** offers body wraps, facials, and massages. Even vacationers staying elsewhere come for the C$55 surf, turf, and sushi dinner buffet of in-house restaurant **Windigo.**

3045 chemin de la Chapelle, Mont-Tremblant, PQ J8E 1E1. ✆ **800/257-7544** or 819/681-7000. Fax 819/681-7099. www.fairmont.com/tremblant. 314 units. Winter C$249–C$369 double; summer from C$249. Children 17 and younger stay free in parent's room. Packages available. AE, DC, DISC, MC, V. Pets accepted, C$25 per day. Valet parking C$18. **Amenities:** Restaurant; cafe in ski season; bar; babysitting; bike rental; children's programs; concierge; executive-level rooms; exercise room; pools (indoor lap and heated outdoor); room service; sauna; spa; access to watersports equipment; Wi-Fi (in lobby, C$18 per day). In room: A/C, TV, hair dryer, Internet (C$18 per day), minibar.

Homewood Suites by Hilton Directly on the pedestrian village at Place St-Bernard, a central gathering space, the Hilton offers direct access to the resort's restaurants, bars, and shops that ring the plaza. It has ski-in-ski-out access to the mountain's slopes, which are just across the plaza, and ski lockers are available to guests. An outdoor pool was added in 2008 and in-suite upgrades were set for completion in 2010. The hotel is made up of several buildings decorated on the outside to look like candy-colored row houses, and all accommodations are crisply furnished suites with fireplaces and equipped kitchens—useful when you want to avoid the village's expensive food venues. Suites range in size from studios to two-bedroom units.

3035 chemin de la Chapelle, Mont-Tremblant, PQ J8E 1E1. © **888/288-2988** or 819/681-0808. Fax 819/681-0331. www.hiltontremblant.com. 103 units. C$200–C$399 suite. Rates include breakfast and afternoon snack and beverages every Mon–Thurs. Children 17 and younger stay free in parent's room. Packages available. AE, MC, V. Self-parking C$10. **Amenities:** Babysitting; hot tub (outdoor salt water); pool (outdoor); room service; Wi-Fi (in dining room, C$10 per day). *In room:* A/C, TV, DVD player available for rent, hair dryer, Internet (free), kitchen.

Hôtel du Lac ★★ (**Kids**) (**Value**) About 3km (2 miles) from the ski mountain's base, this resort is a quieter option than being directly in the pedestrian village hubbub and has a good variety of on-site activities: private lake access and marina, kayaks and paddle-boats, a day camp, the hushed Spa-sur-le-Lac. A needed renovation of rooms and public spaces started in 2008 and continued into 2009. The complex is terraced into a hillside that slopes toward Lac Tremblant and consists of several lodges in muted alpine style. Accommodations offer the greatest of luxuries: space. Most rental units are suites of one or two bedrooms, with prices about equivalent to a single room at many other area resorts. Because the hotel is tucked away, most people take a dinner and breakfast plan. There are no elevators, so ask for a lower level if stairs present an issue. There are a lot of families, conventions, and weddings here.

121 rue Cuttle, Mont-Tremblant, PQ J8E 1B9. © **800/567-8341** or 819/425-2731. Fax 819/425-5617. www.hoteldulac.ca. 122 units. C$249 suite. Children 4 and younger stay free in parent's room. Packages available. AE, MC, V. Free parking. Take Lac Tremblant north and follow signs for less than a mile. Small pets accepted, C$25 per day. **Amenities:** Restaurant; bar; babysitting; bike rental; children's programs (day camp); concierge; exercise room; hot tub (outdoor); pools (indoor and summer-only outdoor); free shuttle to ski mountain; spa; 3 tennis courts; watersports equipment; winter sport equipment rental. *In room:* A/C, TV, hair dryer, kitchen, Wi-Fi (free).

Hôtel Mont-Tremblant (**Value**) A modest hotel in the old village of Mont-Trem-blant, this 22-room property (founded in 1902) is popular both with skiers who want to avoid the resort village's higher prices (a shuttle bus to the slopes stops just across the street) and, in summer, with cyclists who appreciate the location directly on Le P'tit Train du Nord cycling path (p. 179). Most rooms have twin or double beds, and a few have sitting areas. The inn houses the popular restaurant **Le Bernardin,** which was relocated to the second floor in 2009. That made room for a new ground floor Irish pub which the owners outfitted with antiquities and beer draughts from the mother country. Dinner features span French-cut steak with shallots to old-fashioned duck leg with citrus sauce, with main courses priced between C$21 and C$38. Room rates include breakfast and dinner for two.

1900 chemin du Village, Mont-Tremblant, PQ J8E 1K4. © **888/887-1111** or 819/425-3232. Fax 819/425-9755. www.hotelmonttremblant.com. 22 units. C$169 double. Packages available. Rate includes dinner and breakfast for two. AE, MC, V. Free parking. **Amenities:** Restaurant; bar; bike storage; Wi-Fi (in restaurant and pub, free). *In room:* A/C, TV, hair dryer.

Le Grand Lodge ★★ (**Kids**) At a quiet distance from the main resort's frequent clamor, this handsome hotel, which consists mostly of suites, is on the shore of Lake Ouimet and draws families, small conventions, and weddings. It was built in 1998 with the palatial log construction of the north country and units leave little to be desired—what with full kitchens, gas fireplaces, and balconies. Dog sledding directly from the hotel and snowshoeing flesh out the more obvious winter pursuits (for example, skiing), and, in summer, guests partake in tennis, mountain biking, and canoeing and kayaking from a private beach on the lake. There are events for kids every night in the height of the summer and winter ski seasons. A big bar area overlooks the lake, and inside you'll find what the hotel claims is Mont-Tremblant's largest pool. Like it enough and you can buy one of the condos in the complex.

2396 rue Labelle (Rte. 327), Mont-Tremblant, PQ J8E 1T8. ℂ **800/567-6763** or 819/425-2734. Fax 819/425-9725. www.legrandlodge.com. 112 units. C$179–C$299 studio or suite. Children 17 and younger stay free in parent's room. Packages available. AE, DC, DISC, MC, V. Free self-parking; valet parking C$10. Pets accepted, C$25 per night. **Amenities:** Restaurant; bar; babysitting; bike rental; children's programs; concierge; exercise room; pool (indoor); sauna; spa; steam bath; 4 tennis courts; whirlpools (indoor and outdoor); watersports equipment; outdoor ice-skating rink in winter. *In room:* A/C, TV, hair dryer, kitchen, Wi-Fi (free).

Quintessence ★★★ The region's luxury property. All units have views of Lake Tremblant and guests have access to a private beach. Go assuming that virtually every service you might find in a larger deluxe hotel will be available to you—then concentrate on the extras. Hugely comfortable beds have thick feather mattress covers. Bathroom floors are heated, showers are of the drenching rainforest variety, and every unit has a wood-burning fireplace and balcony. If it's warm, you can book a ride on the hotel's gorgeous 1910 mahogany motorboat. There's an outdoor infinity pool and a spa (hotel guests only) that limits the number of visitors to ensure an unhurried atmosphere. Lavish dinners can be taken in the La Quintessence dining room, the intimate Jardin des Saveurs, or outdoors near the pool, and there's a 5,000-bottle wine cellar to draw from. Nature fans will want to consider the one rustic cabin which has a four-poster bed.

3004 chemin de la Chapelle, Mont-Tremblant, PQ J8E 1E1. ℂ **866/425-3400** or 819/425-3400. Fax 819/425-3480. www.hotelquintessence.com. 31 units. Late June to early Sept C$450–C$1,630 suite, C$371–C$536 cabin. Rates include breakfast. Weekends require a 2-night minimum stay. Children 5 and younger stay free in parent's room. Packages available. AE, MC, V. Valet parking C$12. **Amenities:** Restaurant; winebar; babysitting; concierge; health club w/sauna and steam rooms; pool (heated outdoor) and hot tub; room service; spa; Wi-Fi (free); private shoreline w/firepit; 1910 motorboat. *In room:* A/C, TV (upon request), CD player, hair dryer, minibar.

Wyndham Cap Tremblant ★ The Wyndham is a sprawl of handsome condos, both residential and rental, built high into a mountainside with terrific views of Mont-Tremblant, Lake Mercier below, and distances far into the horizon. Units were built in the last few years and rental suites have one to five bedrooms and all the amenities needed for an extended stay: a kitchen, a fireplace, a washer and dryer, a private balcony with a barbecue in summer, and a locker for skis or golf clubs. Outdoor pools include one with a long slide that's popular with kids. The resort's restaurant, **Il Pinnacolo,** is surprisingly good. It's housed in a building at the top of the mountain along with the reception desk, a steep walk from the condos. (The driving isn't easy, either.) There's a shuttle bus to the ski mountain. This is a fine choice if you're looking to be tucked away and left on your own.

400 rue du Mont-Plaisant, Mont-Tremblant, PQ J8E 1L2. ℂ **888/996-3227** or 819/681-8043. Fax 819/681-8086. www.wyndham.com. 170 units. From C$199 suite. Packages available. AE, MC, V. Up the hill from the old village of Mont-Tremblant, off chemin du Village. Free parking. **Amenities:** Restaurant; bar; concierge; exercise room; pools (3 outdoor, 1 heated year-round); steam bath; 4 tennis courts; trails for hiking and cross-country skiing; whirlpools. *In room:* A/C, TV, CD player, hair dryer, kitchen Wi-Fi (free).

Mont-Tremblant's Pedestrian Village

The pedestrian-only resort village (see www.tremblant.ca/village) on Mont-Tremblant's slope is the social hub of winter (and, increasingly, summer) tourism in the Laurentians. From the bottom of the village near the parking lots and bus shuttle, small lanes lead up past clothing shops and more than three dozen restaurants and bars. Along the paths and spread off in all directions are hotels, several of which are described in this chapter.

The village has the prefabricated look of a theme park, but at least planners used the Québécois architectural style of pitched or mansard roofs in bright colors, not ersatz Tyrolean or Bavarian Alpine flourishes. For a sweeping view, take the free gondola from the bottom of the village to the top; it zips over the walkways, candy-colored hotels, and outdoor swimming pools.

Year-round, the village hosts outdoor concerts, barbecues, and events such as the goofy spring Caribou "Splash" Cup, where skiers dress in Halloween costumes, ski down an alpine trail into a pool of cold water, and then run through the village, stopping for shooters and a full glass of beer. Dude!

The resort is owned by Intrawest, a real-estate giant headquartered in Vancouver. The company plans to add two additional villages, a conference center, and 1,200 housing units to the resort within the next 10 years.

Make reservations for lodgings in the resort by contacting the establishments directly, through a central number (© **888/738-1777** U.S. and Canada; 0800/028-3476 U.K.; 514/876-7273), or online at www.tremblant.ca. There are options, too, to rent fully equipped condos and single-family residences.

Where to Dine

Though most Laurentian inns and resorts have their own dining facilities and often require that guests use them (especially in winter), the area does have some good independent dining options for casual lunches or the odd night out. Also keep in mind **La Quintessence** in Quintessence (see above), **Le Bernardin** in Hôtel Mont-Tremblant (p. 187), and **Il Pinnacolo** in the Wyndham Cap Tremblant (p. 188).

Right within the pedestrian village, **Au Grain de Café** (© **819/681-4567;** www.augraindecafe.com), tucked into a corner of the upper village just off Place St-Bernard, is a favorite for coffee and sandwiches. It's open daily from 7:30am until 11pm during ski season, 8am until 9pm the rest of the year.

Also in the pedestrian village, you can browse for baked goods and specialty chocolates at **La Chouquetterie** (116 chemin Kandahar, © **819/681-4509**). If you're lucky, you'll walk in to the aroma of baking croissants, or catch a glimpse of how they're made near the ovens in the cafe area. The desserts are a feast for any adult eye while children may giggle over the souvenir chocolate toothbrushes.

Like most ski mountains, beer is abundant, and there's a worthy reason to trek just beyond the slope-side drink palaces **Le Shack** or **La Forge** to the microbrewery **Microbrasserie La Diable,** housed in a free-standing chalet at 117 chemin Kandahar (© **819/681-4546**). Shoulder up to the bar and the bartender will likely pour a sample or two of the establishment's six home brews.

If you're in the mood for a cocktail, head to **Avalanche Bistro** at 127 chemin Kandahar (✆ **819/681-4727;** www.avalanchebistro.com), just across the path from the microbrewery, where you can choose from more than 30 martinis. There is a small bar that accommodates 10 patrons in winter and outdoor seating in the summer—note that the host may ask for your first and last name upon entering. While more of a place for dining than drinking, the contemporary Japanese menu at **Restaurant Yamada** (100 chemin Kandahar, ✆ **819/681-4141;** www.restaurantyamada.com) offers yet another village option—a wide selection of sake.

Antipasto ITALIAN   Antipasto is housed in an old train station in Centre-Ville Mont-Tremblant. So there's the expected railroad memorabilia on the walls, but the owners have resisted the temptation to play up the theme to excess. Captain's chairs are drawn up to big tables with green Formica tops. The César salad (their spelling) is dense and strongly flavored—the half portion is more than enough as a first course. Individual pizzas are cooked in brick ovens with an enormous range of toppings, including scallops and crabmeat, on a choice of regular or whole-wheat crust; pastas are available in even greater variety. There are outdoor tables in summer.

855 rue de St-Jovite (in Centre-Ville Mont-Tremblant). ✆ **819/425-7580.** Main courses C$12–C$36. AE, MC, V. Daily 11am–10pm.

Aux Truffes ★★ FRENCH CONTEMPORARY   The management and kitchen here are more ambitious than just about any on the mountain, evidenced by a wine cellar that sails through Canadian, Californian, Argentine, Australian, Spanish, and many admirable French bottlings, up to a Château Latour '86 for C$900. (For 9 years running, *Wine Spectator* magazine gave Aux Truffes its award of excellence for its wine list.) Put yourself in the hands of the knowledgeable sommelier and go from there. Seared duck foie gras from the region is a steadfast opener. Imaginative mains include a roasted rack of caribou served shepherd's-pie-style with *chicoutai* berries sauce and braised veal cheek "profiteroles" with grilled apricot sauce and bleu cheese from Québec. Close with selections from the *plateau* of raw-milk Québec cheeses. The service is impeccable, even on the slowest, snowiest days.

Place Saint-Bernard, 3035 chemin de la Chapelle (in the pedestrian village). ✆ **819/681-4544.** www. auxtruffes.com. Main courses C$29–C$46. AE, MC, V. Daily 6–10pm.

Crêperie Catherine BREAKFAST/BRUNCH   This is the spot for those who long for a hot breakfast and bottomless cup of coffee before venturing onto the ski slopes. In addition to both savory and sweet crepes made before your eyes, Crêperie Catherine has cultivated something neighboring restaurants can lack—cozy ambience. A collection of chef figurines can be found in every nook of the wood paneled interior, and each comes with a personal story tied to the restaurant's origins. Don't hesitate to smother your crepe with the house specialty, *sucre a la crème* (a concoction of brown sugar and butter). You can order from any part of the menu any time of day.

113 chemin Kandahar (in the pedestrian village). ✆ **819/681-4888.** www.creperiecatherine.ca. Main courses C$12–C$17, dessert crepes from C$4.95. Daily 8am–9pm.

Le Cheval de Jade FRENCH   Chef Oliver Tali is what is known in the culinary world as a maître canardier, or master chef, in the preparation of duck. In fact, there is only one maître canardier in all of Canada recognized by France's *l'ordre des canardiers,* and he's the one. Normally, that would mean that there's really only one choice: the house specialty, duckling *à la rouennaise.* But, surprise: The bouillabaisse is also a standout. This is a modest-looking roadside restaurant in Centre-Ville Mont-Tremblant with a dozen tables and country decor. If you're interested in having the duck, you have to call in advance to make a special reservation.

688 rue de St-Jovite (in Centre-Ville Mont-Tremblant). ✆ **819/425-5233.** www.chevaldejade.com. Reservations recommended. Main courses C$28–C$35; *table d'hôte* from C$36; 7-course *menu degustation* for 2 C$175. AE, MC, V. Tues–Sat 5:30–10pm.

Patrick Bermand ★ FRENCH/SEAFOOD   If you cherish seafood and have been disappointed by the paucity of finned offerings in the pedestrian village, make dinner reservations here on a Friday or Saturday night. Other nights, it's still a marked improvement over other eateries in Tremblant. Appetizers are especially satisfying and have included garlicky, buttery escargot served in individual ceramic pots, and traditional *soupe à l'oignon* (onion soup). Main courses are good, too, and large—a lot of leftovers leave the building. Opened in 2003 in a roadside log-cabin-style house, the restaurant is in Mont-Tremblant's old village, a short drive from the base of the ski mountain.

2176 chemin du Village (Rte. 327 in the old village). ✆ **819/425-6333.** www.patrickbermand.com. Main courses C$23–C$39; *table d'hôte* from C$26. AE, MC, V. June–August, daily 6–11pm; Sept–May Wed–Sun 6–11pm. Call to confirm hours.

2 CANTONS-DE-L'EST

20–160km (12–99 miles) SE of Montréal, toward Sherbrooke

The rolling countryside of Cantons-de-l'Est has long served as Québec province's breadbasket. Still referred to by most Anglophones as the **Eastern Townships** (and, less frequently, as Estrie), the region is largely pastoral, marked by billowing hills, small villages, a smattering of vineyards, and the 792m (2,598-ft.) peak of Mont-Orford, the centerpiece of a provincial park. Cantons-de-l'Est's southern edge borders Vermont, New Hampshire, and Maine, and just past the Knowlton exit, at Km 100, there's an especially beguiling vista of the Appalachian Mountains that stretches toward New England, not far over the horizon.

Sherbrooke is the gritty, industrial capital at the center of the region, but the highlights noted below are located before you reach it, in an upside-down triangle approximately bordered by the villages of **Bromont** and **North Hatley** in the north (with 62km/38 miles btw. them) and **Dunham** in the south.

Serene glacial lakes attract summer swimmers, boaters, and fishers. Bicyclists zip along rural roads, passing day-trippers touring the region's grape and apple orchards (for wine and cider, natch). Except for a few disheartening signs for fast-food stops, the region is largely advertisement-free.

In winter, skiers who don't head north to the Laurentians come this direction; the Ski Bromont center (see below), just 45 minutes from Montréal, offers 67 illuminated trails for night skiing. (Fun fact: In 1922, Armand Bombardier, who was born near Sherbrooke, invented the prototype for the Ski-Doo, the first snowmobile, to get through the region's unplowed rural roads.)

The Cantons-de-l'Est kick into another gear when spring warmth thaws the ground; crews penetrate every sugar-maple stand to tap the sap and "sugar off." The result? Maple festivals and farms hosting sugaring parties, with guests wolfing down prodigious country repasts capped by traditional maple-syrup desserts. Montréal newspapers and local tourist offices (below) keep up-to-date lists of what's happening and where during the sugaring; most spots are within an hour's drive from the city.

Autumn has its special attractions, too. In addition to the glorious fall foliage (usually best from early Sept–early Oct), the orchards around here sag under the weight of apples of every variety, and cider mills hum day and night to produce Québec's "wine." Particularly special are the ice-cider aperitifs produced by vineyards such as Domaine Pinnacle (see below) from apples that have frosted over. Visitors are invited to help with the harvest and can pay a low price to pick their own baskets of fruit. Cider mills open their doors for tours and tastings.

English town names such as Granby, Sutton, and Sherbrooke are vestiges of the time when Americans loyal to the Crown migrated here during and shortly after the Revolutionary War. Now, however, the population of Cantons-de-l'Est is upwards of 90% French-speaking, with a name to reflect that demographic. A few words of French and a little sign language are sometimes necessary outside hotels and other tourist facilities, since the area draws fewer Anglophone visitors than do the Laurentides.

Best of all for tourists, the Cantons are one of Québec's best-kept secrets: It's mostly Québécois who occupy rental houses here. Follow their lead. For extended stays, consider making your base in one of the several luxury inns along the shores of Lac Massawippi and take day trips from there.

ESSENTIALS
Getting There
BY CAR Leave Montréal by Pont Champlain, a bridge which funnels into arrow-straight Autoroute 10. Go east toward Sherbrooke, and within 30 minutes, you'll be passing silos and fields, clusters of cows, and, in summer, meadows strewn with wildflowers. The exit numbers represent the distance in kilometers that the exit is from Montréal.

BY BUS **Limocar** (which is actually a bus service) offers about 10 trips a day from Montréal through Cantons-de-l'Est as far north as Sherbrooke. Most of the trips are express, while some make stops at Granby, Bromont, Magog, and other towns. Call ℂ 514/842-2281 for schedules from Montréal or visit www.limocar.ca for a complete schedule and prices.

Visitor Information
Tourisme Cantons-de-l'Est (ℂ 800/355-5755; fax 819/566-4445; www.easterntownships. org) provides a slew of information, including updates regarding special packages and promotions.

Driving from Montréal, the first regional **tourist information office** (ℂ 866/472-6292 or 450/375-8774; www.granby-bromont.com) is at exit 68 off Autoroute 10. It's open Monday through Friday 8:30am to 4:30pm and Saturday and Sunday 9am to 5pm (shorter hours in winter).

Telephone area codes in Cantons-de-l'Est are 450 and 819, depending on where you're calling. Towns with a 450 area code are closer to Montréal.

GRANBY
About an hour out of Montréal, north of Autoroute 10 at exit 68, this largely unassuming city (pop. 58,856) offers a few fun activities for children.

First is the **Zoo de Granby,** 300 bd. David-Bouchard (ℂ 877/472-6299 or 450/372-9113; www.zoodegranby.ca). Take exit 68 (or, if you're coming from the east, exit 74) off

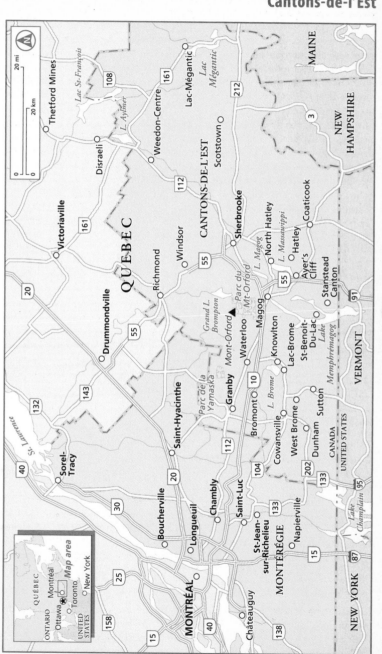

Autoroute 10 and follow the signs. Two roller coasters were added in 2008, and other recent additions include a hippo's river, an outside gorilla park, a "Mayan temple" with jaguars and spectacled bears, a lemur's island, and a tiger's habitat, which can be toured by elevated train. There is also a shark petting area (called a "touch tank" and overseen by an educator), bumper cars, and a Ferris wheel. A massive heated wave pool is a highlight of the water park. The zoo is open daily June through early September and weekends through mid-October, from 10am to 7pm in peak summer months and until 5pm the rest of the season. Admission is C$33 for 13 and older, C$26 for 65 and older, C$22for children 3 to 12, and free for 2 and younger. The fee includes entry to both the zoo and the water park.

Granby is also home to **Parc de la Yamaska** (© 800/665-6527 or 450/776-7182; www.sepaq.com/pq/yam/en), which has a popular beachfront, and opportunities for such activities as swimming, canoeing, hiking, and biking. This is the northern part of the Appalachian mountain range, and it's lush and verdant in summer.

MONT ORFORD

Also on the north side of Autoroute 10 is one of Québec's most popular provincial parks. From mid-September to mid-October, **Parc du Mont-Orford** (© 800/665-6527 or 819/843-9855; www.sepaq.com/pq/mor/en) blazes with autumnal color. Visitors come to try the 18-hole golf course and the 80km (50 miles) of short and long hiking trails in summer; the Route Verte cycling network also passes through the park. In winter, people flock to the slopes to ski, snowboard, or traverse the network of cross-country ski and snowshoe trails. From Autoroute 10, take exit 118 north.

The mountain itself, Mont Orford, is a veteran ski area known as the **Mont Orford ski resort.** It has long provided the preferred slopes of local moneyed families. The resort is composed of three mountains, the contiguous Mont Giroux, Mont Desrochers, and Mont Orford, which is one of the three highest peaks in Québec. Combined, the mountains provide four faces with nine lifts (including a hybrid gondola) and 61 trails. Information is at © 866/673-6731 or 819/843-6548 and www.orford.com.

The area's other ski resorts—**Owl's Head** (© 800/363-3342 or 450/292-3318; www.owlshead.com) and **Mont Sutton** (© 866/538-2545 or 450/538-2545; www.montsutton.com)—are more family-oriented and less glitzy. Mont Sutton is particularly known for its "glade skiing"—or skiing through the woods.

Orford has another claim to fame in the warm months: **Centre d'Arts Orford,** 3165 chemin du Parc (© 800/567-6155 or 819/843-3981; www.arts-orford.org), is a world-class music academy set on an 89-hectare (222-acre) estate. From late June to mid-August each year, the **Festival Orford** presents a series of classical and chamber music concerts. Most tickets are C$37 for professional concerts, with student ("rising-star") performances for just C$5. Concert and dinner packages are available. The center also has an *auberge* with rooms priced between C$36 and C$58 per person. It's also off exit 118 north from Autoroute 10.

Where to Stay
Manoir des Sables ★★ (Kids) This facility is one of the region's most complete resort hotels, and its unofficial motto could be "we have something for everyone." It serves couples, families, golfers, skiers, skaters, fitness enthusiasts, tennis players, kayakers, and business groups who can enjoy snowshoeing, on-site ice skating, and Saturday-night horse-drawn sleigh rides in winter, and canoeing and fishing in the hotel's lake in summer. The spa underwent major renovation in 2009 with the addition of a Turkish *hammam,* a sea salt bath, and more. An 18-hole expert golf course and 9-hole, par-3

executive course are both on-site; in the winter there are groomed cross-country ski trails.
The hotel began life as a Sheraton; the newer Château section contains 24 upscale suites and its own lounge. A huge number of packages allow guests to pick and choose amenities and the cost of their trip in advance.

90 av. des Jardins, Orford, PQ J1X 6M6. (© **800/567-3514** or 819/847-4747. Fax 819/847-3519. www. manoirdessables.com. 141 units. C$178 and up double. Children 16 and younger stay free in parent's room. AE, DC, MC, V. Packages and meal plans available. Free parking. Take exit 118 from Autoroute 10 and follow Rte. 141 north to the hotel, on the right. **Amenities:** 1 restaurant; 2 bars (1 seasonal); babysitting; bike rental; children's programs; 27-hole golf course; health club; pools (indoor and outdoor); room service; spa; outdoor sauna/Nordic baths; steam room; 2 tennis courts; water and winter sports equipment rental. In room: A/C, TV, hair dryer, Wi-Fi (free).

BROMONT

The rest of the towns and attractions in this chapter are all on the southern side of Autoroute 10. Medium-size country roads connect many of them.

Founded in 1964 primarily to accommodate an industrial park and other commercial enterprises, this town of 6,049 at exit 78 is now a popular destination for **Ski Bromont** (© **866/276-6668** or 450/534-2200; www.skibromont.com). In winter, the mountain offers day and extensive night skiing. In summer, it has mountain biking (rent bikes onsite or at the town's entrance, opposite the tourist office) and the Ski Bromont Water Park. A new wave pool, big enough for 700 people, was added in 2009.

Each May since 2001 Bromont has been home to the **La Fête du Chocolat** (Chocolate Festival), with activities for the whole family, including live music and performances, chocolate body painting, chocolate sculpting, and of course—tasting upon tasting. For event details visit www.feteduchocolat.ca or contact the regional tourist office (© **866/472-6292** or 450/375-8774). If you miss the fest, you can stop by the one-room **Musée du Chocolat,** in a red house along in the main stretch of businesses at 679 rue Shefford, opposite the church (© **450/534-3893**). Inside you'll find a display of chocolates both made on the premises and imported from around the world, and a restaurant that serves breakfast and lunch. It's normally open throughout the year Monday through Friday 9am to 6pm and Saturday and Sunday 8am to 5:30pm, with extended hours in the summer.

Bromont is also home to the area's largest **flea market** *(marché aux puces),* where anywhere from a couple dozen to several hundred vendors set up in the local drive-in from 9am to 5pm weekends from April to October. It's at 16 rue Lafontaine (© **450/534-0440**).

Where to Stay & Dine

Château Bromont ★ Kids A landscaped panoramic terrace looks up at the ski mountain across the way, giving this valley hotel a most attractive setting. It sits adjacent to the Château Bromont Golf Club, making this a particularly choice spot for a golf getaway. The hotel coordinates packages with horseback riding or a day at the Granby Zoo (see above), which also appeals to families. For those who just want to relax, an on-site spa features mud and algae baths, a Turkish hammam, and a restaurant that serves healthy lunches. If noise is a concern, you may want to inquire about your room's proximity to the courtyard that surrounds the indoor pool. About a quarter of the rooms have fireplaces.

90 rue Stanstead, Bromont, PQ J2L 1K6. (© **800/304-3433** or 450/534-3433. Fax 450/534-0514. www. chateaubromont.com. 160 units. From C$170 double. Rates include breakfast. Some dates require 2-night minimum stay. Packages available. AE, MC, V. **Amenities:** 2 restaurants; bar; babysitting; exercise room; 18-hole golf course; indoor/outdoor hot tubs; indoor pool and summer-only outdoor pool; racquetball court; spa. In room: A/C, TV, hair dryer, minibar, Wi-Fi (free).

(Finds) **Cantons-de-l'Est: Wine (& Cidre de Glace) Country**

Canada is known more for its beers and ales than its wines, but that hasn't stopped agriculturists from planting vines and transforming fruit into drinkable clarets, chardonnays, and Sauternes. So far, the most successful efforts have blossomed along southern Ontario's Niagara Frontier and in British Columbia's relatively warmer precincts.

Cantons-de-l'Est enjoys the mildest microclimates in the province, and where apples grow, as they do in these parts, so will other fruits, including grapes. Most vintners and fruit-growers are concentrated around **Dunham,** about 103km (64 miles) southeast of Montréal, with several vineyards along Route 202. A stop for a snack or a facility tour makes for a pleasant afternoon. If you're really gung-ho, follow the established **Route des Vins,** which passes 16 vintners (find the map at www.laroutedesvins.ca).

One vineyard on the route is Vignoble de l'Orpailleur, at 1086 Rte. 202 in Dunham (© **450/295-2763;** www.orpailleur.ca). It has guided tours every day from June through October for C$6. Its white wines, such as L'Orpailleur Classique, are popular on Montréal restaurant menus.

Ice cider and ice wine are two regional products that may be new to visitors: They're made from apples and grapes, respectively, left on the trees and vines past the first frost, and served ice-cold with foie gras, cheese, or dessert. One top producer is **Domaine Pinnacle,** at 150 Richford Rd. in Frelighsburg (© **450/298-1226;** www.icecider.com), about 13 km (8 miles) south of Dunham. Its *cidre de glace* is a regular gold medalist in international competitions: It's delightfully smooth and not cloyingly sweet. The farm's tasting room and boutique are open daily from 10am to 6pm May through December.

Other credible wines come out of **Le Cep d'Argent,** at 1257 chemin de la Rivière in Magog (© **877/864-4441** or 819/864-4441; www.cepdargent.com). Many of the vintages produced here are also prizewinners, including the dry white Le Cep d'Argent and the maple-tinged dessert wine L'Archer. There are several tour options, including a "privilege tour" of the champagne cellar that describes the méthode champenoise and includes tastings of six wines with regional products. Cost is C$16 for the 90-minute exploration. Reservations are required.

KNOWLTON & WEST BROME

For a good confluence of countryside, cafes, and antiquing, head to the town of Knowlton, at Brome Lake's southeast corner; it's part of the seven-village municipality known as **Lac Brome** (pop. 5,078). From Autoroute 10, take exit 90, heading south on Route 243 toward Lac Brome.

In the summer season, the Lac Brome **tourist kiosk** (also called a *relais d'information touristique*) is open on Route 243 shortly after you've left Autoroute 10. Knowlton is about 8km (5 miles) past the kiosk, and you'll hug the lake's eastern side for most of the trip. (Be careful: Bikers share the road with nary a shoulder to fall back on.) There is a public parking area and a lake beach, **Plage Douglass,** about 5km (3 miles) into the route, just before Knowlton. You can park to take a dip or do some easy lakeside hiking.

Knowlton is compact, but its two main shopping streets (Lakeside and Knowlton) have about three dozen boutiques and antiques stores that reveal the creeping chic influence of refugees from Montréal. Stores sell toys, gourmet items, quilts, jewelry, pottery, chocolate, and clothing.

Knowlton is one of the last towns in the region where a slim majority of the residents keep English as their mother tongue. Paul Holland Knowlton, a Loyalist from Vermont, settled here in the early 1800s, establishing a farm, general store, and sawmill. He was a member of Parliament for Lower Canada from 1830 to 1834.

The major local sight is **Musée Historique du Comté de Brome (Brome County Historical Museum)** at 130 rue Lakeside (Rte. 243; © **450/243-6782**). It occupies five historic buildings, including the town's first school. Exhibits focus on various aspects of town life, with re-creations of a general store and courthouse. The Martin Annex (1921) is dominated by a 1917 Fokker single-seat biplane, the foremost German aircraft in World War I. Also on the premises are collections of old radios and 18th- to early-20th-century weapons. The museum sells books about the area. Admission is C$5 adults, C$3 seniors, and C$2.50 children. It's open mid-May through mid-September Monday to Saturday 10am to 5pm, Sunday 11am to 5pm. Allow about an hour.

For a quick snack, the funky, barnlike **Station Knowlton Country Store** at 7 Mount Echo Rd. (© **450/242-5862;** www.stationknowlton.com) sells fruit smoothies and healthy sandwiches for less than C$6. You can also buy a variety of the store's hand-produced line of soaps and creams (made by store's owners, David and Josée), in addition to wooden toys and antique replicas of metal signs.

Where to Stay & Dine

Auberge & Spa West Brome   Out in the country, beyond town limits, this quiet property is made up of a grouping of creamy-yellow buildings amid rolling hills. A 1898 farmhouse at the roadside contains the reception desk and restaurant. About 90m (295 ft.) back are more modern structures, where the bedrooms are. A spa with therapeutic baths, massage rooms, and pedicure chairs was added in 2005. Rooms are in three categories: Classic, on the small side but not cramped; Deluxe, with full kitchens, fireplaces, and decks; and Suite, which can accommodate four. The complex is close to the Route des Vins (www.laroutedesvins.ca; p. 196), with many of the vineyards near Dunham. The

---

 Tips   **Biking the Cantons-de-l'Est: Easy on, Easy Off**

The Québec province's new **Route Verte (Green Route),** a 4,000km (2,485-mile) bike network (www.routeverte.com), stretches southeast into the Cantons-de-l'Est on a new 225km (140-mile) circuit called **Véloroute des Cantons** (© **800/355-5755** or 819/820-2020; www.cantonsdelest.com/velo).

The website offers details about where to find picnic areas, restaurants, and bathrooms near the trail; maps; and lists parking areas, bike rental and repair shops, and accommodations catering to cyclists. Day-tripping is easy, but all-inclusive 3- and 4-day bike tours are available for beginners and more advanced bikers. Find current programs on the website by clicking on the "Cycling planners" tab.

Moments **Maple Heaven in Cabanes à Sucre**

For a purely Québec experience that shouldn't be missed, get yourself to a sugar shack. Called *cabanes à sucre* or *érablières* in French, they were once places that merely processed sap from maple trees. When producers realized that they were drawing large audiences, some began offering wider experiences to keep the customers reaching for their wallets, putting in bars and dining rooms where bountiful spreads of simple country food are served at long communal tables. Some even put in dance floors and booked live entertainment.

Originally open only during sugaring-off season, roughly February through April, a few now stay open much longer, even all year. There are hundreds across the province, with small directional signs often positioned at roadsides or on highways.

At most shacks, you can see the rendering room, where sap gathered from maple-tree taps is boiled in a trough called an evaporator, and then cooked further on a stove. After that, the syrup is filtered and poured into cans or bottles.

You can often get your taste at the long, narrow tray of snow that has a wiggly stream of syrup pouring down the middle. This forms a sort of maple taffy, which is rolled up onto popsicle sticks for lollipop-like eating.

At the restaurants, there usually isn't a menu. If there's not a buffet, just sit down at a table and food will start coming. Thick pea soup is standard, as are baked beans, loaves of fragrant bread, sausages, ham slices, home fries, coleslaw, and stacks of pancakes. At the ready are preserves, pickles, and all the maple syrup you can ingest. Total cost rarely exceeds C$25.

Signature products are available in a variety of sizes and forms, primarily syrup and candy. Some folks consider the best syrup to be the clearer and lighter Grade A from the first run of sap, while others prefer the darker, denser Grade B from later in the season.

auberge recycles all glass, metal, and paper items, 80% of which is composted; uses only recycled-paper products and compact fluorescent light bulbs; and bans fertilizers and pesticides from its gardens and lawns.

128 Rte. 139, West Brome, PQ J0E 2P0. © **888/902-7663** or 450/266-7552. Fax 450/266-2040. www.awb. ca. 26 units. C$180–C$215 double; suites from C$245. Rates include full breakfast. Packages available. 2-night minimum stay during peak summer months. AE, MC, V. **Amenities:** Restaurant; bar; fitness room; pool (heated outdoor) and hot tub; spa. *In room:* A/C, TV, hair dryer, Internet (dial-up).

Auberge Lakeview The core structure of this Victorian inn dates from 1874, and a 19th-century flavor has been sustained through many renovations. Leather chairs are arranged around the fireplace in the lobby, tin ceilings prevail, and much of the furniture was crafted in Québec country style. The bedrooms come in several categories of relative comfort—if you go for the best (a Deluxe Studio, C$462 in high season), you get access to a veranda, a heart-shaped whirlpool bathtub, and a sitting area. Since rates include dinner in the dining room, this is the place to sample the area's gourmet treat, Lake Brome duck. The *auberge* is about a half-kilometer (about a third of a mile) from downtown Knowlton and its many boutiques and antiques shops.

50 rue Victoria, Knowlton (Lac Brome), PQ J0E 1V0. ℂ **800/661-6183** or 450/243-6183. Fax 450/243-
0602. www.aubergelakeviewinn.com. 28 units. May–Oct C$334–C$462 double; about C$40 less off sea-
son. Rates include dinner, breakfast, and gratuities for 2. Packages available. AE, MC, V. **Amenities:**
Restaurant; bar; pool (heated outdoor). *In room:* A/C, TV, hair dryer, Internet (dial-up).

MAGOG & LAC MEMPHREMAGOG

As with countless other North American town names, Magog (pop. 24,359) came by its
handle through corruption of a Native Canadian word. The Abenaki name *Memrobagak*
("great expanse of water") somehow became Memphrémagog, which was eventually
shortened to Magog (pronounced *May*-gog).

Confusingly, the town of Magog is not adjacent to Lac Magog, which is about 13km
(8 miles) north. Instead, it's positioned at the northernmost end of the large, long Lac
Memphrémagog (pronounced Mem-*phree*-may-gog), which spills across the U.S.-Cana-
dian border into Vermont on its southern end.

The helpful **Bureau d'Information Touristique Memphrémagog** (ℂ **800/267-2744**
or 819/843-2744; www.tourisme-memphremagog.com), at 55 rue Cabana (via Rte. 112),
in Magog, is open daily 8:30am to 7pm in summer, and 9am to 5pm the rest of the year.

The pretty Magog has a fully utilized waterfront, and in late July to early August each
year, the **Lac Memphrémagog International Swimming Marathon** (ℂ **818/847-
3007;** www.traversee-memphremagog.com) creates a big splash. From 1979 until 2003,
competitors started out in Newport, Vermont, at 6am and swam 42km (26 miles) to
Magog, arriving in midafternoon. Since 2004, the event has become a 34km (21-mile)
race, beginning and ending in Magog.

To experience the lake without such soggy exertion, board a boat. **Croisière Memphrémagog** (ℂ **888/842-8068** or 819/843-8068; www.croisiere-memphremagog.com)
offers lake cruises; one option is a 2½-hour trip to Abbaye de Saint-Benoît-du-Lac (see
below). Boats leave from Point Merry Park, the focal point for many of the town's outdoor activities. Cruises off season depend upon demand; call for times and prices. Several
firms rent sailboats, motorboats, kayaks, and windsurfers; **Marina Le Merry Club,** 201
rue Merry sud (ℂ **819/843-2728;** www.lemerryclub.com) specializes in pontoons,
motor boats, and jet skis.

If you're driving and want to take in **Abbaye de Saint-Benoît-du-Lac** (see below),
Magog itself, and **Bleu Lavande** (p. 203), a lavender farm that's stunning in full bloom
in July and August, take Route 245 from Autoroute 10 and visit the Abbaye first. Then
head north to Magog and south on Route 247. This area, on both the west and east sides
of Lac Memphrémagog, is wonderfully scenic.

Abbaye de Saint-Benoît-du-Lac   There's no mistaking the abbey, with its granite
steeple that thrusts into the sky above Lac Memphrémagog's western shore. Although
Saint-Benoît-du-Lac dates only from 1912, and the monastery was constructed from
1939 to 1941, its serenity is timeless. Some 45 monks live here largely in silence, keeping
the art of Gregorian chant alive in their liturgy. Outsiders are welcome to attend the
45-minute service (sit in back if you want to avoid the otherwise obligatory standing and
sitting during the service).

A blue cheese known as L'Ermite, among Québec's most famous, is produced here,
along with a creamy version and Swiss and cheddar cheeses. They are on sale in a little
shop, which also sells honey, books, tapes of religious chants, and a nonalcoholic cider
produced from fruit from the property's orchard. Visitors that come mid-September to

(Fun Facts   Québec's Own Nessies?

Lac Memphrémagog is known locally for more than just its annual international swimming marathon: Eagle eyes scan the ripples for **Memphre** (pronounced Mem-*phree*), the lake's legendary sea creature. Like the Loch Ness monster, which was first spotted in the Scottish waters in the year 565, Memphre supposedly surfaced for the first time in 1798 but left no hard evidence. Other sightings, it will come as no surprise, have been claimed since then.

Locals in North Hatley whisper about a creature of their own in Lake Massawippi, whom they have dubbed **Wippi.** Like Loch Ness, Lake Massawippi has pockets that go very deep—up to 150m (500 ft.) in some spots. Unlike Loch Ness, however, neither Memphrémagog nor Massawippi has been subjected to teams of scientists bouncing sonar signals to search out the water's depths. Memphre and Wippi are free to surface again in peace.

mid-October may want to help pick apples. And be sure to peek into the tiny stone chapel to the left of the property's entrance, opposite the small cemetery.

The abbey maintains **hostels** for men and women (© **819/843-4080** for men, © **819/843-2340** for women) who are seeking a quiet retreat, spiritual reflection, and have possible interest in the vocation. Suggested donation is C$50 per person for room and board. Room reservations must be made in advance by phone.

Saint-Benoît-du-Lac, J0B 2M0. © **819/843-4080.** www.st-benoit-du-lac.com. Free admission; donations accepted. Daily 5am–9pm; Mass with Gregorian chant daily at 11am; vespers with Gregorian chant at 5pm (7pm Thurs). No vespers Tues July–Aug. Shop: Mon–Sat 9–10:45am and 11:45am–6pm; Sun 10–10:45am and 11:45am–6pm. Exit 106 from Autoroute 10, Rte. 245 south to Bolton center, left on Nicolas Austin Rd. to village of Austin, right on Fisher, follow signs to abbey.

Where to Stay

There are a number of modest B&Bs and small hotels in Magog along the blocks of rue Merry, immediately north and south of its intersection with the main street, rue Principale. Many are listed with **Tourisme Cantons-de-l'Est** (© **800/355-5755;** fax 819/566-4445; www.easterntownships.org). Also consider the hostels at the **Abbaye de Saint-Benoît-du-Lac,** described above. Otherwise, look for accommodations in one of the nearby towns described in this section.

Where to Dine

In addition to the restaurant below, we also recommend the outpost of the popular regional chain **Piazzetta** (p. 232), at 399 rue Principale (© **819/843-4044**).

Boulangerie Owl's Bread ★ (Finds FRENCH   This bakery-restaurant is the kind you wish for in every neighborhood. There are mouth-watering pastries for breakfast, sit-down service for lunch every day, house specialties such as *cassoulet toulousain,* and home-made breads that are sold in a shop at the entrance. The "Eastern Township style" panini with smoked Lake Brome duck breast, blue cheese from nearby Abbaye de Saint-Benoît-du-Lac, Grenoble walnuts, and a touch of maple syrup on a baguette is sandwich making (and eating) at its pinnacle. Service is friendly and there's a menu in English. Due to the Boulangerie's increasing popularity, dinner hours may be added in summer months.

428 rue Principale ouest, Magog, J1X 2A9. ☎ **819/847-1987.** www.owlsbread.com. Most items under C$13. MC, V. Mon–Fri 8.30am–3pm; Sat–Sun 8am–5pm (shop closes daily at 5:30pm); winter hours may differ.

LAKE MASSAWIPPI

Set among rolling hills and fertile farm country, 19km-long (12-mile) Lake Massawippi, with its scalloped shoreline, is easily Cantons-de-l'Est's most desirable resort area. It was settled in the late 19th century by people of wealth and power, including many U.S. Southerners trying to escape their sultry summers (they came up by train and are said to have pulled down their window shades while they crossed through Yankee territory). They built grand estates with verandas and formal gardens on slopes along the lakeshore, with enough bedrooms to house their friends and extended families for months at a time. Several homes have been converted into inns, including the lavish **Auberge Ripplecove & Spa** (see below) and **Manoir Hovey** (see below). For an escape from intensive travel or work, it's difficult to do better than here.

The jewel of Lake Massawippi (which means "deep water" in Abenaki) is the town of **North Hatley** (pop. 780). Only 148km (92 miles) from Montréal and just 34km (21 miles) from the U.S. border, it has a river meandering through it that empties into the lake. See the impressive sunsets over the lake, try the town's very fine restaurants, take advantage of access to 54km (33 miles) of good bike paths, and partake in a summertime program of Sunday-afternoon band concerts. A full listing of activities is online at www.northhatley.net.

Horse lovers will want to know about **Randonnées J. Robidas** at 32 chemin McFarland (☎ **888/677-8767** or 819/563-0166; www.randonneesjrobidas.qc.ca). Guides lead trail rides through forest and meadow beside the Massawippi in summer, with rates starting at C$53 for a 1½-hour ride with two to four people. Buggy and winter sleigh rides are possibilities as well, and there's a discovery farm and nature school on-site.

Where to Stay

The acclaimed gastronomic resort Auberge Hatley burned to the ground in early 2006, and the Groupe Germain, which owned the property, announced later that year that it will not be rebuilding. There are, however, many other lodging options, including the three listed below. These full-service inns won't refuse children, but they have serious dining rooms that can test youngsters' patience. Other meal arrangements should be made for children 12 and younger.

Auberge Ripplecove & Spa ★★★   The staff extends a warm welcome at this handsome inn, and impeccable housekeeping standards are observed throughout. With 4.8 hectares (12 acres) directly on Lake Massawippi's southern end, the *auberge* is a grand miniresort, with a private beachfront and equipment for sailing, water-skiing, and canoeing. In winter, there is cross-country skiing on the property and, on Saturdays, horse-drawn sleigh rides. The core structure dates from 1945, but subsequent expansions have added well-appointed rooms, suites, stand-alone cottages, and, in 2003, a spa with a full range of therapies and an outdoor hot tub with a view of the lake. About half the rooms have private balconies and whirlpools. The award-winning lakeside restaurant fills up in season with diners drawn to the kitchen's reputation for creativity. Members of the same family run **Manoir Hovey,** below. At what's nearly Québec province's most southeastern corner, the inn is only 378km (235 miles) from Boston.

700 chemin Ripplecove, Ayer's Cliff, PQ J0B 1C0. (℡) **800/668-4296** or 819/838-4296. Fax 819/838-5541. www.ripplecove.com. 35 units. Late June to mid-Oct C$316–C$626 double; rest of the year from C$266 double. Rates include dinner, breakfast, gratuities for 2, and use of most recreational facilities. AE, MC, V. Exit 121 from Autoroute 10, take Autoroute 55 south to exit 21, then Rte. 141 south 5 min. to Ayer's Cliff; follow signs to *auberge*. **Amenities:** Restaurant; pub; private beach; bikes for guests' use (free); concierge; exercise room; hot tub; pool (heated outdoor); room service; spa; lit tennis court, watersports equipment (some for fee); Wi-Fi (in main building, free). *In room:* A/C, TV, hair dryer, Internet.

Le Tricorne At the end of a long dirt-and-gravel road deep in the countryside, this family-run inn offers spectacular views of Lake Massawippi and the rolling Canadian Appalachians. While the core of the main house is 145 years old, it looks as if it could have been erected only a few years ago—the exterior is dusty rose and white, and the interior is decked out in *Good Housekeeping* manner, with equestrian-print wallpaper and tartans. A newer building 45m (148 ft.) up the hill has five larger bedrooms decorated in a more sophisticated corporate style. With 37 hectares (92 acres), three small ponds, and a heated outdoor pool, this property offers the peace and quiet of being tucked away in the woods. Some units have wood fireplaces, and about half have jet bathtubs.

50 chemin Gosselin, North Hatley, PQ J0B 2C0. (℡) **819/842-4522.** Fax 819/842-2692. www.manoirle tricorne.com. 17 units. C$125–C$225 double. Rates include full breakfast. AE, MC, V. From North Hatley, take Rte. 108 west; follow the signs. Bringing children 8 or younger is discouraged. **Amenities:** Pool (heated outdoor); sauna (winter only). *In room:* A/C, no phone, Wi-Fi (free).

Manoir Hovey ★★★ Built in 1898 by the owner of paper manufacturer Georgia Pacific, this lakeside manor house, with its broad veranda and ivy-covered white pillars, was inspired by George Washington's home in Mount Vernon, Virginia. This manor manages to maintain a magical balance of feeling like both a genteel estate for a private getaway and a grand resort for a weekend's pampering; it's a member of the exclusive Relais & Châteaux group. Aristocratic touches include tea and scones in the afternoon, a carefully manicured English garden with fresh herbs (used by cooks in the kitchen), and a massive stone hearth in a library lounge with deep chairs and floor-to-ceiling bookshelves. Sumptuously appointed rooms have touches like Italian bathroom tiles and antique sink basins; all feature high-end bedding and CD players with classical discs. Dinner is included; consider the extraordinary caribou with crystallized foie gras taboule that melts into the meat.

575 chemin Hovey, North Hatley, PQ J0B 2C0. (℡) **800/661-2421** or 819/842-2421. Fax 819/842-2248. www.manoirhovey.com. 41 units. Late June to mid-Oct and Christmas week C$320–C$590 double, rest of the year from C$270 double; suites from C$670 double. Rates include 3-course dinner, full breakfast, gratuities, and use of most recreational facilities for 2. Packages available. AE, DC, MC, V. From Autoroute 55 exit 29, take Rte. 108 east, follow the signs. **Amenities:** Restaurant; bar; 2 private beaches; bikes; concierge; exercise room; pool (heated outdoor); room service; ice fishing, snowshoeing, skating rink in winter; tennis court (lit, clay); watersports equipment. *In room:* A/C, TV, CD player, hair dryer, Wi-Fi (free).

Where to Dine

Café Massawippi ★ FRENCH CONTEMPORARY It was daring to open a restaurant in the same small town as the multistarred inns described above, but chef-owner Dominic Tremblay has pulled it off. Contained in a small roadside house with a plain, unassuming interior, the true art appears on the plate. Think seared scallops with blackened watermelon, cilantro pesto, and cantaloupe froth, or veal sweetbread with roasted peaches and orange-cardamom tapioca. The chef recommends the *table d'hôte* for the entire table, served leisurely (plan 2½ hr.), though guests can also order à la carte.

3050 chemin Capelton. ✆ **819/842-4528.** www.cafemassawippi.com. Reservations recommended.
Table d'hôte dinner C$75; C$46–C$56 main courses. AE, DC, MC, V. Late May to early Oct daily 6–10pm, with lunch Thurs–Sun in July–Aug, 11:30am–3pm; rest of year Wed–Sat 6–10pm.

Pilsen Restaurant & Pub INTERNATIONAL   For food less grand and less expensive than that at the establishments described above, head to Pilsen in the center of North Hatley. Housed in a former horse-carriage manufacturing shop from 1900, the restaurant has a deck with tables over a narrow river, the better to watch boats setting out or returning. The place fills up quickly on warm days with patrons enjoying renditions of quesadillas, burgers, pastas, and fried calamari, as well as more adventurous fare, such as the Ploughman's Platter with wild game terrine, St-Benoit-du-Lac blue cheese pâté, onion confit, and apples. There's an extensive choice of beers, including local microbrew Massawippi Blonde and the Czech Pilsner Urquel, for which the restaurant was named. Most nights, the bar stays open well past midnight.

55 rue Main. ✆ **819/842-2971.** www.pilsen.ca. Reservations recommended on weekends. 3-course *table d'hôte* C$24–C$28; C$10–C$27 main courses. AE, MC, V. Mid-May to Nov. Mon–Sat 11:30am–10:30pm; rest of year Thurs–Sun 11:30am–10:30pm. Open 9am Sunday year-round. Closes as early as 8pm in winter and as late as 3am in summer.

STANSTEAD & BEEBE PLAIN

For a brief detour on the drive south to Vermont, explore the border villages that compose the town of Stanstead, at the end of Route 143.

Stanstead (pop. 3,012) was settled in the 1790s and, as a border town, became a commercial center for the Québec-Boston stagecoach route. Many of the society homes from the late 1800s have been preserved.

Canada's largest producer of lavender also happens to be one of the region's most popular destinations. **Bleu Lavande** (✆ **888/876-5851** or 819/876-5851; www.bleu lavande.ca) is a huge farm, a picnic spot, an agricultural discovery center, and a place to buy chocolate, jelly, home-cleaning products, sprays, and an array of other goodies infused with the miraculous properties of *Lavandula*. Hotels in Magog and neighboring towns organize excursions to the farm, which is located on 891 Narrow Road, just 4.4km (2¾ miles) from Route 247 in Stanstead. During peak season, when the lavender blooms in July and August, Bleu Lavande can attract more than 2,000 visitors per day. The website offers a complete list of activities, including times for tours, which run daily June through mid-October. Packages with wine sampling or lunch are available. The boutique is open daily during high season, Monday to Friday during low season, and closed between Christmas and the first week of January.

Fans of geographical oddities will want to stop by the **Haskell Opera House** (✆ **819/876-2020;** www.haskellopera.org). Dating from 1904, it's literally and logistically half-Canadian and half-American: The stage and performers are in Canada, while the audience watches from the U.S. **QNEK Productions** is the resident theatre company, and it's based in Vermont. QNEK ticket information is at ✆ **802/334-2216** and www. qnek.com.

What makes the township of **Beebe Plain** notable is 1km-long (⅔-mile) **Canusa Street.** The north side is in Canada, the south side in the U.S.—hence the name, CANUSA. Check the car license plates on either side. Here, it's long-distance to call a neighbor across the street, and, while folks are free to walk across for a visit, they are expected, at least technically, to report to the authorities if they drive that same distance.

Getting to Know Québec City

Québec City seduces from first view. Situated along the majestic Fleuve Saint-Laurent (St. Lawrence River), much of the oldest part of the city—Vieux-Québec, or, in English, Old Québec—sits atop Cap Diamant, a rock bluff that once provided military defense. Fortress walls still encase the upper city, and the soaring Château Frontenac, a hotel with castlelike turrets, dominates the landscape. Hauntingly evocative of a coastal town in the motherland of France, the tableau is as romantic as any in Europe.

Québec City is, in fact, the soul of New France, and it holds fast to that history. Founded in 1608 by Samuel de Champlain, it was the first significant settlement in Canada. Major sprucing up took place all over the city for the 400th-anniversary celebrations in 2008, including additional pedestrian-friendly access to the waterfront and a new waterside pavilion that serves as a Parks Canada discovery center.

The city is almost entirely French in feeling, spirit, and language. Almost everyone—95% of the population—is Francophone, or French speaking. But many of the 632,000 residents do know some English, especially those who work in hotels, restaurants, and shops. Although it's more difficult in Québec City than in Montréal to get by without French, the average Québécois goes out of his or her way to communicate—in halting English, sign language, simplified French, or a combination of all three. Most of the Québécois are uncommonly gracious.

Because of its beauty, history, and unique stature as the only walled city north of Mexico's Campeche, Québec City's historic district was named a UNESCO World Heritage Site in 1985.

Île d'Orléans is an agricultural and residential island within sight of Vieux-Québec. It's less than 20 minutes from downtown by car and makes a pleasant day trip. Consider, too, a drive along the St. Lawrence's northern coast past the shrine of Ste-Anne-de-Beaupré (p. 278), the waterfalls near Mont Ste-Anne (p. 279), and on to pastoral Charlevoix (p. 285) and the Saguenay River, where whales come to play.

1 ORIENTATION

Almost all of a visit to Québec City can be spent on foot in the old Lower Town, which hugs the river below the bluff, and in the old Upper Town, atop Cap Diamant (Cape Diamond). Many accommodations, restaurants, and tourist-oriented services are based in these places.

The colonial city was first built right down by the St. Lawrence. It was here that the earliest merchants, traders, and boatmen earned their livelihoods. Unfriendly fire from the British and Amerindians in the 1700s moved residents to safer houses atop the cliffs that form the rim of the Cap. The tone and atmosphere of the 17th and 18th centuries still suffuse these areas today.

Basse-Ville (Lower Town) became primarily a district of wharves and warehouses. That trend has been reversed, with small hotels and many attractive bistros and shops bringing life to the area. It maintains the architectural feel of its origins, however, reusing old buildings and maintaining the narrow cobbled streets.

Haute-Ville (Upper Town) turned out to not be immune to cannon fire, as the British General James Wolfe proved in 1759 when he took the city from the French. Nevertheless, the division into Upper and Lower towns persisted for obvious topographical reasons. Upper Town remains enclosed by fortification walls, with a cliff-side elevator *(funiculaire)* and several steep streets connecting it to Lower Town.

ARRIVING

For information about arriving in Québec City by plane, car, train, or bus, see "Getting to Montréal & Québec City," on p. 26 in chapter 3.

VISITOR INFORMATION

High season in Québec City is from June 24 (Jean-Baptiste Day) through Labour Day (the first Mon in Sept, as in the U.S.). For those 11 weeks the city is in highest gear. Tourist office, museums, and restaurants all expand their opening hours, and hotels charge top dollar. This book notes the changes in hours and prices throughout the year for many venues, but it's best to call and confirm opening hours before making a special trip to an attraction or restaurant outside of the high season.

There are several tourist information centers. The most central is in Upper Town, across from the Château Frontenac and directly on Place d'Armes. **Centre Infotouriste de Québec,** 12 rue Ste-Anne (© **877/266-5687;** www.bonjourquebec.com), is run by Québec province's tourism department and is open from 8:30am to 8:30pm daily from June 21 to early September and from 9am to 5pm daily the rest of the year. It has brochures, a lodging reservation service, a currency-exchange office, and information about tours by foot, bus, or boat.

Also in front of the Château is the independent **Kiosque Frontenac** (© **418/692-5483**), which sells tour tickets and exchanges currency. It's in a small kiosk next to the entrance of the cliff-side elevator to Lower Town.

Just outside the Old City walls on Parc des Champs-de-Bataille's northern edge, **Québec City Tourism** has an information office in the Discovery Pavilion at 835 av. Wilfrid-Laurier (© **877/783-1608** or 418/641-6290; www.quebecregion.com). You'll find rack after rack of brochures as well as attendants who can answer questions and make hotel reservations. It's open daily throughout the year, from 8:30am to 7:30pm from June 24 to Labour Day and somewhat shorter hours the rest of the year. The building is marked with a large, blue question mark.

From early June to Labour Day, the tourist office's student staff pilot motor scooters through the tourist districts of Upper and Lower towns, making themselves available for questions. They're also in force on foot during the wintertime Carnaval de Québec. In French, they're called the *service mobile,* and their blue mopeds bear flags with a large question mark. Just hail them as they approach—they're bilingual.

CITY LAYOUT

MAIN AVENUES & STREETS Within the walls of Haute-Ville (Upper Town), the principal streets are **St-Louis** (which becomes **Grande-Allée** outside the city walls), **Ste-Anne,** and **St-Jean.** In Basse-Ville (Lower Town), major streets are **St-Pierre, Dalhousie,**

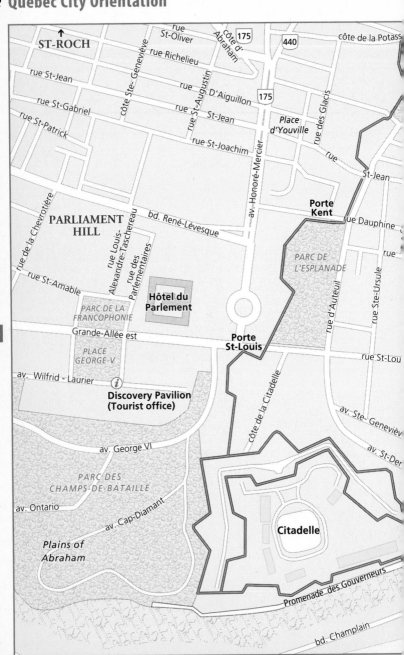

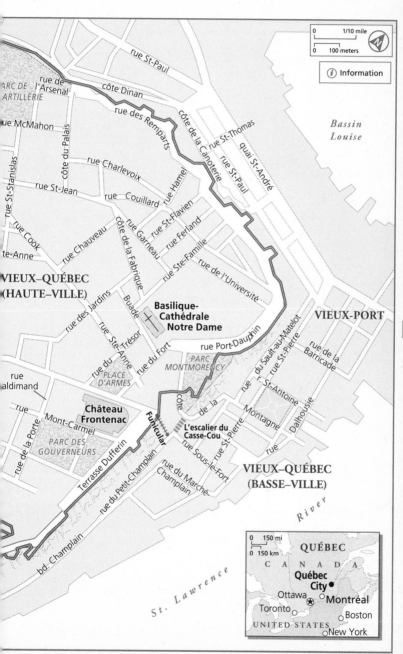

Long May They Wave: The Flags of Canada

With a relatively small population spread over a territory larger than the continental U.S., Canadians' loyalties have always tended to be directed to the cities and regions in which they live, rather than to the nation at large. Part of this comes from the semi-colonial relationship the nation retained with England after the British North America Act made it self-governing in 1867 (Queen Elizabeth II is still on all the currency). Part comes from the fact that Canada's citizens speak two different major languages. Canadians didn't even have a national anthem until "O Canada" was given the honor in 1980.

Local loyalties are reflected in the flags. Québécois began asserting themselves and declaring their regional pride after World War II, and officially adopted their national flag, the Fleurdelisé, in 1950. It employs blue-and-white crossbars with four fleurs-de-lis (one in each resulting quadrant) and is flown prominently in Québec City.

In 1965, the red-and-white maple leaf version of the Canadian flag was introduced, replacing a previous ensign that featured a Union Jack in the upper-left corner.

In the face of decades of hurt and outright hostilities between French and English Canada, there must be occasional sighs of longing in some quarters for the diplomatic display of the flag of Montréal. Adopted way back in 1832, it has red crossbars on a white background. The resulting quadrants have depictions of a rose, a fleur-de-lis, a thistle, and a shamrock. They stand, respectively, for the founding groups of the new nation—the English, French, Scots, and Irish.

St-Paul, and, parallel to St-Paul, **St-André.** Useful maps of Upper and Lower towns and the metropolitan area are available at any tourist office.

FINDING AN ADDRESS   If it were larger, the historic district's winding and plunging streets might be confusing to negotiate. However, the area is very compact. Most streets are only a few blocks long, making navigation and finding a specific address fairly easy.

THE NEIGHBORHOODS IN BRIEF

Vieux-Québec: Haute-Ville Old Québec's Upper Town, surrounded by thick ramparts, occupies the crest of Cap Diamant and overlooks the Fleuve Saint-Laurent (St. Lawrence River). It includes many of the sites for which the city is famous, among them the **Château Frontenac** and the **Basilica of Notre-Dame.** At a still higher elevation, to the south of the Château and along the river, is the **Citadelle,** a partially star-shaped fortress built by the French in the 18th century and augmented often by the English (after their 1759 capture of the city) well into the 19th century.

With most buildings at least 100 years old and made of granite in similar styles, Haute-Ville is visually harmonious, with few jarring modern intrusions. When they added a new wing to the Château Frontenac, for instance, they modeled it after the original—standing policy here.

Terrasse Dufferin is a pedestrian promenade atop the cliffs that attracts crowds in all seasons for its magnificent views of the river and its water traffic, which includes ferries gliding back and forth, cruise ships, and Great Lakes freighters putting in at the harbor below.

Vieux-Québec: Basse-Ville and Vieux-Port Old Québec's Lower Town encompasses **Vieux-Port,** the old port district; the impressive **Museum of Civilization,** a highlight of any visit; **Place Royale,** perhaps the most attractive of the city's many small squares; and the pedestrian-only **rue du Petit-Champlain,** which is undeniably touristy, but not unpleasantly so, and has many agreeable cafes and shops. Visitors travel between Lower and Upper towns by the cliff-side elevator *(funiculaire)* at the north end of rue du Petit-Champlain, or by the adjacent stairway.

Parliament Hill Once you pass through the walls at St-Louis Gate, you're still in Haute-Ville (Upper Town), but no longer in Vieux-Québec. Rue St-Louis becomes **Grande-Allée,** a wide boulevard that passes the stately Parliament building and runs parallel to the broad expanse of the Plains of Abraham, where one of the most important battles in the history of North America took place between the French and the British for control of the city. This is also where the lively Carnaval de Québec is held each winter. Two blocks after Parliament, Grande-Allée becomes lined on both sides with terraced restaurants and cafes. The city's large modern hotels are in this area, too, and the **Musée National des Beaux-Arts** is a pleasant 20-minute walk up the Allée from the Parliament. Here, the neighborhood becomes more residential and flows into the Montcalm district.

St-Roch Northwest of Parliament Hill and enough of a distance from Vieux-Québec to warrant a cab ride, this newly revitalized neighborhood has some of the city's trendiest restaurants and bars. Along the main strolling street, **rue St-Joseph est,** sidewalks have been widened, new benches added, and artists hired to renovate the interiors and exteriors of industrial buildings. It has all brought a youthful pop and an influx of new technology and media companies to the neighborhood.

Much of St-Roch, including what's referred to as Québec's "downtown" shopping district, remains nondescript and a little grubby. But the blocks near the corner of rue St-Joseph and **rue du Parvis** (where Hugo Boss moved in with a massive store) are increasingly home to top-notch restaurants and cute boutiques. *Note:* On older maps, rue du Parvis was called rue de l'Eglise.

2 GETTING AROUND

Once you're within or near the walls of Québec City's Old Town (Haute-Ville), virtually no restaurant, hotel, or place of interest is beyond walking distance. In bad weather, or when you're traversing between opposite ends of Lower and Upper Towns, a taxi might be necessary. But in general, walking is the best way to explore.

QUEBEC CITY BY FUNICULAR

To get between Upper and Lower Town, you can take streets, staircases, or a cliff-side elevator, known as the funicular, which has long operated along an inclined 64m (210-ft.) track.

The upper station is near the front of the city's visual center—Château Frontenac and Place d'Armes—while the lower station is at the northern end of the teeny rue du Petit-Champlain, a pedestrian-only shopping street. The elevator offers excellent aerial views of the historic Lower Town on the short trip and runs daily from 7:30am until 11pm all year, and until midnight in high season. Wheelchairs and strollers are accommodated. The one-way fare is C$1.75. Read about its history at **www.funiculaire-quebec.com**.

QUEBEC CITY BY TAXI

Taxis are everywhere: cruising, parked in front of the big hotels, and in some of Upper Town's larger squares. In theory, they can be hailed, but they are best obtained by locating one of their stands, as in the Place d'Armes or in front of the Hôtel-de-Ville (City Hall). Restaurant managers and hotel bell captains will also summon them upon request. The starting rate is C$3.30, each kilometer costs C$1.45, and each minute of waiting adds C55¢. Tip 10% to 15%. Companies include **Taxi Coop** (© **418/525-5191**) and **Taxi Québec** (© **418/525-8123**).

QUEBEC CITY BY BUS

For travel within the most touristed areas in the warm months, look for the **Ecolobus** (www.rtcquebec.ca). You're likely to see it if you spend any time in Upper Town. It's a free service, and you can get on and get off at any stop.

City bus routes are listed online at **www.rtcquebec.ca**. Buses in Upper Town include no. 7, which travels up and down rue St-Jean, and nos. 10 and 11, which shuttle along Grande-Allée/rue St-Louis. Bus stops sport signs that state the bus numbers and direction of travel for each route. Flag down the bus as it approaches so the driver knows to stop.

The fare is C$2.60 in exact change. One-day passes cost C$6.45, with discounts available for seniors and students with proper ID. The Québec City Museum Card (p. 235) has in the past included 2 days of unlimited public transport in addition to free entrance to museums. The pass is being reorganized for 2010, so confirm before buying.

QUEBEC CITY BY CAR

Québec City is compact, but driving is tricky because there are so few roads between Upper and Lower Town and because many streets are one-way.

On-street parking is very difficult in Québec City's old, cramped quarters. When you find a rare space on the street, be sure to check the signs for hours when parking is permissible. Meters cost C50¢ per 15 minutes, and some meters accept payment for up to 5 hours. Meters are generally in effect Monday through Saturday from 9am to 9pm and Sunday 10am to 9pm. But be sure to double-check: Spots along Parc des Champs-de-Bataille (Battlefields Park) have to be paid for 24 hours a day.

Many of the smaller hotels and B&Bs that don't have their own parking lots maintain special arrangements with local garages, with discounts for guests of a few dollars off the usual C$14 or more per day. Check with your hotel.

If a particular hotel or *auberge* (the French word for "inn") doesn't have access to a garage or lot, plenty of public ones are available and clearly marked on the foldout city map available at tourist offices. The cheapest are, in Upper Town, the lot beneath Hôtel-de-Ville (City Hall), with entrances on rue Ste-Anne and Côte de la Fabrique; and, in Lower Town, the lot across the street from the Musée de la Civilisation, on rue Dalhousie.

Names and contact information for **rental-car** agencies doing business in Québec City are listed on p. 295. Budget and Hertz both have offices in Upper Town on Côte du Palais at rue St-Jean.

Unlike in Montréal, drivers in Québec City are permitted to turn right at red traffic
 lights, but only after coming to a full stop and yielding to pedestrians in the crosswalk. Look out for the occasional sign at busy intersections prohibiting right turns on red.

QUEBEC CITY BY BIKE

Given Vieux-Québec's hilly topography and tight quarters, cycling isn't a particularly attractive option either within the walls or in Lower Town. But beyond the walls is another story. Québec has a great network of cycling paths called the **Route Verte (Green Route),** with both local lanes and access to longer-distance rides. See "Biker's Paradise: The 4,000km Route Verte" on p. 179 in chapter 12. Day trips and longer tours are listed at **www.routeverte.com**.

You can rent bicycles in Lower Town at **Cyclo Services,** 289 rue St-Paul (© **418/692-4052;** www.cycloservices.net), for C$25 for 4 hours, with other increments available. The shop is open daily 8am to 8pm.

Where to Stay in Québec City

Staying in one of the small hotels within or below the walls of Vieux-Québec can be one of your trip's most memorable experiences. Keep in mind, though, that standards of amenities fluctuate wildly from one hotel to another—and even from room to room within a single establishment. It's reasonable to ask to see two or three rooms before making a decision to stay.

Unless otherwise noted, all rooms in the lodgings listed below have private bathrooms—*en suite,* as they say in Canada. Most of the accommodations listed here are completely nonsmoking.

Vieux-Québec has about a dozen bed-and-breakfasts. With rates mostly in the C$85-to-C$135 range, they don't represent substantial savings over the small hotels, but do give you the opportunity to get to know some of the city dwellers. Many will post signs that say COMPLET, meaning full, or VACANT, which means that rooms are available. When calling to make arrangements at a B&B, be very clear about your needs and requirements. A deposit is often required, as are minimum stays of 2 nights. Credit cards may not be accepted.

The *Official Accommodation Guide* put out by Québec City Tourism lists every member of the Greater Québec Area Tourism and Convention Bureau, from B&Bs to five-star hotels, with details about the number of rooms, the prices, and the facilities. It's available at tourist offices (p. 205).

High-rise hotels outside the ancient walls in Parliament Hill are within walking distance or a quick taxi ride from the Old City's attractions. Upscale boutique hotels in Lower Town have greatly enhanced the lodging stock.

If cost is a prime consideration, note that prices drop significantly from October to May, with the exception of the Christmas holiday and winter carnival in February. Many hotels offer special deals through their websites or AAA discounts.

Important note: The prices in the listings below represent rack rates for a double-occupancy room in high season (which includes the warm months, Christmastime, and Carnaval), unless otherwise noted.

See p. 62 for information about the Frommer's star-rating system, price rankings, categories, and taxes.

1 BEST HOTEL BETS

- **Most Romantic Boutique Hotels: Auberge Saint-Antoine,** 8 rue St-Antoine (© **888/692-2211** or 418/692-2211), features a grand wing and archaeological displays from lobby to bedside, and it's hard to beat curling up with a glass of wine beside the fire in one of the cozy lobby alcoves. See p. 218. The sleek **Dominion 1912,** 126 rue St-Pierre (© **888/833-5253** or 418/692-2224), also is a favorite, infusing a pre–World War I building with a cunning modernist flavor, continuing a trend in Basse-Ville's designer hotels and inns. See p. 219.

- **Best Chain Hotel:** The **Courtyard Marriott Québec,** 850 Place d'Youville (© 866/694-4004 or 418/694-4004), gets consistently high marks for its friendly service, comfy rooms, great location, and solid in-house restaurant. See p. 220.
- **Best New Hotel: Hôtel-Musée Premières Nations,** on the nearby Wendake reservation (© 866/551-9222 or 418/847-2222), is built alongside a bank of maple trees and a gently flowing river. It features huge glass windows, animal pelts, and uniquely beautiful furniture of carved woods. See p. 223.
- **Best Location for Peace and Quiet:** The Parc des Gouverneurs, just south of the Château, is a green space just steps from Upper Town's streets, restaurants, and shops. It's quiet, giving visitors a respite from activity at the end of the day. Dozens of B&Bs and small hotels are directly on the park or nearby, including **Cap Díamant,** 39 av. Ste-Geneviève (© 888/694-0303 or 418/692-0303); **Maison du Fort,** 21 av. Ste-Geneviève (© 888/203-4375 or 418/692-4375); **Manoir Sur-le-Cap,** 9 av. Ste-Geneviève (© 418/694-1987); and **Hôtel Château Bellevue,** 16 rue de la Porte (© 800/463-2617 or 418/692-2573). See p. 217, 218, 218, and 217.
- **Best Location for Proximity to Gourmet Pleasures:** Lower Town, hands down. You could have a satisfying visit simply eating your way across this neighborhood.
- **Best Historic Hotel: Fairmont Le Château Frontenac,** 1 rue des Carrières (© 866/540-4460 or 418/692-3861), is the visual star of this city. It was built more than a century ago as one of the first hotels to serve railroad passengers and to encourage tourism at a time when most people stayed close to home. Nothing can beat it for proximity to all the sights. In fact, "the Château" *is* one of the sights. See below.
- **Most Memorable Hotel:** How many chances do you get to sleep in a hotel built completely of ice? On a bed of ice, near a chandelier made of ice, after dancing in a disco made of ice, ice, ice? The **Hôtel de Glace,** Station touristique Duchesnay, 30 minutes outside the city (© 877/505-0423; www.icehotel-canada.com), is open from January to April. See p. 221.

2 VIEUX-QUEBEC: HAUTE-VILLE (UPPER TOWN)

VERY EXPENSIVE

Fairmont Le Château Frontenac ★★★ (Kids) Québec's magical "castle" opened in 1893 and has been wowing guests ever since. Many of the rooms are full-on luxurious, outfitted with elegant château furnishings and marble bathrooms. More than 500 (of 618) rooms were renovated in a 3-year project that finished in 2008. Prices depend on size, location, and view, with river views garnering top dollar. Lower-priced rooms overlooking the inner courtyard are appealing, too: The gabled roofs they face are quite romantic, and children might imagine Harry Potter swooping by. Anyone can stay on the more princely (and pricey) Fairmont Gold floors, which have a separate concierge and a lounge with an honor bar in the afternoons and breakfast in the mornings. Known locally as "the Château," the hotel was built in phases, following the landline, so the wide halls take crooked paths. The **St-Laurent Bar et Lounge** (p. 269) overlooks the river and has live music and dancing on Friday nights in summer.

1 rue des Carrières (at Place d'Armes), Québec City, PQ G1R 4P5. © **866/540-4460** or 418/692-3861. Fax 418/692-1751. www.fairmont.com/frontenac. 618 units. C$259–C$499 double; suites from C$499 and way up. Packages available. AE, DC, DISC, MC, V. Valet parking C$31, self-parking C$26, hybrid vehicles

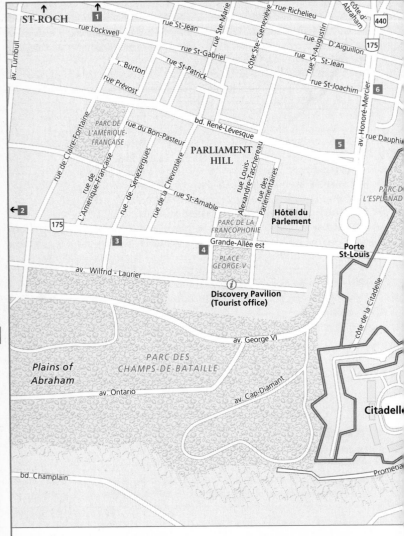

Auberge Internationale de Québec **7**
Auberge Le Vincent **1**
Auberge Place d'Armes **19**
Auberge Saint-Antoine **23**
Cap Diamant **13**
Courtyard Marriott Québec **6**

Dominion 1912 **24**
Fairmont Le Château Frontenac **17**
Hilton Québec **5**
Hôtel Champlain Vieux-Québec **8**
Hôtel Château Bellevue **15**
Hôtel Château Laurier Québec **4**

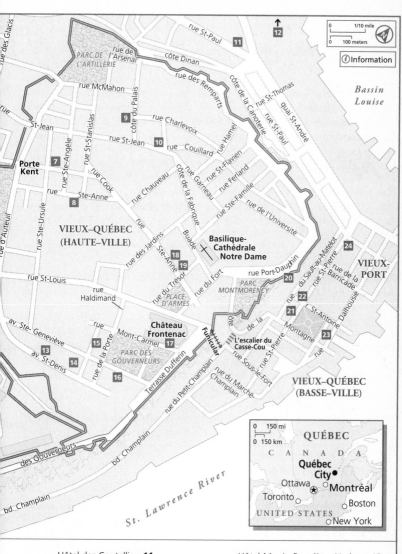

WHERE TO STAY IN QUÉBEC CITY

14

VIEUX-QUÉBEC: HAUTE-VILLE (UPPER TOWN)

Hôtel des Coutellier **11**
Hôtel du Vieux-Québec **10**
Hôtel Le Priori **20**
Hôtel Manoir Victoria **9**
Hôtel Sainte-Anne **18**
Hôtel 71 **21**

Hôtel-Musée Premières Nations **12**
Le Saint-Pierre **22**
Loews Le Concorde **3**
Maison du Fort **14**
Manoir Sur-le-Cap **16**
Relais Charles-Alexander **2**

park free. Pets accepted, C$25 per night. **Amenities:** 3 restaurants; bar; babysitting; children's programs; concierge; executive-level rooms; expansive health club and spa; pools (indoor and kiddie pool w/outdoor terrace); room service. *In room:* A/C, TV, hair dryer, Internet (C$18 per day), minibar.

EXPENSIVE

Hôtel du Vieux-Québec (Kids)   This century-old brick hotel is centrally located and has been renovated with care. The most recent updates were in 2008–09, and furnishings are now mahogany or maple from the province, with reproductions of paintings by Québec artists on the walls. There's a lounge with board games and many rooms have two queen beds, making the hotel understandably popular with families. In addition to its French bistro, **Les Frères de la Côte** (© 418/692-5445) on the ground floor, many moderately priced restaurants and nightspots are nearby. In July and August, the hotel offers a complimentary orientation walk at 9:30am. A page on the website describes the hotel's green activities, including the installation of water-efficient toilets and compact fluorescent light bulbs, use of refurbished furniture, installation of a rooftop garden, and conversion to amenity dispensers—no more little shampoo bottles for guests to use once then throw out.

1190 rue St-Jean (at rue de l'Hôtel Dieu), Québec City, PQ G1R 1S6. © **800/361-7787** or 418/692-1850. Fax 418/692-5637. www.hvq.com. 45 units. May to late Oct C$146–C$266 double; rest of the year from C$94 double. Continental breakfast included with rooms booked directly with hotel. Packages available. AE, MC, V. Pets accepted, C$25 additional per night. **Amenities:** Restaurant, fitness room. *In room:* A/C, TV/DVD, DVD library, hair dryer, Wi-Fi (free).

Hôtel Manoir Victoria ★   With an air of a grand old-timer, Manoir Victoria is formal and proper, from a lobby that features elegant Old World decor to an elaborate formal dining room. Over half the comfortable bedrooms were renovated in 2009 with everything from new mattresses to rugs and curtains, and some now feature gas fireplaces and whirlpool tubs. The hotel has some special touches not normally found in midsize properties: a small indoor pool, rare in this city; a full-service spa that offers massages and Canadian specials such as maple body scrubs; and a pub/bistro in addition to the main restaurant. The hotel is located across the street from the city hospital and around the corner from the busy rue St-Jean restaurant-and-bar scene. Note that there's a steep staircase from the front door to the lobby, although elevators make the trip to most guest rooms.

44 Côte du Palais (at rue St-Jean), Québec City, PQ G1R 4H8. © **800/463-6283** or 418/692-1030. Fax 418/692-3822. www.manoir-victoria.com. 156 units. May to mid-Oct C$175–C$295 double; mid-Oct to Apr C$129–C$245 double. Packages available. AE, DC, DISC, MC, V. Valet parking C$20. **Amenities:** 2 restaurants; bar; babysitting; concierge; exercise room; pool (indoor heated; limited days and hours); room service; spa. *In room:* A/C, TV, hair dryer, minibar, Wi-Fi (free).

MODERATE

Auberge Place d'Armes ★   Renovated with care in 2008, this high-end *auberge* offers 21 sumptuous rooms with stone walls that date from 1640 and handmade artisanal furniture—at surprisingly moderate prices. The auberge swallowed up a museum that had been here previously, and as a result the most eye-popping unit, the Marie Antoinette suite, has actual 17th-century decor from Versailles. A portion of the rooms are done up in blue and white French decor, with the other in red and white British touches. Rooms have high-end flourishes such as heated bathroom floors and flatscreen TVs. There's no elevator, but staff will carry luggage to upper floors. Breakfasts are served in the very good in-house restaurant **Le Pain Béni** (p. 227).

24 rue Ste-Anne (at Place d'Armes), Québec City, PQ G1R 3X3. © **866/333-9485** or 418/694-9485. Fax 418/694-9899. www.aubergeplacedarmes.com. 21 units. Summer C$150–C$200 double; rest of the year from C$90. Continental breakfast included. AE, MC, V. Pets accepted, C$25 a day to max of C$75.

Amenities: Restaurant; babysitting; concierge; room service. *In room:* A/C, CD player, fridge, hair dryer, MP3 docking station, Wi-Fi (free).

Cap Diamant   There are a lot of B&Bs in the quiet, pretty corner of Vieux-Québec behind the Château Frontenac. Owner Florence Guillot has turned this 1826 home into something of a Victoriana showpiece, with antiques and old photos richly decorating common areas and bedrooms. The whole thing is quite grand and romantic. Many rooms feature ornate fireplaces, mantles, heavy gold-edged mirrors, oriental rugs, and glass lamps. There's a small all-season back porch where breakfast is served, and a summer garden. Although it's a B&B, all rooms have private baths. Ask to see the industrial-size dumb waiter that descends from a secret trap door ceiling to carry luggage up to the top floors; the controls are behind a painting in the front hall, like something out of a James Bond movie. Mindboggling!

39 av. Ste-Geneviève (at Ste-Ursule), Québec City, PQ G1R 4B3. ℂ **888/694-0303** or 418/694-0303. Fax 418/692-1375. www.hotelcapdiamant.com. 9 units. Summer C$164–C$174 double; rest of the year from C$114. Continental breakfast included. Packages available. AE, MC, V. Parking C$14. *In room:* A/C, TV, fridge, hair dryer, Wi-Fi (free).

Hôtel Champlain Vieux-Québec ★ (Value)   New owners gave this property a total overhaul in 2006, from decor to bathrooms to beds. Even the smallest rooms have silk curtains, king or queen beds, 300-count cotton sheets, flatscreen TVs, and most units are quite roomy. A midpriced room, no. 13, allows views of stone buildings across the street and feels very French, while guests in no. 47 can see the Château Frontenac from their bed. Windows open, an unusual feature in this city. A self-serve Nuovo Simonelli espresso machine by the front desk provides free cappuccinos any time of day or night, and there's a computer for guests to use for free. Don't be alarmed when you arrive: A bleh 1960s facade hasn't been updated and doesn't reflect the pizazz inside. This is a sister property to **Auberge Place d'Armes** (see above).

115 rue Ste-Anne (near rue Ste-Ursule), Québec City, PQ G1R 3X6. ℂ **800/567-2106** or 418/694-0106. Fax 418/692-1959. www.champlainhotel.com. 50 units. Summer C$179–C$209 double; rest of the year C$109–C$149 double. Continental breakfast included. AE, DISC, MC, V. Limited on-site parking. **Amenities:** Concierge. *In room:* A/C, TV/DVD, fridge, hair dryer, MP3 docking station, Wi-Fi (free).

Hôtel Château Bellevue   Occupying several row houses at the top of the Jardin des Gouverneurs in one of Vieux-Québec's prettiest areas, this 58-room hotel has a helpful staff as well as some of the creature comforts typical of larger facilities. Though units are small and unspectacular, they are quiet for the most part, and a dozen have two double beds. Many rooms were renovated in 2008, so ask for one of them. A few higher-priced units overlook the park. The lobby features free coffee and newspapers as well as an unusual wine machine that dispenses selections by the glass. If this place is full, there are about a dozen other small lodgings within a block in any direction. A sister hotel, **Château Laurier** (p. 222), is outside the walls on Parliament Hill.

16 rue de la Porte (at av. Ste-Geneviève), Québec City, PQ G1R 4M9. ℂ **800/463-2617** or 418/692-2573. Fax 418/692-4876. www.hotelchateaubellevue.com. 58 units. July–Oct C$139–C$245 double; rest of the year from C$99 double. Continental breakfast included Nov–June. Packages available. AE, DC, DISC, MC, V. Valet parking C$18. *In room:* A/C, TV, hair dryer, Wi-Fi (free).

Hôtel Sainte-Anne ★   A find for fans of modern, European-style design. Exposed stone and brick walls are common, and most rooms have a tall, narrow, free-standing cabinet housing a TV near the top, an unstocked fridge, a coffeemaker, and a closet. The effect is spare but clean, and unusual lighting fixtures add drama. Swank, high-design bathrooms feature satisfyingly drenching showers. Breakfast and room service are provided from **Le Grill,** a sleek and vaguely corporate-feeling restaurant. The boutique hotel is housed in a 19th-century row house that fronts a pedestrian block of rue Ste-Anne in Upper Town's historic district.

32 rue Ste-Anne (near rue des Jardins), Québec City, PQ G1R 3X3. ☎ **877/222-9422** or 418/694-1455. Fax 418/692-4096. www.hotelste-anne.com. 28 units. Mid-June to mid-Oct C$189–C$229 double; rest of year from C$119 double. AE, MC, V. **Amenities:** Restaurant (mid-May–Oct). *In room:* AC, TV, fridge, hair dryer, Wi-Fi (free).

INEXPENSIVE

Auberge Internationale de Québec There are 279 beds in this centrally-located youth hostel, which is the largest in Canada. Most beds are in dorm layouts standard to the Hostelling International organization, while others are in modest private rooms for one to five people, with either shared or private bathrooms. There's a laundry room for everyone's use. The facility is open 24 hours and has an excellent four (out of five) star rating by the tourist board for its comfort, range of services, and overall quality. Reservations are necessary in the summers.

19 rue. Ste-Ursule (near rue Ste-Anne), Québec City, PQ G1R 4E1. ☎ **866/694-0950** or 418/694-0755. Fax 418/694-2278. www.aubergeinternationaldequebec.com. 23 private rooms; 279 beds total. C$74–C$87 private room for two; C$4 discount for Hostelling International members. AE, MC, V. **Amenities:** Restaurant; bar; self-service kitchen Wi-Fi (in lobby, free). *In room:* Fan.

Maison du Fort One of the cheeriest B&Bs near Parc des Gouverneurs. The owner is friendly and even the smallest rooms, such as no. 2 on the first floor, are pleasant, with yellow and lime green decor. Tea and muffins are served in the morning. The home was built in 1851 and has a tasteful manner to match its pedigree. There are two resident cats.

21 av. Ste-Geneviève (near rue de la Porte), Québec City, PQ G1R 4B1. ☎ **888/203-4375** or 418/692-4375. Fax 418/692-5257. www.hotelmaisondufort.com. 9 units. C$129–C$189 double. MC, V. *In room:* TV (some units), hair dryer, Wi-Fi (free).

Manoir Sur-le-Cap Continual renovations and sprucing up of units keep this inn on the Parc des Gouverneurs, opposite the Château Frontenac, looking spiffy. All guest rooms have gleaming floors and many feature exposed stone or brick walls. If you require air-conditioning, be sure to request one of the six units that have it. Room no. 8 is one of the least expensive units but has a small balcony; room no. 10 features a king bed, claw-foot tub, and large windows with a view of the Château. Photos of each room are online.

9 av. Ste-Geneviève (near rue de la Porte), Québec City, PQ G1R 4A7. ☎ **418/694-1987.** Fax 418/627-7405. www.manoir-sur-le-cap.com. 14 units. C$105–C$175 double. AE, MC, V. *In room:* AC (some units), TV, hair dryer, Wi-Fi (free).

3 VIEUX-QUEBEC: BASSE-VILLE (LOWER TOWN)/VIEUX-PORT

EXPENSIVE

Auberge Saint-Antoine ★★★ This uncommonly attractive property began life as an 1830 maritime warehouse. It kept the soaring ceilings, dark beams, and stone floors, and is now one of the city's landmark luxury boutique hotels (and a member of the prestigious Relais & Châteaux luxury group). Ancient walls remain in view, and artifacts unearthed during the development are on display throughout the hotel—in public areas, at the door to each room, and bedside, lit with an underwater-blue glow. Bedrooms are modern and sleek with luxury linens, plush robes, Bose sound systems, heated bathroom floors, and bathing nooks with rain-shower nozzles directly overhead. Many have balconies, terraces, fireplaces, or kitchenettes; ask when booking if you want to ensure having any of these features in your room. A striking lounge serves breakfast, lunch, snacks, and drinks, and its high-end restaurant, **Panache** (p. 230), has become one of the best in town.

8 rue St-Antoine (next to the Musée de la Civilisation), Québec City, PQ G1K 4C9. ℰ **888/692-2211** or 418/692-2211. Fax 418/692-1177. www.saint-antoine.com. 95 units. C$169–C$399 double; from C$299 suite. Packages available. AE, DC, MC, V. Valet parking C$23. **Amenities:** 2 restaurants; 2 bars; babysitting; concierge; exercise room; room service. *In room:* TV, hair dryer, minibar, Wi-Fi (free).

Dominion 1912 ★★★ Old Québec meets new in one of the city's most romantic boutique hotels. The owners stripped the 1912 building down to the studs and started over, keeping the angular lines and adding soft touches. Québec-made beds are topped with mattresses that are deep, soft, and enveloping, heaped with pillows and feather duvets. Custom-made bedside tables swing into place or out of the way, and even the least expensive rooms are large. About a third of the rooms have only showers, while the rest include tubs. Room no. 206 is a dandy, with a shower that shares a glass wall with the bedroom and views of the city's centuries-old, formerly industrial buildings. A hearty continental breakfast is set out along with morning newspapers near the fireplace in the handsome lobby, and a machine that dispenses free espresso is available round the clock. A fitness room has been rigged up in the basement.

126 rue St-Pierre (at rue St-Paul), Québec City, PQ G1K 4A8. ℰ **888/833-5253** or 418/692-2224. Fax 418/692-4403. www.hoteldominion.com. 60 units. C$169–C$425 double. Rates include breakfast. AE, DC, MC, V. Parking C$18. Pets accepted, C$30 per night. **Amenities:** Espresso bar; babysitting; concierge; exercise room; room service. *In room:* A/C, TV, CD player, hair dryer, minibar, Wi-Fi (free).

Hôtel 71 ★★ Owned by the same people as the adjacent **Le Saint-Pierre** (see below), the two properties share a bar, but Hôtel 71 is slicker and ultra-contemporary. Room no. 620 is typical, with 4.5m-high (15-ft.) creme-colored walls and curtains that extend nearly floor to ceiling, warmed up with deep-red velveteen chairs and cloth panels that serve as closet doors. Bathrooms are in the open style common to the area's boutique hotels, with sea-foam-green glass separating the shower from the sink area and shower nozzles of the big-disk variety (all rooms have showers; four have bathtubs as well). Rooms are on floors four to seven and many feature bird's-eye views of the tops of the 19th-century buildings of Old Québec, the St. Lawrence River, or the ramparts of the fortress wall. The small but stylish **Café 71,** on the first floor, is open for breakfast and for snacks during the day.

71 rue St-Pierre (near rue St-Antoine), Québec City, PQ G1K 4A4. ℰ **888/692-1171** or 418/692-1171. Fax 418/692-0669. www.hotel71.ca. 40 units. C$180–C$290. Rates include breakfast. Packages available. AE, DC, MC, V. Valet parking C$20. **Amenities:** Restaurant; bar; babysitting; concierge; exercise room w/ spectacular river view; room service. *In room:* A/C, TV/DVD, CD player, hair dryer, Wi-Fi (free).

MODERATE

Hôtel des Coutellier ★ In a quiet nook across from the city's market and down the block from the train station, Coutellier does lots of small things right. As a result, it boasts of having one of the highest occupancy rates in the city. It gets lots of repeat business travelers but also caters to vacationers who appreciate the personal touch that can come with a 24-room operation. Breakfasts of croissant, yogurt, and orange juice are delivered each morning in a basket that hangs from the front doorknob. A few rooms have brick walls and the odd angles that are common to the refurbished 19th century warehouses of the neighborhood. For bicyclists, the hotel offers free indoor bike storage. Charmingly, a *pétanque* pit (similar to boule and boccie) in front of the hotel brings out local players in the afternoons.

253 rue St-Paul (at Quai St-André), Québec City, PQ G1K 3W5. ℂ 888/523-9696 or 418/692-9696. Fax 418/692-4050. www.hoteldescoutellier.com. 24 units. C$195–C$255. Rates include breakfast delivered in basket to door. AE, DISC, MC, V. **Amenities:** Room service (from adjacent restaurant Môss). *In room:* A/C, TV, hair dryer, minibar, MP3 docking station, Wi-Fi (free).

Hôtel Le Priori ★ A playful Art Deco interior sets the mood for this renovated 1726 house—you'll find conical stainless-steel sinks in the bedrooms and, in four units, claw-foot tubs beside duvet-covered queen-size beds. Several units, including no. 10, are quite masculine, with brown walls, animal-skin rugs, and fur throws. Suites include sitting rooms with wood-burning fireplaces, kitchens, and Jacuzzis. Rooms face either the small street out front or a leafy, pretty, inner courtyard. The inventive in-house restaurant **Toast!** (p. 231) moves into the courtyard on summer nights.

15 rue Sault-au-Matelot (at rue St-Antoine), Québec City, PQ G1K 3Y7. ℂ 800/351-3992 or 418/692-3992. Fax 418/692-0883. www.hotellepriori.com. 26 units. Summer C$199–C$259 double, winter C$129–C$189 double; suites from C$250. Rates include breakfast. Packages available. AE, MC, V. Valet parking C$15. **Amenities:** Restaurant; bar; babysitting; concierge; room service. *In room:* A/C, TV/DVD, CD player, hair dryer, Wi-Fi (free).

Le Saint-Pierre ★ One of the city's country-cozy *auberge* options—though recent renovations have sleeked up the hotel. Most rooms are surprisingly spacious, and the even more commodious suites are a luxury on a longer visit, especially since they have modest kitchen facilities. The made-to-order furnishings suggest traditional Québec style, and units have wood floors and original brick or stone walls. All rooms are on the fourth to seventh floors, and some have a river view. All rooms also have whirlpool baths, a nice treat after days spent walking. The full breakfasts, included in the price, are cooked to order.

79 rue St-Pierre (behind the Musée de la Civilisation), Québec City, PQ G1K 4A3. ℂ 888/268-1017 or 418/694-7981. Fax 418/694-0406. www.le-saint-pierre.ca. 41 units. C$199–C$289 double. Rates include full breakfast. Packages available. AE, DC, MC, V. Valet parking C$20. **Amenities:** Bar; babysitting; concierge. *In room:* A/C, TV, hair dryer, Wi-Fi (free).

4 PARLIAMENT HILL/ON OR NEAR GRANDE-ALLEE

EXPENSIVE

Courtyard Marriott Québec ★★ Value The Courtyard Marriott has become a hot property in recent years, due in part to across the board raves on online boards for its friendly staff, comfortable rooms, and fair prices. Someone here is paying attention to the right details, because the hotel has also been named tops among all Courtyard hotels in staff service for 5 straight years. Beds have been given the deluxe treatment and are piled with five pillows and sheet-cover duvets. All rooms have either a sofa bed or an oversized chair that pulls out into a single bed, and all feature ergonomic chairs at the

(Moments) **Québec's Ice Hotel: The Coldest Reception in Town**

For C$16 you can visit, but for C$325 per person (and up) you can have dinner and spend the night. Tempted? Québec's **Ice Hotel** (© **877/505-0423;** www. icehotel-canada.com) is built each winter at the Station touristique Duchesnay, a woodsy resort a half-hour outside of Québec City. It celebrates its 10th anniversary in 2010.

The *Hôtel de Glace* is crafted each year from 500 tons of ice, and nearly everything is ice, from the ice chandelier in the 5.4m (18-ft.) vaulted main hall to the thick ice shot glasses in which vodka is served to the pillars and arches and furniture. That includes the frozen slabs they call beds; deer skins and sleeping bags provide insulation.

Nighttime guests get their rooms at 9pm, after the last tours, and have to clear out by 8am, before the next day's arrivals. Some rooms are themed and vaguely grand: The Chess Room, for instance, features solid-ice chess pieces the size of small children at each corner of the bed. Other rooms bring the words "monastic" or "cell block" to mind.

Bear in mind that except for in the hot tub, temperatures everywhere hover between 23° and 27°F (–5° to –3°C). Refrigerators are used not to keep sodas cold but to *keep them from freezing.* And to whomever dreamed up the luxury suite with a real fireplace that somehow emits no heat: There is a special circle in hell for you.

The hotel has 36 rooms and suites, a wedding chapel, and a disco for guests to shake the chill from their booties. Open each January, it takes guests until early April—after that, it's destroyed.

Locals have a bemused reaction to all the fuss. A waitress down the road told one guest, "I would have charged you half as much and let you sleep in a snowbank behind the pub."

desks. The in-house restaurant, **Que Sera Sera,** is well regarded. Note that the hotel is right on the central Place d'Youville, which is often noisy at night. Ask for a room higher up or towards the back if that's a concern.

850 Place d'Youville (near rue St-Jean), Québec City, PQ G1R 3P6. © **866/694-4004** or 418/694-4004. Fax 418/694-4007. www.marriott.com. 111 units. C$160–C$299 double. Packages available. AE, DC, MC, V. Valet parking C$20, self-parking C$17. **Amenities:** Restaurant; bar; exercise room and whirlpool; room service. *In room:* A/C, TV, fridge, hair dryer, Internet (free).

Hilton Québec ★ (Kids) Renovations in 2008 spruced up about half of the rooms in this Hilton, so insist on one of them. They feature luxe bedding, big desks, ergonomic work chairs, and sand-colored walls. The idea: less clutter, more Zen. Older rooms, on the other hand, are stale and in need of updating, and can sour a visit quickly. Views facing the St. Lawrence River and Vieux-Québec are spectacular and provide views of sunrise over the Citadelle. The busy boulevard René-Lévesque provides a steady hum of cars but is only particularly noticeable during morning rush hour. The heated outdoor pool (plain, with a spare concrete patio) is open year-round; you can take a swim during a snowstorm. The hotel is connected to the Place Québec shopping complex and the convention center.

1100 bd. René-Lévesque est, Québec City, PQ G1R 4P3. (C) **800/447-2411** or 418/647-2411. Fax 418/647-6488. www.hiltonquebec.com. 571 units. C$175–C$400 double. Packages available. AE, DC, DISC, MC, V. Valet parking C$29. **Amenities:** Restaurant; babysitting; bar; concierge; executive-level floors; exercise room w/sauna; pool (outdoor, heated, year-round); room service. *In room:* A/C, TV, hair dryer, Internet (C$12 per day).

Loews Le Concorde Hotel ★ (Kids) The skyscraper that houses this hotel rises discordantly from a neighborhood of late-Victorian town houses. But for guests, no matter: With all rooms on the fifth floor and above, the hotel offers spectacular views of the river and the Old City. It's also adjacent to the Grande-Allée restaurant and party scene on one side and the pristine Joan of Arc garden in Parc des Champs-de-Bataille on the other. **L'Astral** (p. 269), the hotel's revolving rooftop restaurant with a bar and live piano music on weekends, is definitely worth a stop and has better food than usually can be expected of sky-high venues. For kids, there's a lending library of toys.

1225 Cours du Géneral de Montcalm (at Grande-Allée), Québec City, PQ G1R 4W6. (C) **800/463-5256** or 418/647-2222. Fax 418/647-4710. www.loewsleconcorde.com. 406 units. C$139–C$399 double. Packages available. AE, DC, DISC, MC, V. Self-parking C$23, valet parking C$28. Pets accepted, C$25 per stay. **Amenities:** Restaurant (revolving rooftop); 2 bars; babysitting; concierge; well-equipped health club w/sauna; pool (outdoor heated); room service. *In room:* A/C, TV, hair dryer, minibar, Wi-Fi (C$13).

MODERATE

Hôtel Château Laurier Québec ★ Right on action-filled Grande-Allée, this property has perked up considerably in recent years. A saltwater pool and Finnish sauna opened in 2007, and the health center and the restaurant were renovated that same year. Eight categories of rooms and suites are available thanks to nearly continual expansion in recent years; getting one of the better rooms can make or break your stay here. Newer units, such as those on executive floors, are more desirable than those in the plainer and more cramped original wing and come with sizable desks and leather sitting chairs with reading lamps. Some units feature working fireplaces, whirlpools, and king-size beds; all enjoy the comforts and doodads of a first-class hotel. Many rooms on the higher floors have views of the Citadelle and the St. Lawrence River. The hotel is 2 blocks west of the fortress wall and St-Louis Gate.

1220 Place Georges-V ouest (at Grande-Allée), Québec City, PQ G1R 5B8. (C) **800/463-4453** or 418/522-8108. Fax 418/524-8768. www.oldquebec.com. 291 units. C$159–C$319 double. Children 17 and younger stay free in parent's room. Packages available. AE, DC, MC, V. Parking C$20. **Amenities:** Restaurant; babysitting; concierge; executive-level floors; exercise room; pool (indoor saltwater); room service; sauna (Finnish). *In room:* A/C, TV, hair dryer, Internet (free).

INEXPENSIVE

Relais Charles-Alexandre (Value) This little hotel is close to the Musée des Beaux-Arts du Québec and the pleasant shopping street avenue Cartier. Its proximity to the Plains of Abraham makes it a good choice, too, if you're visiting for one of the festivals held there. Rooms are very basic but crisply maintained. Spend the extra C$10 for one of the nicer units.

91 Grande-Allée est (2 blocks east of av. Cartier), Québec City, PQ G1R 2H5. (C) **418/523-1220.** Fax 418/523-9556. www.quebecweb.com/rca. 23 units. May–Oct and Carnaval C$129–C$139 double; Nov–Apr C$89–C$99 double. Rates include breakfast. MC, V. Parking C$8. **Amenities:** Breakfast room. *In room:* A/C, TV, hair dryer, Wi-Fi (free).

5 ST-ROCH

Until about 2000, there were few reasons for travelers to include Québec's St-Roch neighborhood in their plans, but that's changing. Young restaurateurs, artists, and media techies have settled in and dubbed the area "Le Nouvo St-Roch" (proper spelling would be too traditional).

MODERATE

Auberge Le Vincent ★ Value The emerging St-Roch neighborhood has restaurants worth going out of your way for (p. 233) and nestled in this neighborhood of tech companies, skateboard punks, and well-heeled hipsters is the Van Gogh–inspired Le Vincent, which opened its 10 rooms in 2006. Housed in a renovated 100-year-old building, the sophisticated accommodations represent a terrific value, considering all the luxe features: goose duvets, 400-count sheets, custom-made dark cherry-wood furniture, generous lighting options, and local art. Breakfast, which is included, is served in a brick-walled seating area off the lobby (note the lobby's floor, which is painted in Van Gogh–style sunbursts and roiling blue curves). Bike storage is available. Rooms are up either one or two flights of stairs.

295 rue St-Vallier est (corner of rue Dorchester), Québec City, PQ G1K 3P5. ✆ **888/523-5005** or 418/523-5000. Fax 418/523-5999. www.aubergelevincent.com. 10 units. C$199–C$229 double. Rates include full breakfast. Packages available. AE, MC, V. Parking C$15. *In room:* A/C, TV/DVD, CD player, fridge, hair dryer, Wi-Fi (free).

6 JUST OUTSIDE THE CITY

MODERATE

Hôtel-Musée Premières Nations ★ Fifteen minutes from Québec City is a First Nations reservation called Wendake. It's here that a beautifully airy, earthy hotel that shows off native furnishings opened in early 2008. The hotel is tucked into a grove of maple trees along the shores of the Akiawenrahk River, and each room overlooks the river and has a small balcony with seating. An onsite museum celebrates Huron-Wendat culture year-round, and in July and August packages are available that include an outdoor show of traditional dance and music called **Kiugwe** (www.tourismewendake.com), which is presented at a nearby amphitheatre. A high-end restaurant features First Nations–inspired cuisine such as elk, bison, and smoked mackerel, and includes a four-course *table d'hôte* for C$38. There also are shops and a few restaurants in Wendake for guests to poke around. Nature fans will find this hotel an intriguing option for visiting Québec City while staying in the woods.

5 Place de la Rencontre, Wendake, Québec, PQ G0A 4V0. ✆ **866/551-9222** or 418/847-2222. Fax 418/847-2903. www.hotelpremieresnations.ca. 55 units. C$149–C$179 double. Packages available. AE, MC, V. Free parking. Rte. 175 north, exit 154 for rue de la Faune, enter Wendake reservation and follow signs to hotel. **Amenities:** Restaurant; bar; babysitting; bike rental; room service. *In room:* A/C, TV, fridge, hair dryer, Wi-Fi (free).

Where to Dine in Québec City

With a little research, it's possible to eat extraordinarily well in Québec City. It used to be that this gloriously scenic town had no *temples de cuisine* comparable to those of Montréal. That has changed. There are now restaurants equal in every way to the most honored establishments of any North American city, with surprising numbers of creative, ambitious young chefs and restaurateurs bidding to achieve similar status.

By sticking to any of the many competent bistros and a couple of jazzy fusion eateries, you'll likely be more than content. Another step up, a half-dozen enterprises tease the palate with hints of higher achievement.

Even the blatantly touristy restaurants along rue St-Louis in Upper Town and around the Place d'Armes, many of them with hawkers outside and accordion players and showy tableside presentations inside, can produce decent meals. The less extravagant among them are entirely satisfactory for breakfast or lunch.

The best dining deals are the *table d'hôte* (fixed-price) meals. Nearly all full-service restaurants offer them. As a rule, they include at least soup or salad, a main course, and a dessert. Some places add in an extra appetizer and/or a beverage. The total price ends up being approximately what you'd pay for the main course alone.

At the better places, and even at some that might seem inexplicably popular, reservations are all but essential during traditional holidays and the festivals that pepper the social calendar. Other times, it's necessary to book ahead only for weekend evenings. In the listings below, where no mention is made of reservations, they shouldn't be necessary. Dress codes are rarely stipulated, but "dressy-casual" works almost everywhere.

The evening meal tends to be served earlier in Québec City than in Montréal, at 6 or 7pm rather than 8pm. In the winter months, when tourist traffic slows, restaurants sometimes close early or cut down on their days, so it's best to confirm opening hours.

Smoking in restaurants, bars, and most other public places in Québec province has been prohibited since 2006.

1 BEST DINING BETS

- **Best Restaurants for a Special Evening: Laurie Raphaël,** 117 rue Dalhousie (© **418/692-4555**), is sophisticated and endlessly eclectic; you never know what Daniel Vézina's kitchen will have in store. See p. 230. **Initiale,** 54 rue St-Pierre (© **418/694-1818**), is hushed and elegant, with less sizzle but equally top-notch cuisine. See p. 230. New to this list is **Panache,** 10 rue St-Antoine (© **418/692-1022**), which may be the most romantic of the three. See p. 230. These stellar restaurants are just blocks from each other in Lower Town.

- **Best Bistros:** In a city that specializes in the informal bistro tradition, **L'Echaudé,** 73 rue Sault-au-Matelot, near rue St-Paul (© **418/692-1299**), is a star. The classic dishes are all in place, from confit de canard to steak frites, and the tone is casual sophistication. See p. 231. **Le Clocher Penché Bistrot,** 203 rue St-Joseph est (© **418/640-0597**), offers a cozy atmosphere and a good reason to explore the trendy St-Roch neighborhood. See p. 234.

- **Best Overall Value:** Just steps from Place d'Armes, the epicenter of Upper Town, the handsome **Le Pain Béni,** 24 rue Ste-Anne (© **418/694-9485**) serves up adventurous, locally-sourced food in healthy portions at fair prices. See p. 227.

- **Best Big View:** Revolving rooftop restaurants rarely dish out food as elevated as their lofty venues. **L'Astral** in the Loews Le Concorde Hotel, 1225 Cours du Général de Montcalm (© **418/647-2222**), is an exception. The food is above average and the revolving view one of a kind. It's open daily for all meals, with a C$18 Sunday brunch. See p. 269.

- **Best Idyllic Terrace:** The crimson red main room is sexy, but try to get onto the leafy enclosed back terrace of Lower Town's **Toast!,** 17 rue Sault-au-Matelot (© **418/692-1334**), which is a haven. See p. 231.

- **Best Rockin' Hot Spot:** You don't have to be young and gorgeous to get into the **VooDoo Grill,** 575 Grande-Allée est (© **418/647-2000**), but there seems to be a lot of self-selecting going on. The noise level can get brutal and the pace frantic, making the good food all the more surprising. See p. 232.

- **Best Restaurant in St-Roch:** Utopie, 226½ rue St-Joseph est (© **418/523-7878**), is the restaurant worth traveling outside the tourist orbit for. It recently added a tapas and wine bar called **Le Cercle** right next door. See p. 233 and 267.

- **Best Afternoon Bargain:** Dinner at **Aux Anciens Canadiens,** 34 rue St-Louis (© **418/692-1627**), can set you back C$50 or more, but from noon until 5:45pm daily the purveyor of classic Québécois fare offers a three-course meal with a glass of wine or beer for C$20. See p. 226.

- **Best Sugar Pie:** We have to go with **Aux Anciens Canadiens** (see above) for this category as well. Québec's favorite dessert reaches its apogee at this admittedly tourist-heavy venue in central Upper Town. Think maple syrup with a crust, or pecan pie without the pecans. See p. 226.

- **Best Family Meal on a Holiday:** Large (it seats more than 200) and jovial, **Le Café du Monde,** 84 rue Dalhousie (© **418/692-4455**), manages the nearly impossible: classic French food *and* fast service without a compromise in quality—even on crowded holiday weekends. See p. 232.

- **Best Breakfast with Locals:** In the residential neighborhood of Montcalm, not far from the Musée des Beaux-Arts du Québec, **Café Krieghoff,** 1091 av. Cartier (© **418/522-3711**), gets a mix of families, singles, and artsy folks of all ages. See p. 233.

- **Best Regional Chain:** Twenty years ago, **Piazzetta** opened its first gourmet pizza restaurant at 63 rue St. Paul (© **418/692-2962**) in Vieux-Port. It has expanded to about two dozen restaurants throughout Québec province and is a dependably good choice. See p. 232.

- **Best Heart-of-it-All Location:** At the bottom of Breakneck Stairs right next to the funicular, the terrace of **Le Marie-Clarisse,** 12 rue du Petit-Champlain (© **418/692-0857**), offers an unsurpassed observation point. See p. 231.

2 RESTAURANTS BY CUISINE

Bistro
L'Echaudé ★★ (Basse-Ville/
Vieux-Port, $$$, p. 231)
Le Clocher Penché Bistrot ★★
(St-Roch, $$, p. 234)
Mistral Gagnant ★ (Basse-Ville/
Vieux-Port, $$, p. 232)

Contemporary Pizza
Piazzetta ★ (Basse-Ville/Vieux-Port,
$$, p. 232)

Contemporary Québécois
Initiale ★★★ (Basse-Ville/
Vieux-Port, $$$$, p. 230)
Laurie Raphaël ★★★ (Basse-Ville/
Vieux-Port, $$$$, p. 230)
Le Pain Béni ★ (Haute-Ville, $$,
p. 227)
Panache ★★ (Basse-Ville/Vieux-Port,
$$$$, p. 230)
Toast! ★ (Basse-Ville/Vieux-Port, $$$,
p. 231)
Utopie ★ (St-Roch, $$$, p. 233)

Continental
Versa (St-Roch, $$, p. 234)
VooDoo Grill ★ (Parliament Hill, $$,
p. 232)

Traditional French
Le Café du Monde ★ (Basse-Ville/
Vieux-Port, $$, p. 232)

Italian
Ristorante Il Teatro (Haute-Ville, $$,
p. 227)

Light Fare
Café Krieghoff (Parliament Hill, $,
p. 233)
Paillard (Haute-Ville, $, p. 227)

Seafood
Le Marie-Clarisse ★ (Basse-Ville/
Vieux-Port, $$$, p. 231)
Poisson d'Avril (Basse-Ville/
Vieux-Port, $$$, p. 231)

Sushi
Yuzu Sushi ★ (St-Roch, $$, p. 234)

Traditional Québécois
Aux Anciens Canadiens ★
(Haute-Ville, $$$, p. 226)

Vegetarian
Le Commensal (Parliament Hill, $,
p. 233)

Key to Abbreviations: $$$$ = Very Expensive $$$ = Expensive $$ = Moderate $ = Inexpensive
The prices within each review refer to the cost in Canadian dollars of individual main courses, using the
following categories: Very Expensive ($$$$), main courses at dinner average more than C$35; Expensive
($$$), C$25 to C$35; Moderate ($$), C$15 to C$25; and Inexpensive ($), C$15 and less.
Restaurants are listed alphabetically at the end of the index in the back of this book.

3 VIEUX-QUEBEC: HAUTE-VILLE (UPPER TOWN)

EXPENSIVE
Aux Anciens Canadiens ★ TRADITIONAL QUEBECOIS   Inundated by travelers during peak months, this venerable restaurant with costumed servers is in what's
probably the city's oldest house (1677); its front windows are small because their original

glass came over from France packed in barrels of molasses. Surprisingly, it's one of the best places in La Belle Province at which to sample cooking that has its roots in New France's earliest years. Ancient Québécois recipes are done well here, and servings are large enough to ward off hunger for a week. Caribou figures into many of the dishes, as does maple syrup, which goes into, for example, the duckling, goat-cheese salad, and luscious sugar pie. Prices are high but the restaurant's afternoon special, from noon to 5:45pm, is a terrific bargain: soup, a main course, a dessert, and a glass of beer or wine for C$20.

34 rue St-Louis (at rue des Jardins). ☎ 418/692-1627. www.auxancienscanadiens.qc.ca. Reservations recommended. Main courses C$29–C$68; *table d'hôte* dinner C$40–C$79; *table d'hôte* lunch C$20. AE, DC, MC, V. Daily noon–9pm.

MODERATE

Le Pain Béni ★★ (Value) CONTEMPORARY QUEBECOIS When one person is in the mood for adventurous taste combinations but others want something simple, head to Pain Béni, located in the touristic heart of Upper Town. Everyone will be happy. There are pizzas and pastas and a filet mignon with scalloped potatoes. But there also are Québécois classics with modern twists, such as wild boar over creamy risotto, or sweetbreads and red tuna caramelized in honey and soy with a vanilla-perfumed artichoke purée. Desserts are especially creative, as with rum-flambéed banana crème brûlée with grilled coconut, or "lemon pie splash" featuring a lemony homemade marshmallow—sublime. The menu changes three times a year. Pain Béni, which is inside the **Auberge Place d'Armes** (p. 216), is handsome, friendly, and fairly priced. Unlike some of the restos in this touristed area, it's open year-round.

24 rue Ste-Anne (at rue du Trésor). ☎ 418/694-9485. www.aubergeplacedarmes.com. Main courses C$14–C$45; *table d'hôte* cost of main plus C$9. AE, DC, MC, V. Daily 11:30am–1:30pm and 5:30–9:30pm most of the year, with longer hours in high-season summer months and closed Sunday in winter.

Ristorante Il Teatro ★ (Value) ITALIAN There's so much to like about this convivial Italian restaurant. There's its huge menu (22 types of pasta and 6 types of risotto, for instance). There are its generous portions and fair prices (most main courses are under C$20). There's its large sidewalk cafe, directly on the hopping Place d'Youville. And there's its general ambiance: friendly, bustling, and never snooty. Teatro also offers a *table du soir*, making it one of the few places to get a meal until 11pm or even later—if it's busy, the kitchen will stay open until 2am and the bar until 3am. Actors, musical performers, and theater staff from the adjoining **Le Capitole** theater (p. 267) and other nearby arts venues often stop in after their shows.

972 rue St-Jean (at Place d'Youville). ☎ 418/694-9996. www.lecapitole.com/en/restaurant.php. Main courses C$12–C$36. AE, DC, MC, V. Daily 7am–2am.

INEXPENSIVE

Paillard LIGHT FARE Keep this bright, cavernous sandwich shop in mind when you're looking for healthy, fast food to eat in or take out. Hot and cold sandwiches on hearty ciabatta, baguettes, or croissants are the main event, and natural sodas, satisfying espresso drinks, and a yummy selection of pastries and gelato fill out the menu. There are small tables as well as communal seating at large tables.

1097 rue St-Jean (near rue St-Stanislas). ☎ 418/692-1221. www.paillard.ca. All items cost less than C$10. MC, V. Daily 7:30am–7pm; until 10pm in summer.

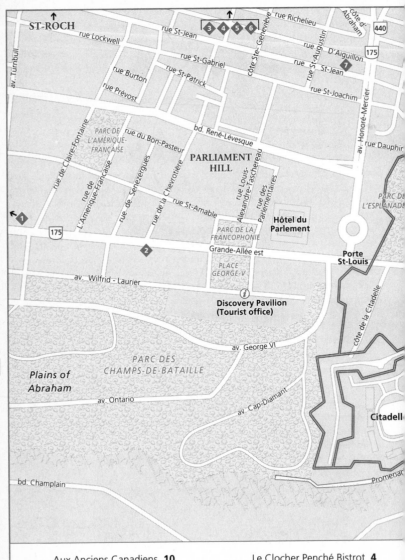

Aux Anciens Canadiens **10**	Le Clocher Penché Bistrot **4**
Café Krieghoff **1**	Le Commensal **7**
Initiale **13**	L'Echaudé **18**
Laurie Raphaël **17**	Le Marie-Clarisse **12**
Le Café du Monde **16**	Le Pain Béni **11**

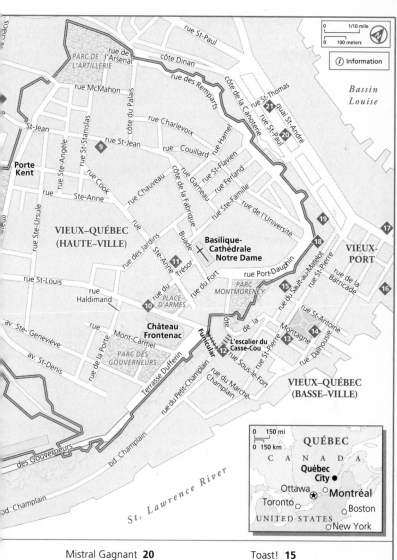

Mistral Gagnant **20**
Paillard **9**
Panache **14**
Piazzetta **19**
Poisson d'Avril **21**
Ristorante Il Teatro **8**

Toast! **15**
Utopie **5**
Versa **6**
VooDoo Grill **2**
Yuzu Sushi **7**

4 VIEUX-QUEBEC: BASSE-VILLE (LOWER TOWN)/VIEUX-PORT

VERY EXPENSIVE

Initiale ★★★ CONTEMPORARY QUEBECOIS   Initiale is not only one of the elite restaurants of Québec City, but one of the best in the entire province. The palatial setting of tall windows, columns, and a deeply recessed ceiling sets a gracious tone, and the welcome is both cordial and correct. Lighting is subdued and the buzz barely above a murmur. This is a good place to cast economy to the winds and go with one of the prix-fixe menus. Dinner might start with a buckwheat crepe folded around an artichoke, a round of crabmeat with a creamy purée of onions, and a flash-fried leaf of baby spinach all arrayed on the plate as on an artist's palette. It might continue with grilled tuna supported by sweet garlic, salsify, and lemon marmalade, and a swirl of pasta with marguerite leaves. Québec cheeses are an impressive topper. Men should wear jackets, and women can pull out the stops.

54 rue St-Pierre (corner of Côte de la Montagne). © **418/694-1818.** www.restaurantinitiale.com. Reservations recommended on weekends. Main courses C$45; *table d'hôte* dinners C$49–C$119. AE, DC, MC, V. Tues–Fri 11:30am–2pm; Tues–Sat 6–9pm.

Laurie Raphaël ★★★ CONTEMPORARY QUEBECOIS   The owners of this smashingly creative restaurant, long one of the city's most accomplished kitchens, tinker relentlessly with their handiwork, building Willy Wonka–style concoctions. Silky-smooth foie gras arrives on a teeny ice cream paddle, drizzled with a port-and-maple-syrup reduction. Alaskan snow crab is accompanied by a bright-pink pomegranate terrine. An egg-yolk "illusion" of thickened orange juice encapsulated in a pectin skin is served in a puddle of maple syrup in an Asian soup spoon. And so on. Service is friendly and correct, and the meal's pace is spot-on. The sophisticated decor is tempered by dashes of eye-popping red and electric pink. A second locale of the same name opened in Montréal in 2007, but only at the Québec location does chef/owner Daniel Vézina give cooking classes (p. 37).

117 rue Dalhousie (at rue St-André). © **418/692-4555.** www.laurieraphael.com. Reservations recommended. Main courses C$38–C$54; 3-course chef's inspiration C$60 (at lunch, C$23); gourmet dinner C$94. AE, DC, DISC, MC, V. Tues–Fri 11:30am–2pm; Tues–Sat 5:30–10pm.

Panache ★★ CONTEMPORARY QUEBECOIS   The restaurant of the superb **Auberge Saint-Antoine** (p. 218) is housed in a former 19th-century warehouse delineated by massive wood beams and rough stone walls. A wrought-iron staircase winds up to a second dining level, where tables feel like they're tucked into the eaves of a secret attic. A center fireplace, velvet couches, generous space between tables, and good acoustics enhance the inherent romantic aura, and service is flawless. Aiming to serve *cuisine Québécoise revisitée*—French-Canadian cuisine with a twist—the frequently changing menu is heavy on locally sourced game, duck, fish, and vegetables. A slip of a bar seats about a dozen. **Café Artefact,** a separate lounge just off the hotel's main lobby, provides a casual and cozy pre-meal meeting spot. If the steep dinner prices put you off, try Panache for a more modestly priced lunch.

10 rue St-Antoine (in Auberge Saint-Antoine). © **418/692-1022.** www.saint-antoine.com. Reservations recommended. Main courses C$43–C$50; 7-course signature menu C$169; lunch main courses from C$14. AE, DC, MC, V. Mon–Fri 6:30–10:30am; Sat–Sun 7–10am; Wed–Fri noon–2pm; daily 6–10pm.

EXPENSIVE

L'Echaudé ★★ BISTRO The most polished of the necklace of restaurants adorning this Vieux-Port corner, L'Echaudé is like a well-worn cashmere sweater—it goes well with both silk trousers and your favorite pair of jeans. Grilled meats and fishes and the seafood stews are an excellent value. Among classics on the menu are steak frites, duck confit, and salmon tartare. Less expected are the grilled horse meat fillet or the Cornish hen with lobster juice and ginger. The owner keeps an important cellar with hundreds of wines, with the full list posted online. The bistro is frequented mostly by locals of almost all ages (the very young are rarely seen) and visitors are attended to by a highly efficient staff. In summer, the small street in front of the patio becomes pedestrian only.

73 rue Sault-au-Matelot (near rue St-Paul). ⓒ **418/692-1299.** www.echaude.com. Reservations suggested on weekends. Main courses C$25–C$35; table d'hôte dinner cost of the main course plus C$18. AE, DC, MC, V. Mon–Sat 11:30am–2:30pm; Sun 10:30am–2:30pm; daily 5:30–10pm.

Le Marie-Clarisse ★ SEAFOOD This spot, at the bottom of Breakneck Stairs and perched overlooking the pedestrian-only rue du Petit-Champlain, sits where the streets are awash with day-trippers and shutterbugs. Location is key: On a summer afternoon, a more pleasant hour cannot be passed anywhere in Québec City than on the terrace here, over a platter of shrimp or pâtés. The menu changes daily, so look closely at the specials posted on chalkboards. The inside rooms are formed of rafters, brick, and stone walls that are more than 340 years old, evoking the feel of a small country inn. In winter, sit aside the stone fireplace and indulge in the dense bouillabaisse—a stew of mussels, scallops, tuna, tilapia, and shrimp.

12 rue du Petit-Champlain (at the funicular). ⓒ **418/692-0857.** www.marieclarisse.qc.ca. Table d'hôte from C$38. AE, MC, V. Summer Mon–Fri 11:30am–2:30pm; daily 6–10pm in summer. Dinner only the rest of the year.

Poisson d'Avril SEAFOOD Nautical trappings that include model ships, marine prints, and mounted sailfish make the intention clear here: The menu is packed with seafood, including some combinations of costly crustaceans responsible for the stiffer prices in the range given below. A crowded bouillabaisse Provençal fits in calamari, scallops, shrimp, mussels, and *rouille* (a savory garnish). Mixed grills and pastas are also available. In good weather, there's a covered dining terrace. The restaurant also runs **Cafe Riviera**, at 155 rue Abraham-Martin, just across the marina, which offers a grand view of the city's Old Port district.

115 quai Saint-André (in Vieux-Port). ⓒ **418/692-1010.** www.poissondavril.net. Reservations recommended. Main courses C$13–C$67; table d'hôte C$31–C$80. AE, DC, MC, V. Daily 5–10pm.

Toast! ★ CONTEMPORARY QUEBECOIS This zesty restaurant adjoins **Hôtel Le Priori** (p. 220). The kitchen has its base in the French idiom, but takes off in many directions. There's rabbit stuffed with blood sausage served with homemade gnocchi. Cod with an almond crust and eggplant purée. For dessert, cheesecake—made with Parmesan reggiano. Dishes are like that: sprightly, with joined tastes and textures. The interior room glows crimson from a wall of fire-engine-red tiles, retro-modern lights, and red Plexiglas window paneling. The outdoor dining terrace in back, with wrought-iron furniture and big leafy trees overhead, is an oasis. The only pity is that after many years offering lunch and weekend brunch, it's now open for dinner only.

17 rue Sault-au-Matelot (at rue St-Antoine). ⓒ **418/692-1334.** www.restauranttoast.com. Reservations recommended on weekends. Table d'hôte only, C$65, C$75, or C$85. AE, DC, MC, V. Daily 6–10:30pm (until 11pm Thurs–Sat).

MODERATE

Le Café du Monde ★ ⓥ Value TRADITIONAL FRENCH A longtime and entirely convivial eating venue, Café du Monde is a large, Parisian-style space, seating more than 100 inside and nearly that number on a terrace overlooking the St. Lawrence River, adjacent to Le Terminal de Croisières—the cruise terminal. The staff is amiable and the food creative but still within bistro conventions. The long menu features classic French preparations of pâtés, duck confit, onion soup, smoked salmon tartare, and mussels with frites. Even on busy holiday weekends, brunch plates—such as scrambled eggs with salmon, dill potatoes, fruit, and a croissant—come out fast.

84 rue Dalhousie (next to the cruise terminal). ℭ 418/692-4455. www.lecafedumonde.com. Reservations recommended. Main courses C$14–C$30; *table d'hôte* C$30–C$34. AE, DC, MC, V. Mon–Fri 11:30am–11pm; Sat–Sun and holidays 9:30am–11pm.

Mistral Gagnant ★ ⓥ Value BISTRO This "restaurant Provençal" channels the spirit of a modest village cafe in France, in both its sunny decor and its friendly atmosphere. Better yet, the food is fairly priced and tasty. The menu changes daily. One offering, *duo de poissons a l'huile de basilica,* turned out to be a full plate of flakey white sea bass with pesto, salmon, scalloped potatoes, carrot mousse, and cauliflower—all fresh and well seasoned. With soup to start, a slice of sublime lemon pie to close, and a price of less than C$15, lunch here can be the best bargain in the area. "Le Mistral" appears to attract mostly locals.

160 rue St. Paul (near rue Rioux). ℭ 418/692-4260. www.mistralgagnant.ca. Main courses C$15–C$31; *table d'hôte* dinner C$24–C$37; lunch and 3-course early bird special 5:30–6:30pm C$11–C$15. AE, MC, V. Tues–Sat 11:30am–2pm and 5:30–9:30pm.

Piazzetta ★ CONTEMPORARY PIZZA We studiously avoided this restaurant for years, figuring why give in to gourmet pizza and pop music with so many classic French options just steps away? But on a night when most restaurants were wanting for customers and we were wanting for a salad, Piazzetta was bustling with smart-looking 30- and 40-something Québécois, so in we went. And boy did we feel dopey for not giving it a go sooner. The decor is cheerful, with quirks: beamed ceiling painted lime green, chandeliers surrounded by lampshades. The staff is friendly. Best of all, the food is great: fresh, generously portioned, well seasoned—there are seven salads to choose from, along with 22 pizzas. Piazzetta opened at this spot in 1989 and has expanded to about two dozen restaurants throughout Québec City, Montréal, and outlying areas.

63 rue St. Paul (at rue Sault-au-Matelot). ℭ 418/692-2962. www.lapiazzetta.ca. Main courses C$7.50–C$31. AE, MC, V. Daily 11:30am–10:30pm (until 11:30 Fri and Sat).

5 PARLIAMENT HILL/ON OR NEAR GRANDE-ALLEE

MODERATE

VooDoo Grill ★ CONTINENTAL Of all the unlikely places to expect a decent meal, let alone one that surpasses most of what can be found at more conventional local restaurants, VooDoo takes the laurels. Female waitstaff are clad in sleeveless halter tops even when temperatures are arctic outside, African carvings adorn the walls, thumping music sets the pace, and conga drummers circulate nightly—a tremendous distraction. It

(Finds) **Picnic Fare**

Halles du Petit-Cartier is a mall for foodies, with about a dozen merchants in open-fronted shops who trade in cheeses, pâtés, terrines, glistening produce, pastries, fresh meats, and fancy picnic items. A few counters make sandwiches to order and there's a small grocery store in back. It's open 7 days a week and located just outside the tourist orbit, west of Parliament Hill, in the Montcalm residential neighborhood, at 1191 av. Cartier (1 block off Grande Allée). It celebrated its 25th birthday in 2009.

is all loud, young, and casual. The menu has been reworked to bring prices down substantially, and nearly everything is under C$20. There's a disco upstairs, **Maurice** (p. 268), an attached cigar lounge, the **Société Cigare,** and a chichi bar called the **Charlotte Lounge.**

575 Grande-Allée est (corner of rue de la Chevrotiére). ✆ **418/647-2000.** www.voodoogrill.com. Reservations recommended. Main courses C$9–C$22. AE, DC, MC, V. Mon–Fri 11:30am–11pm; Sat–Sun 5–11pm.

INEXPENSIVE

Café Krieghoff LIGHT FARE   Walk down Grande-Allée about 10 minutes from the Parliament building, and turn right on avenue Cartier. This 5-block strip is the heart of the Montcalm residential neighborhood, with bakeries, boutiques, and a mini-mall of food shops (see "Picnic Fare," below). In the middle of the hubbub is the cheerful Krieghoff, which features an outdoor terrace a few steps up from the sidewalk. On weekend mornings it's packed with artsy locals of all ages, whose tables get piled high with bowls of café au lait and huge plates of egg dishes, sweet pastries, or steak frites. Service is efficient and good-natured. There's a modest *auberge* upstairs, with seven rooms (C$110–C$150).

1091 av. Cartier (north of Grande-Allée). ✆ **418/522-3711.** www.cafekrieghoff.qc.ca. Most items cost less than C$12. MC, V. Daily 8am–10pm.

Le Commensal (Value) VEGETARIAN   Like its sister outpost in Montréal (p. 84), this large restaurant presents a vegetarian buffet, where you pay for your food by weight. Options include stir-fries, Chinese seitan, hazelnut cake, and sugar pie.

860 rue St-Jean (at av. Honoré-Mercier). ✆ **418/647-3733.** www.commensal.com. Pay by weight; most meals cost less than C$10. A, MC, V. Daily 11am–9pm (until 10pm Thurs–Sat).

6 ST-ROCH

EXPENSIVE

Utopie ★ CONTEMPORARY QUEBECOIS   Utopie continues to have the essential ingredients for its considerable success: The food isn't same-old, the clientele has a stylish sheen, the interior is almost painfully chic, and the location is sufficiently out of the way to require that customers are those in the know. Stands of birch trunks march down the middle of the high-ceilinged space, and blown-up photos of bark line one wall. Food is ambitious: Daïkon vanilla cream soup opened one meal, while at another, sautéed *lotte* (monkfish) was joined with translucent baby bok choy and wild asparagus no thicker than bean sprouts. There are two all-out meal options: a nine-course *menu degustation* for C$90 (C$150 with wine pairing), and the *menu bouteille,* with six courses built around a wine grape of the moment, for C$55 plus the cost of the wine. Lunch is a bargain. A tapas and wine bar next door, **Le Cercle** (p. 267), is a sister operation and serves food until 1am daily.

226¹/₂ rue St-Joseph est (near rue Caron). ℂ **418/523-7878.** www.restaurant-utopie.com. Reservations recommended on weekends. Main courses C$26–C$33; 9-course tasting dinner C$90; *menu bouteille* C$55 per person plus the cost of the wine; *table d'hôte* dinner C$35–C$65 dinner, lunch C$22. AE, MC, V. Thurs–Fri 11:30am–2pm; Tues–Sun 6–10pm.

MODERATE

Le Clocher Penché Bistrot ★★ (**Value** BISTRO   Open since 2000, the development of this unpretentious neighborhood bistro parallels the polishing up of the overall neighborhood during the same period. With its caramel-toned woods, tall ceilings, and walls serving as gallery space for local artists, Clocher Penché has a laid-back European sophistication. There's a huge wine list, with the majority of the bottles organic or "biodynamic." The short menu changes regularly and can include duck confit or a terrific blood sausage *(boudin noir),* which we had with a delicate pastry, caramelized onions, and yellow beets. The menu touts that nearly everything is sourced locally. Service reflects the food—amiable and without flourishes.

203 rue St-Joseph est (at rue Caron). ℂ **418/640-0597.** Reservations recommended. Main courses C$19–C$26; *table d'hôte* lunch and weekend brunch C$16. MC, V. Tues–Fri 11:30am–2pm; Sat–Sun 9am–2pm; Tues–Sat 5–10pm.

Versa CONTINENTAL   Looking more like a club than a restaurant, Versa is a destination to remember when with a group in a partying mood. A communal table sits beneath a teak oval ceiling illuminated by pin lights and a basketball-size disco ball, seats have a '60s Swedish mien, and the translucent panels behind the back bar pulse with a rainbow of colors, highlighting the pride of the barkeeps, their inventive roster of cocktails. A wide selection of appetizers invites grazing: salmon tartar with Rice Krispies and wasabi, perhaps, or minihamburgers. The windows along the front open in good weather, and the evening action floats between here, **Yuzu Sushi** (see below), and the **Boudoir Lounge** (p. 268) across the street from both, a busy nightspot in the heart of what locals call "Le Nouvo St-Roch" (new atmosphere demands new spelling).

432 rue du Parvis (at rue St-Françoise). ℂ **418/523-9995.** www.versarestaurant.com. Main courses C$14–C$30; *table d'hôte* dinner C$25–C$33, lunch C$10–C$20. MC, V. Mon–Fri 11:30am–midnight; Sat–Sun 5pm–midnight.

Yuzu Sushi ★ SUSHI   At the epicenter of the renovated portion of St-Roch, where pockets of chic shops and restaurants are giving a youthful pop to otherwise dreary office buildings and low-key retail, Yuzu focuses on sushi and Japanese preparations, with a long sushi menu, a chef's choice Japanese tasting, and house specialties that include bluefin tuna with green shiso pesto.

438 rue du Parvis (at bd. Charest). ℂ **418/521-7253.** www.yuzu.ca. Reservations recommended. Sushi C$3.75–C$15; main courses C$12–C$40; tasting menus C$69 and C$84. AE, DC, MC, V. Mon–Fri 11:30am–2:30pm; daily 5:30–10pm (to 11pm Thurs–Sat).

Exploring Québec City

Wandering the streets of Vieux-Québec is a singular pleasure, comparable to exploring a provincial capital in Europe. You might happen upon an ancient convent, gabled houses with steeply pitched roofs, a battery of 18th-century cannons in a leafy park, or a bistro with a blazing fireplace on a wintry day.

The Old City, Upper and Lower, is so compact that it's hardly necessary to plan precise sightseeing itineraries. Start at Terrasse Dufferin alongside the Château Frontenac and go off on a whim, down Breakneck Stairs (L'Escalier du Casse-Cou) to the Quartier du Petit-Champlain and Place-Royale, or out of the walls to the military fortress of the Citadelle that overlooks the mighty St. Lawrence River and onto the Plains of Abraham, where generals James Wolfe of Britain and Louis-Joseph, marquis de Montcalm of France, fought to their mutual deaths in a

20-minute battle that changed the continent's destiny.

Most of the historic sights are within the city walls of Vieux-Québec's Haute-Ville (Upper Town) and Basse-Ville (Lower Town). While Upper Town is hilly, with sloping streets, it's nothing like, say, San Francisco, and only people with physical limitations are likely to experience difficulty. Other sights are outside Upper Town's walls, along or just off the boulevard called Grande-Allée. If rain or ice discourages exploration on foot, tour buses and horse-drawn calèches are options.

If you're planning to visit several museums, consider the **Québec City Museum Card** (© **418/641-6290;** www.museo capitale.qc.ca). It's being reorganized for 2010, but in the past it has provided entry to 10 museums over 3 consecutive days for C$50.

1 THE TOP ATTRACTIONS

VIEUX-QUEBEC: BASSE-VILLE (LOWER TOWN)

Musée de la Civilisation ★★★ **Kids** Try to set aside at least 2 hours for a visit to this terrifically engrossing museum. Open since 1988, it's an innovative presence on the waterfront of historic Basse-Ville. Its precise mission has never been entirely clear: Recent temporary exhibits, for example, have focused on extraterrestrials (the 10-ft. Alien Queen from the movie *Aliens* greeted visitors) and the concept of free time. No matter. Through imaginative display techniques, hands-on devices, and holograms, curators ensure that visitors will be so enthralled by the experience that they won't pause to question its intent.

A dramatic atrium-lobby sets the tone with a representation of the St. Lawrence River with an ancient ship beached on the shore. If nothing else, definitely take in "People of Québec . . . Then and Now," a permanent exhibit that is a sprawling examination of Québec history, moving from the province's roots as a fur-trading colony to the turbulent movement for independence from the 1960s to the present, providing visitors with a rich sense of Québec's daily life over the generations. Another permanent exhibition, "Encounter with the First Nations," examines the culture of the aboriginal tribes that

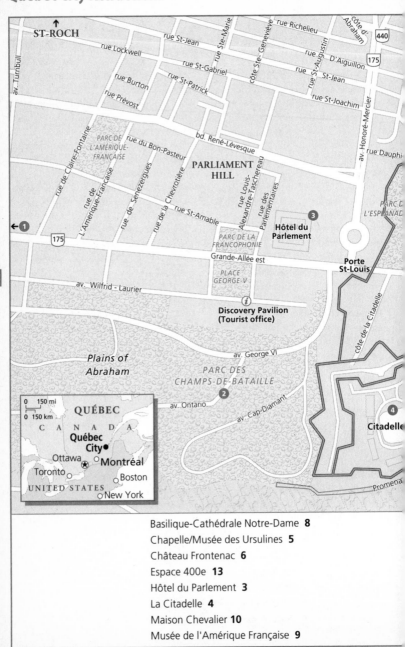

Basilique-Cathédrale Notre-Dame **8**

Chapelle/Musée des Ursulines **5**

Château Frontenac **6**

Espace 400e **13**

Hôtel du Parlement **3**

La Citadelle **4**

Maison Chevalier **10**

Musée de l'Amérique Française **9**

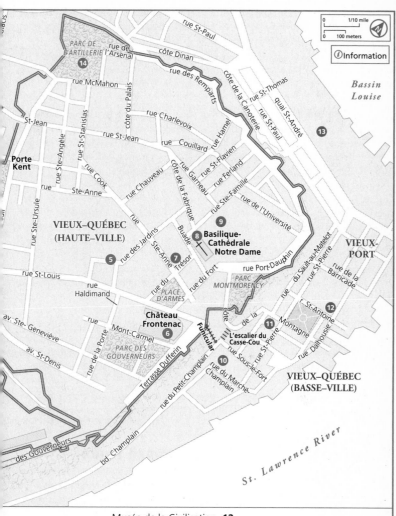

Musée de la Civilisation **12**

Musée National des
  Beaux-Arts du Québec **1**

Québec Expérience **7**

Parc de l'Artillerie **14**

Parc des Champs-de-Bataille **2**

Parks Canada Discovery Centre **13**

Place-Royale **11**

inhabited the region before the Europeans arrived and still live in Québec today. A show on mummies runs through April 4, 2010.

Exhibit texts are in French and English, and there's a second-floor cafe. Through the glass wall behind the ticket counter, you can see the Maison Estèbe, which dates from 1752. It's now restored and houses the museum shop.

85 rue Dalhousie (at rue St-Antoine). ℂ **418/643-2158.** www.mcq.org. Admission C$11 adults, C$10 seniors, C$8 students 17 and older, C$4 children 12–16, free for children 11 and younger; free to all on Tues Nov 1–May 31, and Sat 10am–noon Jan–Feb. Late June to early Sept daily 9:30am–6:30pm; rest of the year Tues–Sun 10am–5pm.

Place-Royale ★★★ (Kids) This small but picturesque plaza is considered by Québé-cois to be the literal and spiritual heart of Basse-Ville—in grander terms, the birthplace of French America. There's a **bust of Louis XIV** in the center. In the 17th and 18th centuries, Place-Royal, or "Royal Square," was the town marketplace and the center of business and industry and was populated by many rich merchants.

Eglise Notre-Dame-des-Victoires dominates the plaza. It's Québec's oldest stone church, built in 1688 after a massive fire in Lower Town destroyed 55 homes in 1682. The church was restored in 1763 and again in 1969. Its paintings, altar, and large model boat suspended from the ceiling were votive offerings brought by early settlers to ensure safe voyages. The church is open daily to visitors May through October and admission is free. Sunday Masses are held at 10:30am and noon.

Commercial activity here began to stagnate around 1860, and by 1950 this was a poor, rundown district. Rehabilitation began in 1960, and all the buildings on the square have now been restored, though only some of the walls are original.

For years, there was an empty lot behind the stone facade on the west side, which now is a whole building again housing the **Centre d'Interprétation de Place-Royale** on the ground floor. Inside, a 20-minute multimedia show and other exhibitions detail the city's 400-year history. Guided tours explaining the plaza's role are available in both English and French. When you exit, turn left and at the end of the block, turn around to view a *trompe l'oeil* mural depicting citizens of the early city.

Free admission to the Place-Royale and Eglise Notre-Dame-des-Victoires. Centre d'Interprétation de Place-Royale, 27 rue Notre-Dame. ℂ **866/710-8031** or 418/646-3167. www.mcq.org. Admission C$6 adults, C$5 seniors, C$4 students, C$2 ages 12–16, free for children 11 and younger; free to all Tues Nov–May. June 24–Sept 6 daily 9:30am–5pm; Sept 7–June 23 Tues–Sun 10am–5pm.

VIEUX-QUEBEC: HAUTE-VILLE (UPPER TOWN)

La Citadelle ★★ The duke of Wellington had this partially star-shaped fortress built at the south end of the city walls in anticipation of renewed American attacks after the War of 1812. Some remnants of earlier French military structures were incorporated into the Citadelle, including a 1750 magazine. Dug into the Plains of Abraham high above Cap Diamant (Cape Diamond), the rock bluff adjacent to the St. Lawrence River, the fort has a low profile that keeps it all but invisible until walkers are actually upon it. The facility has never actually exchanged fire with an invader but continues its vigil for the state. It's now a national historic site, and since 1920 has been home to Québec's **Royal 22e Régiment,** the only fully Francophone unit in Canada's armed forces. That makes it North America's largest fortified group of buildings still occupied by troops.

You can only enter by guided tour, which provides access to the Citadelle and its 25 buildings, including the small regimental museums in the former powder house and prison. The hour-long walk is likely to test the patience of younger visitors and the legs of many older people. For them, it might be better simply to attend the ceremonies of the **changing of the guard** (daily at 10am July 24 to Sept 6) or **beating the retreat,** a sunset ceremony to call in the troops (Fri and Sat at 7pm July and Aug).

Côte de la Citadelle (enter off rue St-Louis). ✆ **418/694-2815.** www.lacitadelle.qc.ca. Admission C$10 adults, C$9 students and senior citizens, C$5.50 children 17 and younger. June 24–Sept 6 daily 9am–6pm; shorter hours rest of the year. May be canceled in the event of rain.

PARLIAMENT HILL/NEAR GRANDE-ALLEE

Musée National des Beaux-Arts du Québec ★★★ Kids Toward the southwestern end of Parc des Champs-de-Bataille (Battlefields Park) and a half-hour walk from Upper Town is the city's major art museum. Musée du Québec, as it's known, occupies a former prison and includes a soaring glass-roofed Grand Hall.

A central reason to visit is to see the Inuit art assembled over the years by Québécois Raymond Brousseau and acquired by the museum in 2005. Much of the 2,635-piece collection was produced in the 1980s and 1990s, and some 285 works are on display. Look for the small, whimsical statue called *Woman Pulling out Grey Hairs.*

The 1933 **Gérard-Morisset Pavilion** houses much of the rest of the museum's permanent collection, North America's largest aggregation of Québécois art. The museum tilts toward the modern as well as the indigenous, with a permanent exhibition of works by famed Québec abstract expressionist and surrealist Jean-Paul Riopelle. Included is his *L'Hommage à Rosa Luxemburg,* a triptych made up of 30 individual paintings that include ghostly spray-painted outlines of birds and handyman tools.

The 1867 **Charles-Baillairgé Pavilion** is a former prison (one cellblock has been left intact as an exhibit). Keep climbing until you reach the tower room, a small widow's walk accessible only by spiral staircase. The petite space holds a massive wooden sculpture of a body in motion by Irish artist David Moore and offers expansive views of the city in every direction. For children, there's a craft-projects room; check in advance to find out about creative workshops for kids.

Parc des Champs-de-Bataille, near where av. Wolfe-Montcalm meets Grande Allée ✆ **866/220-2150** or 418/643-2150. www.mnba.qc.ca. Free admission to permanent collection. Admission for special exhibitions C$15 adults, C$12 seniors, C$7 students, C$4 ages 12–17, free for children 11 and younger. June 1 to Labour Day daily 9am–6pm (until 9pm Wed); day after Labour Day to May 31 Tues–Sun 10am–5pm (until 9pm Wed). Bus: 11.

Parc des Champs-de-Bataille ★★ Kids Covering 108 hectares (267 acres) of grassy hills, sunken gardens, monuments, fountains, and trees, Québec's Battlefields Park was Canada's first national urban park. A section called the **Plains of Abraham** is where Britain's General James Wolfe and France's Louis-Joseph, marquis de Montcalm, engaged in their short but crucial battle in 1759 which resulted in the British defeat of the French troops. It's also where the national anthem, "O Canada," was first performed. Today, the park is a favorite place for Québécois when they want sunshine or a bit of exercise.

From spring through fall, visit the **Jardin Jeanne d'Arc (Joan of Arc Garden),** just off avenue Wilfrid-Laurier near the Loews le Concorde Hotel. This spectacular garden combines French classical design with British-style flower beds. In the rest of the park, nearly 6,000 trees of more than 80 species blanket the fields and include the sugar maple, Norway maple, American elm, and American ash. Also in the park are two Martello towers, cylindrical stone defensive structures built between 1808 and 1812 when Québec feared an American invasion.

Céline et Paul: Music in the Park

The Plains of Abraham in Parc des Champs-de-Bataille is the site of some of the city's major outdoor concerts, and few were more spectacular than those held in 2008 for the 400th anniversary celebrations. On August 22, Céline Dion, the biggest French-Canadian star on the planet, performed in front of 250,000 fans. The wildly successful concert was recorded and released as a DVD, "Céline sur les Plaines." A month earlier, Paul McCartney also played a glorious show, although some sniffed that an English artist—and a knight, to boot!—was not quite what they had in mind for French celebrations. "The presence of your English-language music on the most majestic part of Battlefields Park, as beautiful as it might be, can't help but bring back painful memories of our Conquest," wrote Québec City painter and sculptor Luc Archambault in an open letter. Said McCartney: "Music is a good way to celebrate an anniversary like this. It's a universal language which unites everyone." He also showed up able to speak a little French, which smoothed out some of the ruffled feathers. Videos of both shows are on YouTube.

On the eastern end of the park, the **Discovery Pavilion of the Plains of Abraham,** at 835 av. Wilfrid-Laurier (© **418/648-4071**) has a tourist office and a multimedia exhibit called "Odyssey: A Journey through History on the Plains of Abraham." It's presented in English, French, Spanish, and Japanese.

Parc des Champs-de-Bataille. www.ccbn-nbc.gc.ca. Odyssey show C$10 adults, C$7 seniors and ages 13–17, C$3 12 and younger; discount prices mid-Sept to mid-June. Daily 10am–5pm.

2 MORE ATTRACTIONS

VIEUX-QUEBEC: HAUTE-VILLE (UPPER TOWN)

Basilique Cathédrale Notre-Dame de Québec ★ Notre-Dame Basilica, representing the oldest Christian parish north of Mexico, has weathered a tumultuous history of bombardment, reconstruction, and restoration. Parts of the existing basilica date from the original 1647 structure, including the bell tower and portions of the walls, but most of today's exterior is from the reconstruction completed in 1771. The interior, a re-creation undertaken after a fire in 1922, is flamboyantly neo-baroque, with glinting yellow gold leaf and shadows wavering by the fluttering light of votive candles. Paintings and ecclesiastical treasures still remain from the time of the French regime, including a chancel lamp given by Louis XIV. More than 900 people are buried in the crypt, including four governors of New France.

16 rue Buade (at Côte de la Fabrique). © **418/694-0665.** www.patrimoine-religieux.com. Free admission for worshippers, donations encouraged. Daily 8:30am–5pm. Guided tours of cathedral and crypt May–Oct daily. Tour C$3 adults, C$2 children and students.

Chapelle/Musée des Ursulines Marie de l'Incarnation arrived in Québec City in 1639 and her Ursuline convent, originally built as a girls' school in 1642, is North

America's oldest. The museum tells the story of the nuns, who were also pioneers and artists. On display are vestments woven with gold thread and a cape made of the drapes from the bedroom of Anne of Austria, which was given to the 40-year-old Marie de l'Incarnation when she left for New France. There are also musical instruments and Amerindian crafts, including the *flèche*, or arrow sash, which is still worn during the winter carnival. A new permanent exhibition, launched in 2009, explores the history of the facility as a boarding school.

The chapel is significant for the wooden sculptures in its pulpit and two richly decorated altarpieces, created by Pierre-Noël Levasseur between 1726 and 1736. Although the present building dates only from 1902, much of the interior decoration is nearly 200 years older. Marie de l'Incarnation's tomb is to the right of the entry. She was beatified by Pope John Paul II in 1980.

12 rue Donnacona (at rue des Jardins). ✆ **418/694-0694.** www.museocapitale.qc.ca/014a.htm. Free admission to chapel. Museum C$6 adults, C$5 seniors, C$4 students, C$3 ages 12–16, free for children 11 and younger. Museum May–Sept Tues–Sat 10am–5pm, Sun 1–5pm; Oct–Apr Tues–Sun 1–5pm.

Château Frontenac ★ **Kids**   Visitors curious about the interior of Québec City's emblem, its Eiffel Tower, can take a 50-minute guided tour. Tours are led by costumed guides—maybe a "chambermaid," maybe a "wealthy guest." Designed as a version of a Loire Valley palace, the hotel opened in 1893 to house railroad passengers and encourage tourism. It's visible from almost every quarter of the city, commanding its majestic position atop Cap Diamant, the rock bluff that once provided military defense. Reservations required. See p. 213 for hotel information.

1 rue des Carrières, at Place d'Armes. ✆ **418/691-2166.** www.tourschateau.ca. Tours C$8.50 adults, C$8 for seniors, C$6 children 6–16, free for children 5 and younger. May 1–Oct 15 daily 10am–6pm; Oct 16–Apr 30 Sat–Sun noon–5pm. Departures on the hour.

Excavation under Terrasse Dufferin   Excavation alongside the Château Frontenac took place from 2005 to 2009 as part of a project to perform maintenance work on the promenade and the fortification wall beneath it. Remnants of forts and other buildings dating back to 1620 were unearthed, and visitors can now stroll through the site on self-directed walks. Parks Canada guides are on hand to answer questions.

Terrasse Dufferin. www.pc.gc.ca/lhn-nhs/qc/fortifications/ne/index_E.asp. Free. May to mid-Oct daily.

Musée de l'Amérique Française ★   Located on the site of the Québec Seminary, which dates from 1663, the "Museum of French America" highlights the evolution of French culture in Canada and the U.S. It reopened in October 2008 after a year of renovation, and exhibits are a touch more high-tech, accompanied by clever photo montages, atmospheric lighting, and a few interactive displays (the museum is run by the Musée de la Civilisation). The complex includes the chapel of the seminary, which has beautiful *trompe l'oeil* ornamentation, and an exhibition pavilion a short walk away. Shows there have focused on the Huguenots (French Protestants) of New France and the settling of French Americans in New England, and there's a permanent exhibit on the heritage of the seminary and its founding of Laval University. In the summer, there are five tours a day of the seminary itself. The language of the tour (French or English) is determined by the first registered visitor.

2 Côte de la Fabrique (next to Basilique Notre-Dame). ✆ **418/692-2843.** www.mcq.org. Admission C$7 adults, C$6 seniors, C$4.50 students, C$2 children 12–16, free for children 11 and younger; free to all Tues Nov–May. June 24–Sept 6 daily 9:30am–5pm; Sept 7–June 23 Tues–Sun 10am–5pm.

Musée du Fort (Kids) A multimedia show combines light, sound, and a 36-sq.-m (400-sq.-ft.) scale model of the city to tell the story of Québec's 18th-century battles. It's short enough (30 min) and sufficiently engrossing enough to keep the attention of all but the very young. English- and French-language shows alternate.

10 rue Ste-Anne, Place d'Armes. ✆ **418/692-2175.** www.museedufort.com. Admission C$8 adults, C$6 seniors, C$5 students. Apr–Oct daily 10am–5pm; Feb–Mar Thurs–Sun 11am–4pm; closed Nov–Jan.

Parc de l'Artillerie A complex of defensive buildings erected by the French in the 17th and 18th centuries make up Artillery Park. They include an ammunition factory that was functional until 1964 (it was staffed by Canadian Rosie the Riveter–type women during World War II). An iron foundry, officers' mess and quarters, and a scale model of the city created in 1806 are on view. It may be a blow to romantics and history buffs to learn that the nearby St-Jean Gate in the city wall was built in 1940, the fourth in a series that began with the original 1693 entrance, which was replaced in 1747, and then replaced again in 1867.

2 rue d'Auteuil (near Porte St-Jean). ✆ **888/773-8888** or 418/648-4205. www.pc.gc.ca/artillerie. Admission C$3.90 adults, C$3.40 seniors, C$1.90 ages 6–16, free ages 5 and younger. Additional fees for audio guide, tea ceremony, special activities. May to mid-Oct daily 10am–5pm (until 5pm June 24–Sept 6).

Québec Expérience (Kids) A 3D show that re-creates the grand but more often grim realities of the evolution of the city—the difficult weather conditions endured by the European explorers in the 17th century; the disease and fire that plagued immigrant workers in Old Port in the 18th century; the wars between French and British troops in the 19th century; and modern construction disasters in the 20th. Guns and cannons point at audiences, a simulated bridge comes crashing down, and faux flames and screams fill the hall. All in all, it's quite vivid. Take a padded bench seat at least half way back to get the full experience, and prepare to leave expecting an anvil or piano to land on your head.

8 rue du Trésor. ✆ **418/694-4000.** www.quebecexperience.com. Admission C$7.50 adults, C$5 students and seniors, free for ages 5 and younger. Mid-May to Sept daily 10am–10pm; Oct to mid-May daily 10am–5pm. English and French shows alternate throughout the day.

VIEUX-QUEBEC: BASSE-VILLE (LOWER TOWN)

L'Escalier du Casse-Cou These stairs connect Terrasse Dufferin at the top of the cliff with rue Sous-le-Fort at the base. The name translates to **"Breakneck Stairs,"** and they lead—very steeply, although hardly neck-break-inducing anymore—from Haute-Ville to the Quartier du Petit-Champlain in Basse-Ville. A stairway has existed here since the settlement began. In 1698, the town council had to explicitly forbid citizens from taking their animals up or down the stairway, and those who didn't comply were punished with a fine.

Parks Canada Discovery Center At the site of what used to be an old-fashioned interpretation center, this all-new waterfront pavilion was opened in the summer of 2008 as the central location for Québec's 400th-anniversary celebrations. Purposely raw-looking, it's a vast glass, metal, and concrete space ideal for avant-garde, dreamlike exhibits. Throughout 2008 it was called Espace 400e. It was to reopen in 2009 as a Parks Canada venue, but the opening was delayed until the summer of 2010. Check the website or tourist office for current information.

100 quai St-Andre (at rue Rioux). ✆ **418/648-3300.** www.pc.gc.ca and search for "discovery centre Quebec" in the "Parks Canada Agency" category. Check for hours and prices.

Hôtel du Parlement   Since 1968, what the Québécois call their "National Assembly" has occupied this imposing Second-Empire château constructed in 1886. Twenty-two bronze statues of some of the most prominent figures in the province's tumultuous history grace the facade. Inside, highlights include the Assembly Chamber and the Legislative Council Chamber, where parliamentary committees meet. Throughout the building, representations of the fleur-de-lis and the initials VR (for Victoria Regina) remind visitors of Québec's dual heritage. Guided tours are available weekdays year-round from 9am to 4:30pm, and weekends in summer from 10am to 4:30pm. Enter at door no. 3.

The grand Beaux Arts style restaurant **Le Parlementaire** (© **418/643-6640**) is open to the public as well as parliamentarians and visiting dignitaries. Featuring Québec products and cuisine, it serves breakfast and lunch Monday through Friday most of the year.

Entrance at corner of Grande-Allée est and av. Honoré-Mercier. © **866/337-8837** or 418/643-7239. www.assnat.qc.ca. Free admission. Guided tours June 24–Labour Day Mon–Fri 9am–4:30pm, Sat–Sun and holidays 10am–4:30pm; rest of the year Mon–Fri 9am–4:30pm.

3 ESPECIALLY FOR KIDS

Children who have responded to Arthurian tales of fortresses and castles or to Harry Potter's adventures will delight in walking around this storybook city and the **Château Frontenac,** which offers tours (see above). Start at **Terrasse Dufferin** in Upper Town, where there are coin-operated telescopes, street entertainers, and ice-cream stands. If military sites might be appealing, take them to see the colorful ceremonies at **La Citadelle,** the changing of the guard and beating the retreat (p. 238).

To help young ones run off excess energy, head for **Parc des Champs-de-Bataille (Battlefields Park,** also called the **Plains of Abraham;** p. 239), adjacent to the Citadelle. Acres of grassy lawn provide room to roam and are perfect for a family picnic.

The **Musée du Fort** (see above), at 10 rue Ste-Anne, is a kid-friendly presentation of the city's military history. Halfway down **Breakneck Stairs** (L'Escalier du Casse-Cou; see above) are giant **cannons** ranged along the battlements. The gun carriages are impervious to the assaults of small humans, so kids can scramble all over them at will. At the bottom of Breakneck Stairs is a glass-blowing workshop, the **Verrerie La Mailloche.** It's somewhat less impervious to assaults but is still kid-friendly. In the downstairs room, craftsmen give intriguing and informative glass-blowing demonstrations.

In Lower Town, the **Musée de la Civilisation** (p. 235) presents exhibits for families and has a shop and cafe. Given that it's free for children 11 and younger, it's a good value for families.

When in doubt, head to the water. **Montmorency Falls** (p. 276) makes a terrific day trip for children of all ages. It's just 10 minutes north of the city by car, and there are bus tours to the site as well. On Wednesdays and Saturdays from late July to mid-August, the falls are host to a grand fireworks competition, **Les Grands Feux Loto-Québec** (p. 23). It pits international pyrotechnical teams against each other in a contest for who can make the biggest and brightest presentation.

Canyon Ste-Anne (p. 279) is a 45-minute drive northeast and offers thrilling bridge walks over a rushing waterfall. It's particularly spectacular in spring when the snow begins to melt.

Village Vacances Valcartier (© 888/384-5524; www.valcartier.com) in St-Gabriel-de-Valcartier, about a half-hour northwest of the city, is a major manmade water park. In summer, it boasts 35 slides, a gigantic wave pool, a huge pirate ship, and a faux Amazon River to go tubing down. In winter, the same facilities are put to use for "snow rafting" on inner tubes and skating.

Québec City is also close to where whales come out to play each summer. For a **whale-watching cruise,** travel northeast about 207km (129 miles) along the St. Lawrence River into the Charlevoix region. Boats leave from the towns of Baie Ste-Catherine and Tadoussac and typically spend 2½ hours out with the giants. Buses from the city can take you up and back in a (long) day. Or, if you have a car, consider booking an overnight stay at Hôtel Tadoussac (p. 288) and get a package that includes a cruise. See p. 287 for more information.

4 ORGANIZED TOURS

Québec City is small enough to get around with a good map and a guidebook, but a tour is tremendously helpful for getting background information about the city's history and culture, for grasping the lay of the land, and, in the case of bus tours, for seeing those attractions that are a bit of a hike or require wheels to reach.

Below are some agencies and organizations that have proved to be reliable. Arrange tours by calling the companies directly or by stopping by the large tourist center at the Place d'Armes in Upper Town.

BUS TOURS

Buses are convenient if extensive walking is difficult, especially in hilly Upper Town. Among the established tour operators, **Dupont,** which also goes by the name **Old Québec Tours** (© 800/267-8687 or 418/664-0460; www.tourdupont.com), offers English-only tours, which are preferable to bilingual tours since twice as much information is imparted in the same amount of time. The company's city tours are in small coaches, while day trips out of the city are in full-size buses. The company also offers a **whale-watching excursion** hours north into the Charlevoix region. The 12-hour day includes a 3-hour cruise among the belugas (p. 287).

HORSE-DRAWN CARRIAGE TOURS

A romantic if somewhat expensive way to see the city at a genial pace is in a horse-drawn carriage, called a calèche. Carriages will pick you up or can be hired from locations throughout the city, including at Place d'Armes. The 35-minute rides cost C$80 plus tip for four people maximum. Carriages operate year-round, rain or shine. Companies include **Calèches du Vieux-Québec** (© 418/683-9222; www.calecheduvieuxquebec.com), **Calèches de la Nouvelle-France** (© 418/692-0068; www.calechesquebec.com), and **Calèches Royales du Vieux-Québec** (© 418/687-6653).

RIVER CRUISES

Croisières AML (© 800/563-4643 or 418/692-1159 in season; www.croisieresaml.com) offers a variety of cruises. Its *Louis Jolliet* is a three-decked 1930s ferry-boat-turned–excursion-vessel which carries 1,000 passengers and is stocked with bilingual guides, full dining facilities, and a bar. The company offers brunch and dinner cruises as well as jaunts that take in the fireworks or the Image Mill presentation. The boats dock at quai Chouinard, at 10 rue Dalhousie in Vieux-Port.

WALKING TOURS

Times and points of departure for walking tours change, so get up-to-date information at any tourist office (addresses are listed on p. 205). Many tours leave from the Place d'Armes in Upper Town, just in front of the **Château Frontenac.**

Tours Voir Québec (© 866/694-2001; www.toursvoirquebec.com) specializes in English-only guided tours of the Old City. "The Grand Tour," which is available year-round, is a 2-hour stroll that covers the architecture, events, and cultural history of the city. Tours are limited to 15 people. Cost is C$18 adults, C$15 students, C$10 children 6 to 12, and free for children 5 and younger. The company also offers private tours. Call or go online to inquire about rates.

One way to split the difference between being out on your own and signing up for a tour is to use **Map Old Québec** (www.oldquebecmap.com), a website which offers a beautifully designed map and MP3 files. After you purchase the map you can download a tour onto your MP3 player and go at your own pace.

5 SPECTATOR SPORTS

Québec has not had a team in any of the major professional leagues since the NHL Nordiques left in 1995. Since 1999, though, it has been represented by **Les Capitales de Québec** (**Québec Capitales;** www.capitalesdequebec.com), a baseball club in the Can-Am League. Home games take place at Stade Municipal (Municipal Stadium), 100 rue du Cardinal Maurice-Roy (© 877/521-2244 or 418/521-2255), not far beyond the St-Roch neighborhood. Tickets C$8–C$16.

6 OUTDOOR ACTIVITIES

Inside the city, **Parc des Champs-de-Bataille (Battlefields Park)** is the most popular park for bicycling and strolling.

Outside the city, lakes and hills provide countless opportunities for outdoor recreation, including swimming, rafting, fishing, skiing, snowmobiling, and sleigh riding. There are three centers in particular to keep in mind, all within a 45-minute drive from the capital. The provincial **Parc de la Jacques-Cartier** (© 800/665-6527; www.sepaq. com/pq/jac/en) is off Route 175 north; **Station touristique Duchesnay** (© 877/511-5885; www.sepaq.com/duchesnay) is a resort in the town of Ste-Catherine-de-la-Jacques-Cartier; and **Parc du Mont Ste-Anne** is northeast of the city toward the Charlevoix region (see p. 280 for details about Parc Mont Ste-Anne). All three centers are mentioned in the listings below.

From mid-November to late April, the **Taxi Coop Québec** shuttle service (© 418/525-5191; www.taxicoop-quebec.com) picks up passengers at Québec City hotels in the morning to take them to Parc Mont Ste-Anne and Station Stoneham (where Parc de la Jacques-Cartier is), with return trips in the late afternoon.

WARM-WEATHER ACTIVITIES

Biking

Given Upper Town's hilly topography, biking isn't a particularly attractive option in that area. But there are lots of places to go for a couple hours right in the city, either along the river or up in Parliament Hill in Parc des Champs-de-Bataille (Battlefields Park). Rentals are available at a shop across from the Marché du Vieux-Port (Old Port Market) in flatter Lower Town: **Cyclo Services,** 289 rue St-Paul (© **418/692-4052;** www.cyclo services.net) rents bikes for C$25 for 4 hours, with other increments available. The company also conducts guided bicycle tours with several route options.

A marked path for cyclists (and in-line skaters) along the waterfront follows the second half of the route described in "Walking Tour 2: Lower Town (Vieux-Québec: Basse-Ville & Vieux-Port; p. 255). The path was new in 2008 and is well-maintained. It extends both directions alongside and heading out of the city. Tourist information centers provide bicycle trail maps and can point out a variety of routes depending on your timing and interests.

Camping

The greater Québec City area has 21 campgrounds. One has just 16 campsites, while another has 703 (most have fewer than 200). Most have toilets and showers. For a list of sites and their specs, go to **www.quebecregion.com** and click on "Camping."

Canoeing

The lakes and rivers of **Parc de la Jacques-Cartier** are easy to reach yet still seem to be in the midst of wilderness. You can rent canoes in the park. The **Station touristique Duchesnay** resort is on the shores of Lac Saint-Joseph and rents out canoes, kayaks, and pedal boats. See intro above for contact information.

Fishing

The river that flows through **Parc de la Jacques-Cartier** is home to trout and salmon, and fishing there is allowed. Permits are required and can be purchased at many sporting-goods stores. Check with the park for details; see intro above for contact information.

Golf

An 18-hole course, **Golf de la Faune** (© **418/627-1576;** www.golfdelafaune.com), opened in June 2008, 10 minutes from downtown, at the Four Points by **Sheraton Québec** (© **418/627-8008;** www.fourpoints.com/quebec). The course has eight water hazards and 45 sand traps. Green fees start at C$35.

About 40 minutes north of the city, **Le Grand Vallon** (© **888/827-4579** or 418/827-4653; www.legrandvallon.com) at Parc Mont Ste-Anne is an 18-hole, par-72 course with tree-lined stretches, four lakes, and 40 sand traps. Rates start at C$38 and include a golf cart, access to the driving range, and practice balls.

Swimming

Those who want to splash around during their visit should plan to stay at one of the handful of hotels with pools. **Fairmont Le Château Frontenac** has one, as do **Hôtel Manoir Victoria, Hilton Québec, Loews Le Concorde,** and **Hôtel Château Laurier.** They're all listed in chapter 14. **Village Vacances Valcartier** (p. 244), an all-season recreational center a half-hour from the city, has an immense wave pool and water slides.

COLD-WEATHER ACTIVITIES
Cross-Country Skiing

Parc des Champs-de-Bataille (Battlefields Park), where Carnaval de Québec establishes its winter playground during February, has a network of groomed cross-country trails in winter. Equipment can be rented at the **Discovery Pavilion** (p. 240), near the Citadelle. Thirty minutes outside the city, **Station touristique Duchesnay** (p. 245) offers extensive trails and ski rentals. This is where the **Ice Hotel** (p. 221) is built each winter. The resort also has a spa, other hotel accommodations, and a bistro, Le Quatre-Temps. The **Association of Cross-Country Ski Centers of Québec Area** (www.rssfrq.qc.ca) maintains a website with venues and maps.

Dog Sledding

Aventure Inukshuk (✆ 418/875-0770; www.aventureinukshuk.qc.ca), is located in Station touristique Duchesnay, in the town of Ste-Catherine-de-la-Jacques-Cartier, near where the Ice Hotel is built each winter. Guides show you how to lead a sled pulled by six dogs. Even on the shortest 1-hour trip, you go deep into a hushed world of snow and thick woods, past rows of Christmas trees, and over a beaver pond. The 285-plus dogs live in a field of individual pens and houses under evergreen trees and work up an enormous cacophony of howls whenever a team of dogs is harnessed up and set to go. Guides train and care for their teams themselves. Overnight camping trips are available, too. The 1-hour trip, which includes an additional half-hour of training, costs C$91 in December, January, and March and C$100 in February. Children ages 6 to 12 are half price, and ages 2 to 5 go free (children younger than 2 aren't allowed). It's expensive, especially for families, but the memory stays with you.

Ice-Skating

In winter, outdoor rinks (with skate rentals) are set up in Place d'Youville just outside the Upper Town walls. Check with the tourist office for more information.

Skiing

Foremost among the nearby downhill centers is **Mont Ste-Anne,** which offers eastern Canada's largest total skiing surface, with 66 trails (17 are lit for night skiing). See p. 280 for more information.

Snowmobiling

Snowmobiles, known here as "ski-doos," are hugely popular. It's said, in fact, that there are more trails for snowmobiling than there is asphalt in Québec City. Many restaurants and hotels outside the city accommodate snowmobile touring, making it possible to tour from locale to locale. Check the tourist office for current options.

Tobogganing

An old-fashioned toboggan run called *Les Glissades de la Terrasse* (✆ 418/829-9898) is set up on the steep wooden staircase at Terrasse Dufferin's south end in winter. The slide extends almost to the Château Frontenac. Next to the ticket booth, a little sugar shack sells sweet treats. Cost is C$2 per person.

Québec City Strolls

The many pleasures of walking in picturesque French Québec are entirely comparable to walking in similar *quartiers* in northern European cities. Stone houses rub shoulders with each other, carriage wheels creak behind muscular horses, sunlight filters through leafy canopies, drinkers and diners lounge in sidewalk cafes, childish shrieks of laughter echo down cobblestone streets. Not common to other cities, however, is the bewitching vista of river and mountains that the higher elevations bestow.

In winter especially, Vieux-Québec takes on a Dickensian quality, with a lamp glow flickering behind curtains of falling snow. The man who should know—Charles Dickens himself—described the city as having "splendid views which burst upon the eye at every turn."

An alternative to these guided strolls is to simply "walk the walls" of the city, an endeavor which takes about an hour. In most spots you're on a path alongside the fortress wall, while in some sections you are literally on top of it. There's a little creative guesswork involved in figuring out how to follow the route. Because of the number of stairs and occasional .6m (2-ft.) gap to traverse, walking the wall rates as moderately strenuous and isn't for young children. But it's easy to get on and off the path, and the trek offers wonderful views of the city.

WALKING TOUR 1	UPPER TOWN (VIEUX-QUEBEC: HAUTE-VILLE)
START:	Château Frontenac, the castlelike hotel that dominates the city.
FINISH:	Hôtel du Parlement, on Grande-Allée, just outside the walls.
TIME:	2 to 3 hours, depending on whether you take all the optional diversions.
BEST TIMES:	Anytime, although early morning when the streets are emptier is most atmospheric.
WORST TIMES:	None.

The Upper Town (Haute-Ville) of Old Québec (Vieux-Québec) is surrounded by fortress walls. This section of the city overlooks the St. Lawrence River and includes much of what makes Québec so beloved. Buildings and compounds along this tour have been carefully preserved, and most are at least a century old. We start at the grand Château Frontenac, the visual heart of the city.

❶ Château Frontenac

The original section of the famous edifice that defines the Québec City skyline was built as a hotel from 1892 to 1893 by the Canadian Pacific Railway Co. The architect, an American named Bruce Price, raised his creation on the site of the governor's mansion and named it after Louis de Buade, comte de Frontenac, an early governor general of New France. In 1690, Monsieur le Comte was faced with the threat of an English fleet under Sir William Phips during King William's War. Phips sent a messenger to demand Frontenac's surrender, but Frontenac replied, "Tell your lord that I will reply with the mouths of my cannons." He did, and Phips sailed away. Known locally as "the Château," the hotel today has 618 rooms (p. 213). Guided tours are available (p. 241).

Walk around to the river side of the Château, where there is a grand boardwalk called:

❷ Terrasse Dufferin

With its green-and-white-topped gazebos in warm months, this boardwalk promenade looks much as it did 100 years ago, when ladies with parasols and gentlemen with top hats and canes strolled along it on sunny afternoons. It offers vistas of river, watercraft, and distant mountains, and is particularly romantic at sunset.

Walk south on Terrasse Dufferin, past the Château. If you're in the mood for some exercise, go to the end of the boardwalk and continue up the stairs—there are 310 of them—walking south along the:

❸ Promenade des Gouverneurs

This path was renovated in 2007 and skirts the sheer cliff wall, climbing up and up past Québec's military Citadelle, a fort built by the British army between 1820 and 1850 that remains an active military garrison. The promenade/staircase ends at the grassy **Parc des Champs-de-Bataille,** about 15 minutes away. If you go to the end, return back along the path to Terrasse Dufferin to continue the stroll.

Walk back on the terrace as far as the battery of ancient (but not original) cannons on the left, which are set up as they were in the old days. Climb the stairs toward the obelisk into the:

❹ Parc des Gouverneurs

Just southwest of the Château Frontenac, this park stands on the site of the mansion built to house the French governors of Québec. The mansion burned in 1834 and the ruins lie buried under the great bulk of the Château. B&Bs and small hotels now border the park on two sides.

The **obelisk monument** is dedicated to both generals in the momentous battle of September 13, 1759, when Britain's General James Wolfe and France's Louis-Joseph, marquis de Montcalm, fought for what would be the ultimate destiny of Québec (and,

quite possibly, of all of North America). The French were defeated and both generals died. Wolfe, wounded in the fighting, lived only long enough to hear of England's victory. Montcalm died a few hours after Wolfe. Told that he was mortally wounded, Montcalm replied, "All the better. I will not see the English in Québec."

Walk up rue Mont-Carmel, which runs between the park and Château Frontenac. Turn right onto rue Haldimand. At the next corner, rue St-Louis, stands a white house with blue trim. This is:

❺ Maison Kent

Built in 1648, this might be Québec's oldest building. It's most famous for being the building in which France signed the capitulation to the British forces. Its name comes from the duke of Kent, Queen Victoria's father. He lived here for a few years at the end of the 18th century, just before he married Victoria's mother in an arranged liaison. His true love, it is said, was with him in Maison Kent. Today, the building houses France's consulate general, as the tricolor over the door attests.

To the left and diagonally across from Maison Kent, at rue St-Louis and rue des Jardins, is:

❻ Maison Jacquet

This small, white dwelling with crimson roof and trim dates from 1677 and now houses a popular restaurant called **Aux Anciens Canadiens** (p. 226). Among the oldest houses in the province, it has sheltered some prominent Québécois, including Philippe Aubert de Gaspé, the author of *Aux Anciens Canadiens,* which recounts Québec's history and folklore. He lived here from 1815 to 1824.

> **TAKE A BREAK**
> Try Québécois home cooking right here at the restaurant named for de Gaspé's book, **Aux Anciens Canadiens,** 34 rue St-Louis. Consider caribou in blueberry-wine sauce or Québec meat pie, and don't pass up the maple sugar pie with cream. See p. 226 for more information.

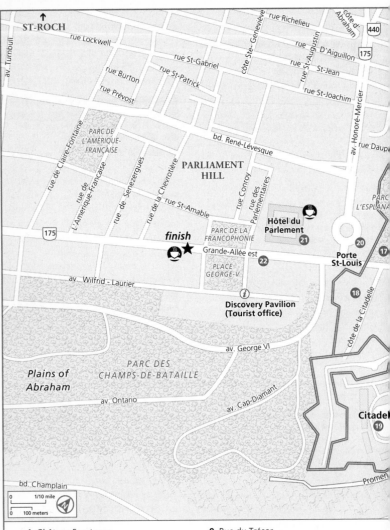

1	Château Frontenac	**9**	Rue du Trésor
2	Terrasse Dufferin	**10**	Basilique Notre-Dame
3	Promenade des Gouverneurs	**11**	Séminaire de Québec
4	Parc des Gouverneurs	**12**	Hôtel-de-Ville (City Hall)
5	Maison Kent	**13**	Anglican Cathedral of the Holy Trinity
6	Maison Jacquet	**14**	Chapelle/Musée des Ursulines
7	Maison Maillou	**15**	Cannonball
8	Place d'Armes	**16**	Hôtel d'Esplanade

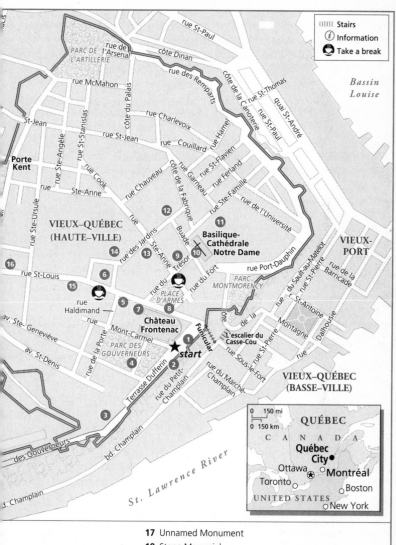

17 Unnamed Monument
18 Stone Memorial
19 Citadelle
20 Site of Winter Carnival
21 Hôtel du Parlement
22 Grand-Allée

Leaving the restaurant, turn back toward Maison Kent and walk along rue St-Louis to no. 17:

7 Maison Maillou

This house's foundations date from 1736, though the house was enlarged in 1799 and restored in 1959. It's best seen from the opposite side of the street. Maison Maillou was built as an elegant luxury home and later served as headquarters of militias and armies. Note the metal shutters used to thwart weather and unfriendly fire.

Continue on rue St-Louis to arrive at the central plaza called:

8 Place d'Armes

This plaza was once the military parade ground outside the governors' mansion (which no longer exists). In the small park at the center is the fountain **Monument to the Faith,** which recalls the arrival of the Recollet monks from France in 1615. France's king granted them a large plot of land in 1681 on which to build their church and monastery.

Facing the square is the **monument to Samuel de Champlain,** who founded Québec in 1608. Created by French artists Paul Chevre and Paul le Cardonel, the statue has stood here since 1898. Its pedestal is made from stone that was also used in the Arc de Triomphe and Sacré-Coeur Basilica in Paris.

Near the Champlain statue is the diamond-shaped **UNESCO monument** designating Québec City as a World Heritage Site, a rare distinction. Installed in 1986, the monument is made of bronze, granite, and glass.

The city's major **tourist information center** faces the plaza, at 12 rue Ste-Anne.

Just adjacent to the Restaurant Le Relais is the narrow pedestrian lane called:

9 Rue du Trésor

Artists hang their prints and paintings of Québec scenes on both sides of the walkway. In decent weather, it's busy with browsers and sellers. Most prices are within the means of the average visitor.

Follow rue du Trésor down to rue Buade and turn left. On the right, at the corner of rue Ste-Famille is the:

10 Basilique Notre-Dame

The basilica's interior is ornate and its air rich with the scent of burning candles. Many artworks remain from the time of the French regime. The chancel lamp was a gift from Louis XIV, and the crypt is the final resting place for most of Québec's bishops. The basilica dates back to 1647 and has suffered a tumultuous history of bombardment and reconstruction; see p. 240 for more information.

As you exit the basilica, turn a sharp right to enter the grounds and, a few steps in, the all-white inner courtyard of the historic:

11 Séminaire de Québec

Founded in 1663 by North America's first bishop, Bishop Laval, this seminary had grown into Laval University by 1852. During summer, visitors can take a 1-hour tour of the old seminary's grounds and some of its buildings, which reveal lavish decorations of stone, tile, brass, and gilt-framed oil paintings. The tours are conducted by the **Musée de l'Amérique Française** (© **418/692-2843l;** www.mcq. org), based inside the seminary grounds. There are five tours a day with the language of the tour (French or English) determined by the first registered visitor.

Head back to the basilica. Directly across the small park from the church is:

12 Hôtel-de-Ville (City Hall)

The park next to City Hall is often converted into an outdoor show area in summer, especially during the **Festival d'Eté (Summer Festival)** with concerts and other staged programs (p. 23).

> **TAKE A BREAK**
> This part of town is a great place to sit and watch the world go by. Grab a sidewalk table and enjoy something to drink or eat. One option is **Restaurant Le Relais,** the red-roofed building with a mock-Tudor façade at 16 rue Ste-Anne.

As you face City Hall, the tall building to the left is **Edifice Price,** Old City's tallest building at 18 stories. It was built in 1929 in Art Deco style with geometric motifs and a steepled copper roof. When it was built, it inadvertently gave a bird's-eye view into the adjacent Ursuline Convent, and a "view tax" had to be paid to the nuns to appease them. It is dramatically lit at night.

Facing the front of Hôtel-de-Ville, walk left on rue des Jardins toward Édifice Price. On your left, you'll pass a small statue celebrating the city's connections to *le cirque* and its performers. Cross over rue Ste-Anne. On the left are the spires of the:

⑬ Anglican Cathedral of the Holy Trinity

Modeled after London's St-Martin-in-the-Fields, this building dates from 1804 and was the first Anglican cathedral to be built outside the British Isles. The interior is simple but spacious and bright, with pews of solid English oak from the Royal Windsor forest and a latticed ceiling with a gilded-chain motif. Lucky visitors may happen upon an organ recital or choral rehearsal.

One block up rue des Jardins, turn right at the small square (triangle-shaped, actually) and go a few more steps to 12 rue Donnacona, the:

⑭ Chapelle/Musée des Ursulines

Handiwork by Ursuline nuns from the 17th, 18th, and 19th centuries is on display here along with Amerindian crafts and a cape that was made for Marie de l'Incarnation, a founder of the convent, when she left for New France in 1639.

Peek into the restored chapel if it's open. The tomb of Marie de l'Incarnation, who died in 1672, is here. The altar created by sculptor Pierre-Noël Levasseur between 1726 and 1736 is worth a look. See p. 240 for more details.

From the museum, turn right on rue Donnacona to walk past the **Ursuline Convent,** originally built in 1642. The present complex is actually a succession of different buildings added and repaired at

various times until 1836, as frequent fires took their toll. A statue of Marie is outside. The convent is now a private girls' school and not open to the public.

Continue left up the hill along rue du Parloir to rue St-Louis. Turn right. At the next block, rue du Corps-de-Garde, note the tree on the left side of the street with a:

⑮ Cannonball

Lodged at the base of the trunk, one story says that the cannonball landed here during the Battle of Quebec in 1759 and over the years became firmly embraced by the tree. Another story says that it was placed here on purpose to keep the wheels of horse-drawn carriages from bumping the tree when making tight turns.

Continue along St-Louis another 2 blocks to rue d'Auteuil. The house on the right corner is:

⑯ Hôtel d'Esplanade

Notice that many of the windows in the facade facing rue St-Louis are blocked by stone. This is because houses were once taxed by the number of windows they had, and the frugal homeowner who lived here found this way to get around the law—even though it cut down on his view.

Continue straight on rue St-Louis toward the Porte St-Louis, a gate in the walls. Before the gate on the right is the Esplanade powder magazine, part of the old fortifications. Just before the gate is an:

⑰ Unnamed Monument

This monument commemorates the 1943 meeting in Québec of U.S. President Franklin D. Roosevelt and British Prime Minister Winston Churchill. It remains a soft-pedaled reminder to French Québécois that it was the English-speaking nations that rid France of the Nazis.

Just across the street from the monument is a small road, Côte de la Citadelle, that leads to La Citadelle. Walk up that road. On the right are headquarters and barracks of a militia district, arranged around an inner court. Near its entrance is a:

⑱ Stone Memorial

This marks the resting place of 13 soldiers of General Richard Montgomery's American army, felled in the unsuccessful assault on Québec in 1775. Obviously, the conflicts that swirled for centuries around who would ultimately rule Québec didn't end with the British victory after its 1759 battle with French troops.

Continue up the hill to:

⑲ La Citadelle

The impressive star-shaped fortress just beyond view keeps watch from a commanding position on a grassy plateau 108m (354 ft.) above the banks of the St. Lawrence. It took 30 years to complete, by which time it had become obsolete. Since 1920, the Citadelle has been the home of the French-speaking **Royal 22e Régiment,** which fought in both world wars and in Korea. With good timing and weather, it's possible to watch a **changing of the guard** ceremony, or, as it's called, "beating the retreat." See p. 238 for more details.

Return to rue St-Louis and turn left to pass through Porte St-Louis, which was built in 1873 on the site of a gate dating from 1692. Here, the street broadens to become Grande-Allée. To the right is a park that runs alongside the city walls.

⑳ Site of Winter Carnaval

One of the most captivating events on the Canadian calendar, the 17-day **Carnaval de Québec** happens every February and includes outdoor games, snow-tubing, dogsled races, canoe races, and more. A palace of snow and ice rises on this spot just outside the city walls, with ice sculptures throughout the field. Colorfully clad Québécois come to admire the palace and dance the nights away at outdoor parties. On the left side of Grande-Allée, a carnival park of games, food, and music is set up on Parc des Champs-de-Bataille. See p. 21 for more about the festivities.

Fronting the park, on your right, stands Québec province's stately:

㉑ Hôtel du Parlement

Constructed in 1884, this government building houses what Québécois call their "National Assembly" (note the use of the word "national" and not "provincial").

The massive fountain in front of the building, **La Fontaine de Tourny,** was commissioned by the mayor of Bordeaux, France, in 1857. Sculptor Mathurin Moreau created the dreamlike figures on the fountain's base. It was installed in 2007 as a gift from the Simons department store to the city for its 400th anniversary in 2008.

In the sumptuous Parliament chambers, the fleur-de-lis symbol and the initials VR (for Victoria Regina) are reminders of Québec's dual heritage. If the crown on top is lit, Parliament is in session. Along the exterior facade are 22 bronze statues of prominent figures in Québec's tumultuous history.

Guided tours are available weekdays year-round from 9am to 4:30pm, and weekends in summer from 10am to 4:30pm. See p. 243 for more information.

TAKE A BREAK
Le Parlementaire restaurant (📞 **418/643-6640**), in the Hôtel du Parlement at 1045 rue des Parlementaires, is done up in regal Beaux Arts decor and open to the public (as well as parliamentarians and visiting dignitaries) for breakfast and lunch Monday through Friday most of the year. Or, continue down Grande-Allée to find plenty of other options.

Continue down:

㉒ Grand-Allée

Just past Hôtel du Parlement is a park called Place George-V, and behind the park are the charred remains of the **1885 Armory.** A major visual icon and home to the country's oldest French-Canadian regiment, the Armory was all but destroyed in an April 2008 fire. The stone facade still stands. The destruction was a huge blow to the city, and discussions over what kind of rebuilding to do are still continuing.

To the left of the armory is a building that houses **a tourist information office** and the **Discovery Pavilion** (p. 240), where a multimedia exhibit called "Odyssey: A Journey through History on the Plains of Abraham" is presented.

After the park, the street becomes lined with cafes, restaurants, and bars on both sides. This strip really gets jumping at night, particularly in the complex that includes **VooDoo** restaurant (p. 232) and **Maurice** nightclub (p. 268), at no. 575.

One food possibility is **Chez Ashton,** at 640 Grande-Allée est. The Québec fastfood restaurant makes what many consider the town's best *poutine*—french fries with cheese curds and brown gravy.

A great way to end the stroll is with a stop at **L'Astral,** the restaurant and bar

atop Loews le Concorde Hotel, at the corner of Grande-Allée est and Cours du Général-De Montcalm. The room spins slowly (it takes about 1½ hours for a full rotation) and lets you look back at all the places you've been and all the places still to go. See p. 269 for information.

The city bus along Grande-Allée can return you to the Old City, or turn left at Loews and enter the **Parc des Champs-de-Bataille** (**Battlefields Park;** p. 239) at the Joan of Arc Garden. If you turn left in the park and continue along its boulevards and footpaths, you'll end up at the Citadelle. If you turn right, you'll reach the **Musée des Beaux-Arts du Québec** (p. 239).

WALKING TOUR 2	LOWER TOWN (VIEUX-QUEBEC: BASSE-VILLE & VIEUX-PORT)

START:	Either in Upper Town at Terrasse Dufferin, the boardwalk in front of Château Frontenac, or, if you're already in Lower Town, at the funicular, the cable car that connects the upper and lower parts of the Old City.
FINISH:	Place-Royale, the restored central square of Lower Town.
TIME:	1½ hours.
BEST TIMES:	Anytime during the day. Early morning lets you soak up the visual history, though shops won't be open.
WORST TIMES:	Very late at night.

The Lower Town (Basse-Ville) part of Old Québec (Vieux-Québec) encompasses the city's oldest residential area—now flush with boutique hotels, high-end restaurants, and touristy shops and cafes—and Vieux-Port, the old port district. The impressive Museum of Civilization is here, and if you have time, you may want to take a pause from the tour for a visit. We start at the cliff-side elevator *(funiculaire)* that connects Upper and Lower towns.

If you're in Upper Town, descend to Lower Town by one of two options:

❶ Funicular (Option A)

This cable car's upper terminus is on Terrasse Dufferin near the Château Frontenac. As the car descends the steep slope, its glass front provides a broad view of Basse-Ville (Lower Town).

Or, if you prefer a more active (and free) means of descent, use the stairs to the left of the funicular, the:

❶ L'Escalier du Casse-Cou (Option B)

"Breakneck Stairs" is the self-explanatory name given to this stairway (although

truth be told, they're not *that* harrowing anymore). Stairs have been in place here since the settlement began. In 1698, the town council had to forbid citizens from taking their animals up and down the stairway.

Breakneck Stairs and the funicular arrive at the intersection of rues Petit-Champlain and Sous-le-Fort. At the bottom of the last set of stairs on the left is the:

❷ Verrerie La Mailloche

In the downstairs room, craftsmen give glass-blowing demonstrations—intriguing and informative, especially for children who haven't seen this ancient craft. The glass is melted at 2,500°F (1,350°C) and is worked at 2,000°F (1,100°C). There are displays of the results and a small shop in which to purchase them.

Outside the glass-blowing shop, look at the building from which the funicular passengers exit:

❸ Maison Louis Jolliet

This building is now the funicular's lower terminus and full of tourist trinkets and geegaws, but it has an auspicious pedigree. It was built in 1683 and was home to Louis Jolliet, the Québec-born explorer who, along with a priest, Jacques Marquette, was the first person of European parentage to explore the Mississippi River's upper reaches.

Walk down the pretty little street here:

❹ Rue du Petit-Champlain

Allegedly North America's oldest street, this pedestrian-only lane swarms with restaurant-goers, cafe-sitters, strolling couples, and gaggles of schoolchildren in the warm months. Many of the shops listed in chapter 18 are here. In winter, it's a snowy wonderland with ice statues and twinkling white lights.

> **TAKE A BREAK**
> Though it's early in the stroll, there are so many eating and shopping options here that you might want to pause for a while. Look for the sign with the flying rabbits for **Le Lapin Saute**, at 52 rue du Petit-Champlain, a country-cozy bistro with hearty food in generous portions. A lovely terrace overlooks a small garden and, in the warm months, street musicians serenade diners.

At the end of Petit-Champlain, turn left onto boulevard Champlain. A lighthouse from the Gaspé Peninsula used to stand across the street, but it has been returned to its original home, leaving just an anchor and cannons to stand guard (rather forlornly) over the river.

Follow the street's curve; this block offers pleasant boutiques and cafes. At the corner is the crimson-roofed:

❺ Maison Chevalier

Dating from 1752, this was once the home of merchant Jean-Baptiste Chevalier. Note the wealth of windows, more than 30 in front-facing sections alone. In 1763, the house was sold at auction to ship owner Jean-Louis Frémont, the grandfather of Virginia-born John Charles Frémont (1813–90). John Charles went on to become an American explorer, soldier, and politician who mapped some 10 Western and Midwestern territories.

The Chevalier House was sold in 1806 to an Englishman, who in turn rented it to a hotelier, who transformed it into an inn. In 1960, the Québec government restored the house, and it became a museum about 5 years later. It's overseen by the Musée de la Civilisation, which mounts temporary exhibitions. Entrance is free.

Just past the Maison's front door, turn left and walk up the short block of rue Notre-Dame to rue Sous-le-Fort. Take in the carefully restored stone and brick streets and buildings. Turn right, and walk 1 block to the:

❻ Royal Battery

Fortifications were erected here by the French in 1691 and the cannons added in 1712 to defend Lower Town from the British. The cannons got their chance in 1759, but the English victory silenced them and eventually, they were left to rust. Sunken foundations were all that remained of the battery by the turn of the 20th century, and when the time came for restorations, it had to be rebuilt from the ground up.

From the Royal Battery, walk back up rue Sous-le-Fort. This is a good photo opportunity, with the imposing Château Frontenac on the cliff above framed between ancient houses.

Turn right on rue Notre-Dame. Half a block up the grade is the heart of Basse-Ville, the small:

❼ Place-Royale

Occupying the center of New France's first permanent colony, this small and still very

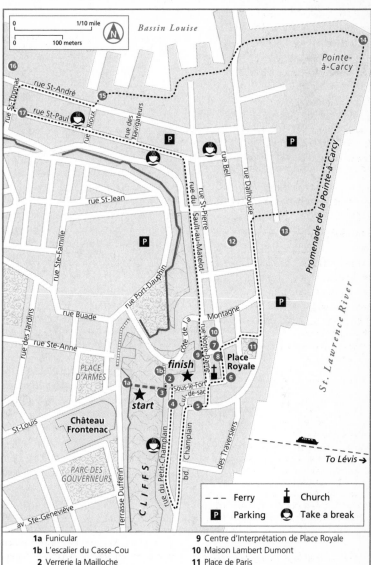

Bassin Louise

Pointe-à-Carcy

Promenade de la Pointe-à-Carcy

St. Lawrence River

To Lévis →

PLACE D'ARMES

Château Frontenac

PARC DES GOUVERNEURS

CLIFFS

Place Royale

start

finish

- - - Ferry
P Parking
† Church
Take a break

1a Funicular	**9** Centre d'Interprétation de Place Royale
1b L'escalier du Casse-Cou	**10** Maison Lambert Dumont
2 Verrerie la Mailloche	**11** Place de Paris
3 Maison Louis Jolliet	**12** Musée de la Civilisation
4 Rue du Petit-Champlain	**13** Vieux-Port (Old Port)
5 Maison Chevalier	**14** Pointe-à-Carcy
6 Royal Battery	**15** Parks Canada Discovery Centre
7 Place Royale	**16** Marché du Vieux-Port
8 Église Notre-Dame-des-Victoires	**17** Rue St-Paul and antique shops

much European-feeling enclosed square served as the town marketplace. It went into decline around 1860 and by 1950 had become a derelict, run-down part of town. Today, it has been restored to very nearly recapture its historic appearance. The prominent bust is of Louis XIV, the Sun King, a gift from the city of Paris in 1928 that was installed here in 1931. The striking 17th- and 18th-century houses once belonged to wealthy merchants. Note the ladders on some of the steep roofs used to fight fire and remove snow. See p. 238 for more information about the square.

Facing directly onto the square is:
❽ Eglise Notre-Dame-des-Victoires
Named for French naval victories over the British in 1690 and 1711, Québec's oldest stone church was built in 1688 after a massive Lower Town fire destroyed 55 homes in 1682. The church was restored in 1763 after its partial destruction by the British in the 1759 siege. The white-and-gold interior has a few murky paintings and a large model boat suspended from the ceiling, a votive offering brought by early settlers to ensure safe voyages. On the walls, small prints depict the stages of the Passion. The church is open to visitors 9am to 5pm from May through October. See p. 238 for more information.

Walk straight across the plaza, passing the:
❾ Centre d'Interprétation de Place-Royale
For decades, this space was nothing but a propped-up facade with an empty lot behind it, but it has been rebuilt to serve as an interpretation center with shows and exhibitions about this district's history; it's good for kids as well as adults (p. 238).

At the corner on the right is the:
❿ Maison Lambert Dumont
This building now houses Geomania, a store selling rocks and crystals. In earlier years, though, it was home to the Dumont family and one of several residences in the

square. To the right as you're facing it once stood a hotel where U.S. President William Taft would stay as he headed north to vacation in the picturesque Charlevoix region.

Walk about 15m (50 ft.) past the last building on your left and turn around; the entire end of that building is a *trompe l'oeil* mural of streets and houses and depictions of citizens from the earliest colonial days to the present, an amusing splash of fool-the-eye trickery. Have your photo taken here—nearly everyone does!

Return to Place-Royale and head left toward the water, down two small sets of stairs to the:
⓫ Place de Paris
This plaza contains a discordantly bland white sculpture that resembles three stacked Rubik's Cubes. It's called *Dialogue avec L'Histoire* and was a gift from the city of Paris in 1987.

Continue ahead to rue Dalhousie, a main street for cars, and turn left. A few short blocks up and on the left is the:
⓬ Musée de la Civilisation
This wonderful museum, which opened in 1988, may be housed in a lackluster gray-block building, but there is nothing plain about it once you enter. Spacious and airy, with ingeniously arranged multidimensional exhibits, it's one of Canada's most innovative museums. If there is no time now, put it at the top of your must-see list for later. See p. 235 for museum details.

Across the street from the museum is:
⓭ Vieux-Port (Old Port)
In the 17th century, this 29-hectare (72-acre) riverfront area was the port of call for European ships bringing supplies and settlers to the new colony. With the decline of shipping by the early 20th century, the port fell into precipitous decline. But since the mid-1980s, it has experienced a rebirth, becoming the summer destination for international cruise ships. It got additional sprucing up for Québec's 400th anniversary in 2008.

> **TAKE A BREAK**
> If you're doing this stroll in the colder months, you might want to head indoors at this point. **Le 48 Saint-Paul,** named after its address, is just steps from the corner of rue Dalhousie and rue St-Paul, 1 block past the museum. It's sleek and affordable, with creative burgers and pizzas, most under C$10. To continue the tour, head back to rue Dalhousie and cross over toward Terminal de Croisières to the waterfront.

From the museum, head across the parking lot to the river and turn left at the water's edge. After Terminal de Croisières, the cruise terminal, you'll pass the **Agora,** an outdoor theater, and, behind it, the city's **Customs House,** built between 1830 and 1839.

Continue along the river's promenade, past the Agora, to the small landscaped:

⑭ **Pointe-à-Carcy**

The bronze statue of a sailor here is a memorial to Canadian merchant seamen who lost their lives in World War II. From the point, you can look out across Louise Basin to the Bunge of Canada grain elevator, which stores wheat, barley, corn, and soybean crops that are produced in western Canada before they are shipped to Europe. These silos make up the massive "screen" upon which the nightly show the **Image Mill** is projected on summer nights (see p. 266).

The bridge to rural **Île d'Orléans** can be seen in the distance from here. Île d'Orléans is the island that supplies Québec with much of its fresh fruits and vegetables. It's an easy day trip from the city (p. 270).

The water below is the launch area for a wild canoe race across the ice floes during **Carnaval de Québec** (p. 21).

Follow the walkway left from Pointe-à-Carcy along the Louise Basin. You'll pass

the **Musée Naval de Québec,** which has 259 been closed for years of renovation and is set to reopen in the summer of 2010, in time to celebrate the Navy's centennial birthday. In the warm months, you can board a scenic river cruise here.

At the end of the basin, take a short jog left, and then right to stay along the water's edge. Up ahead is a modern glass building, the:

⑮ **Parks Canada Discovery Center**

This new building was the central location for Québec's 400th-anniversary celebrations in 2008, when it went by the name Espace 400e. It will reopen in 2010 as a Discovery Center. (p. 242).

From the Discovery Center, continue 1 block to:

⑯ **Marché du Vieux-Port**

This colorful market at 160 quai St-André has jaunty teal-blue roofs and, in summer, rows and rows of booths heaped with fresh fruits and vegetables, regional wines and ciders, soaps, pâtés, jams, handicrafts, cheeses, chocolates, fresh fish, and meat. Cafes and kiosks offer options for a meal or sweet treat.

(As you approach the market, you'll see, farther down the street, the city's grand train station, designed in 1916 by New York architect Bruce Price. He designed the Château Frontenac in 1893 and used his signature copper-turned-green spires here, too.)

Leaving the market, cross rue St-André at the light and walk a short block to:

⑰ **Rue St-Paul**

Turn left onto this street, home to galleries, craft shops, and about a dozen antiques stores. They include **Maison Dambourgès,** at no. 155, which sells folk art and pine furniture, and **l'Héritage Antiquité,** at no. 109, which has old postcards, bits of china sets, and the like. Rue St-Paul manages to maintain a sense of unspoiled neighborhood.

> **TAKE A BREAK**
> **Mistral Gagnant,** at 160 rue St-Paul, is a sunny Provençal restaurant that features hearty food such as omelets, escargot, bouillabaisse, and outrageously good lemon pie. **Café le Saint Malo,** at 75 rue St-Paul, has low ceilings, rough stone walls, and storefront windows that draw patrons in.

From here, return to the heart of Lower Town—Place-Royale and the funicular—by turning right off rue St-Paul onto either rue du Sault-au-Matelot or the parallel rue St-Pierre. Both are quiet streets with galleries and restaurants. Meander along and settle into the relaxed pace of this nook of the city.

Québec City Shopping

Vieux-Québec's compact size, with its upper and lower sections, makes it especially convenient for browsing and shopping. Much of the merchandise is of high quality.

1 THE SHOPPING SCENE

Vieux-Québec's Lower Town, particularly the area known as **Quartier du Petit-Champlain,** offers many possibilities—clothing, souvenirs, gifts, household items, collectibles—and is avoiding (so far) the trashiness that can afflict heavily touristed neighborhoods. The area is just around the corner from the funicular entrance.

In Upper Town, wander along **rue St-Jean,** both within and outside the city walls, and on **rue Garneau** and **Côte de la Fabrique,** which branch off the east end of St-Jean. For T-shirts, postcards, and other souvenirs, check out the myriad shops that line **rue St-Louis.**

If you're heading to St-Roch to eat, build in a little time to stroll **rue St-Joseph,** which, for a few blocks, has new boutiques alongside cafes and restaurants.

Outside the walls, just beyond the strip of eateries and nightspots that line Grande-Allée, **avenue Cartier** has shops and restaurants of some variety, from clothing and ceramics to housewares and gourmet foods. The 5 blocks attract crowds of youngish and middle-aged locals. The area remains outside the tourist orbit, but it's an easy walk: Head up wide, tree-lined Grande-Allée and turn right onto Cartier.

Most stores are open Monday through Wednesday from 9 or 10am to 6pm, Thursday and Friday until 9pm, and Saturday from 10am to 5pm. Many stores are now also open on Sunday from noon to 5pm.

THE BEST BUYS

Indigenous crafts, handmade sweaters, and **Inuit art** are among the desirable items specific to Québec. An official igloo trademark identifies authentic Inuit (Eskimo) art, though the differences between the real thing and the manufactured variety become apparent with a little careful study. Inuit artwork, which is usually in the form of carvings in stone or bone, is an excellent purchase not for its low price, but for its high quality. Expect to pay hundreds of dollars for even a relatively small piece.

You're bound to see a lot of the **Inukshuk** figurine, which looks like a human figure made of stacked rocks. It's the centerpiece of the logo of the 2010 Winter Olympics, taking place in Vancouver in February and March (see www.vancouver2010.com).

Maple syrup products make sweet gifts, as do **regional wines** and **jams.**

Apart from a handful of boutiques, Québec City does not offer the high-profile designer clothing showcased in Montréal.

2 SHOPPING FROM A TO Z

Listed with the address for each shop below is its neighborhood: Lower Town or Upper Town in Vieux-Québec, or Montcalm, the residential neighborhood just west of Parliament Hill.

ANTIQUES ROW

About a dozen antiques shops line rue St-Paul in Lower Town. They're filled with knick-knacks, Québec country furniture, candlesticks, old clocks, Victoriana, Art Deco and Art Moderne objects, and the increasingly sought-after kitsch and housewares of the early post–World War II period. Among the shops is **De Retour,** 273 rue St-Paul (✆ **418/692/5501**), which is filled with Scandinavian and American chairs, lamps, and other furniture from the 1950s—*très moderne.*

ARTS & CRAFTS

Artisans Canada   Crafts predominate in the front of this shop, all a little on the expensive side. There are plenty of fur hats, slippers, coats, jewelry, toy soldiers, and soapstone carvings. Plus a chess set of French and British Generals Montcalm and Wolfe, so you can reenact the battle that sealed the political fate of all of Canada. 30 Côte de la Fabrique, Upper Town. ✆ 418/692-2109. www.artisanscanada.com.

Boutique Métiers d'Art   In a stone building at the corner of Place-Royale, this carefully arranged store displays works by scores of Québécois craftspeople, at least some of which are likely to appeal to almost any customer. Among these objects are wooden boxes, jewelry, graphics, and a variety of gifts. When departing, be sure to turn left, walk past the end of the building and turn around—it's a surprise! 29 rue Notre-Dame, Lower Town. ✆ 418/694-0267. www.metiers-d-art.qc.ca.

Dugal   One of the owners works in wood, carving sinuous and remarkably comfortable rocking chairs, while the other creates jewelry featuring black pearls set in gold and silver. 15 rue Notre-Dame, Lower Town. ✆ 418/692-1564.

Galerie Brousseau et Brousseau   In 2005, the important Inuit art collection assembled over 30 years by Québécois Raymond Brousseau was acquired by the Musée des Beaux-Arts du Québec, and 285 works from the 2,635-piece collection are on display at that museum. Here, you can buy Native Canadian carvings selected by the same family to take home. This is the most prominent of the city's art dealers, and it offers certificates of authenticity. Prices are high but competitive for merchandise of similar quality. The shop is set up like a gallery, so feel free just to browse. 35 rue St-Louis (at rue des Jardins), Upper Town. ✆ 418/694-1828. www.sculpture.artinuit.ca.

Galerie d'Art du Petit-Champlain   The superbly detailed carvings of Roger Desjardins, who applies his skills to meticulous renderings of waterfowl, are featured here. The inventory also includes lithographs and paintings. 88 rue du Petit-Champlain (near bd. Champlain), Lower Town. ✆ 418/692-5647. www.gapc.ca.

Rue du Trésor Outdoor Gallery   Sooner or later, everyone passes this outdoor alley near the Place d'Armes. Artists gather along here much of the year to exhibit and sell their work. Most of the prints on view are of Québec scenes and can make attractive souvenirs. The artists seem to enjoy chatting with interested passersby. Rue du Trésor (btw. rues Ste-Anne and Buade), Upper Town.

Sachem Fur hats, baby moccasins, carvings, and jewelry are all packed into this compact boutique, which specializes in *"arts Indien esquimau."* Included are a variety of miniature Inukshuk human figurines, which look like they've been made of stacked rocks. The Inukshuk is part of the logo of the 2010 Winter Olympics being held in Vancouver and will be ubiquitous for awhile. 17 rue des Jardins (near Hôtel-de-Ville), Upper Town. ℂ 418/692-3056.

BATH & BODY

Fruits & Passion You'll find outposts of this Québec-based chain throughout the region. It features lotions, shampoos, candles, foods, and even dog-care items. Its Cuchina hand-care line uses olive leaf extract with scents ranging from fig to lime zest. 75 rue du Petit-Champlain, Lower Town. ℂ 418/692-2859. www.fruits-passion.com.

CLOTHING

Atelier La Pomme Just steps from the funicular in Lower Town, this cute boutique of women's clothes specializes in chic dresses by Québécois designers and *vêtements de cuir,* or leather clothing. 47 Sous-Le-Fort (near rue du Petit-Champlain), Lower Town. ℂ 418/692-2875.

Crocs (Kids) The recipe behind Crocs, the rubbery, marshmallowy, candy-colored clogs that took the world by storm in 2003, originated in Québec. Many of the shoes, in fact, were made in the province—that is, until 2008, when the Montréal factory was closed by U.S. corporate owners. Not surprisingly, you'll hear fewer praises in these parts now for the once locally produced product. 1071 rue St-Jean (at rue St-Stanislas), Upper Town. ℂ 418/266-0262. www.crocs.ca.

Fourrures du Vieux-Port The fur trade underwrote the development and exploration of Québec and the vast lands west, and continues to be important to the region to this day. This Lower Town merchant has as good a selection as any, including knit furs and shearlings, along with designer coats by Nicole Miller, Christia, and Olivieri. 55 rue St-Pierre, (at Côte de la Montagne), Lower Town. ℂ 866/692-6688. www.quebecfourrure.com.

Harricana Montréal designer Mariouche Gagné, who was born on Île d'Orléans in 1971, is a leader of the so-called ecoluxe movement. Her company recycles old fur, silk scarves, and even wedding dresses to create new coats, winter hats, tops, and skirts. One favorite on a recent visit: a white aviator hat of recycled fur and scraps of a lace wedding gown, for C$250. 44 Côte de la Fabrique, Upper Town. ℂ 418/204-5340. www.harricana.qc.ca.

La Maison Darlington The popular emporium in this ancient house (it was built in 1775) comes on strong with both tony and traditional clothing for men and women produced by such makers as Dale of Norway, Geiger, and Ballantyne. Inventory includes high-quality and tasteful men's and women's hats, scarves, and sweaters, especially in cashmere and other wools. As appealing are the hand-smocked, locally made dresses for little girls. 7 rue de Buade (near Place d'Armes), Upper Town. ℂ 418/692-2268.

LOGO Sport (Kids) The top spot for sports jerseys: hockey, of course, but soccer, baseball, and basketball as well. 1047 rue St-Jean (at rue Ste-Angèle), Upper Town. ℂ 418/692-1351.

Marie Dooley A teeny boutique featuring the chic, youthful women's clothing of Dooley, a Québec-born designer. 3B bd. René-Lévesque est (1 block northeast of av. Cartier), Montcalm. ℂ 418/522-7597. www.mariedooley.com.

QUÉBEC CITY SHOPPING

18

SHOPPING FROM A TO Z

Michael Fashionable women's clothing for work or for play featuring the chic Animale and Sandwich labels. A store by the same name for men is next door, at no. 1060. 1066 rue St-Jean (near rue Ste-Angèle), Upper Town. ☏ 418/692-5666.

Murmure Off the tourist track on avenue Cartier, this small boutique features casual dresses, jackets, and skirts, primarily for 30- to 50-something women. (For designer jeans and skimpy jackets for younger women, visit **Urbain,** directly across the street.) 989 av. Cartier (at bd. René-Lévesque), Montcalm. ☏ 418/522-1016.

Simons Kids Old Québec's only department store opened here in 1840. Small by modern standards, Simons has two floors for men's and women's clothing, emphasizing sportswear for adults and teens. Most of it is pretty basic. 20 Côte de la Fabrique (near the Hôtel-de-Ville), Upper Town. ☏ 418/692-3630. www.simons.ca.

Zazou This boutique focuses primarily on casual and dressy fashions from Québécois designers, including wool sweaters with nature motifs and silk scarves. 31 Petit-Champlain (near the funicular), Lower Town. ☏ 418/694-9990. www.quartierpetitchamplain.com.

FOOD

Canadian Maple Delights Kids This maple-syrup foods boutique stocks everything from maple chocolate and maple crystals to gift bottles of syrup and freshly made pastries and cookies. Maple-sweetened gelatos come in flavors such as hazelnut, mocha, and—mmm—meringue. This is one of the few shops where you'll find the English translation of the name getting as much prominence in signage as the French translation, Les Délices de l'Erable. 1044 rue St-Jean (near rue Ste-Angèle), Upper Town. ☏ 418/692-3245. www.mapledelights.com.

Choco-Musée Erico Kids Gourmet chocolates in an old-timey shop which includes a small room with historical information about how chocolate is made. Flavors include Szechuan, jasmin, balsamic vinegar, and chai cardamom. You can also buy ice cream here, in portions as small as C$1. 634 rue St-Jean (5 blocks outside Upper Town walls), Parliament Hill. ☏ 418/524-2122. www.chocomusee.com.

Epicerie J.A. Moisan A true food emporium. There must be close to 30 olive oils to choose from, for instance, making this *épicerie* a special spot. For one thing, it's a step back in time, dating to 1871 (it claims to be the oldest grocery store in North America). As engagingly, it maintains an international selection of foods whose expanse is usually only found in shops 20 times its size. 699 rue St-Jean (4 blocks outside Upper Town walls), Parliament Hill. ☏ 418/522-0685. www.jamoisan.com.

Epicerie Richard Keep this small, centrally-located shop in Upper Town in mind if you need a nibble and aren't quite hungry enough for a full meal or if you're looking for picnic foods. It carries a good selection of meats, cheeses, pâtés, sandwiches, and prepared meals. There are vegetarian options, too, including lentil salad, couscous, and tabbouleh. Beer and wine are also available. It's open until 11pm daily. 42 rue des Jardins (near rue St-Louis), Upper Town. ☏ 418/692-1207.

La Petite Cabane à Sucre Kids Canada is the biggest producer of maple syrup in the world, and Québec is the source of 75% of Canada's share. "The little sugar shack," as this store's name translates into English, sells ice cream, honey, maple syrup, maple candy, and related products, including tin log cabins that pour syrup from their chimneys. 94 rue du Petit-Champlain (near bd. Champlain), Lower Town. ☏ 418/692-5875. www. petitecabaneasucre.com.

Marché du Vieux-Port By the water near the train station, this market is a year- round operation that blossoms in spring and summer with farmers' bounty from Île d'Orléans and beyond. In addition to fresh fruits and vegetables, you'll find relishes, jams, honey, wines, meats, cheeses, and handicrafts. 160 quai Saint-André (near the train station), Lower Town. ℂ 418/692-2517. www.marchevieuxport.com.

HOUSEWARES

Zone Located in a residential area of Québec City walking distance from Upper Town, Zone is a nifty housewares store featuring colorful bowls and plates, clocks and frames, and small lamps and vases. 999 av. Cartier (at the corner of bd. René-Lévesque), Montcalm. ℂ 418/522-7373. www.zonemaison.com.

LEATHER GOODS

Ibiza This leather store sells coats, hats, gloves, slippers, and handbags. It also stocks knives by the company Laguiole. 57 rue du Petit-Champlain (midblock), Lower Town. ℂ 418/692-2103. www.quartierpetitchamplain.com.

MUSIC

Archambault (**Kids**) Part of a Canadian chain, Archambault stocks two large floors with CDs, books, magazines, and some toys for children. 1095 rue St-Jean, Upper Town. ℂ 418/694-2088. www.archambault.ca.

NEWSPAPERS & MAGAZINES

Maison de la Presse Internationale As its name implies, this large store in the midst of the St-Jean shopping and nightlife bustle offers up racks and racks of magazines and a good assortment of newspapers from around the world, in many languages. It also has adapter plugs and converters. It's open daily from 7am (except Sun, at 8am) until 11pm. 1050 rue St-Jean (at the corner of rue Ste-Angèle), Upper Town. ℂ 418/694-1511.

SHOPPING COMPLEXES

Shopping malls on a grand scale aren't found in or near Old Town. For that, it's necessary to travel to the neighboring municipality of **Sainte-Foy.** The malls there differ little from their cousins throughout North America in terms of layout and available products. With 350 shops, **Laurier Québec,** at 2700 bd. Laurier in Sainte-Foy (ℂ 418/651-5000; www.laurierquebec.com) is the biggest, and it attracts some 13 million shoppers each year. It offers a shuttle bus from several hotel stops in Québec City from mid-May through mid-October; call ℂ 418/664-0460 for schedule information. The smaller **Place Québec** is a mall attached to the convention center and the Hilton hotel just outside the city walls.

WINES

Société des Alcools du Québec Liquor and other spirits can only be sold in stores operated by this provincial agency. SAQ outlets are supermarkets of wines and spirits, with thousands of bottles in stock. Québec's unique ice cider *(cidre de glace),* made from apples left on trees after the first frost, can be purchased here for around C$25. Look for the VQA logo, for Vintners Quality Alliance, which is posted on wines that have received the state seal of approval for quality. 1059 av. Cartier (near rue Fraser), Montcalm. ℂ 418/643-4334. www.saq.com.

Québec City After Dark

Though Québec City has fewer nighttime diversions than exuberant Montréal, there are more than enough activities to occupy visitors' evenings during an average stay. Apart from theatrical productions, which are almost always in French, knowledge of the language is rarely necessary to enjoy the range of entertainment.

There are two terrifically innovative events to plan summer evenings around: Through 2013, **Cirque du Soleil** will be putting on free performances on city streets every weekday evening from June 24 to Labour Day. Spectators will meet up with bands of circus performers at designated spots and then travel the streets with the troupes. Later at night, the 40-minute show the **Image Mill** will be projected in Vieux-Port along the Bunge grain silos. A highlight of the 400th anniversary celebrations in 2008, the show will be presented Wednesdays through Sundays, also for free. For a taste of the Image Mill project, there are photos at the website of its creator Robert LePage, at www.lacaserne.net. Details about both programs are at the city's website, **www.quebecregion.com**.

The neighborhood for each venue below is listed with the address: Lower Town and Upper Town in Vieux-Québec; Vieux-Port, adjacent to Lower Town; Parliament Hill; Montcalm, the residential neighborhood just west of Parliament Hill; and St-Roch.

1 THE PERFORMING ARTS

CLASSICAL MUSIC, OPERA & DANCE

The region's premier classical groups are **Orchestre Symphonique de Québec** (✆ 418/643-8486; www.osq.org), Canada's oldest symphony, which performs at the Grand Théâtre de Québec (see below), and **Les Violons du Roy** (✆ 418/692-3026; www.violonsduroy.com), a string orchestra which just celebrated its 25th year. It features musicians in the early stages of their careers and performs at the centrally located Palais Montcalm (p. 267).

CONCERT HALLS & PERFORMANCE VENUES

Many of the city's churches host sacred and secular music concerts, as well as special Christmas festivities. Look for posters on outdoor kiosks around the city and check with the tourist office (p. 205) for listings.

Colisée Pepsi   Rock concerts by Metallica and a gathering of military bands called the Québec City Military Tattoo were among the awfully thin number of offerings in 2009 at this 15,300-seat arena. The stadium is a 10-minute drive northwest of Parliament Hill. 250 bd. Wilfrid-Hamel (ExpoCité), north of St-Roch. ✆ 800/900-SHOW or 418/691-7110. www.expocite.com.

Grand Théâtre de Québec ★★★   Classical music concerts, opera, dance, jazz, blues, klezmer, and theatrical productions are presented in two halls. Visiting conductors, orchestras, and dance companies perform here in addition to resident companies such as the Orchestre Symphonique de Québec. 269 bd. René-Lévesque est (near av. Turnbull), Parliament Hill. ✆ 418/643-8131. www.grandtheatre.qc.ca.

Le Capitole   Big musical productions such as *Les Misérables* and *Sherazade* keep this historic 1,262-seat theater on Place d'Youville buzzing along. (Productions are in French.) More intimate shows such an homage to Johnny Cash and *Rock Story… La Suite* featuring classic hits of the 1970s and '80s are put on in the attached Le Cabaret du Capitole. 972 rue St-Jean (at Place d'Youville), Parliament Hill. (C) 800/261-9903 or 418/694-4444. www.lecapitole.com.

Palais Montcalm ★   Recent renovations made this venue bigger and more modern, and it's now a hub of the city's cultural community. The main performance space is the 979-seat Raoul-Jobin Theatre, which presents a mix of dance programs, plays, and classical music concerts by Les Violons du Roy and others. More intimate recitals happen in a 125-seat cafe-theater. 995 Place d'Youville (near Porte Saint-Jean), Parliament Hill. (C) 418/641-6411. www.palaismontcalm.ca.

2 THE CLUB & MUSIC SCENE

Québec City's **Festival d'Eté (Summer Festival)** bills itself as Canada's largest outdoor arts festival. It's held in Vieux-Québec and St-Roch for 11 days each July. Highlights include the free jazz and folk combos who perform in an open-air theater next to City Hall. The festival hosts more than 400 shows with performers from Africa, Asia, Europe, and North America showcasing theater, music, and dance. For details, call (C) 888/992-5200, or check www.infofestival.com.

BOITES A CHANSONS & OTHER MUSIC CLUBS

Boîtes à chansons (literally, "boxes with songs") are small clubs for a casual evening of music from singer-songwriters. They're popular throughout the Québec region.

If you just want to stroll, there are three principal streets to choose from for nightlife: **rue St-Jean** inside and outside the walls, **Grande-Allée** outside the walls, and **avenue Cartier** in the Montcalm neighborhood.

Largo Resto-Club (Finds) ★   An attractive restaurant and jazz club, Largo is one of a growing number of businesses sprucing up a blocks-long strip of rue St-Joseph in the St-Roch district. It combines the old and the new beautifully: High ceilings and chandeliers give it old-time class, while blond-wood floors, clean angles, and contemporary art make it modern. There's jazz on Fridays, Saturdays, and occasional other evenings, free most nights for diners. Main courses range from C$17 to C$24. 643 rue St-Joseph est, St-Roch. (C) 418/529-3111. www.largorestoclub.com.

Le Cercle   This tapas and wine bar opened in 2008 adjacent to its sister restaurant, the worthy **Utopie** (p. 233). In the evenings, stylish snacks are only half the deal: Three or four nights each week, there's live music in the space, which holds upwards of 300 people. Performers run the gamut from post-punk to post-modern. Music starts around 10pm, with the cover charge from about C$5 to C$20. In addition to serving food until 1am daily, it's also open for weekend brunch, from 10am to 2pm. 228 St-Joseph est (near rue Caron), St-Roch. (C) 418/948-8648. www.lecerclesurst-joseph.com.

Le Pape-Georges (Finds)   A cozy wine bar in a 325-year-old stone-and-beamed room that features *chanson* (a French-cabaret singing style), along with other music genres, Friday through Sunday at 10pm (and in summer on Thurs and occasionally Wed). Light fare is available along with up to 15 choices of wine by the glass (the bar's motto: "Save water; drink wine!"). 8 rue Cul-de-Sac (near bd. Champlain), Lower Town. (C) 418/692-1320. www.papegeorges.com.

Les Voûtes Napoléon Down a flight of stairs that's tucked behind the terrace cafes and general bustle of Grande-Allée, this amicable *boîtes à chansons* has music 7 nights a week starting around 10:30pm and is always free. Stone arches and a low ceiling give the front room a cavelike feel, and there's a postage-stamp-size stage for the Québécois singer-songwriters passing through town. 680 Grande-Allée, Parliament Hill. ✆ **418/640-9388.**

Théâtre du Petit-Champlain Québécois and French singers alternate with jazz and rock groups in this roomy cafe and theater in Lower Town. Performances take place most Wednesdays through Saturdays at 8pm. Tickets run about C$20 to C$40. There's a pretty outdoor patio for pre-show drinks. 68 rue du Petit-Champlain (near the funicular), Lower Town. ✆ **418/692-2631.** www.theatrepetitchamplain.com.

DANCE CLUBS

Boudoir Lounge ★ The hottest club in St-Roch, Boudoir is open daily from noon until 3am, with DJs working sound systems from 10pm on Thursdays, Fridays, and Saturdays. Live music is occasionally featured. In warm weather, there's a terrace on the pedestrian street in front of its doors. The signature Boudoir martini features vodka, triple sec, ice wine, champagne, and peach syrup. 441 rue du Parvis (at bd. Charest est), St-Roch. ✆ **418/524-2777.** www.boudoirlounge.com.

Le Drague Cabaret Club Catering mostly to gay and lesbian clientele, "the Drag" has been around since 1983 and features two dance rooms and a cabaret with drag shows on Sunday nights. Other nights bring live shows, karaoke, and country-music dancing. 815 rue St-Augustin (just off rue St-Jean), Parliament Hill. ✆ **418/649-7212.** www.ledrague.com.

Maurice Find this club in the triple-tiered enterprise that occupies a converted mansion at the thumping heart of the Grande-Allée scene. It includes a surprisingly good restaurant (**VooDoo Grill**, p. 232), a couple of bars, and music that tilts heavily toward Latin. In winter, it has been known to set up a sidewalk-level "Icecothèque" with a bar made completely of ice, ice sculptures, and roaring music. Theme nights are frequent, and crowds of hundreds are not unusual. 575 Grande-Allée est, Parliament Hill. ✆ **418/647-2000.** www.mauricenightclub.com.

3 BARS

If you're young and looking for fun, keep in mind the **Grande-Allée** strip just past Place George-V, where a beery collegiate atmosphere can sometimes rule as the evening wears on. The bars listed here are removed from Grande-Allée's melee. Note that smoking has been banned in bars throughout the province since 2006.

Aviatic Club A good locale to visit when you're coming or going by train, as it's right inside the station. Food ranges from sushi to Tex-Mex, to go along with local and imported beers. It celebrated its 20th year in 2009. 450 de la Gare-du-Palais (near rue St-Paul), Lower Town. ✆ **418/522-3555.** www.aviatic-club.com.

Brûlerie St-Roch A bar, yes, but a hipster *coffee* bar, in the heart of the St-Roch neighborhood. A wall of coffee bean bins lines one wall, a coffee roaster works its magic in a corner, and folks chat or work on glowing laptops at tables and tall chairs along a front window. Daily from 6:30am to 11pm (to midnight Thurs–Sat). 375 rue St-Joseph est (near rue Dorchester), St-Roch. ✆ **418/529-1559.**

Summer Fireworks

From late July to mid-August, the city hosts a grand fireworks competition, **Les Grands Feux Loto-Québec,** at scenic Montmorency Falls 10 minutes north of city center. Tickets are C$8 to C$29. See p. 23 for more details.

La Ninkasi du Faubourg A relaxed go-to spot if you're young and gay or just happy to be livin' la vida loca. With a tagline "bieres et culture," the Ninkasi features 200 Québécois microbrews. In warm months it sometimes lays sod grass over the asphalt on the outdoor terrace. Daily from 11am. 811 rue St-Jean (1 block west of av. Honoré-Mercier), Parliament Hill. ℂ **418/529-8538.** www.ninkasi.ca.

L'Astral ★ Spinning slowly above a city that twinkles below like tangled necklaces, this restaurant and bar atop the **Hôtel Loews le Concorde** (p. 222) unveils a breathtaking 360-degree panorama. The restaurant is high-quality (look for the classic French-Canadian dessert *pudding chômeur,* a pound cake soaked with maple syrup and brown sugar), but you can also come just for drinks and the sunset view. The bar is open daily from noon until 11pm. A popular Sunday buffet brunch costs C$18. 1225 Cours du Général de Montcalm (at Grande-Allée), Parliament Hill. ℂ **418/647-2222.**

Pub St-Patrick An Irish pub that seats 300 and just keeps on getting on. Pints of Guinness are the steadiest pour, of course, and food is available. The music of the Ould Sod is the big draw, too. For that, show up on Friday and Saturday starting at 9:30pm. 1200 rue St-Jean (at rue Couillard), Upper Town. ℂ **418/694-0618.** www.pubsaintpatrick.com.

Ristorante Il Teatro ★ This friendly Italian restaurant (p. 227) directly on the Place d'Youville just outside the Upper Town walls is open from 7am to at least 2am every day. It's part of a complex that includes **Le Capitole** theater (p. 267), and actors, musical performers, and theater staff often come in for a drink or a meal after shows. A *table du soir* offers a truncated menu until 11pm or later. 972 rue St-Jean (at Place d'Youville), Upper Town. ℂ **418/694-9996.** www.lecapitole.com/en/restaurant.php.

Saint Alexandre Pub ★ Roomy and sophisticated, this is one of the best-looking bars in town. It's done in British-pub style: polished mahogany, exposed brick, and a working fireplace that's particularly comforting during the 8 cold months of the year. Bartenders serve more than 40 single-malt scotches and 250 beers, along with hearty bar food (chicken wings, steak and kidney pie, fish and chips). Check the schedule for the occasional live music—rock, blues, jazz, or Irish. 1087 rue St-Jean (near rue St-Stanislas), Upper Town. ℂ **418/694-0015.** www.pubstalexandre.com.

St-Laurent Bar et Lounge A swank little room inside Québec's magical castle, the Château Frontenac. Dark wood and marble lend an air of elegance, and a bank of windows overlooks the river. The crowd is older and well-heeled, reflected in the drink options: 19 types of single malt, 15 wines by the glass, and 30 mixed drinks including the signature St-Laurent Club, with muddled blueberries, Tanqueray #10 Gin, and lemon juice. There's a small food menu. Friday nights in the summer months, there's live music from 6 to 10pm. Château Frontenac, 1 rue des Carrières (at Place d'Armes), Upper Town. ℂ **418/692-3861.** www.fairmont.com/frontenac.

Side Trips from Québec City

The first four excursions described below can be combined and completed in a day. Admittedly, it will be a morning-to-night undertaking, especially if much time is taken to explore each destination, but the farthest of the four destinations is only 42km (26 miles) from Québec City. Just over a bridge outside the city, bucolic **Île d'Orléans,** with its maple groves, orchards, farms, and 18th- and 19th-century houses, is an unspoiled mini-oasis. The waterfalls of **Montmorency** and **Canyon Ste-Anne** make for dazzling fun, especially in the spring when winter thaws make them thunder. And **Ste-Anne-de-Beaupré** is home to one of Canada's most visited basilicas.

With 2 or more days, you can continue along the northern shore of the St. Lawrence River to **Charlevoix,** where the stunning expanse of the river, high-end inns, and a wide variety of outdoor activities, including whale-watching in summer and fall, invite an overnight stay. There's an option to take the ferry across the river so that you can explore different riverside villages as you make your way back to Québec City.

Although it's preferable to drive in this region, tour buses go to Montmorency Falls and the shrine of Ste-Anne-de-Beaupré, circle the Île d'Orléans, and make the trek all the way up to **Tadoussac** for whale-watching cruises.

For more information, visit the Québec City website at **www.quebecregion.com**. Note that prices listed for hotels in this chapter are the rack rate for double occupancy during the busy skiing and summer-vacation months, unless otherwise noted.

1 ÎLE D'ORLEANS

16km (10 miles) NE of Québec City

Île d'Orléans was first inhabited by native people and then settled by the French as one of their initial outposts of New France in the 17th century. Jacques Cartier had landed here in 1535 and first named the island Bacchus, in celebration of its many grape vines, but renamed it later to honor the Duke of Orléans. Long isolated from the mainland, the island's 7,000 or so current residents firmly resist development, so far preventing the potential of becoming just another sprawling bedroom community. Many of the island's oldest houses are intact, and it remains a largely rural farming area. Notable are the many red-roofed homes.

Until 1935, the only way to get to Île d'Orléans was by boat (in summer) or over the ice in sleighs (in winter). The highway bridge built that year has allowed the island's fertile fields to become Québec City's primary market garden. During harvest periods, fruits and vegetables are picked fresh on the farms and trucked into the city daily.

In mid-July, hand-painted signs posted by the main road announce FRAISES: CUEILLIR VOUS-MEME (STRAWBERRIES: YOU PICK 'EM). The same invitation to pick-your-own is made during apple season, August through October. Farmers hand out baskets and quote

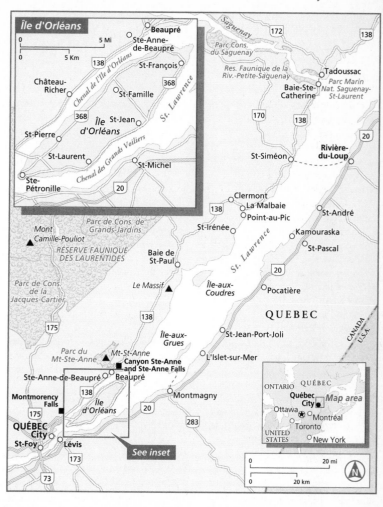

the price, and you pay when the basket's full. Bring along a bag or box to carry away the bounty.

Other seasonal highlights include the visit of thousands of migrating snow geese, ducks, and Canada geese in April and May and again in late October. It's a spectacular sight when they launch in flapping hordes so thick that they almost blot out the sun. Late May also brings the blooming of the many apple trees on the island.

Look for the cookbook *Farmers in Chef Hats* (www.farmersinchefhats.com), which in 2008 received a Gourmand World Cookbook award for "Best in the World" in the local-growers category. The bilingual book has 50 recipes featuring 50 products from Île d'Orléans, as well as an agrotourism map.

ESSENTIALS

Getting There

BY CAR   The drive from Québec City to the island is short. Get on Autoroute 440 east, in the direction of Ste-Anne-de-Beaupré. In about 15 minutes, the Île d'Orléans bridge will be on your right. Take exit 325. If you'd like to hire a guide, **Maple Leaf Guide Services** (© 418/622-3677; www.mapleleafservices.com) can provide one in your car or theirs.

Biking over the bridge is not recommended, given the bridge's narrow and precarious pedestrian sidewalk. Cyclists can park their cars at the tourist office for C$5 per day, or in any of the parking lots of the island's churches for free.

BY BUS   **Dupont,** which also goes by the name **Old Québec Tours** (© 800/267-8687or 418/664-0460; www.tourdupont.com), offers a 6½-hour tour with stops at a sugar shack, an apple orchard, and a *chocolaterie.*

Visitor Information

After arriving on the island, follow the "?" signs and turn right on Route 368 east toward Ste-Pétronille. The **Bureau d'Accueil Touristique,** or Tourist Information Center (© 866/941-9411 or 418/828-9411; www.iledorleans.com) is in the house on the right corner. Pick up the useful map that has most of the restaurants, farms, and accommodations marked. The bureau is open daily from about 9am to 5pm, with longer hours in the peak summer months and somewhat shorter hours in winter. Note that there are a limited number of restrooms on the island.

The tourist office offers a 2-hour audio tour on CD for rent (C$17), and brochures that detail a "Gourmet Route" driving tour, "Artists and Artisans" tour, and "Historic and Cultural Sites" tour.

A coast-hugging road—Route 368, also called chemin Royal and, in a few stretches, chemin de Bout-de-l'Ile—circles the island, which is 34km (21 miles) long and 8km (5 miles) wide. Another couple of roads bisect the island. Farms and picturesque houses dot its east side, and abundant apple orchards enliven the west side.

The island has six tiny villages, originally established as parishes, and each has a church as its focal point. Some are stone churches that date from the days of the French regime, and with fewer than a dozen such churches left in all of Québec province, this is a particular point of pride for the islanders.

It's possible to make a circuit of Île d'Orléans in a half-day, but you can justify a full day if you eat a good meal, visit a sugar shack, do a little gallery hopping, or just skip stones from the beach. If you're strapped for time, loop around as far as St-Jean, and then drive across the island on route du Mitan ("middle road"). You'll get back to the bridge by turning left onto Route 368.

Many of the attractions on the island are closed or have limited hours from October through May. This includes the historical venues as well as the agricultural ones. Check before making a special trip for any one place. There are 18 restaurants on the island, and as with the attractions, many have limited hours in the off-season.

Lodgings include *auberges,* with rooms and full-service restaurants open to nonguests, as well as B&Bs and *gîtes* (homes with a room or two available to travelers). You can see brief details about many of these offerings on the tourist office's website, **www.ile dorleans.com**. Many lodgings also provide leaflets to the tourist office.

For much of the year, you can meander the roads of the island at 40kmph (25 mph), pulling over only occasionally to let a car pass. There is no bike path, which means that bikers share the narrow rural roads. Both drivers and cyclists need to move with care in the busy summer months.

Important navigational note: Street numbers on the ring road called "chemin Royal" start anew in each village, so that you could pass a no. 1000 chemin Royal in one stretch and then another no. 1000 chemin Royal a few minutes later. Be sure that you know not just the number of your destination, but which village it's in as well.

STE-PETRONILLE

The first village reached on the recommended counterclockwise tour is Ste-Pétronille, only 3km (2 miles) from the bridge (take a right turn off the bridge). Note that in this village, Route 368, which is called chemin Royal on most of the island, is called chemin du Bout-de-l'Île.

When the British occupied the island in 1759, General James Wolfe had his headquarters here before launching his successful attack on Québec City. At the end of the 19th century, this parish was a top vacation destination for the Québécois.

The village is now best known for its Victorian inn, **La Goéliche** (see below), and also claims North America's northernmost stand of **red oaks,** which dazzle in autumn. The houses were the summer homes of wealthy English in the 1800s, and the church dates from 1871. Many of the homes sport red roofs, which made for better visibility from the river, especially when traveling through rain or snow.

Drive down to the water's edge to take in the view back to Québec City. One possibility is to turn right onto the small rue Horatio-Walker, which goes past the former workshop of Walker, a successful painter who spent his summers in Ste-Pétronille from the late 1800s to his death in 1938. Another option is to turn off at the sign for La Goéliche, the inn. Adjacent to the property is a small public area with benches and views of Québec City.

For a light snack, the **Chocolaterie de l'Île d'Orléans,** 150 chemin du Bout-de-l'Île (© 418/828-2250), sells soups, sandwiches, and pizza-like meals called *tartes flambées* (the *saumon fume,* smoked salmon, is good), along with homemade chocolates and ice cream. Unlike many operations on the island, it's open year-round.

Where to Stay & Dine

La Goéliche ★   On a rocky point of land at the southern tip of Île d'Orléans stands this romantic country inn and restaurant with a wraparound porch. The building is a virtual replica of the 1880 Victorian house that stood here until a 1996 fire, which burned it to the ground. The new building re-creates the period flavor with tufted chairs, Tiffany-style lamps, and antiques. All rooms face the water, and first-floor units have small terraces. There are two apartments suitable for groups or longer stays. The river slaps at the foundation of the glass-enclosed terrace dining room, which is a grand observation point from which to watch cruise ships and Great Lakes freighters steaming past. Nonguests can come for breakfast, lunch, or dinner. (A *goéliche,* by the way, is a small schooner. Until the mid-1900s, they transferred goods from the St. Lawrence River's shore to larger boats.)

22 chemin du quai, Ste-Pétronille, PQ G0A 4C0. © **888/511-2248** or 418/828-2248. Fax 418/828-2745. www.goeliche.ca. 16 units. C$128–$283 double. Rates include breakfast. Packages available. AE, DC, MC, V. Free parking. **Amenities:** Restaurant; bar; babysitting; pool (heated outdoor); golf and tennis nearby. *In room:* Hair dryer, minibar (some rooms), Wi-Fi (free).

ST-LAURENT

From Ste-Pétronille, continue on Route 368, which continues to be called chemin du Bout-de-l'Île in this village. There are a few restaurants and art galleries in this stretch,

> ⓘ Tips   **Economuseums: A Local (Tourism) Tradition**
>
> The Québec province is enamored of minimuseums, especially museums of food products. Called *economusées* or interpretation centers, they're often simply a room or two attached to a store. Usually they display tools used in production and feature photographs and explanatory text in French and (usually) English. Examples include, on Île d'Orléans, Chocolaterie de l'Île d'Orléans in Ste-Pétronille (see above) and Cassis Monna et Filles in St-Pierre (see below) and, in Québec City, Canadian Maple Delights (p. 264) and Choco-Musée Erico (p. 264). Designed both to educate and provide tourist oomph, they're rarely worth a visit on their own but usually provide a few minutes of interesting reading if you've stopped to shop. A list of many of them is online at www.economusee.com.

and bicycle rentals at **Ecolocyclo,** 1979 chemin Royal (ⓒ **418/828-0370;** www.ecolocyclo. net). After 7km (4⅓ miles), you'll arrive at St-Laurent, founded in 1679, once a boat-building center turning out ships that could carry up to 5,300 tons for Glasgow ship owners.

To learn about the town's maritime history, visit **Le Parc Maritime de St-Laurent** (ⓒ **418/828-9672;** www.parcmaritime.ca), an active boatyard from 1908 to 1967. Before the bridge was built, islanders journeyed across the river to Québec City by boat from here. The maritime park incorporates the old Godbout Boatworks and offers demonstrations of the art of building flat-bottomed schooners. It's open daily from 10am to 5pm mid-June through mid-October. Cost is C$3 per person, and free for children 12 and younger.

Where to Stay & Dine

Le Moulin de Saint-Laurent ★   A former flour mill, in operation from 1720 to 1928, has been transformed into one of the island's most romantic restaurants. Rubble-stone walls and hand-wrought beams form the interior, with candlelight glinting off the hanging copper and brass pots. On a warm day, try for a table on the shaded terrace beside the waterfall that tumbles down a small hill. Lunch, daily from 11:30am to 2:30pm, might be a quiche, a plate of assorted cheeses, or a fillet of pork. Main courses at dinner range from C$15 to C$28. The restaurant is closed from November to April, but the owners rent 10 cottage chalets at the shore year-round. Each has a fully equipped kitchen and some have a fireplace and a washing machine.

754 chemin Royal (Rte. 368), St-Laurent, PQ G0A 3Z0. ⓒ **888/629-3888** or 418/829-3888. Fax 418/829-3716. www.moulinstlaurent.qc.ca. 10 units. C$190–C$260 double. Rates include dinner and breakfast. Packages available. AE, DC, MC, V. Free parking. Pets allowed in some units for no additional charge. **Amenities:** Restaurant; pool (small outdoor heated pool in summer); terrace next to waterfall. *In room:* TV, kitchen.

ST-JEAN

St-Jean, 6km (3¾ miles) from St-Laurent, was home to sea captains. That might be why the houses in the village appear more luxurious than others on the island. The creamy-yellow "Scottish brick" in the facades of several of the homes was ballast in boats that came over from Europe and was considered a sign of luxury and wealth. The village church was built in 1734, and the walled cemetery is the final resting place of many fishermen and seafarers.

On the left as you enter St-Jean is the well-preserved Manoir Mauvide-Genest, 1451 chemin Royal (© 418/829-2630; www.manoirmauvidegenest.com), the manor home of Jean Mauvide, a French surgeon who settled here in 1720. Mauvide went on to acquire much of the western part of the island and built this small estate in 1752, becoming one of New France's leading figures. This fine home, built right at the edge of the road, is unlike any other building on the island. Take it in from across the street to really grasp its grandeur. It's filled with authentic and reproduction furnishings from Mauvide's era and is classified as a historic monument. It's open daily 10am to 5pm from mid-May to mid-October. Admission is C$6 for ages 13 and older and C$2 for children 6 to 12, with an additional C$2 per person for a guided tour.

For a sweet treat, keep your eyes out for *cabanes à sucre,* traditional "sugar shacks," where maple syrup is made and casual all-you-can-eat meals are available. One that is open in March and April is La Sucrerie Blouin, 2967 chemin Royal (© 418/829-2903; www.sucrerieblouin.com), run by a family of bakers who have lived on the island for 300 years. They offer demonstrations of the syrup-making equipment and explanations about the process that turns tree sap into syrup.

A gorgeous bed-and-breakfast option is Dans les bras de Morphée, 225 chemin Royal (© 866/220-4061 or 418/829-3792; www.danslesbrasdemorphee.com). The five star B&B was awarded Grand Prize in 2009 in its category by the provincial tourist board. With just four rooms, it is a stunning country cottage in splendid style, at C$138 to C$162.

If you're pressed for time, you can pick up the route du Mitan here. It crosses Île d'Orléans to St-Famille, back near the bridge. The road is marked (barely) with a small sign on the left just past the church in St-Jean. Even if you're continuing the full loop, you might want to make a short detour down the road to see the farmland and forest here. To continue the tour, return to St-Jean and proceed east on Route 368.

ST-FRANÇOIS

St-François is at the island's most northeastern tip. Both potatoes and leeks are grown on this part of the island, which lead some to dub this "the village of vichyssoise." The 9km (5⅗-mile) drive from St-Jean to St-François exposes vistas of the Laurentian Mountains on the other side of the river. Mont Ste-Anne can be seen on the opposite side of the river in the distance, its slopes scored by ski trails.

The St. Lawrence River is 10 times wider here than when it flows past Québec City and can be viewed especially well from the town's observation tower, which you'll pass on your right. You can park here and climb for a view. The town's original church from 1734 burned in 1988. It was replaced in 1992.

After you've looped around the island's northern edge, the road stops being Route 368 east and becomes Route 368 west.

STE-FAMILLE

Founded in 1661, Ste-Famille is the island's oldest parish. It's 8km (5 miles) from St-François. Across the road from the triple-spired church (1743) is the convent of Notre-Dame Congregation, founded in 1685 by Marguerite Bourgeoys, one of Montréal's prominent early citizens (for more about her, see p. 111).

SIDE TRIPS FROM QUÉBEC CITY

ÎLE D'ORLÉANS

For a satisfying low-key meal, stop into roadside **La Crêpe Cochonne,** 3963 chemin Royal (© **418/829-3656**). You'll find a wide selection of dessert crepes, filled with maple syrup, homemade chocolate, or fruit; and savory crepes, with make-your-own options from ham to cheese to asparagus. Crepes cost C$4 to C$9 each. A back deck has a river view.

Maison de Nos Aïeux, 3907 chemin Royal (© **418/829-0330;** www.fondationfrancois lamy.org), is a genealogy center with minimovies about some of the island's oldest families and information about the island's history. **Parc des Ancêtres,** a riverside green space with picnic tables, is adjacent, and the Pub le Mitan, 3887 chemin Royal (© **418/829-0408**), a microbrewery with a deck that overlooks the river, shares the same parking lot.

Other potential stopping points in Ste-Famille are **Les Fromages de l'Isle d'Orléans,** 4696 chemin Royal (© **418/829-0177**), an artisanal dairy that makes a 17th-century-style cheese called Paillasson, and the adjacent **Maison Drouin,** 4700 chemin Royal (© **418/ 829-0330;** www.fondationfrancoislamy.org), a beautifully preserved home from the 1730s that has never been modernized. It is the oldest house on the island open to visitors.

ST-PIERRE

When you reach St-Pierre, you're nearly back to where you started. If you haven't stopped at any of the orchards that beckoned on your tour, **Bilodeau** at 2200 chemin Royal (© **418/828-9316;** www.cidreriebilodeau.qc.ca; daily 9am–5pm year-round) makes a satisfying final stop. It produces some of Île d'Orléans's regular ciders and *cidre de glace,* a sweet wine made from apples left on the trees until after the first frost. Visitors can partake of samples (try the hazelnut-and-apple-syrup mustard), guided facility tours, apple-picking (mid-Aug to mid-Oct), and a shop.

Another wine option is **Cassis Monna et Filles,** 721 chemin Royal (© **418/828- 2525;** www.cassismonna.com). Black currants are grown here, and a chic shop features a display on how the currants are harvested and transformed into beverages such as Crème de Cassis, the key element to a Kir. It's open daily May to October.

St-Pierre's central attraction is its original church, the island's oldest (1717). Services are no longer held there, but there's a large **handicraft shop** in the back, behind the altar. This room dates back to 1695, making it even older than the church. Look for the stone church on your right (followed immediately by a larger, newer church) and a small blue and white sign for "Corporation des artisans" at 1249 chemin Royal. Although the church's front doors are locked, you can get inside for a viewing from an entrance at the shop.

2 MONTMORENCY FALLS

11km (7 miles) NE of Québec City

Back on the mainland, the impressive **Montmorency Falls** are visible from Autoroute 440. At 83m (272 ft.) tall, they're 30m (98 ft.) higher than Niagara Falls—a boast no visitor is spared. These falls, however, are far narrower. They were named by Samuel de Champlain for his patron, the duke of Montmorency, to whom he dedicated his voyage of 1603.

On summer nights, the plunging water is illuminated. Two nights a week from late July to mid-August, an international fireworks competition, **Les Grands Feux Loto-Québec,** is held at the falls (p. 23). In winter there's a particularly impressive sight: The freezing spray sent up by crashing water builds a mountain of white ice at the base, nicknamed *pain de sucre* (sugarloaf). It grows as high as 30m (98 ft.) and attracts ice climbers. The yellow cast of the falls comes from the high iron content of the riverbed.

ESSENTIALS
Getting There
BY BUS **Dupont,** which also goes by the name **Old Québec Tours** (© **800/267-8687** or 418/664-0460; www.tourdupont.com), offers tours to the falls.

BY CAR Take Autoroute 440 east out of Québec City. After 10 minutes, watch for exit 325 for the falls and the parking lot. If you miss the exit, you'll see the falls on your left and will be able to make a legal U-turn.

VIEWING THE FALLS
The falls are surrounded by the provincial **Parc de la Chute-Montmorency** (© **418/ 663-3330;** www.sepaq.com/chutemontmorency), where visitors can take in the view and have a picnic. The grounds are accessible year-round.

Montmorency Falls ★ Kids There are a couple ways to see the 83m (272-ft.) falls, which are visible from Autoroute 440. A path from the lower parking area leads to the base of the falls, where the water comes crashing down, and the view is spectacular in all seasons from here. Stairs ascend from here to near the top, with viewing platforms along the way. At the top, a footbridge spans the water just where it flows over the cliff. If you don't want to walk, a cable car runs from the parking lot to a terminal above the falls, with a pathway that leads close the water's edge. At that top terminal is **Manoir Mont-morency,** a villa that contains an interpretation center, a cafe, and a restaurant. The dining room and porch have a side view of the falls; reservations are suggested. Parking is available at the top of the falls by the villa, too.

2490 av. Royale, Beauport. © **418/663-3330.** www.sepaq.com/chutemontmorency. Admission to the falls is free, though parking costs C$9.50. Round-trip fares on the cable car cost C$12 for adults, C$5.75 for ages 6 to 16, and free for age 5 and younger. Cable car operates throughout the day late Apr to late Aug, and on a more limited schedule the rest of the year.

3 STE-ANNE-DE-BEAUPRE

33km (21 miles) NE of Québec City; 22km (14 miles) NE of Montmorency Falls

The village of Ste-Anne-de-Beaupré is a religious destination, centered around a two-spired basilica that is one of Canada's most famous shrines. Some 1.5 million people make the pilgrimage each year to the complex.

Legend has it that French mariners were sailing up the St. Lawrence River in the 1650s when they ran into a terrifying storm. They prayed to their patroness, St. Anne, to save them, and when they survived, they dedicated a wooden chapel to her on the north shore of the St. Lawrence, near the site of their perils. Not long afterward, a chapel laborer was said to have been cured of lumbago, the first of many documented miracles. Since that time, believers have made their way here to pay their respects to St. Anne, mother of the Virgin Mary and grandmother of Jesus.

Route 138 travels along the river, which is tidal. At low tide, the beach can become speckled with hundreds of birds, such as purple sandpipers, pecking for food. Look for them behind the houses, gas stations, and garages that pepper the road.

Getting There

BY BUS **Dupont,** also called **Old Québec Tours** (☎ **800/267-8687**or 418/664-0460; www.tourdupont.com) offers tours that include Ste-Anne-de-Beaupré.

BY CAR Autoroute 440 turns into Autoroute 40 at Montmorency Falls and then becomes Route 138 almost immediately. Continue on Route 138 to Ste-Anne-de-Beaupré. The church and exit are visible from the road.

A RELIGIOUS TOUR

Basilica and Shrine of Ste-Anne-de-Beaupré ★

The towering basilica that dominates this small village is the most recent building raised here in St. Anne's honor. After the French sailors' first modest wooden chapel (1658) was swept away by a flood, another chapel was built on higher ground. Floods, fires, and the ravages of time dispatched later buildings, until a larger structure was erected in 1887. In 1926, it, too, lay in ruins, gutted by fire. The present basilica is constructed in stone, following an essentially neo-Romanesque scheme, and was consecrated on July 4, 1976.

Inside the front doors, look for the two columns dressed with racks of canes—presumably from people cured of their ailments and no longer in need of assistance—that go 9m (30 ft.) high. There are several Masses per day, and in the summer, daily outdoor candlelight processions at 8:30pm.

Other parts of the shrine complex include the **Scala Santa Chapel** (1891); the **Memorial Chapel** (1878), with a bell tower and altar from the late 17th and early 18th centuries, respectively; and the **Way of the Cross,** which is lined with life-size bronze figures depicting Christ's life. There's also a church store and the **Musée Sainte-Anne,** a small facility housing paintings and sculptures. The church runs the **Auberge La Basilique** for visiting pilgrims. Double-occupancy rooms cost C$58.

The basilica and town are particularly busy on Ste-Anne's Novena (July 17–25) and Ste-Anne's Feast Day (July 26), days of saintly significance.

10018 av. Royale, Ste-Anne-de-Beaupré. ☎ **418/827-3781.** www.ssadb.qc.ca. Admission to basilica and chapels is free; admission to museum C$2, free for children 5 and younger. Basilica daily 7am–8pm; museum daily 9am–4pm May 4–Oct 12 (open only to groups by reservation the rest of the year).

Where to Stay & Dine

Auberge La Camarine ★

This inn has a kitchen that is equaled by only a handful of restaurants in the region and quirky bedrooms full of personality and bathed in sunny, Provence-style yellows and blues. First, the food: Creative, well-coordinated combinations can include smoked salmon and gravlax in fennel and artichoke salad, or butternut-squash soup with rabbit and horseradish cream. Main courses run C$24 to C$34; *tables d'hote* start at C$40. Second, the rooms: Bathrooms are uniformly roomy, beds are comfortable, and decor blends antique and contemporary notions. Nineteen of the 31 rooms have wood-burning fireplaces. Normally, units facing the river would have the most appeal, but given the inn's locale just above busy Route 138, back rooms like nos. 43 and 49, which face quiet fields, can be more relaxing. There's a free washer and dryer for guest use.

10947 bd. Ste-Anne (Rte. 138), Beaupré, PQ G0A 1E0. ☎ **800/567-3939** or 418/827-5703. Fax 418/827-5430. www.camarine.com. 31 units. C$129–C$165 double. Packages available. AE, DC, MC, V. Free parking. Pets accepted. **Amenities:** Restaurant; computer for guest use (free). *In room:* A/C (some rooms), TV, hair dryer, Wi-Fi (free).

4 CANYON STE-ANNE, STE-ANNE FALLS & PARC MONT STE-ANNE

42km (26 miles) NE of Québec City; about 9km (6 miles) NE of Ste-Anne-de-Beaupré

After Ste-Anne-de-Beaupré, the road enters into thick evergreen woods, and the frenetic pace of urban life begins to slip away. A short drive off Route 138 is Canyon Ste-Anne, a deep gorge and powerful waterfall created by the Ste-Anne-du-Nord River. Unseen from the main road, the canyon and its falls are an exhilarating attraction.

A bit inland is the Parc Mont Ste-Anne, which surrounds an 800m-high (2,625-ft.) peak. In winter, it's the area's busiest ski mountain, while summertime invites camping, hiking, and biking.

Birders will want to visit the **Cap Tourmente National Wildlife Area** (© 418/827-4591; www.followthegeese.com), on the coast of the St. Lawrence River. Over 300 different species of birds have been seen here, but it's the great snow geese who are the stars. During migration season, usually late April to mid-May and early October into mid-November, tens of thousands of geese stop at the cape, making it an important ornithological site. Naturalists lead walks through the marshes. It's open daily late April to November, and January to March. There's a sign on Route 138 to the area.

ESSENTIALS
Getting There
BY BUS From mid-November until late April, the **Taxi Coop Québec** (© 418/525-5191; www.taxicoop-quebec.com) shuttle service picks up passengers at Québec City hotels in the morning to take them to Parc Mont Ste-Anne, returning them to Québec City in the late afternoon.

BY CAR Continue along Route 138 from Ste-Anne-de-Beaupré. To get to the waterfalls and other destinations in this chapter, stay on Route 138. A marked entrance to the falls will be on your left. To get to the park and ski mountain, exit onto Route 360 east. Château Mont Sainte-Anne (see below) will be on your left, with the entrance to the park directly after it.

OUTDOOR FUN
Canyon Ste-Anne Waterfalls ★★★ (Kids) Perhaps it's because these falls are tucked into the woods, but they don't get the attention that the Montmorency Falls do, and it's a shame. They're spectacular and kitsch-free. Follow the narrow road from Route 138 through the woods to a parking lot, picnic grounds, and a building containing a cafeteria, a gift shop, and the ticket booth. The falls are less than a 10-minute walk from the entrance, but an open-sided shuttle bus is also available to drive visitors to the top of the falls. Trails go down both sides to the bottom.

Part of the excitement comes from the approach: You hear the falls before you see them, and you step out of the woods practically beside them. Three (optional) footbridges go directly across the falls. The first crosses the narrow river just before the water starts to drop. The second, and most thrilling, crosses right over the canyon, from the top of the rock walls that drop straight down to the water. Being so close to the thundering, unending force crashing over massive rocks is likely to induce vertigo in even the most stable of nerves. The final suspension bridge starts at the gorge's base, just 9m (30 ft.) or so above the water where the river starts to flatten out again, and ends at an observation platform. The very brave-hearted can ride a zipline across the canyon harnessed onto a cable wire, for C$20 (information at www.aventurex.net).

Along the trails are eight platforms that jut over the water and well-written information plaques. Management has wisely avoided commercial intrusions along the trails, letting the powerful natural beauty speak for itself.

The falls are 74m (243 ft.) high and at their most awe-inspiring in the spring, when melt-off of winter snows bloats the rivers above and sends 100,000 liters (more than 26,000 gal.) of water over *per second.* (The volume drops to 10,000L/2,600 gal. per second in Aug and Sept.) So voluminous is the mist coming from the fall that it creates another wall of miniwaterfalls on the side of the gorge.

From 1904 to 1965, the river was used to float logs from lumbering operations, and part of the dramatic gorge was created by dynamiting in 1917, to reduce the amount of literal log-jams.

Those who have difficulty walking can see the falls without going too far from the bus. Those with a fear of heights can stay on the side trails, strolling amid the poplar trees and away from the bridges altogether. A visit takes about 1½ hours.

206 Rte. 138 East, Beaupré. ✆ 418/827-4057. www.canyonsa.qc.ca. Admission C$11 adults, C$8 ages 13–17, C$5 ages 6–12, free for age 5 and younger. May to late Oct daily 9am–4:30pm, and until 5:30pm from June 24 until Labor Day. Hours subject to change due to weather, so call to confirm.

Parc du Mont Ste-Anne ★ (Kids)   The area's premiere wilderness resort surrounds an 800m-high (2,625-ft.) peak and is an outdoor enthusiast's dream. In winter, **downhill skiing** on Mont Ste-Anne is terrifically popular. Just 40 minutes from Québec City, this is the region's largest and busiest mountain, named by *Ski Canada* magazine the best destination in the east for spring skiing. There are 66 trails on three sides, and about a third of the resort is expert terrain. At night, 17 trails are lit. Lift tickets cost C$60 for adults, C$50 for seniors, C$47 for ages 13 to 17, and C$34 for ages 7 to 12.

Also in the winter, the park offers Canada's largest network of **cross-country skiing** trails—208km (129 miles) of them. A day ticket is C$20 for adults, C$15 for age 65 and older, C$14 for ages 13 to 17, C$9 for children 7 to 12, and free for children 6 and younger. There's an inn for cross-country skiers in the middle of the trails called L'Auberge du Fondeur (✆ **800/463-1568**). Other winter options include **dog-sledding, snowshoeing, snowmobiling, ice-canyoning,** and **winter paragliding.**

In summer and early fall, the park offers **camping, hiking,** and **golfing.** A panoramic **gondola** operates daily from late May to mid-October, weather permitting. Details about these activities are listed seasonally on the Mont Ste-Anne website.

Mont Ste-Anne is especially well known for its huge network of trails for both hardcore **mountain biking** and milder day-tripping (bikes can be rented). It will be host to the 2010 Mountain Bike and Trial World Championships from August 30 through September 6 (www.montsainteanne2010.com).

From mid-November to late April, **Taxi Coop Québec** (✆ **418/525-5191;** www.taxicoop-quebec.com) provides daily shuttle service from Québec City.

2000 bd. Beau-Pré, Beaupré. ✆ **888/827-4579** or 418/827-4561. www.mont-sainte-anne.com. General admission to the site is C$9 for a family in a car or, individually, C$3.55 for adults and C$1.75 for children 7–17 years old. Gondola ticket prices are C$17 for adults, C$15 for 65 and older, C$14 for ages 7–17, and free for age 6 and younger, with a variety of family rates.

In addition to the resort below, **Chalets-Village** (© 800/461-2030; www.chalets-village.com) offers condo rentals at the base of the mountain. Rates start at C$200.

Château Mont Sainte-Anne ★ **Kids**   Tucked into the base of its namesake mountain and just next to Parc du Mont Ste-Anne, this resort provides the closest overnight location for all mountain activities. New owners took over in 2005 and have made renovations in the years since, including makeovers to 47 units in 2008 (ask for one of them). The resort's primary identity is as a ski lodge, with ski-in-ski-out accessibility at the base of the gondola lift. But golf courses and an internationally regarded network of mountain biking trails bring summer business. All rooms have either kitchenettes or full kitchens, and 40 have fireplaces. Prices rise and fall depending on occupancy and time of year.

500 bd. Beau-Pré, Beaupré, PQ G0A 1E0. © 800/463-4467 or 418/827-5211. Fax 418/827-5072. www.chateaumsa.ca. 240 units. From C$109 double. Children 17 and younger stay free in parent's room. Packages available. AE, DC, DISC, MC, V. Free parking. Pets accepted in some units. **Amenities:** 2 restaurants; bar/bistro; golf courses; health club; Jacuzzis; pools (indoor and outdoor). *In room:* A/C, TV, hair dryer, kitchenette, Wi-Fi (free).

5 CENTRAL CHARLEVOIX: BAIE-ST-PAUL, ST-IRENEE & LA MALBAIE

Baie-St-Paul: 93km (58 miles) NE of Québec City; St-Irénée: 125km (78 miles) NE of Québec City; La Malbaie: 140km (87 miles) NE of Québec City

The Laurentians move closer to the shore of the St. Lawrence River as they approach the mouth of the intersecting Malbaie River. U.S. President William Howard Taft, who had a summer residence in the area, said that the air here was "as intoxicating as champagne, but without the morning-after headache." Taft was among the political and financial elite of Canada and the eastern U.S. who made Murray Bay, or La Malbaie, a wildly popular vacation destination in the early and mid–19th century.

Charlevoix first blossomed under the British regime in the 18th century. In 1762, Scottish officers in the British Army, John Nairne and Malcolm Fraser, built sawmills and flour mills here. They attracted French-speaking Catholics, making the region a combination of Old France and Old Scotland.

Grand vistas over the St. Lawrence abound, and there are many farms in the area. Moose sightings are not uncommon, and the rolling, dark green mountains with their white ski slope scars offer numerous places to hike and bike in the warm months and ski when there's snow. (It's not unheard of, by the way, for it to snow in May.)

In 1988, Charlevoix was named a UNESCO World Biosphere Reserve, which means that it's a protected area for cross-disciplinary conservation-oriented research, with development balanced against environmental concerns. It was one of the first populated areas to get the designation.

ESSENTIALS
Getting There
BY CAR   Take Route 138 to Baie-St-Paul. Turn onto Route 362 to go into downtown Baie-St-Paul. To continue northeast, you have the option of taking either Route 138 or the smaller, more scenic Route 362, which travels closer to the water and lets you visit St-Irénée on the way to La Malbaie.

Baie-St-Paul has a year-round **tourist office** directly on Route 138 (✆ **800/667-2276** or 418/665-4454) that's open daily from 9am to 4pm, and until 7pm in the summer. It's on a dramatic hill approaching the village and is well marked from the highway. (Beware, though: It's an extremely sharp turnoff.) Stop here for one of the grandest vistas of the river and town below.

There are other tourism offices throughout the region, including one in La Malbaie on the water at 495 bd. de Comporté, Route 362 (✆ **800/667-2276** or 418/665-4454). It's open daily 8:30am to 4:30pm. Regional information is also available at **www. tourisme-charlevoix.com**.

BAIE-ST-PAUL & ISLE-AUX-COUDRES

The first town of any size in Charlevoix via Route 138, Baie-St-Paul is an attractive, funky community of 7,317 that continues to earn its century-old reputation as an artists' retreat. Some two dozen boutiques and galleries and a couple of small museums show the works of local painters and artisans. Given the setting, it isn't surprising that many of the artists are landscapists, but other styles and subjects are represented, too. Work runs the gamut from hobbyist to highly professional. Options include the **Maison de René-Richard,** 58 rue St-Jean-Baptiste (✆ **418/435-5571**), which celebrates the Swiss-born artist who made Baie-St-Paul his home until his 1982 death. Richard painted many of his well-regarded semi-abstract landscapes here. (Note that during July and August, the town can get thick with tourists, turning the main street into a near parking lot.)

For **bicycling,** pop off the mainland by taking the free 15-minute car ferry to the small island of Isle-aux-Coudres ("island of hazelnuts"). Popular paths offer a 23km (16-mile) loop around the island. From May to September, single bikes, tandems, and quadricycles for up to six adults and two small children can be rented from **Vélo-Coudres** (✆ **418/ 438-2118;** www.charlevoix.qc.ca/velocoudres). The island also has a smattering of boutiques and hotels. The ferry leaves from the town of St. Joseph-de-la-Rive, along Route 362 just east of Baie-St-Paul.

Many of Canada's elite skiers train at **Le Massif** (✆ **877/536-2774** or 418/632-5876; www.lemassif.com), the area's largest ski mountain. It has 49 trails, and many give skiers the illusion that they're heading directly into the adjacent St. Lawrence.

There are rumblings of a major project for the area: Daniel Gauthier, a founder of Cirque du Soleil, has been working for years to further develop Le Massif by adding 400 lodging units and refurbishing a train line to allow travelers to get to and throughout the area without driving.

Where to Stay

La Maison Otis A central location and a terrific dining room make Otis an easy choice. A long porch fronts Baie-St-Paul's colorful main street, and rooms in the rambling collection of connecting buildings offer cozy combinations of fireplaces, whirlpools, and four-poster beds. An overhaul of the restaurant in 2009 set aside the more formal menu and brought in a venue where guests can come for either a full meal or a snack. A 130-seat basement-level **cabaret** presents music on occasional Fridays and Saturdays, and an adjacent **spa** has a large menu of massage services and facials, available daily by appointment.

23 rue St-Jean-Baptiste, Baie-St-Paul, PQ G3Z 1M2. ✆ **800/267-2254** or 418/435-2255. Fax 418/435-2464. www.maisonotis.com. 30 units. C$125–C$210 double; C$265 suite. Packages available. MC, V. Free

parking. Pets accepted, C$10 per night. Cabaret info at www.lecafedesartistes.com/cabaret.htm. **Ameni-**
ties: 2 restaurants; pool (indoor); spa (adjacent). *In room:* A/C, TV/DVD, hair dryer, MP3 docking station,
Wi-Fi (free).

Where to Dine

Foodies will want to consider visits to some of the region's food producers. **La Ferme
Basque de Charlevoix,** 813 rue St-Edouard in St-Urbain, just west of Baie-St-Paul
(*©* **418/639-2246;** www.lafermebasque.ca), is a small-scale family farm that raises ducks
and makes foie gras sold throughout the province. Tours are C$4. **La Maison d'Affinage
Maurice Dufour,** 1339 bd. Mgr-de-Lavel (Rte. 138) Baie-St-Paul (*©* **418/435-5692;**
www.fromagefin.com), is a *fromagerie* that makes Le Ciel de Charlevoix, an artisanal
cheese that is a highlight of the region (and 2009 champion in the Canadian Cheese
Grand Prix).

Café des Artistes   In addition to its formal restaurant, the hotel La Maison Otis runs
this appealing attached bistro. Pizzas with wafer-thin crusts are exceptional, and there are
15 types to choose from. Other options include the pâté du jour, *Hot-Dogs Français* with
sauces made in town, and paninis. The cafe does good business with locals and artist
types. Because it's small and features a bar, patrons must be at least 18 years old.

25 rue St-Jean-Baptiste, Baie-St-Paul. *©* **418/435-5585.** www.lecafedesartistes.com. Most items cost
less than C$12. MC, V. Daily 9:30am–midnight.

Le Saint-Pub   This casual restaurant is part of the town's *microbrasserie,* or microbrewery. There's always a selection of over a dozen brews made on-site, and visitors sometimes
get to try test beverages. The kitchen serves up solid renditions of bar food, Québécois-
style. Specialties include barbecue chicken and concoctions cooked with beer (beer-and-
onion soup, wild boar burger marinated in beer, chocolate-and-stout pudding, sugar pie
with beer). There's a patio in summer.

2 rue Racine, Baie-St-Paul. *©* **418/240-2332.** www.microbrasserie.com. Main courses C$11–C$25; *table
d'hôte* C$21–C$33. MC, V. Mon–Fri 11:30am–2pm; daily 5–8pm.

ST-IRENEE

From Baie-St-Paul, take Route 362 northeast toward La Malbaie. The air is scented by
sea salt and rent by the shrieks of gulls, and Route 362 roller-coasters over bluffs above
the river, with wooded hills and well-kept villages. This stretch of the road, from Baie-St-
Paul to La Malbaie, is one of the most scenic in the entire region and is dubbed the *Route
du Fleuve,* which means "river route." (It can be treacherous in icy weather, though, so
in colder months, opt for the flatter Rte. 138.)

In 32km (about 20 miles) is St-Irénée, a cliff-top hamlet of just 743 year-round residents. Apart from the setting, the best reason for dawdling here is the 60-hectare (148-acre)
property and estate of **Domaine Forget** (*©* **888/336-7438** or 418/452-3535; www.
domaineforget.com). The facility is a performing-arts center for music and dance and offers
an **International Festival** from mid-June through August. Concerts are staged in a 604-
seat concert hall, with **Sunday musical brunches** on an outdoor terrace that has spectacular views of the river. The program emphasizes classical music with solo instrumentalists
and chamber groups, but is peppered with jazz and dance. Most tickets are C$20 to C$40.

From September to May, Domaine rents its **student dorms** to the general public.
They're clean and well-appointed studios, with cooking areas and beds for two to five
people. They start at C$70 for double occupancy, with discounts for longer stays, and
they include access to studio work areas.

Kayaking ecotours from a half-day to 5 days can be arranged through several companies in the area. **Katabatik** (📞 **800/453-4850** or 418/665-2332; www.katabatik.ca), based in La Malbaie, offers trips that combine kayaking with information about the bays of the St-Lawrence estuary. A half-day tour costs C$50 for adults, C$40 for children 14 to 17, and C$30 for children 13 and younger. Tours start at various spots along the coast and run from March through October.

LA MALBAIE

From St-Irénée, Route 362 starts to bend west after 10km (6¼ miles), as the mouth of the Malbaie River starts to form. La Malbaie (or "Murray Bay," as it was called by the wealthy Anglophones who made this their resort of choice from the Gilded Age through the 1950s) is the collective name of five former municipalities: Pointe-au-Pic, Cap-à-l'Aigle, Rivière-Malbaie, Sainte-Agnès, and Saint-Fidèle. At its center is a small, scenic bay. The 9,130 inhabitants of the region justifiably wax poetic about their wildlife and hills and trees, the place where the sea meets the sky.

A Casino & a Museum

Casino de Charlevoix Established in 1994, the casino is about as tasteful as such establishments get. Cherrywood paneling and granite floors enclose 950 slot machines and 24 tables, including Texas hold 'em blackjack, roulette, and minibaccarat. A 200-seat bar has live pop music on Friday and Saturday nights. Visitors must 18 years old.

183 av. Richelieu (follow the many signs). 📞 **800/665-2274** or 418/665-5300. www.casino-de-charlevoix. com. Free admission (18 and older only). Daily 11am–midnight (until 3am Fri–Sat) with extended hours in summer.

Musée de Charlevoix ★ A terrific little museum. One of the three gallery spaces is devoted to a marvelous permanent exhibition called *Appartenances* ("Belonging") about the history and culture of Charlevoix. Included are photographs from the 1930s of beluga whale-hunting and frontierswomen skinning eels; artifacts from the Manoir Richelieu before its major fire in 1928; folk art from the 1930s and '40s; and engaging descriptive text in English and French.

10 chemin du Havre (at the corner of Rte. 362). 📞 **418/665-4411.** www.museedecharlevoix.qc.ca. Admission C$7 adults, C$5 seniors and students. June to mid-Oct daily 9am–5pm; mid-Oct to May Mon–Fri 10am–5pm, Sat–Sun 1–5pm.

Where to Stay & Dine

Fairmont Le Manoir Richelieu ★★★ (Kids) This is the region's grand resort. Since 1899, there has been a hotel at the river's edge here, first serving the swells who summered in this aristocratic haven with spectacular views of the St. Lawrence River. After waves of renovations, the decor of the hotel long ago dubbed "the castle on the cliff" is reminiscent of its posh heritage, and many rooms meet deluxe standards. A project that finished in 2006 molded the golf course into a glorious 27-hole expanse overlooking the St. Lawrence on one side and the hills and mountains of Charlevoix on the other. In winter, snowmobile rentals are available to use on the area's extensive network of "ski-doo" trails. Guests run the gamut, from young couples and families drawn to the resort's many sporting activities for children to gamers from the casino next door and older folks who have been coming here forever.

181 rue Richelieu, La Malbaie, PQ G5A 1X7. 📞 **866/540-4464** or 418/665-3703. Fax 418/665-8131. www. fairmont.com/richelieu. 405 units. Summer from C$269 double; Nov–May from C$159 double; suites from C$399. Packages available. AE, DC, MC, V. Free self-parking, valet parking C$19. Pets accepted.

Amenities: 4 restaurants; bar; babysitting; children's programs; concierge; executive-level rooms; golf club; health club; room service; pools (indoor and outdoor); spa; watersports equipment; Wi-Fi (in lobby). *In room:* A/C, TV, hair dryer, Internet (C$14 a day), minibar.

La Pinsonnière ★★★   Romance with a princely touch, in 18 pristine rooms. The 2006 renovation of this Relais & Châteaux Association inn created six deluxe rooms (up from one) with spectacular vistas of the St. Lawrence River. These most expensive units deliver a serious "wow" factor and offer the most transporting visit, featuring handsome linens, private terraces, and huge bathrooms with oversized whirlpools, private saunas, and/or steam showers. Newer decor is contemporary and streamlined, while older rooms are classic Queen Anne. All have fireplaces, either gas or wood. An indoor pool, unspoiled river beach at the bottom of the property, and attentive service make this tiny resort a regional star. Dinners featuring extraordinary tartares and local products cost C$72, C$92, or C$125, with menus changing daily. Wines are a particular point of pride, with 750 labels in the 12,000-bottle cellar. Taking in La Pinsonnière's understated luxury is, simply, pure contentment.

124 rue St-Raphaël, La Malbaie, PQ G5A 1X9. (C) **800/387-4431** or 418/665-4431. Fax 418/665-7156. www.lapinsonniere.com. 18 units. C$345–C$495 double May–Oct and holiday season; C$295–C$445 double rest of the year. Packages available. Minimum 2-night stay on weekends, 3 nights on holiday weekends. AE, MC, V. Free parking. Pets accepted. **Amenities:** Restaurant; bar; babysitting; concierge; health club nearby; pool (heated indoor); room service; spa (small, for massages and treatments). *In room:* A/C, TV, hair dryer, minibar, Wi-Fi (free).

6 UPPER CHARLEVOIX: ST-SIMEON, BAIE STE-CATHERINE & TADOUSSAC

St-Siméon: 173km (107 miles) NE of Québec City; Baie Ste-Catherine: 207km (129 miles) NE of Québec City; Tadoussac: 214km (133 miles) NE of Québec City

After visiting La Malbaie, you have several options. You can return back to Québec City the same way you came—it's only 140km (87 miles) along the river's north shore. Or, you can continue up Route 138 for 33km (20 miles) to St-Siméon and cross the St. Lawrence by ferry, landing at Rivière-du-Loup on the opposite shore a little over an hour later and returning to Québec City along the river's south shore.

But if it's summer or early fall and you have more time—a full afternoon or an extra day to stay overnight—consider continuing on to Baie Ste-Catherine and Tadoussac. Here at the northern end of Charlevoix is one of the world's richest areas for **whale-watching.** The confluence of the St. Lawrence and Saguenay rivers attracts 10 to 12 species each summer—as many as 1,500 minke, humpback, finback, and blue whales, who join the 1,000 or so sweet-faced beluga (or white) whales who are here year-round. Add to that the harbor porpoises who visit, and there can be 5,000 creatures diving and playing in the waters. Many can be seen from land mid-June through late October, and up close by boat or kayak.

Springtime comes to this area in May and June—yellow forsythia in May, lilacs in June. *Note:* In winter and spring, when the whales are gone and the temperatures are lower, most of the very few establishments between St-Siméon and Tadoussac are closed. If you're driving, pack some snacks and water, take bathroom breaks when they're available, and make sure you've got enough gasoline.

Getting There

BY CAR Route 138 leads to both the ferry at St-Siméon and to the northern end of Charlevoix, at Baie Ste-Catherine. The highway dead-ends at the dramatic Saguenay River, with the town of Tadoussac just across the river. There is a free car ferry for the 10-minute passage.

Visitor Information

St-Siméon maintains a seasonal **tourist office** at 494 rue St-Laurent, open daily from 10am to 6pm between mid-June and Labour Day. Visit **www.tourisme-charlevoix.com** for more information.

ST-SIMEON

To get to the ferry that crosses the St. Lawrence to return to Québec City along the river's south shore, follow the signs directing cars and trucks to the terminal. Capacity is 100 cars and boarding is on a first-come, first-served basis. The daily number and times of departures vary substantially from month to month, so check at ℂ **418/638-2856** or www.traverserdl.com for the schedule. One-way fares are C$39 for a car, C$15 for each passenger age 12 to 64 years, slightly less for folks 65 and older and children 5 to 11, and free for children younger than 5. Arrive at least 90 minutes before departure in summer and on holidays. Voyages take about 1 hour.

Even though this isn't a whale-watching cruise, passengers may enjoy a sighting on the passage from late June to September, when whales are most active. The ferry steams through the area they most enjoy, making sightings an ever-present possibility.

BAIE STE-CATHERINE & TADOUSSAC

The teeny Baie Ste-Catherine (pop. 229) sits alongside the meeting point of the St. Lawrence River and the Saguenay River, which comes down from the northwest. Tadoussac (pop. 913), just across the Saguenay, is the southernmost point of the Manicouagan tourist region.

Tadoussac is known as "the Cradle of New France." Established in the 1600s, it's the oldest permanent European settlement north of Florida and became a stop on the fur-trading route. Missionaries stayed until the middle of the 19th century. The hamlet might have vanished soon after had a resort hotel, now called **Hôtel Tadoussac** (see below), not been built in 1864. Thanks to it, a steamship line brought wealthy vacationers from Montréal and points farther west and deposited them here for stays that often lasted all summer.

Apart from the hotel, the town is made up of not much more than a whaling educational center, a beach and boardwalk, and some dozen small motels and B&Bs. This is raw country, where the sight of a beaver waddling up the hill from the ferry terminal is met with only mild interest. Still, Tadoussac has more to offer than Baie Ste-Catherine for visitors and is the recommended choice for a stopover.

For 4 days in June, Tadoussac swells into the thousands when it hosts the annual **Festival de la Chanson,** a festival of French song. See **www.chansontadoussac.com**.

Route 138 dead-ends at the Saguenay River and picks up again on the other side. Passage in between is courtesy of a free 10-minute car ferry (ℂ **877/787-7483**). Departure times vary according to season and demand, but figure every 15 minutes from 8am to 8pm in summer, and less frequently the other 12 hours and in low season. (The ferry is the reason that trucks travel in convoys on the highway, pouring out in groups after each ferry crossing.)

The vista on the crossing is dramatic and nearly worth a trip to Tadoussac on its own: Palisades with evergreens poking out of rock walls rise sharply from both shores. So extreme is the natural architecture, in fact, that the area is often referred to as a fjord.

Whale-Watching

From mid-May to mid-October, a number of companies offer trips to see whales or cruise the majestic Saguenay.

Cruise companies use different sizes and types of watercraft, from stately catamarans and cruisers that carry up to 500 to powered inflatables called Zodiacs that carry 10 to 25 passengers. The larger boats have snack bars and naturalists onboard to describe the action. Zodiacs don't provide food or narration, but they are more maneuverable, darting about at each sighting to get closer to the rolling and breaching behemoths.

Zodiac passengers are issued life jackets and waterproof overalls, but should expect to get wet. It's cold out there, too, so layers and gloves are a good idea. People on the large boats sit at tables inside or ride the observation bowsprit, high above the waves.

Two of the biggest companies are **Croisières AML** (© 866/856-6668; www.croisieres aml.com) and **Group Dufour** (© 800/463-5250; www.dufour.ca). Both offer departures from wharves in both Baie Ste-Catherine and Tadoussac (other companies send tours out of St-Siméon, to the south). In high season, each offers about six daily whale-watching trips. Fares are comparable: 3-hour tours on the larger boats cost C$62 for adults, C$57 for seniors and students, C$28 for children 6 to 16, and free for children 5 and younger. Two-hour Zodiac trips cost C$48 to C$58 for adults, C$52 for seniors and students, and C$32 to C$42 for children 6 to 16. Children younger than 6 are not permitted. Check with each company for exact times, prices, and trip options.

Kayak trips that search out whales are available from **Mer et Monde Ecotours** (© 866/637-6663 or 418/232-6779; www.mer-et-monde.qc.ca). Visitors report that they *felt* the whales before they saw them—imagine being out from the shore and feeling a vibration under the kayak hull! The company is based in Les Bergeronnes, a coastal town 20 km (12 miles) north of Tadoussac, and offers tours in summer that start at the bay of Tadoussac just beyond Hôtel Tadoussac's lawn. A 3-hour trip costs C$43 for adults, C$31 for those 15 and younger.

Although the St. Lawrence is a river, it's tidal and often called the "sea" (you'll see references to "sea-kayaking.") The waters here are in a marine park, which was designated as a conservation area to protect the whales and their habitat.

A Whale Center

Centre d'Interprétation des Mammifères Marins (Kids) Start here when you arrive to learn why Tadoussac is such a paradise for whale researchers. At this interpretation center directly on the Saguenay River's edge, there's a small exhibition room (plaques are in French with English booklets for translation), an exhilarating 15-minute video about the whales who visit each summer (the video is in French, with English translation by headphone), and a bilingual expert who answers questions and explains what the team who works upstairs—as many as 50 people in summer—are up to. There's also a shop with books, cuddly toys, and clothing. The center is run by the nonprofit GREMM, a scientific research group that studies the St. Lawrence's marine mammals and posts updates about local whale activity at www.whales-online.net.

108 rue de la Cale Sèche (on the waterfront), Tadoussac. ☎ **418/235-4701.** www.gremm.org. Admission C$8 adults, C$6 seniors, C$4 children 6–12, free for children 5 and younger. Daily 9am–8pm in summer; noon–5pm in spring and fall. Closed mid-Oct until mid-May.

Where to Stay & Dine

Hôtel Tadoussac (Kids)   Established in 1864 and now housed in a building from 1942, this handsome old-time hotel is king of the (small) hill that is Tadoussac. A large front lawn overlooks the river and the comings and goings of whale-watching boats. Public spaces and bedrooms have a shambling, country-cottage appearance—there's no pretense of luxury here—and their maple furnishings were made in Québec. If you've traveled far to get here, you'll likely want one of the river-view rooms. There are 51 of them, so book one and pay the worthwhile C$40 premium. Meals in the large dining room are resort-pricey (C$25 for a cold buffet dinner, for instance) and agreeable enough, though short of impressive. If you're planning to whale-watch, kayak, or get a spa treatment, check out the many package deals.

165 rue Bord de l'Eau, Tadoussac, PQ G0T 2A0. ☎ **800/561-0718** or 418/235-4421. Fax 418/235-4607. www.hoteltadoussac.com. 149 units. C$204–C$244 double in peak months; C$124–C$164 double in low season. Packages available. AE, DC, MC, V. Free parking. Closed mid-Oct to early May. **Amenities:** 3 restaurants when busy, otherwise 2 open; bar; babysitting; children's programs in peak months; pool (heated outdoor); spa; tennis court; Wi-Fi (free in lobby); 1 computer for guest use. *In room:* Overhead fan, TV, hair dryer.

Where to Dine

Café Bohème   Just a few steps from Hôtel Tadoussac is a cheery 1892 house with a white picket fence and mansard roof. Here, Café Bohème holds court as a dependable stop for healthy food, pastries, good coffee, and groovy world music. The eatery is clean and arty, with wooden floors, benches, tables, and counter seating. The *charlevoisien* panini has goat cheese, aged cheddar, pesto, tomatoes, and green peppers, while home-made ice creams and sherbets can include flavors like mango and chocolate-cardamom. Breakfast, served until 11:30am, includes waffles.

239 rue des Pionniers, Tadoussac. ☎ **418/235-1180.** Main courses C$7.50–C$15; *table d'hôte* C$15–C$22. MC, V. Daily 8am–10pm. Closed mid-Oct to mid-May.

Fast Facts, Toll-Free Numbers & Websites

1 FAST FACTS: MONTREAL & QUEBEC CITY

AREA CODES The Montréal area codes are **514** and **438,** and the Québec City code is **418.** Outside of Montréal, the area code for the southern Laurentides is **450** and the northern Laurentides, from Val-David up, uses **819.** The Cantons de l'Est are the same: **450** or **819,** depending on how close you are to Montréal. Starting in October 2010, new telephone numbers in the 450 region may be given the area code 438. Outside Québec City, the area code for Île d'Orléans and north into Charlevoix is **418,** the same as in the city. You always need to dial the three-digit area code in addition to the seven-digit number. Numbers that begin with **800, 866, 877,** or **888** are free to call from both Canada and the U.S.

AUTOMOBILE ORGANIZATIONS Members of the **American Automobile Association (AAA)** are covered by the **Canadian Automobile Association (CAA)** while traveling in Canada. Bring your membership card and proof of insurance. The 24-hour hot line for emergency road service is ✆ **800/222-4357.** The AAA card will also provide discounts at a wide variety of hotels and restaurants in Québec province. Visit www.caaquebec.com for more information.

BUSINESS HOURS Most **stores** in the province are open from 9 or 10am until 6pm Monday through Wednesday, 9am to 9pm on Thursday and Friday, 9am to 5pm on Saturday, and Sunday from noon to 5pm. Since November 2008, stores in downtown Montréal have been able to stay open until 8pm on Saturdays and Sundays, an 18-month change in law that's part of a government-sanctioned pilot project to stimulate tourism. **Banks** are usually open Monday through Friday from 8 or 9am to 4pm and are closed for the entire weekend. Bankers' hours in Québec City are shorter, from 10am to 3pm. **Post office** hours vary wildly by location, but are generally open from 9:30am to 5:30pm on weekdays. Some are open 9:30am to 5pm on Saturdays, and most are closed on Sundays. While many **restaurants** are open all day between meals, some shut down between lunch and dinner. Most restaurants serve until 9:30 or 10pm. **Bars** stay open until 2 or 3am, while some "after hours" clubs open when other clubs are closing and keep people dancing until noon.

DRINKING LAWS The legal drinking age in the province is 18. All hard liquor and spirits in Québec are sold through official government stores operated by the Québec Société des Alcools (look for maroon signs with the acronym SAQ). Wine and beer are available in grocery stores and convenience stores, called *dépanneurs.* Bars can pour drinks as late as 3am, but often stay open later.

Penalties for drunk driving in Canada are heavy. Provisions instituted in 2008 include higher mandatory penalties including a minimum fine of C$1,000 for a first offense, and for a second offense, a minimum of 30 days in jail. Drivers caught under the influence face a maximum life sentence if they cause death, and a maximum 10-year sentence if they cause bodily harm.

DRIVING RULES See the "Getting Around" sections in chapters 5 & 13.

DRUGSTORES & PHARMACIES A pharmacy is called a *pharmacie;* a drugstore is a *droguerie.* A large chain in Montréal is **Pharmaprix.** Its branch at 5122 Côte-Des-Neiges (© **514/738-8464;** www.pharmaprix.ca) is open 24 hours per day, 7 days per week, and has a fairly convenient location. In Québec City, **Louis-Phillippe & Jacques Royer,** at 57 rue Dalhousie, in Vieux-Port (© **418/694-1262;** www.brunet.ca), is open 9am to 7pm on weekdays, 9am to 5pm on Saturday, and 11am to 5pm Sunday, and delivers to hotels in the Old City.

ELECTRICITY Like the U.S., Canada uses 110 to 120 volts AC (60 cycles), compared to the 220 to 240 volts AC (50 cycles) used in most of Europe, Australia, and New Zealand. If your small appliances use 220 to 240 volts, you'll need a 110-volt transformer and a plug adapter with two flat parallel pins to operate them in Canada. They can be difficult to find in Canada, so bring one with you.

EMBASSIES & CONSULATES Embassies are located in Ottawa, Canada's capital, but there are consulate offices throughout the Canadian provinces, including Québec. The U.S. Embassy information line © **888/840-0032** costs C$1.59 per minute. The U.S. has a consulate in Montréal at 1155 rue St-Alexandre (© **514/398-9695**) where nonemergency American citizen services are provided by appointment only. There is also a U.S. consulate in Québec City, on Jardin des Gouverneurs at 2 rue de la Terrasse-Dufferin (© **418/692-2095**). The U.K.'s consulate in Montréal is at 1000 rue de la

Gauchetière ouest, Ste. 4200 (© **514/866-5863**), and in Québec City in the St-Amable Complex, 1150 Claire-Fontaine, Ste. 700 (© **418/521-3000**).

For contact information for other embassies and consulates, search for "Foreign Representatives in Canada" at www.international.gc.ca.

EMERGENCIES Dial © **911** for police, firefighters, or an ambulance.

GASOLINE (PETROL) Gasoline in Canada is more expensive than in the U.S., even considering the steep rise in U.S. costs over the past few years. Europeans will find the prices inexpensive. Gas is sold by the liter, and 3.78 liters equals 1 gallon. Recent prices of C93¢ per liter are the equivalent of about US$2.85 per gallon.

HOLIDAYS Canada's important public holidays are New Year's Day (Jan 1); Good Friday and Easter Monday (Mar or Apr); Victoria Day (the Mon preceding May 25); St-Jean-Baptiste Day, Québec's "national" day (June 24); Canada Day (July 1); Labour Day (first Mon in Sept); Canadian Thanksgiving Day (second Mon in Oct); and Christmas (Dec 25). For more information on holidays see "Montréal & Québec City Calendar of Events," in chapter 3.

HOSPITALS In Montréal, hospitals with emergency rooms include **Hôpital Général de Montréal,** 1650 rue Cedar (© **514/934-1934**), and **Hôpital Royal Victoria,** 687 av. des Pins ouest (© **514/934-1934**). **Hôpital de Montréal pour Enfants,** 2300 rue Tupper (© **514/412-4400**), is a children's hospital. All three are associated with McGill University.

In Québec City, go to the **Centre Hospitalier Hôtel-Dieu de Québec,** 11 Côte du Palais (© **418/525-4444**).

INSURANCE Medical Insurance Medical treatment in Canada isn't free for foreigners, and hospitals make you pay your bills at the time of service.

Check whether your insurance policy covers you while traveling in Canada, especially for hospitalization abroad. U.S. Medicare and Medicaid programs do not provide coverage for hospital or medical costs outside the U.S. Many other policies require you to pay for services upfront and, if they reimburse you at all, will only do so after you return home. Carry details of your insurance plan with you and leave a copy with a friend at home.

U.K. nationals also have to pay for medical treatment in Canada. Carry a European Health Insurance Card (EHIC), which replaced the E111. More details are at **www.dh.gov.uk/travellers**.

As a safety net, you may want to buy travel medical insurance. Options include **MEDEX Assistance** (© 800/537-2029; www.medexassist.com) or **Travel Assistance International** (© 800/821-2828; www.travelassistance.com).

Travel Insurance The cost of travel insurance varies widely, depending on the destination, the cost and length of your trip, your age and health, and the type of trip you're taking, but expect to pay between 4% and 8% of the cost of the vacation. You can get estimates from various providers at **www.insuremytrip.com**. Enter your trip cost and dates, your age, and other information, for prices from more than a dozen companies.

U.K. citizens and their families who make more than one trip abroad per year may find that an annual travel insurance policy works out to be a better deal. Check **www.moneysupermarket.com**, which compares prices across a wide range of providers for single- and multi-trip policies.

Most big travel agents offer their own insurance and will probably try to sell you their package when you book a holiday. **Britain's Consumers' Association** recommends that you insist on seeing the policy and reading the fine print before buying. **The Association of British Insurers** (© 020/7600-3333; www.abi.org.uk)

gives advice by phone and publishes *Holiday Insurance and Motoring Abroad,* a free guide to policy provisions. You might also shop around for better deals: Try **Columbus Direct** (© 0870/033-9988; www.columbusdirect.net).

Trip Cancellation Insurance Trip-cancellation insurance will help retrieve your money if you have to back out of a trip or depart early, or if your travel supplier goes bankrupt. Trip cancellation usually covers such events as sickness and natural disasters. The latest news in trip-cancellation insurance is the availability of any-reason cancellation coverage, which costs more but covers cancellations made for any reason. You won't get back 100% of your trip's cost, but you'll be refunded a substantial portion. **TravelSafe** (© 888/885-7233; www.travelsafe.com) offers both types of coverage. Expedia also offers any-reason cancellation coverage for its air-hotel packages. For details, contact one of the following recommended insurers: **Access America** (© 800/284-8300; www.accessamerica.com); **Travel Guard International** (© 800/826-4919; www.travelguard.com); **Travel Insured International** (© 800/243-3174; www.travelinsured.com); or **Travelex Insurance Services** (© 800/228-9792; www.travelex-insurance.com).

For more information on medical insurance while traveling, travel insurance, and trip-cancellation insurance, visit www.frommers.com/planning.

INTERNET ACCESS See "Internet & E-mail," in chapter 3.

LANGUAGE Canada is officially bilingual, but Québec province has laws that make French mandatory in signage. About 80% of Montréal's population has French as its first language (about 95% of Québec City's population does). An estimated four out of five Francophones (French speakers) speak at least some English. Hotel desk staff, sales clerks, and telephone operators nearly always greet people initially in French, but usually switch to English quickly if necessary. Outside of Montréal, visitors are more likely to encounter residents who don't speak English. If smiles and sign language don't work, look around for a young person—most of them study English in school.

LAUNDROMATS Laundromats aren't thick upon the ground in tourist districts. In Montréal, one option is **Buanderie Chez Bobette** in the Plateau Mont-Royal neighborhood at 850 rue Duluth est (© **514/522-2612**). **Kanji Laundry** offers free pick-up and delivery within metro Montréal (© **514/501-3577**; www. kanjilaundry.com) and can launder or dry clean within 24 hours. In Québec City, try **La Lavandiere,** at 625 rue St-Jean (© **418/523-0345**), just outside the Old City walls in the Parliament Hill area. Ask your hotel for options, too—many provide laundry service.

LEGAL AID If you are arrested, your country's embassy or consulate can provide the names of attorneys who speak English. See "Embassies & Consulates" above for more information.

MAIL All mail sent through **Canada Post** (© **866/607-6301** or 416/979-8822; www.canadapost.ca) must bear Canadian stamps. That might seem painfully obvious, but apparently a large number of visitors use stamps from their home countries. A letter or postcard to the U.S. requires C98¢. A letter or postcard to anywhere else costs C$1.65. To mail within Canada, letters cost C54¢. **FedEx** (© **800/463-3339**; www.fedex.com/ca) offers service from Canada. Call or go to its website to find locations.

MAPS Good city maps are available for free from the tourist offices (p. 52). The best detailed street guide of Montréal is the pocket-size atlas published by JDM Géo and MapArt (www.mapart.com), which also makes useful maps for all the regions outside Montréal and Québec City

that are mentioned in this book. You can buy them online and in shops and gas stations throughout Canada.

NEWSPAPERS & MAGAZINES Montréal's primary English-language newspaper is the **Montréal Gazette** (www. montrealgazette.com). For information about current arts happenings in Montréal, pick up the Friday or Saturday edition. **The Globe and Mail** (www. theglobeandmail.com) is a national English-language paper. The leading French-language newspaper is **La Presse** (www. cyberpresse.ca/actualites/regional/montreal), with a sister publication, **Le Soleil** (www.cyberpresse.ca/le-soleil), published in Québec City. Most large newsstands and those in larger hotels carry the *New York Times, Wall Street Journal,* and *International Herald Tribune.*

PASSPORTS See www.frommers.com/ planning for information on how to obtain a passport.

For other information, contact the following agencies:

For Residents of Australia Contact the **Australian Passport Information Service** at © **131-232,** or visit the government website at www.passports.gov.au.

For Residents of Ireland Contact the **Passport Office,** Setanta Centre, Molesworth Street, Dublin 2 (© **01/671-1633**; www.irlgov.ie/iveagh).

For Residents of New Zealand Contact the **Passports Office** at © **0800/225-050** in New Zealand or 04/474-8100, or log on to www.passports.govt.nz.

For Residents of the United Kingdom Visit your nearest passport office, major post office, or travel agency or contact the **United Kingdom Passport Service** at © **0870/521-0410** or www.ukpa. gov.uk.

For Residents of the United States To find your regional passport office, either check the U.S. State Department at **www.**

travel.state.gov or call the **National Passport Information Center** ($\textcircled{c}$ **877/487-2778**) for automated information.

POLICE Dial $\textcircled{c}$ **911** for police, firefighters, or an ambulance.

SMOKING Smoking was banned in the province's bars, restaurants, clubs, casinos, and some other public spaces in 2006. Most small inns and many larger hotels have become entirely smoke-free over the past few years as well. Check before you book if you're looking for a room in which you can smoke.

TAXES Most goods and services in Canada are taxed 5% by the federal government (the GST, or Goods and Services Tax). On top of that, the province of Québec tacks on an additional 7.5% tax (the TVQ). A 3% accommodations tax is in effect in Montréal.

Nonresident visitors used to be able to apply for a tax rebate, but that practice was eliminated in 2007. A Foreign Convention and Tour Incentive Program provides limited rebates on the GST for services used during foreign conventions held in Canada, for nonresident exhibitors, and for the short-term accommodations portion of tour packages for nonresident individuals and tour operators. Details are at **www.cra-arc.gc.ca/visitors**.

TELEPHONES See "Telephones," p. 37.

TIME Montréal, Québec City, and all the regions listed in this book as side trips are on Eastern Standard Time. Daylight saving time is observed by moving clocks ahead an hour on the second Sunday in March and back an hour on the first Sunday in November.

TIPPING Tipping practices in the province are similar to those in large Western cities. In hotels, tip **bellhops** C$1 per bag and tip the **chamber staff** C$3 to C$5 per day. Tip the **doorman** or **concierge** only if he or she has provided you with some specific service (for example, calling a cab

for you or obtaining difficult-to-get theater tickets). Tip the **valet-parking attendant** C$1 every time you get your car.

In restaurants, bars, and nightclubs, tip **waiters** 15% to 20% of the check, tip **checkroom attendants** C$1 per garment, and tip **valet-parking attendants** C$1 per vehicle.

Other service personnel: Tip **taxi drivers** 15% of the fare; tip **skycaps** at airports C$1 per bag; and tip **hairdressers** and **barbers** 15% to 20%.

TOILETS You won't find public toilets on the streets in Montréal or Québec City, but they can be found in tourist offices, museums, railway and bus stations, service stations, and large shopping complexes. Restaurants and bars in heavily visited areas often reserve their restrooms for patrons.

VISAS See "Visas," p. 25.

VISITOR INFORMATION The terrific website **www.tourisme-montreal.org** offers a broad range of information for Montréal visitors, while **www.quebecregion.com** serves Québec City travelers. The equally good **www.bonjourquebec.com** is run by Québec province's tourism department.

In Montréal, the main tourist center in downtown is the large **Infotouriste Centre,** at 1255 rue Peel ($\textcircled{c}$ **877/266-5687** or 514/873-2015; Métro: Peel). It's open daily and the bilingual staff can provide suggestions for accommodations, dining, car rentals, and attractions. In Vieux-Montréal, there's a small **Tourist Information Office** at 174 rue Notre-Dame est, at the corner of Place Jacques-Cartier (Métro: Champ-de-Mars). It's open daily in warmer months, Wednesday through Sunday in winter.

In Québec City, the most central tourist office is in Upper Town, across from the Château Frontenac and directly on Place d'Armes. **Centre Infotouriste de Québec,** 12 rue Ste-Anne ($\textcircled{c}$ **877/266-5687;** www.bonjourquebec.com), is open from

9am to 7pm daily from June 21 to early September and from 9am to 5pm daily the rest of the year. It has brochures, a lodging reservation service, a currency-exchange office, and information about tours by foot, bus, or boat.

The travel blog **A Key in the Door** (www.akeyinthedoor.com) offers an insider's perspective on international travel and is written by Herbert Bailey Livesey, who authored *Frommer's Montréal & Québec City* for over a decade.

2 AIRLINE, HOTEL & CAR-RENTAL WEBSITES

MAJOR AIRLINES

Air Canada
www.aircanada.ca

Air France
www.airfrance.com

American Airlines
www.aa.com

British Airways
www.british-airways.com

Continental Airlines
www.continental.com

Delta Air Lines
www.delta.com

Lufthansa
www.lufthansa.com

Olympic Airlines
www.olympicairlines.com

Swiss Air
www.swiss.com

United Airlines
www.united.com

US Airways
www.usairways.com

MAJOR HOTEL & MOTEL CHAINS

Best Western International
www.bestwestern.com

Clarion Hotels
www.choicehotels.com

Courtyard by Marriott
www.marriott.com/courtyard

Crowne Plaza Hotels
www.ichotelsgroup.com/crowneplaza

Days Inn
www.daysinn.com

Doubletree Hotels
www.doubletree.com

Econo Lodges
www.econolodge.com

Embassy Suites
www.embassysuites.com

Farfield Inn by Marriott
www.farfieldinn.com

Hampton Inn
www.hamptoninn1.hilton.com

Hilton Hotels
www.hilton.com

Holiday Inn
www.holidayinn.com

Howard Johnson
www.hojo.com

Hyatt
www.hyatt.com

InterContinental Hotels & Resorts
www.ichotelsgroup.com

Loews Hotels
www.loewshotels.com

Marriott
www.marriott.com

Omni Hotels
www.omnihotels.com

Quality
www.QualityInn.ChoiceHotels.com

Radisson Hotels & Resorts
www.radisson.com

Residence Inn by Marriott
www.marriott.com/residenceinn

Rodeway Inns
www.RodewayInn.com

Sheraton Hotels & Resorts
www.starwoodhotels.com/sheraton

Super 8 Motels
www.super8.com

Travelodge
www.travelodge.com

Westin Hotels & Resorts
www.starwoodhotels.com/westin

Wyndham Hotels & Resorts
www.wyndham.com

CAR-RENTAL AGENCIES

Advantage
www.advantage.com

Alamo
www.alamo.com

Avis
www.avis.com

Budget
www.budget.com

Dollar
www.dollar.com

Enterprise
www.enterprise.com

Hertz
www.hertz.com

National
www.nationalcar.com

Payless
www.paylesscarrental.com

Thrifty
www.thrifty.com

INDEX

See also Accommodations and Restaurant indexes, below.

NOTES